稲垣理一郎

Riichiro Inagaki

Believe it or not, I really like milk. In the summertime, I drink a liter a day. What good does this do for me? I have never broken a bone in my body. I think that the dairy board ought to give me some sort of recognition. Members of the dairy board, please contact me at Jump's editorial department.

Eyeshield 21 is the hottest gridiron manga to hit the scene. A collaborative effort between writer Riichiro Inagaki and artist Yusuke Murata, *Eyeshield 21* was originally serialized in Japan's *Weekly Shonen Jump*. An OAV created for Shueisha's Anime Tour is available in Japan, and the *Eyeshield 21* hit animated TV series debuted in spring 2005!

EYESHIELD 21
Vol 5: Powerful
The SHONEN JUMP ADVANCED Graphic Novel Edition

STORY BY RIICHIRO INAGAKI
ART BY YUSUKE MURATA

Translation & English Adaptation/Allison Markin Powell
Touch-up Art & Lettering/James Gaubatz
Cover and Graphic Design/Sean Lee
Editor/Andy Nakatani

Managing Editor/Elizabeth Kawasaki
Director of Production/Noboru Watanabe
Vice President of Publishing/Alvin Lu
Vice President & Editor in Chief/Yumi Hoashi
Sr. Director of Acquisitions/Rika Inouye
Vice President of Sales & Marketing/Liza Coppola
Publisher/Hyoe Narita

EYESHIELD 21 © 2002 by Riichiro Inagaki, Yusuke Murata.
All rights reserved. First published in Japan in 2002 by SHUEISHA
Inc., Tokyo. English translation rights in the United States of America
and Canada arranged by SHUEISHA Inc. Some scenes have been
modified from the original Japanese edition. The stories, characters
and incidents mentioned in this publication are entirely fictional.

Printed in the U.S.A.

Published by VIZ Media, LLC
P.O. Box 77010
San Francisco, CA 94107

SHONEN JUMP ADVANCED Graphic Novel Edition
10 9 8 7 6 5 4 3 2 1
First printing, November 2005

www.viz.com

THE WORLD'S MOST
CUTTING-EDGE MANGA
SHONEN
JUMP
ADVANCED
www.shonenjump.com

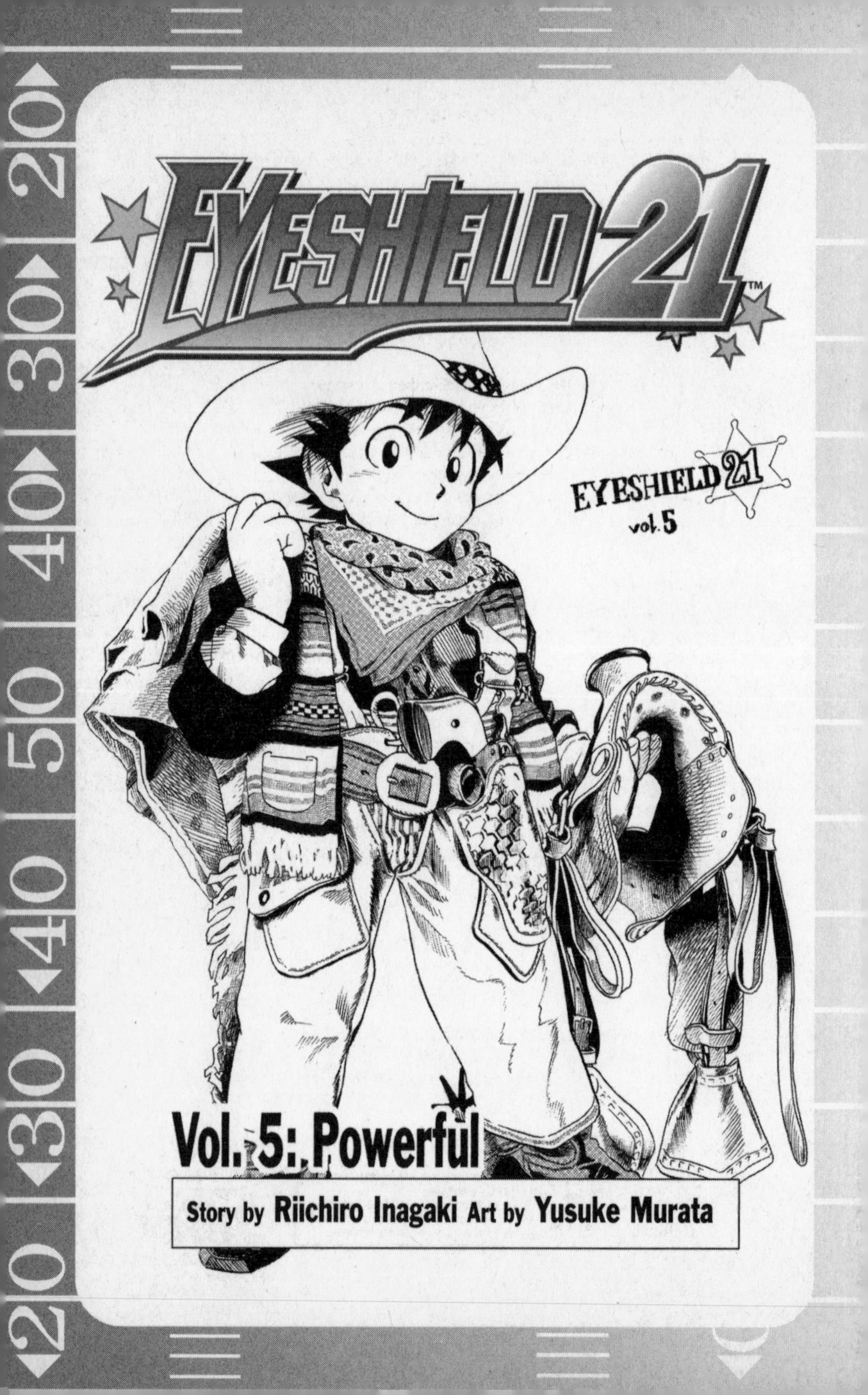
EYESHIELD 21™
EYESHIELD 21
vol.5
Vol. 5: Powerful
Story by Riichiro Inagaki Art by Yusuke Murata

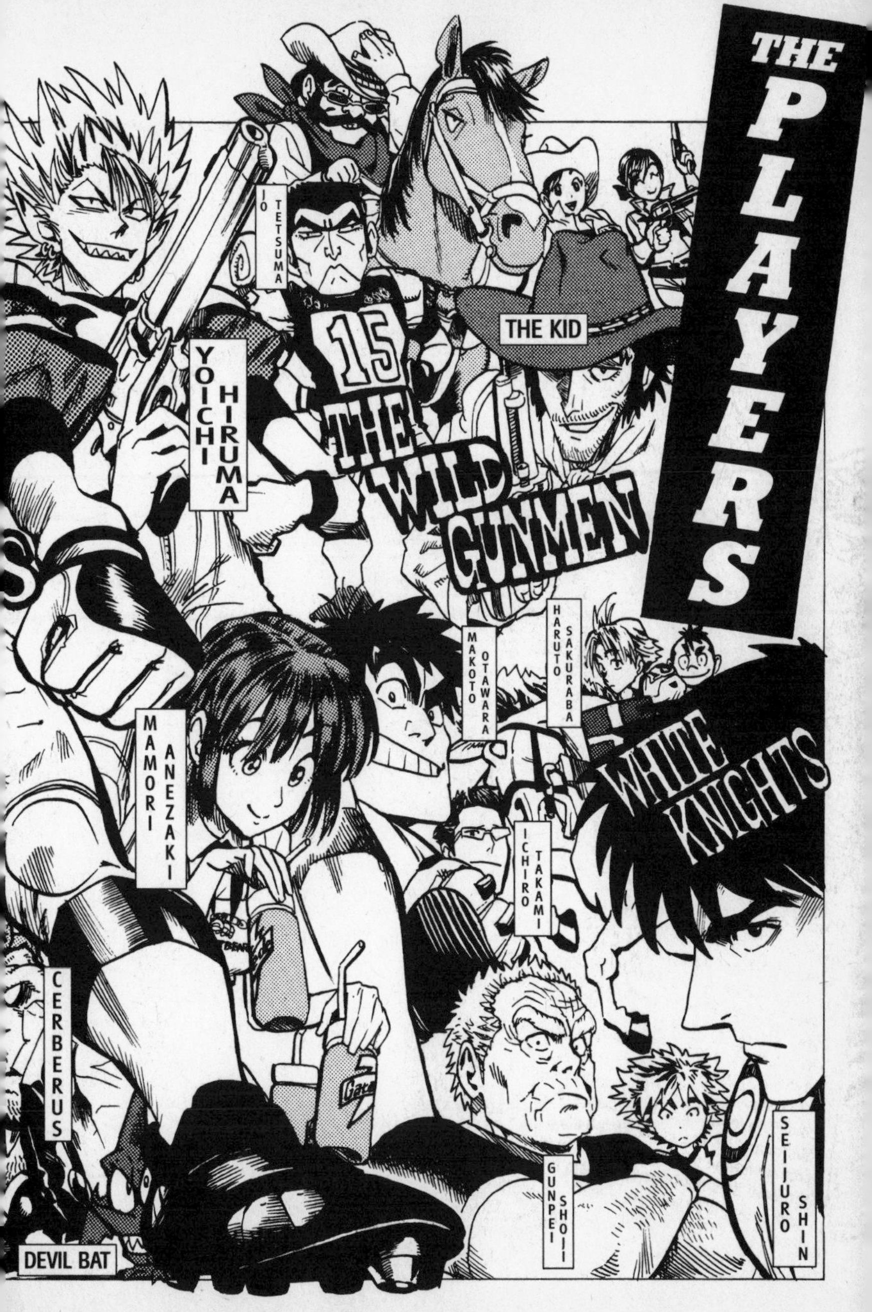
THE PLAYERS
THE WILD GUNMEN
THE KID
JO TETSUMA
YOICHI HIRUMA
WHITE KNIGHTS
HARUTO SAKURABA
MAKOTO OTAWARA
ICHIRO TAKAMI
MAMORI ANEZAKI
SEIJURO SHIN
GUNPEI SHOJI
CERBERUS
DEVIL BAT

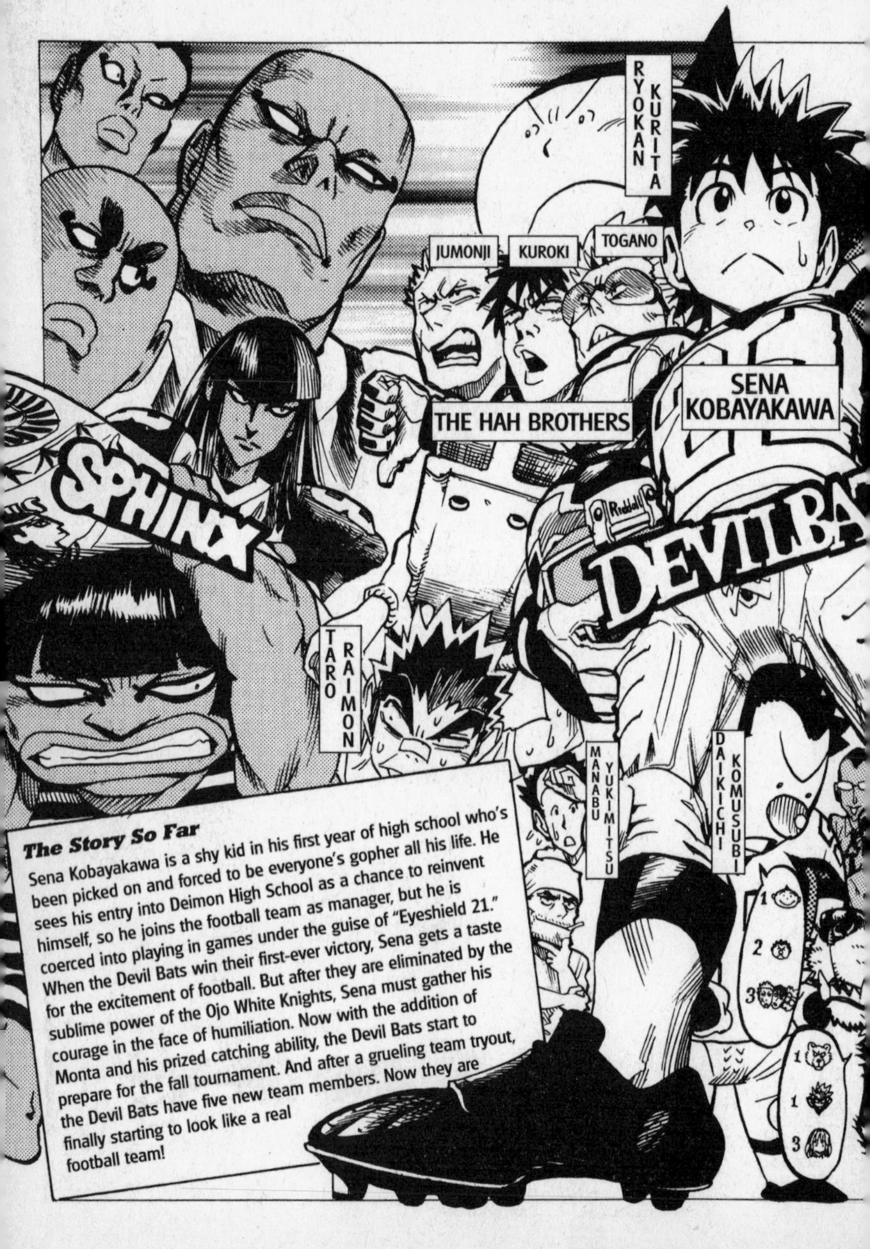

RYOKAN KURITA
SENA KOBAYAKAWA
TOGANO
KUROKI
JUMONJI
THE HAH BROTHERS
SPHINX
DEVILBA
TARO RAIMON
DAIKICHI KOMUSUBI
MANABU YUKIMITSU

The Story So Far

Sena Kobayakawa is a shy kid in his first year of high school who's been picked on and forced to be everyone's gopher all his life. He sees his entry into Deimon High School as a chance to reinvent himself, so he joins the football team as manager, but he is coerced into playing in games under the guise of "Eyeshield 21." When the Devil Bats win their first-ever victory, Sena gets a taste for the excitement of football. But after they are eliminated by the sublime power of the Ojo White Knights, Sena must gather his courage in the face of humiliation. Now with the addition of Monta and his prized catching ability, the Devil Bats start to prepare for the fall tournament. And after a grueling team tryout, the Devil Bats have five new team members. Now they are finally starting to look like a real football team!

EYESHIELD 21

Vol. 5
Powerful

CONTENTS

Chapter 35

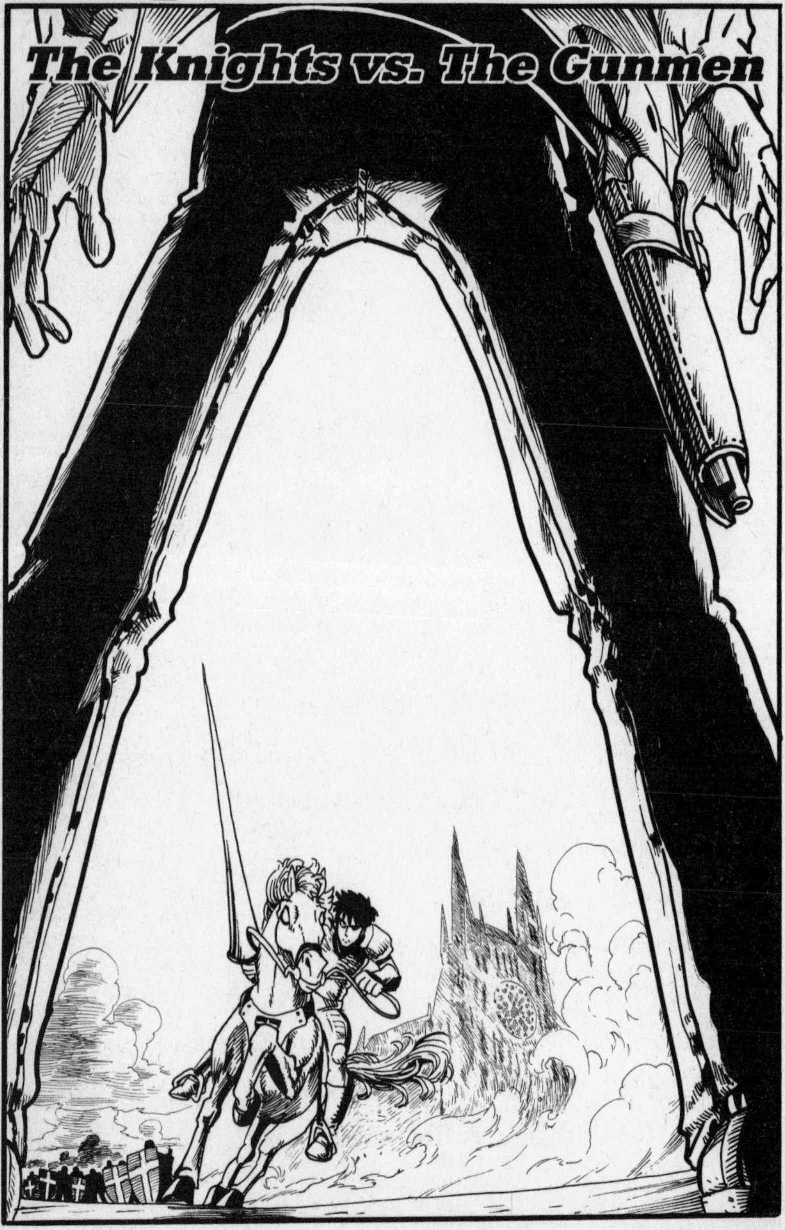
The Knights vs. The Gunmen

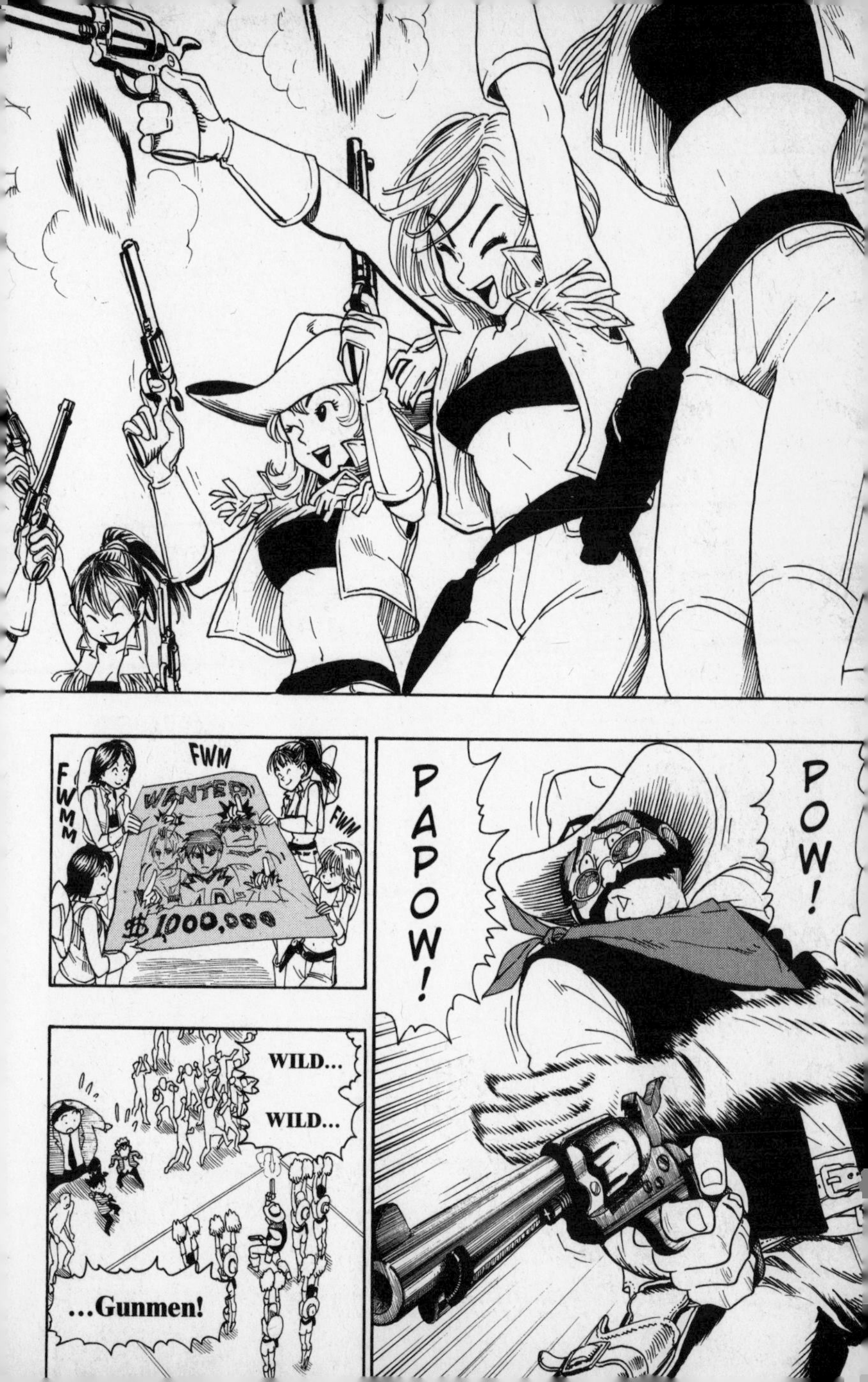
POW!
PAPOW!
FWM
FWM
FWMM
WANTED
$1000,000
WILD...
WILD...
...Gunmen!

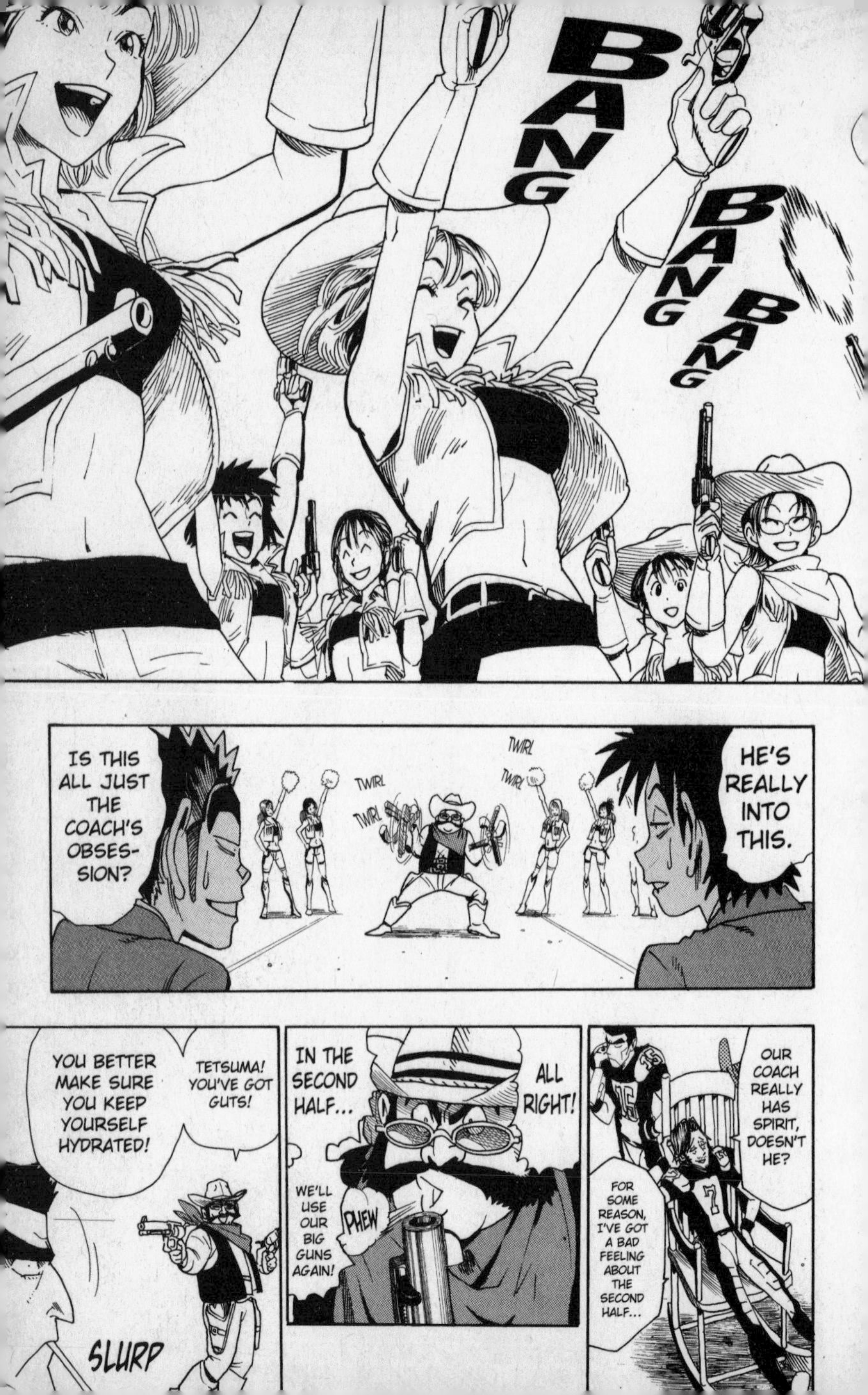
BANG
BANG
BANG
HE'S REALLY INTO THIS.
TWIRL
TWIRL
TWIRL
TWIRL
IS THIS ALL JUST THE COACH'S OBSESSION?
OUR COACH REALLY HAS SPIRIT, DOESN'T HE?
FOR SOME REASON, I'VE GOT A BAD FEELING ABOUT THE SECOND HALF...
ALL RIGHT!
IN THE SECOND HALF...
WE'LL USE OUR BIG GUNS AGAIN!
PHEW
TETSUMA! YOU'VE GOT GUTS!
YOU BETTER MAKE SURE YOU KEEP YOURSELF HYDRATED!
SLURP

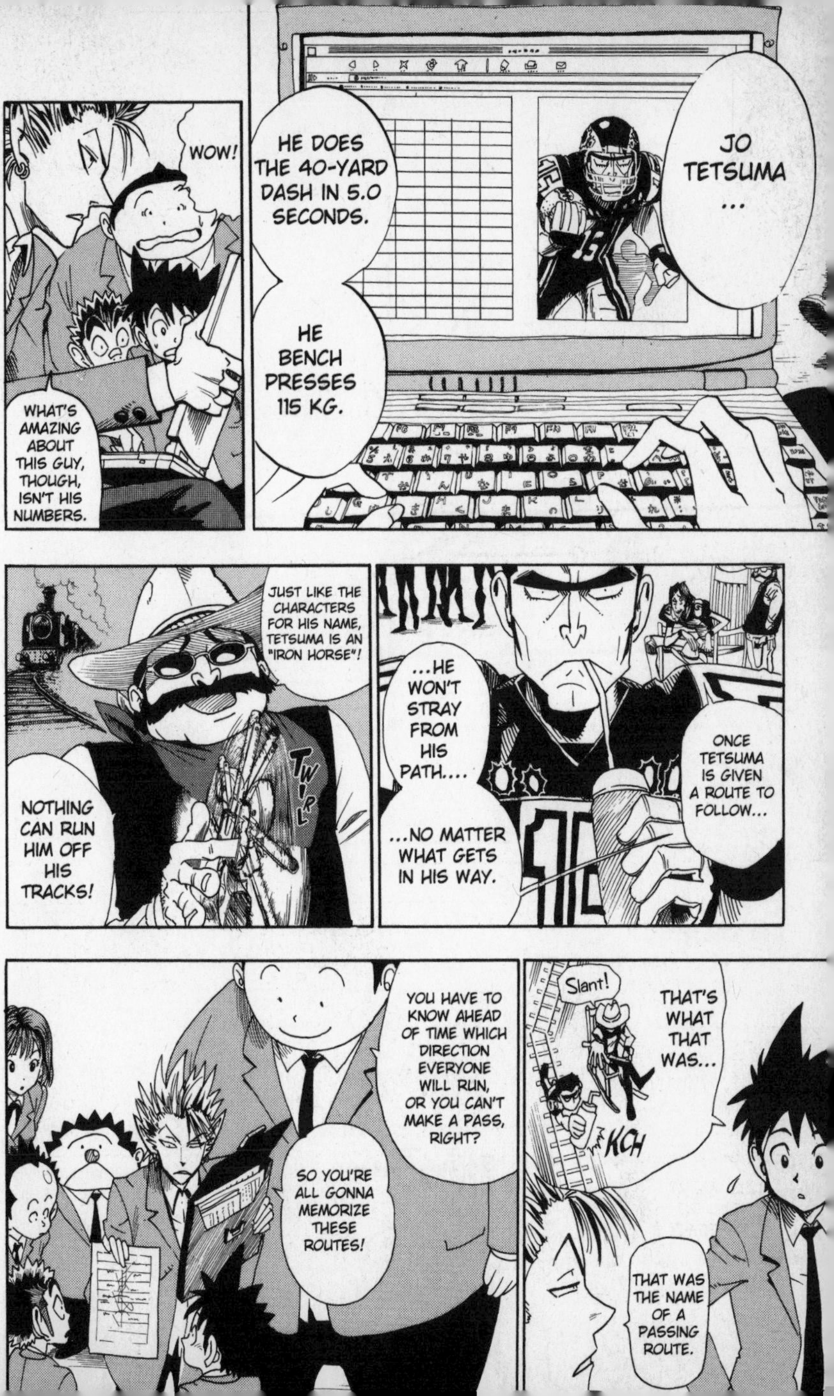
JO TETSUMA ...
HE DOES THE 40-YARD DASH IN 5.0 SECONDS.
HE BENCH PRESSES 115 KG.
WOW!
WHAT'S AMAZING ABOUT THIS GUY, THOUGH, ISN'T HIS NUMBERS.
ONCE TETSUMA IS GIVEN A ROUTE TO FOLLOW...
...HE WON'T STRAY FROM HIS PATH....
...NO MATTER WHAT GETS IN HIS WAY.
JUST LIKE THE CHARACTERS FOR HIS NAME, TETSUMA IS AN "IRON HORSE"!
TWIRL
NOTHING CAN RUN HIM OFF HIS TRACKS!
Slant!
THAT'S WHAT THAT WAS...
KCH
THAT WAS THE NAME OF A PASSING ROUTE.
YOU HAVE TO KNOW AHEAD OF TIME WHICH DIRECTION EVERYONE WILL RUN, OR YOU CAN'T MAKE A PASS, RIGHT?
SO YOU'RE ALL GONNA MEMORIZE THESE ROUTES!

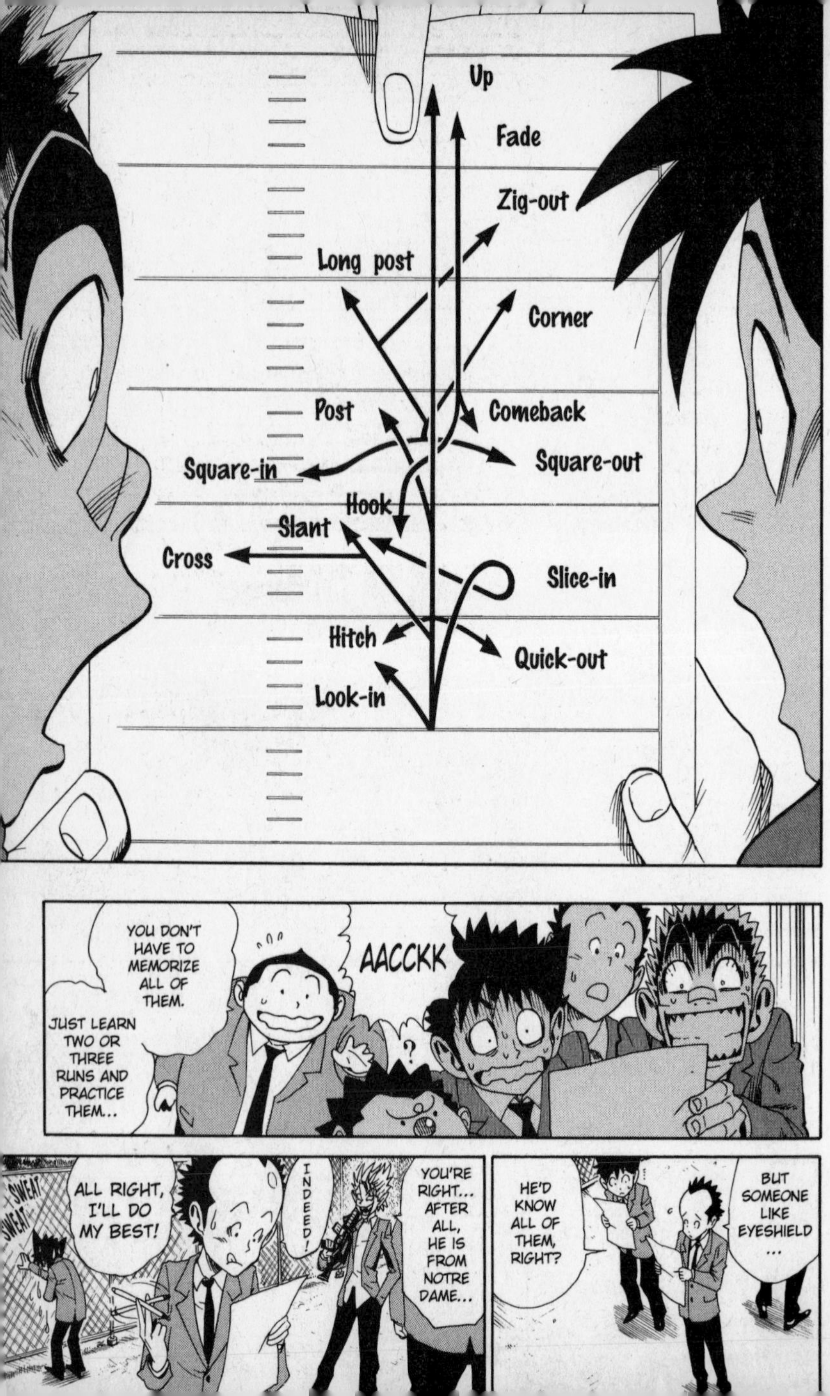
Up
Fade
Zig-out
Long post
Corner
Post
Comeback
Square-in
Square-out
Hook
Slant
Cross
Slice-in
Hitch
Quick-out
Look-in
AACCKK
YOU DON'T HAVE TO MEMORIZE ALL OF THEM.
JUST LEARN TWO OR THREE RUNS AND PRACTICE THEM...
?
BUT SOMEONE LIKE EYESHIELD...
HE'D KNOW ALL OF THEM, RIGHT?
YOU'RE RIGHT... AFTER ALL, HE IS FROM NOTRE DAME...
INDEED!
ALL RIGHT, I'LL DO MY BEST!
SWEAT
SWEAT

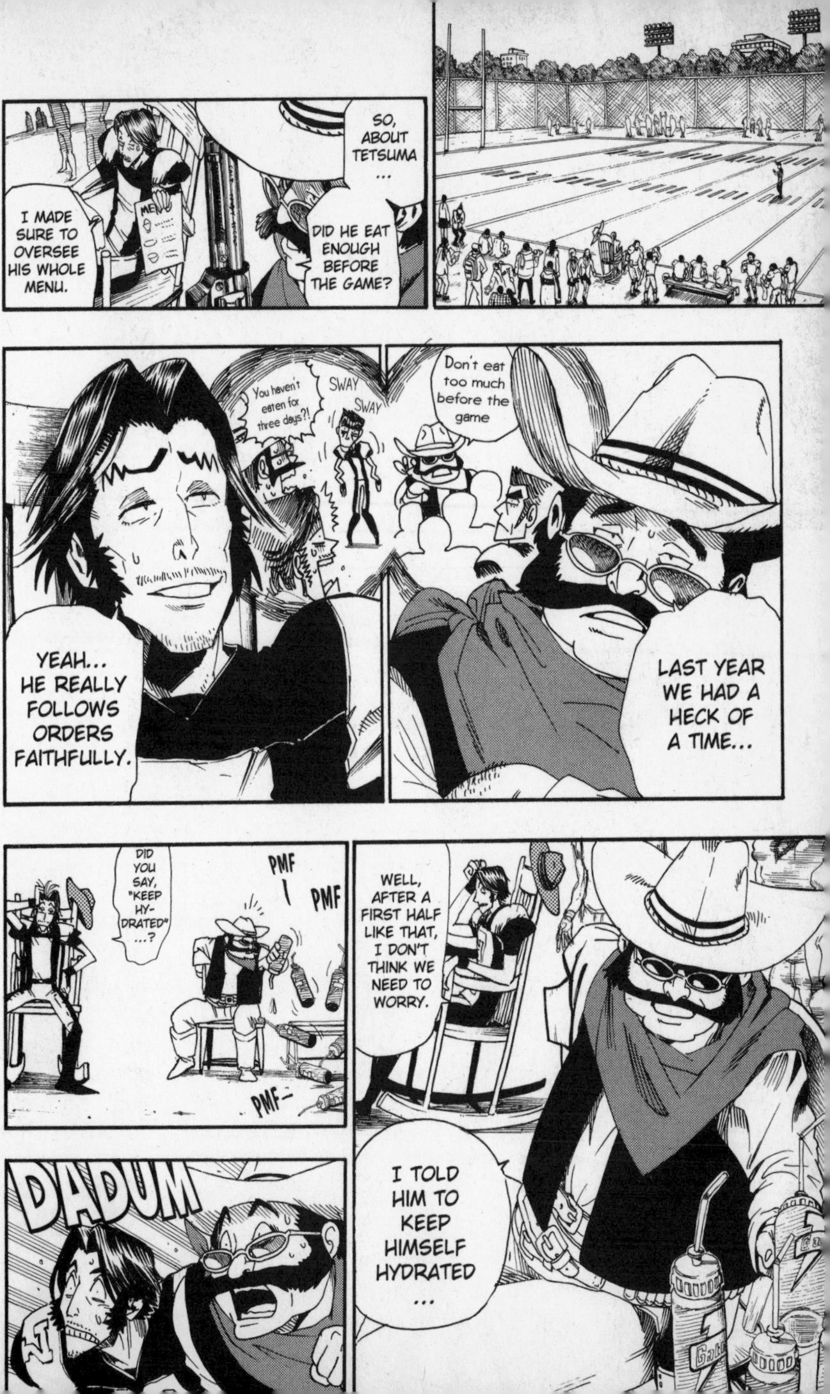
SO, ABOUT TETSUMA...
DID HE EAT ENOUGH BEFORE THE GAME?
I MADE SURE TO OVERSEE HIS WHOLE MENU.
Don't eat too much before the game
LAST YEAR WE HAD A HECK OF A TIME...
SWAY
SWAY
You haven't eaten for three days?!
YEAH... HE REALLY FOLLOWS ORDERS FAITHFULLY.
WELL, AFTER A FIRST HALF LIKE THAT, I DON'T THINK WE NEED TO WORRY.
I TOLD HIM TO KEEP HIMSELF HYDRATED...
PMF
PMF
DID YOU SAY, "KEEP HY-DRATED"...?
PMF
DADUM

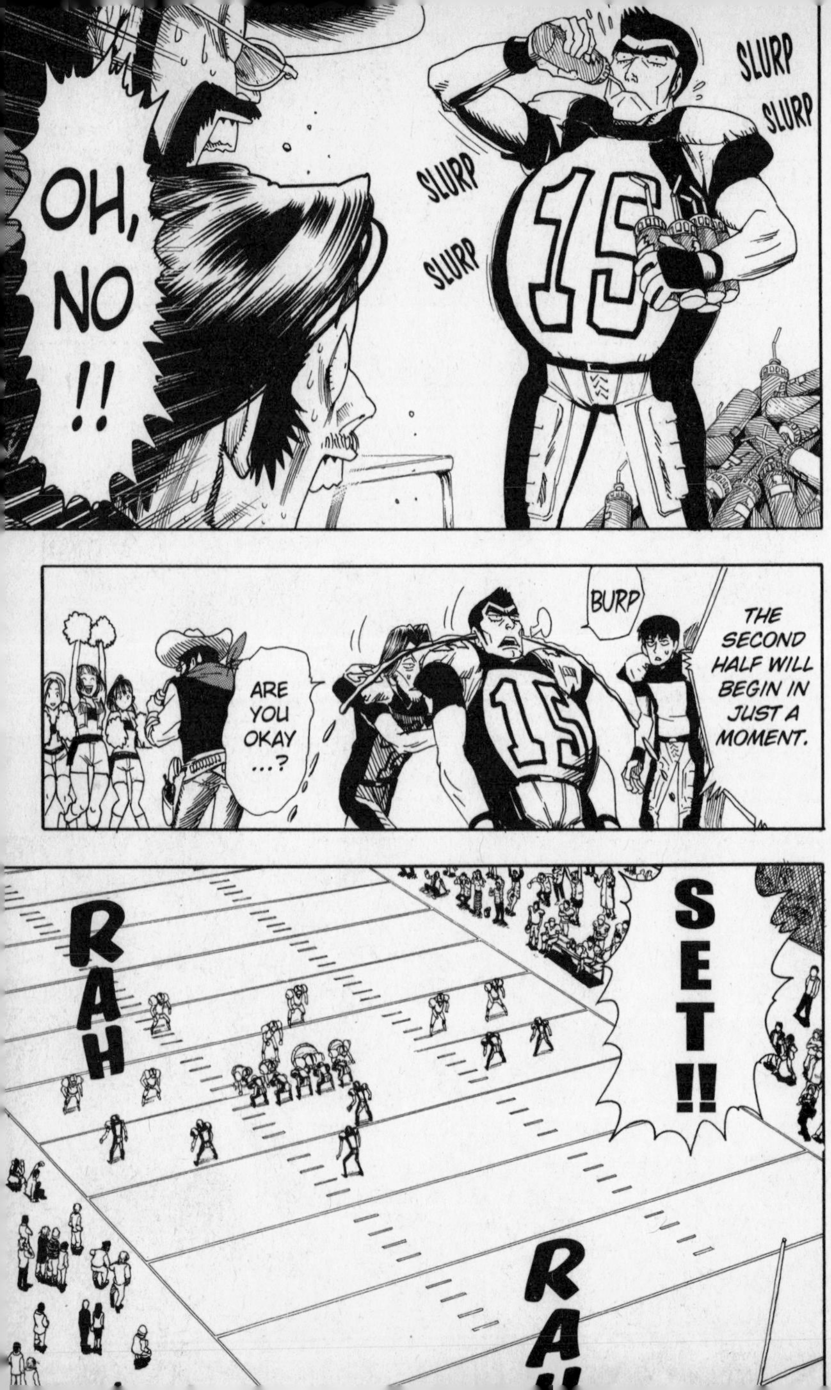
SLURP
SLURP
SLURP
SLURP
OH, NO!!
THE SECOND HALF WILL BEGIN IN JUST A MOMENT.
BURP
ARE YOU OKAY ...?
SET!!
RAH
RA

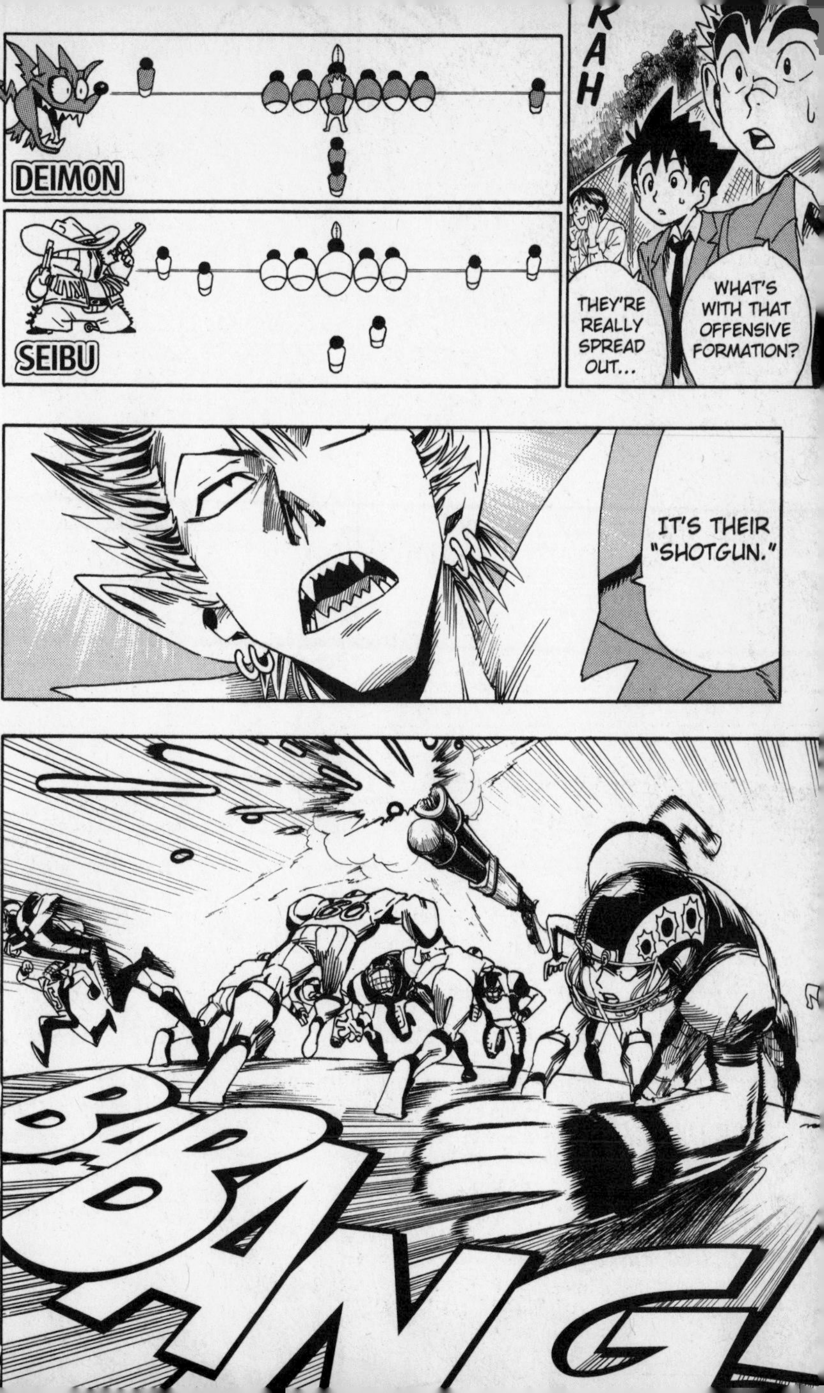
KAH
WHAT'S WITH THAT OFFENSIVE FORMATION?
THEY'RE REALLY SPREAD OUT...
DEIMON
SEIBU
IT'S THEIR "SHOTGUN."
BANG

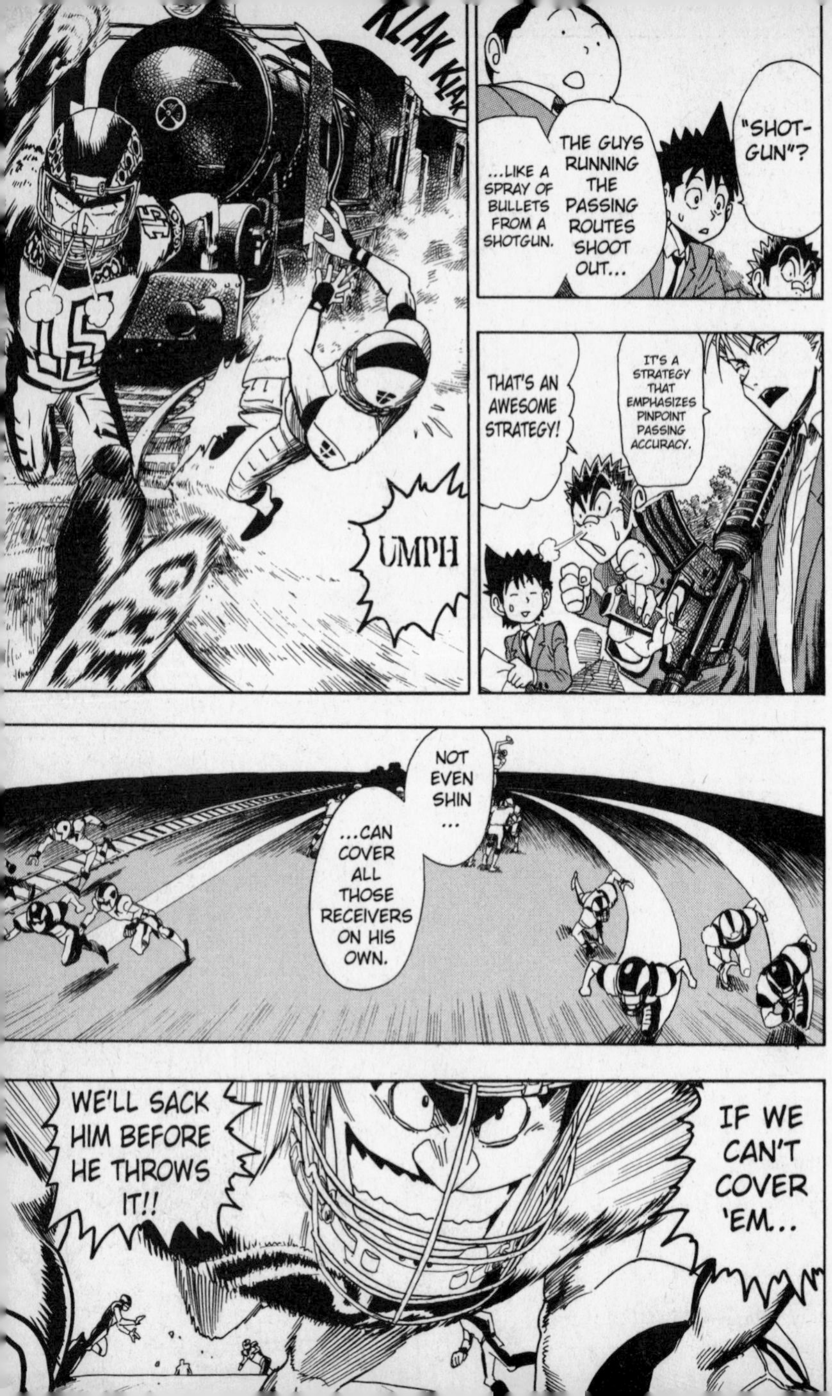
"SHOT-GUN"?
THE GUYS RUNNING THE PASSING ROUTES SHOOT OUT...
...LIKE A SPRAY OF BULLETS FROM A SHOTGUN.
IT'S A STRATEGY THAT EMPHASIZES PINPOINT PASSING ACCURACY.
THAT'S AN AWESOME STRATEGY!
KLAK KLAK
UMPH
NOT EVEN SHIN...
...CAN COVER ALL THOSE RECEIVERS ON HIS OWN.
IF WE CAN'T COVER 'EM...
WE'LL SACK HIM BEFORE HE THROWS IT!!

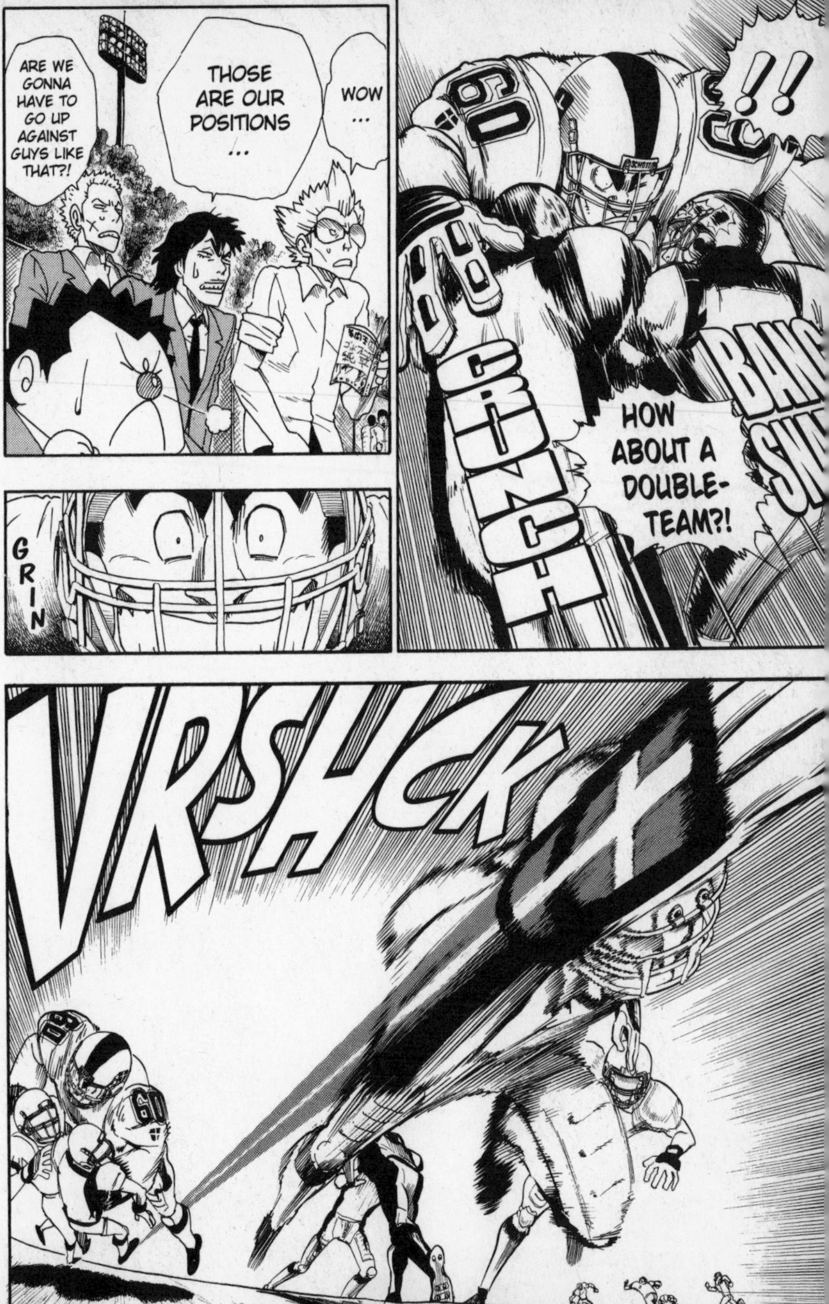
!!
CRUNCH
HOW ABOUT A DOUBLE-TEAM?!
WOW ...
THOSE ARE OUR POSITIONS ...
ARE WE GONNA HAVE TO GO UP AGAINST GUYS LIKE THAT?!
GRIN
VRSHCK

WOOSH

VWUOSH

ALL RIGHT, IT'S A SACK!

HE DOESN'T EVEN HAVE TIME TO JUST THROW THE BALL AWAY.

IT'S ALMOST TOO GOOD TO BE TRUE...

HATE TO SAY IT...

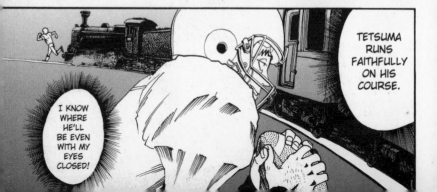

TETSUMA RUNS FAITHFULLY ON HIS COURSE.

I KNOW WHERE HE'LL BE EVEN WITH MY EYES CLOSED!

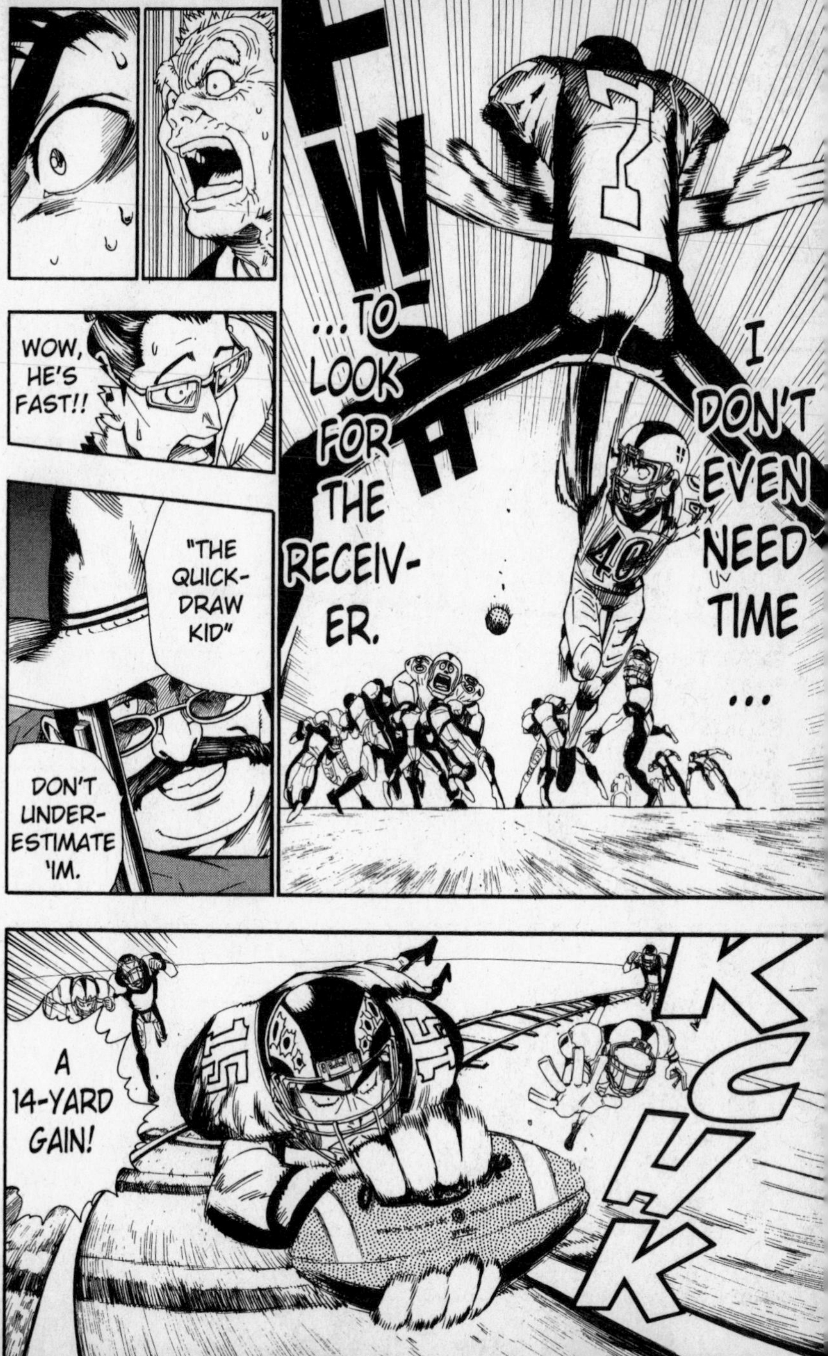
FWH
I DON'T EVEN NEED TIME ...
...TO LOOK FOR THE RECEIV-ER.
WOW, HE'S FAST!!
"THE QUICK-DRAW KID"
DON'T UNDER-ESTIMATE 'IM.
KCHK
A 14-YARD GAIN!

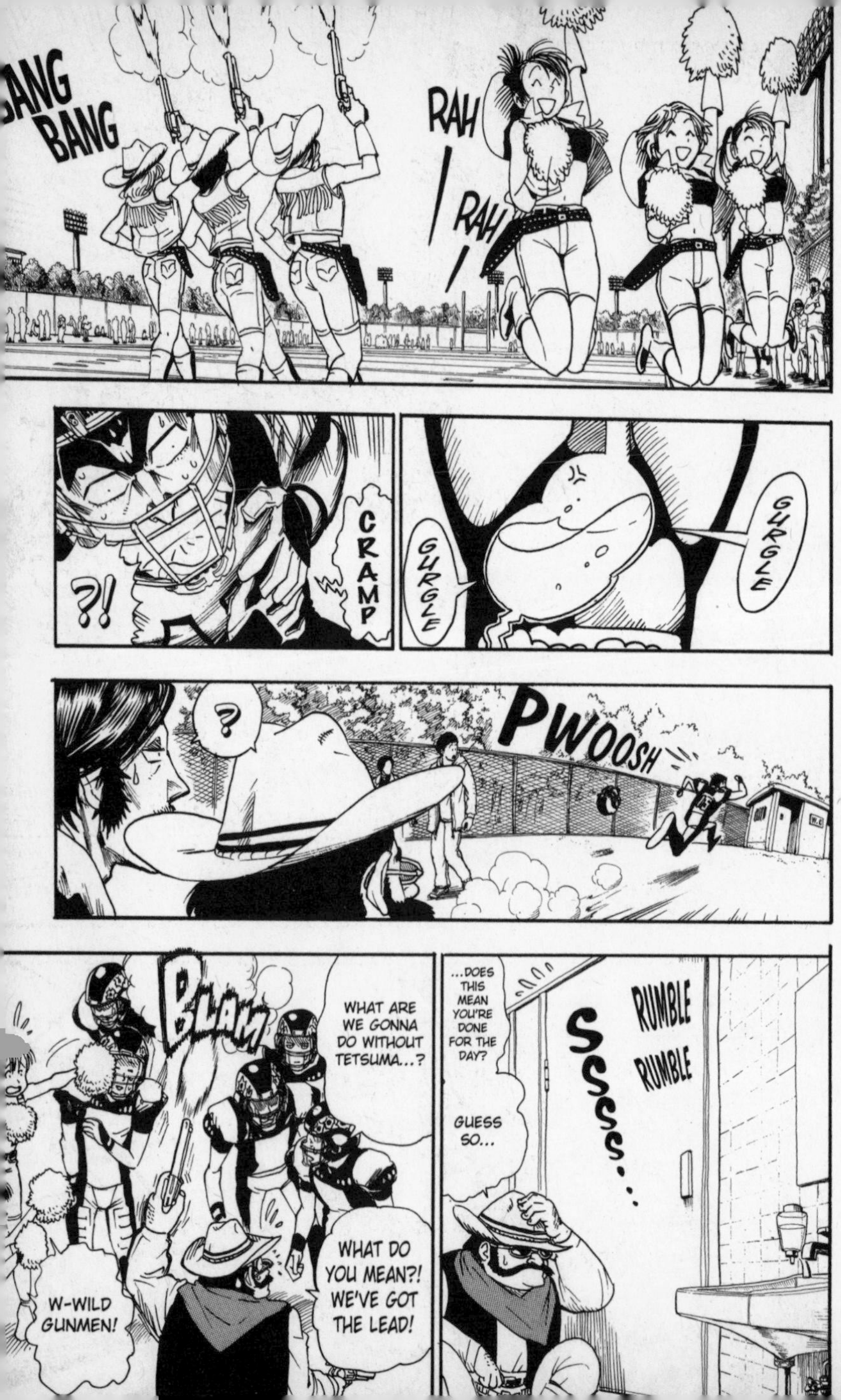
RAH
RAH
BANG
BANG
GURGLE
GURGLE
CRAMP
?!
PWOOSH
?
RUMBLE
RUMBLE
...DOES THIS MEAN YOU'RE DONE FOR THE DAY?
SSSS...
GUESS SO...
WHAT ARE WE GONNA DO WITHOUT TETSUMA...?
BLAM
WHAT DO YOU MEAN?! WE'VE GOT THE LEAD!
W-WILD GUNMEN!

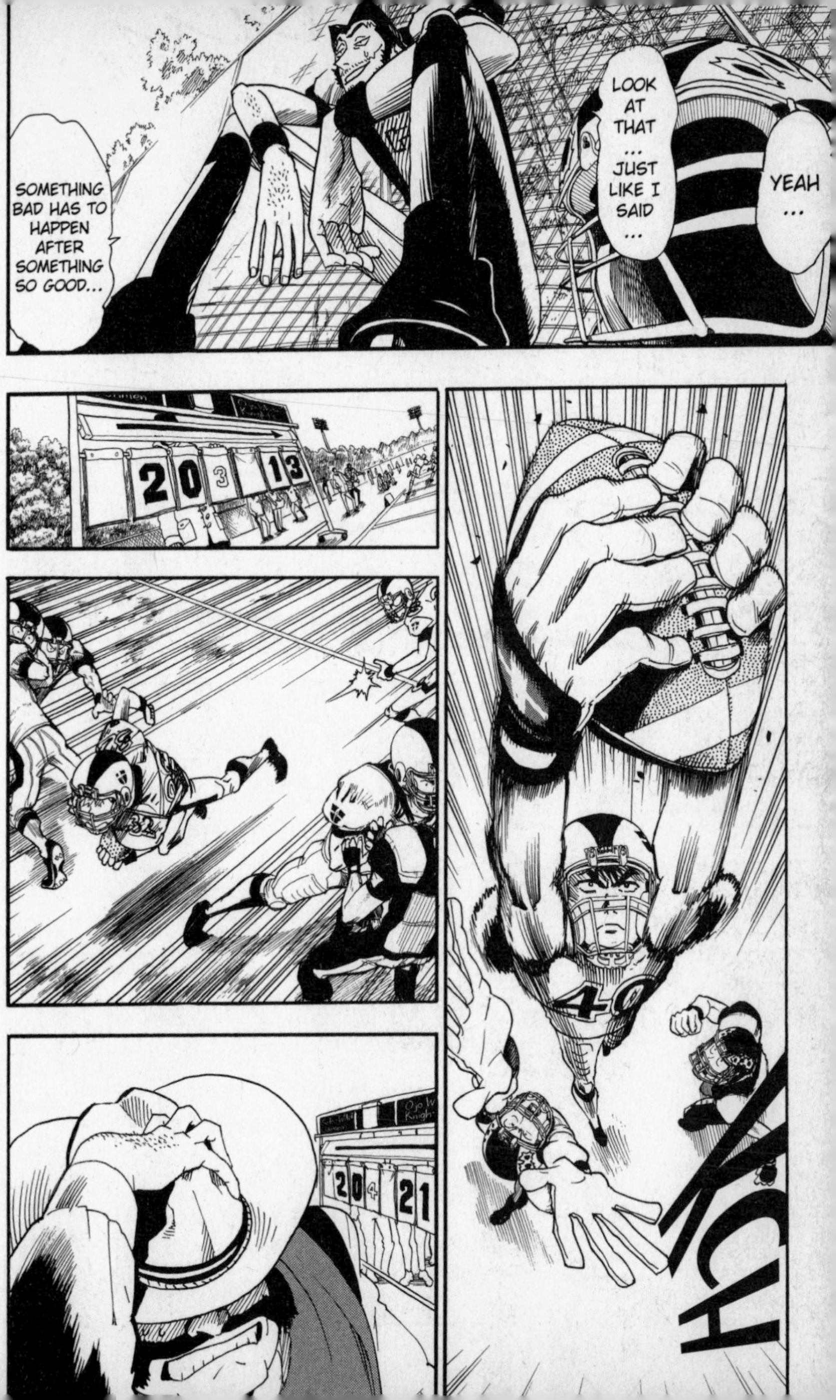
YEAH ...
LOOK AT THAT ... JUST LIKE I SAID ...
SOMETHING BAD HAS TO HAPPEN AFTER SOMETHING SO GOOD...

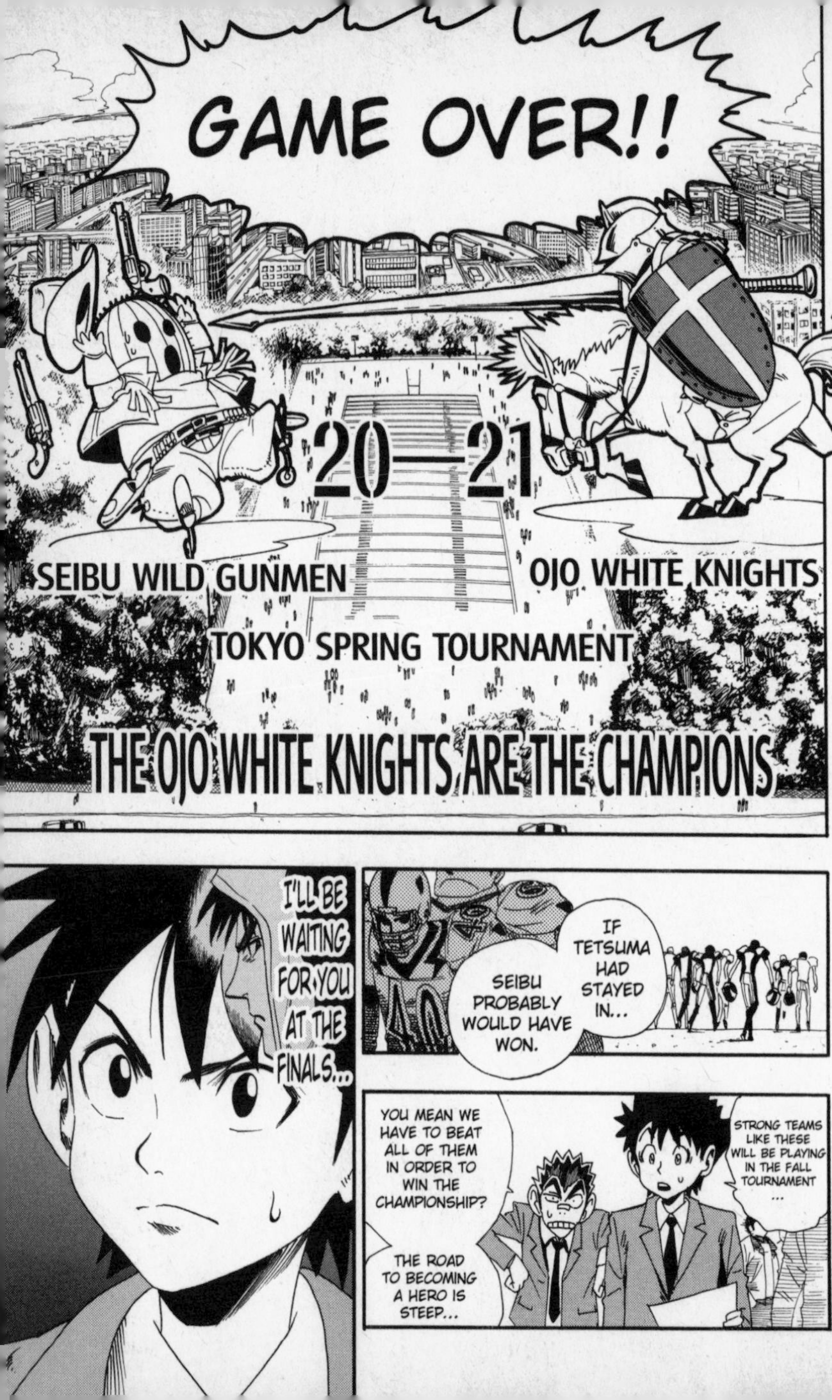
GAME OVER!!
20—21
OJO WHITE KNIGHTS
SEIBU WILD GUNMEN
TOKYO SPRING TOURNAMENT
THE OJO WHITE KNIGHTS ARE THE CHAMPIONS
IF TETSUMA HAD STAYED IN...
SEIBU PROBABLY WOULD HAVE WON.
STRONG TEAMS LIKE THESE WILL BE PLAYING IN THE FALL TOURNAMENT ...
YOU MEAN WE HAVE TO BEAT ALL OF THEM IN ORDER TO WIN THE CHAMPIONSHIP?
THE ROAD TO BECOMING A HERO IS STEEP...
I'LL BE WAITING FOR YOU AT THE FINALS...

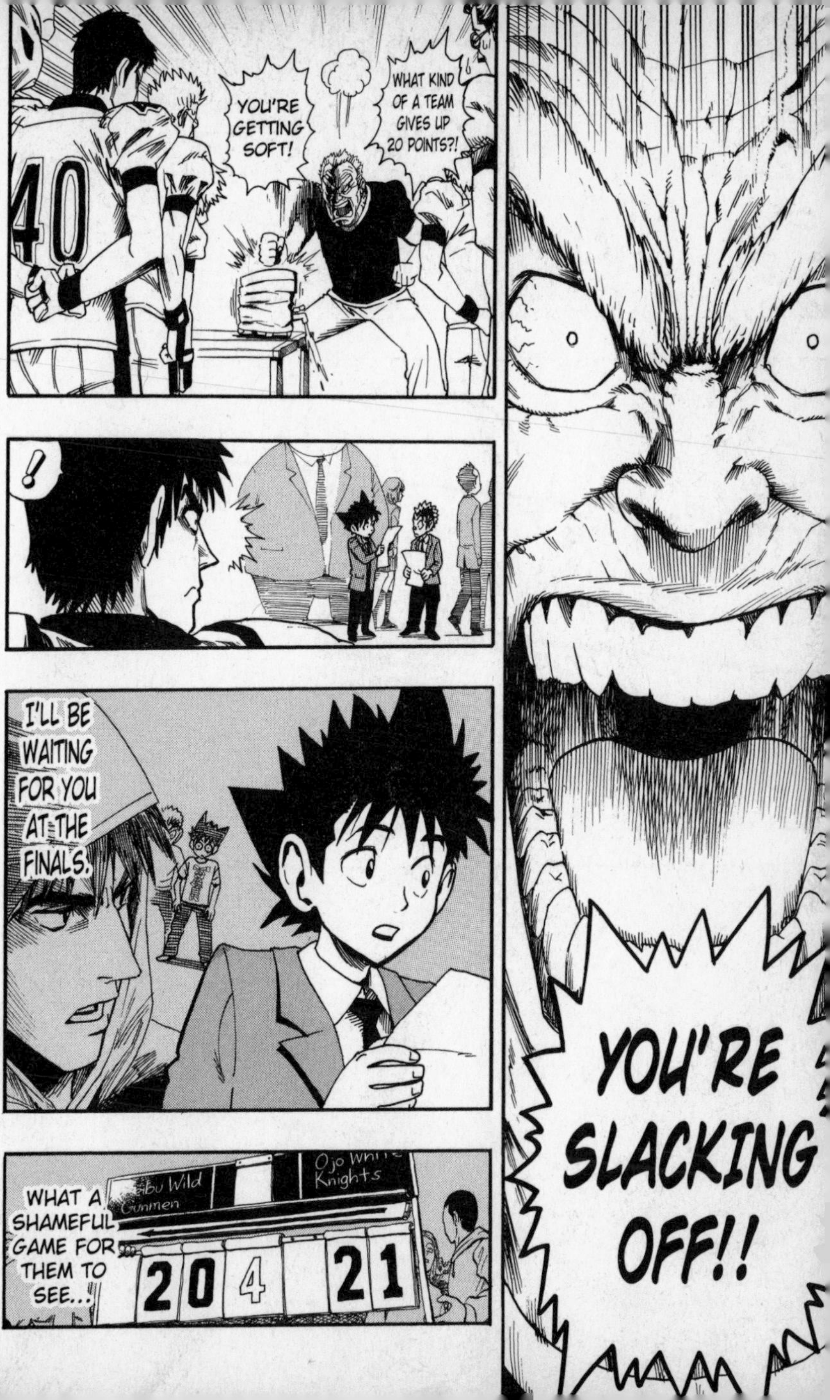
YOU'RE SLACKING OFF!!
WHAT KIND OF A TEAM GIVES UP 20 POINTS?!
YOU'RE GETTING SOFT!
!
I'LL BE WAITING FOR YOU AT THE FINALS.
WHAT A SHAMEFUL GAME FOR THEM TO SEE...
20 4 21

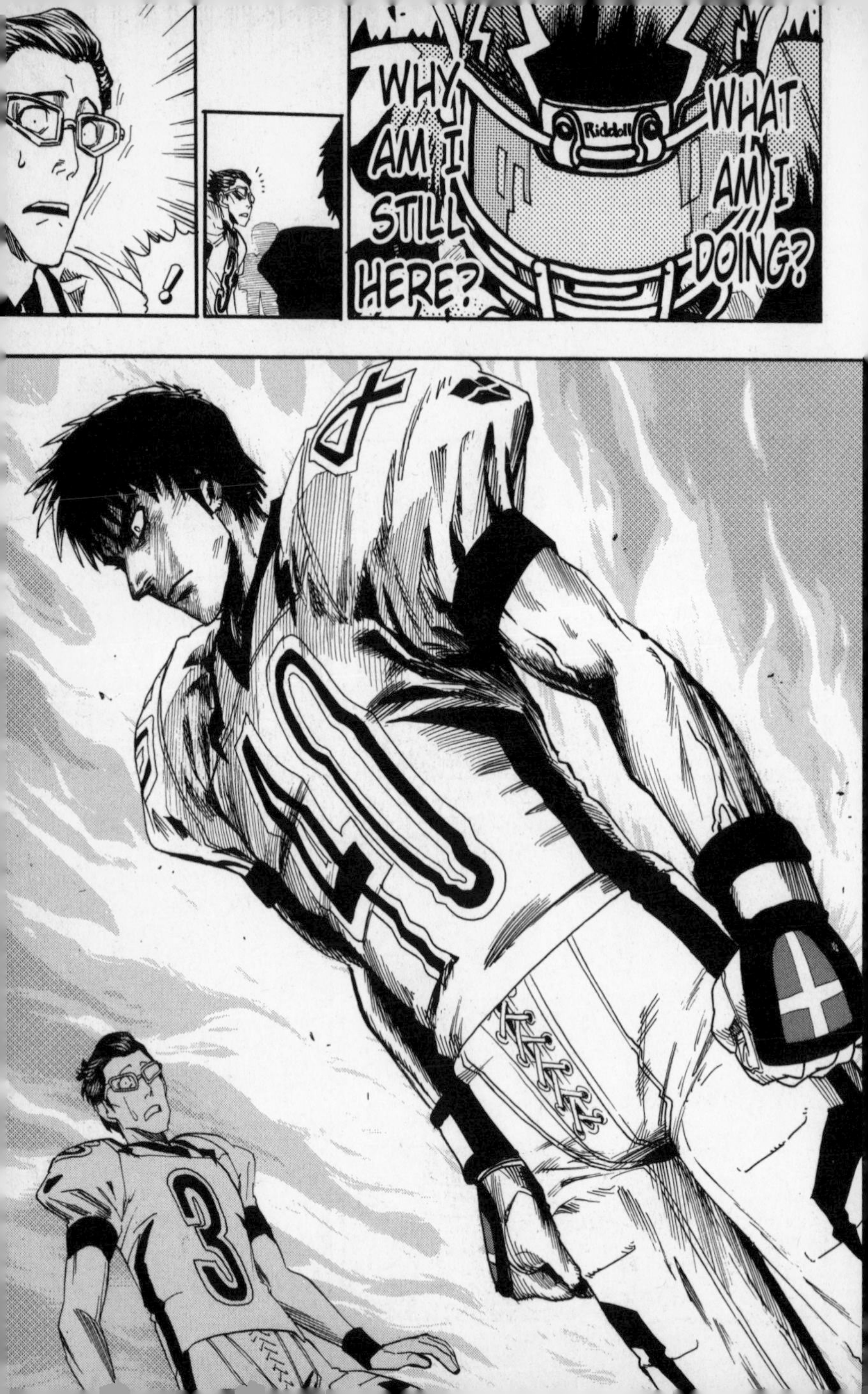
WHAT AM I DOING?
WHY AM I STILL HERE?
!

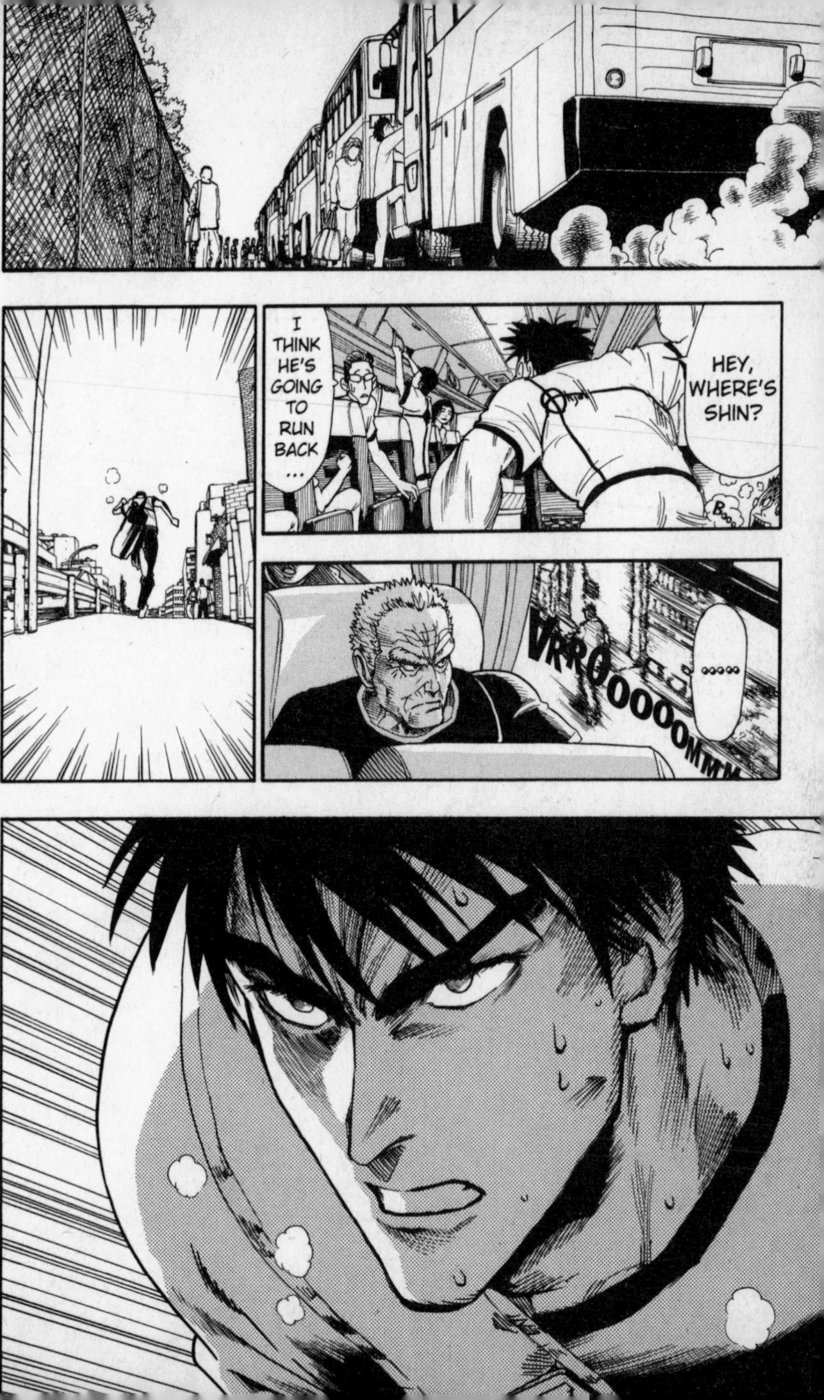
HEY, WHERE'S SHIN?
I THINK HE'S GOING TO RUN BACK...
VRROOOOOOMMM
.....

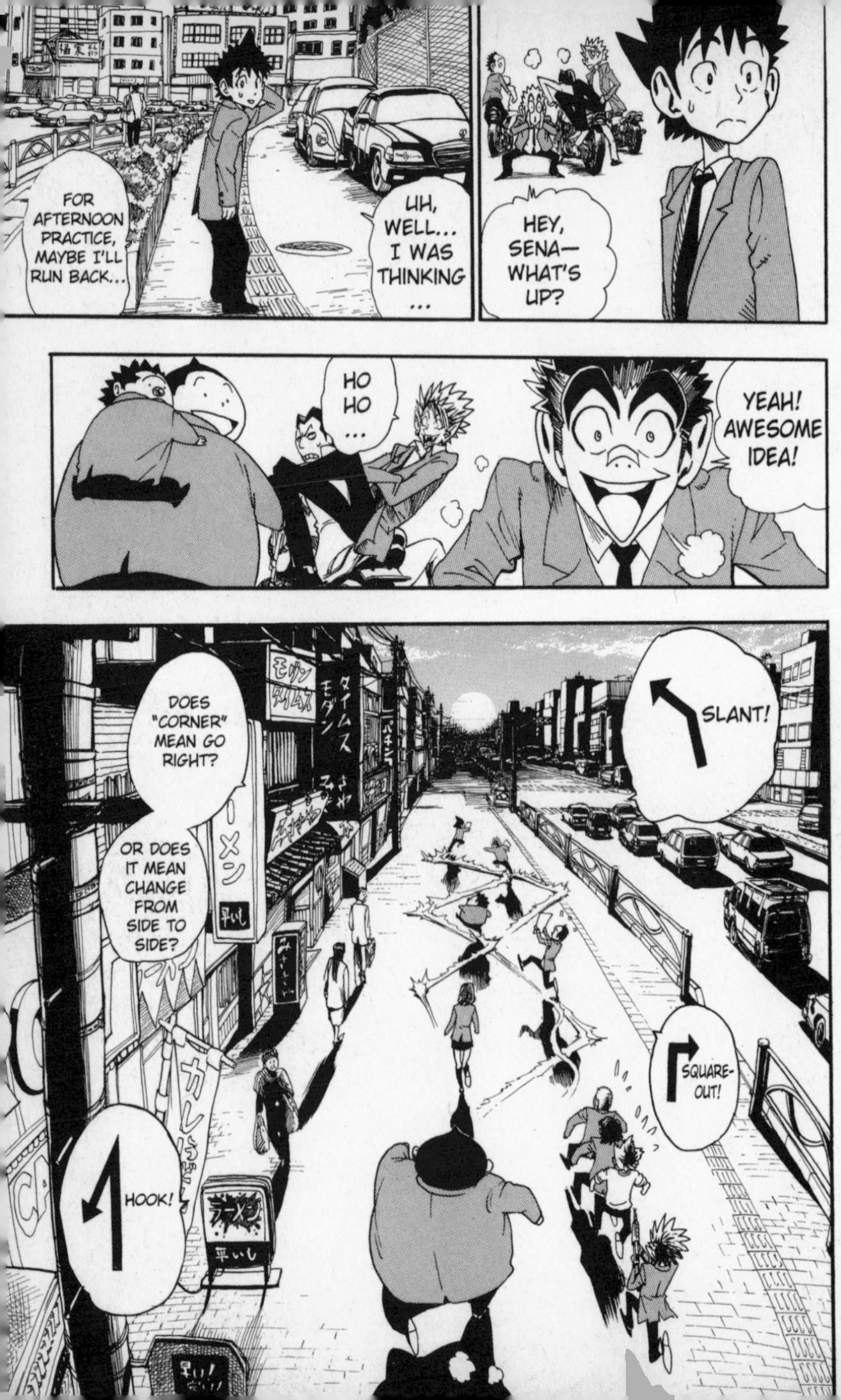
HEY, SENA—WHAT'S UP?
UH, WELL... I WAS THINKING ...
FOR AFTERNOON PRACTICE, MAYBE I'LL RUN BACK...
YEAH! AWESOME IDEA!
HO HO ...
SLANT!
DOES "CORNER" MEAN GO RIGHT?
OR DOES IT MEAN CHANGE FROM SIDE TO SIDE?
SQUARE-OUT!
HOOK!

DEIMON HIGH SCHOOL

SURPRISE SCHOOL BAG INSPECTION

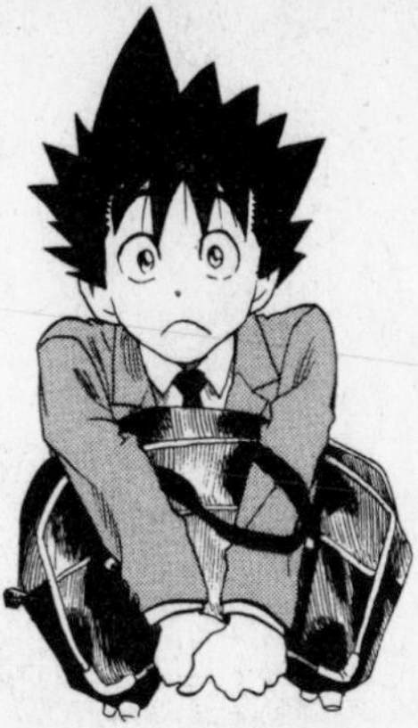

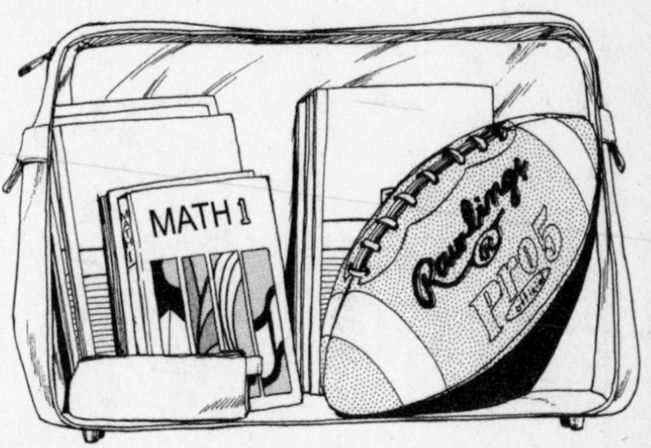
MATH 1
Rawlings
PRO5

Sena Kobayakawa

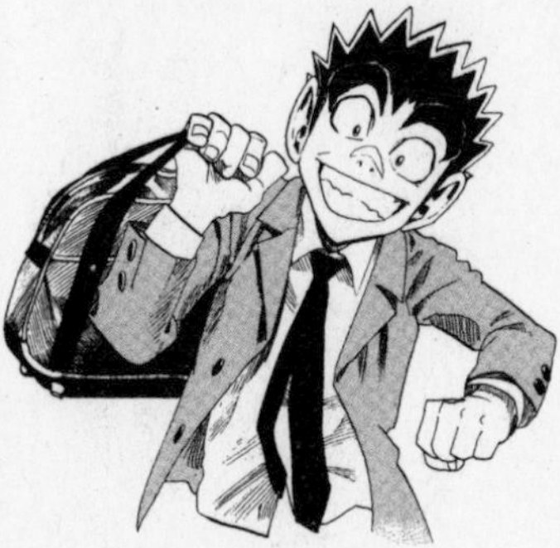

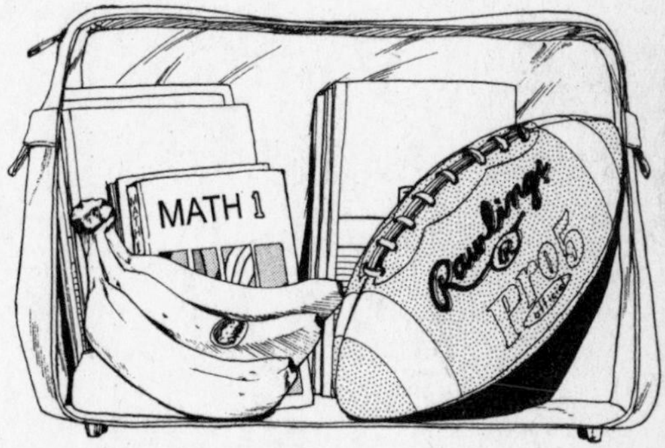
MATH 1
Rawlings
PRO5

Taro Raimon

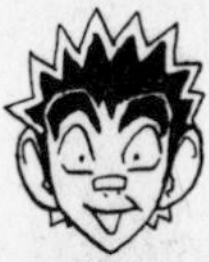

HEY, THE CONTENTS ARE EXACTLY THE SAME!

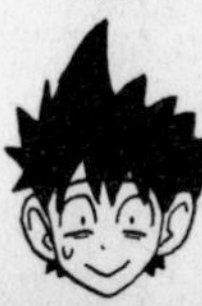

UH, NO, THERE IS ONE BIG DIFFERENCE...

Chapter 36

A Hero Has a Solid Foundation

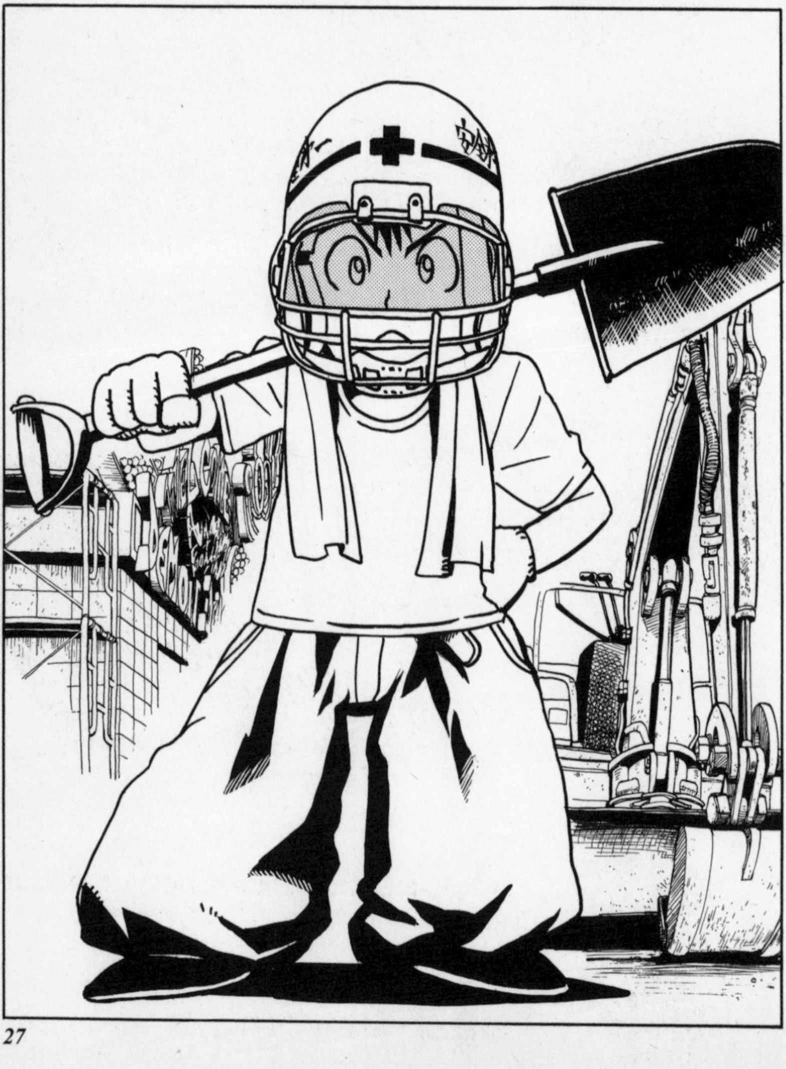

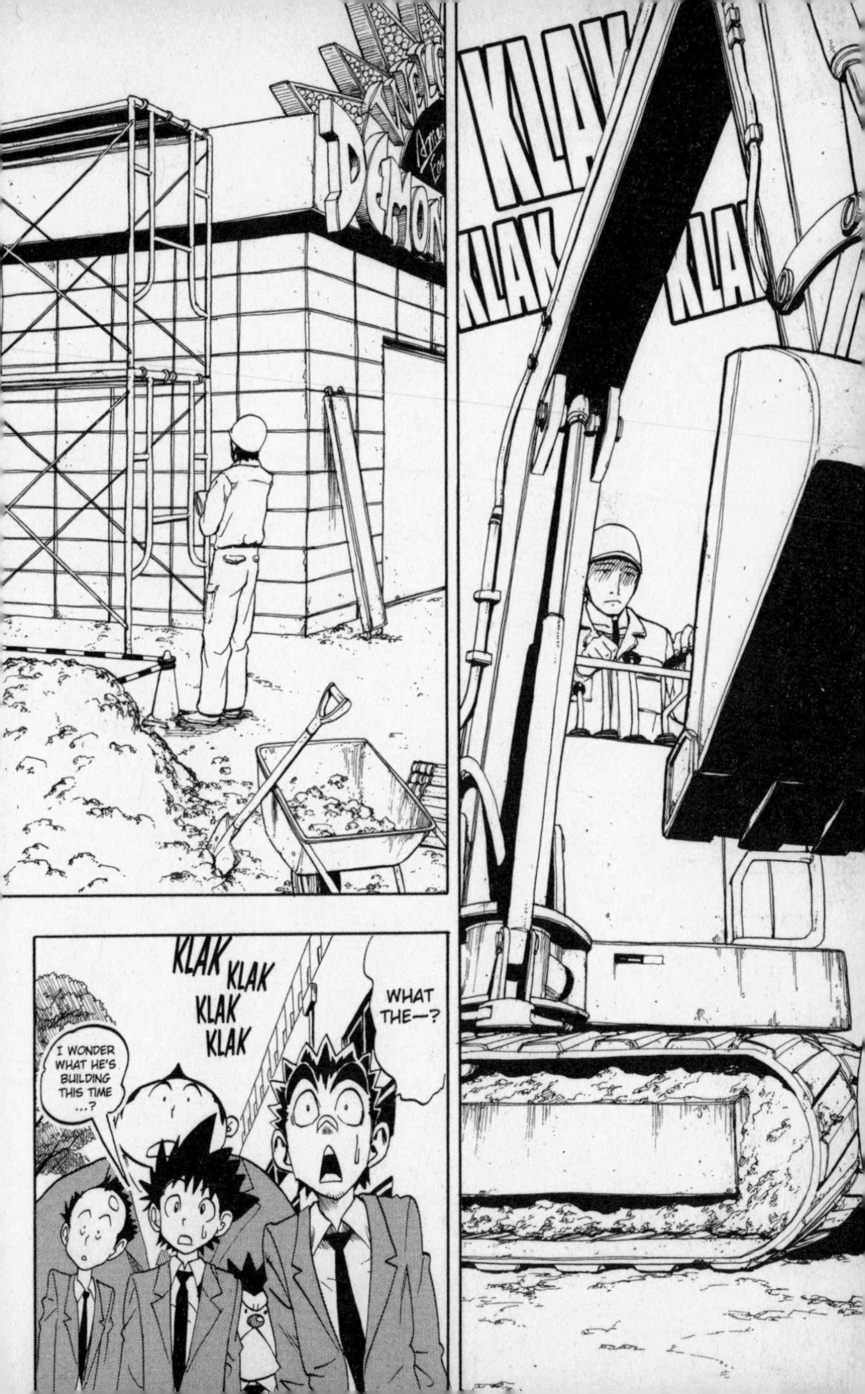
KLAK
KLAK
DEMON
WHAT THE—?
KLAK KLAK KLAK KLAK
I WONDER WHAT HE'S BUILDING THIS TIME ...?

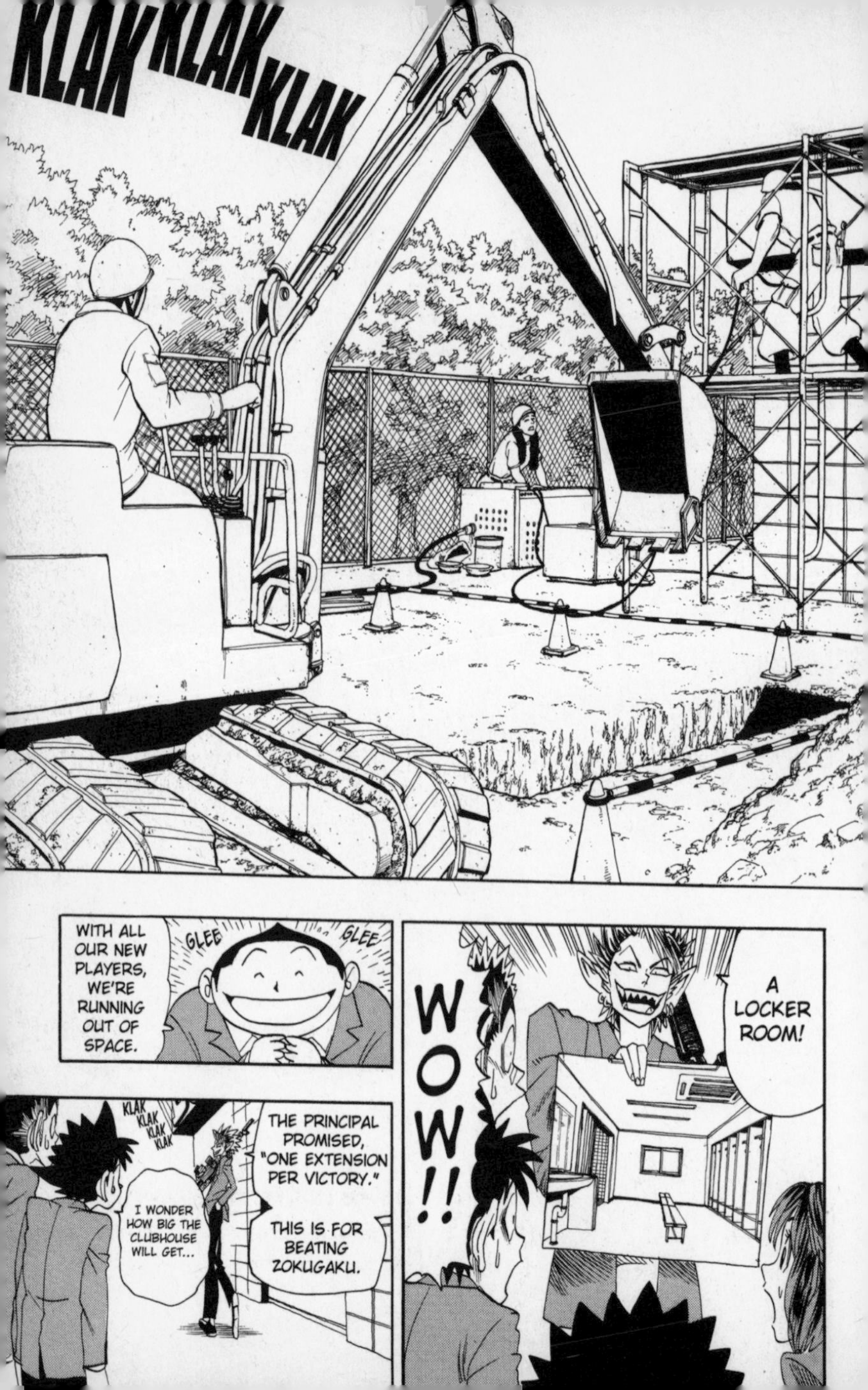
KLAK KLAK KLAK KLAK
A LOCKER ROOM!
WOW!!
GLEE GLEE
WITH ALL OUR NEW PLAYERS, WE'RE RUNNING OUT OF SPACE.
THE PRINCIPAL PROMISED, "ONE EXTENSION PER VICTORY."
THIS IS FOR BEATING ZOKUGAKU.
KLAK KLAK KLAK KLAK
I WONDER HOW BIG THE CLUBHOUSE WILL GET...

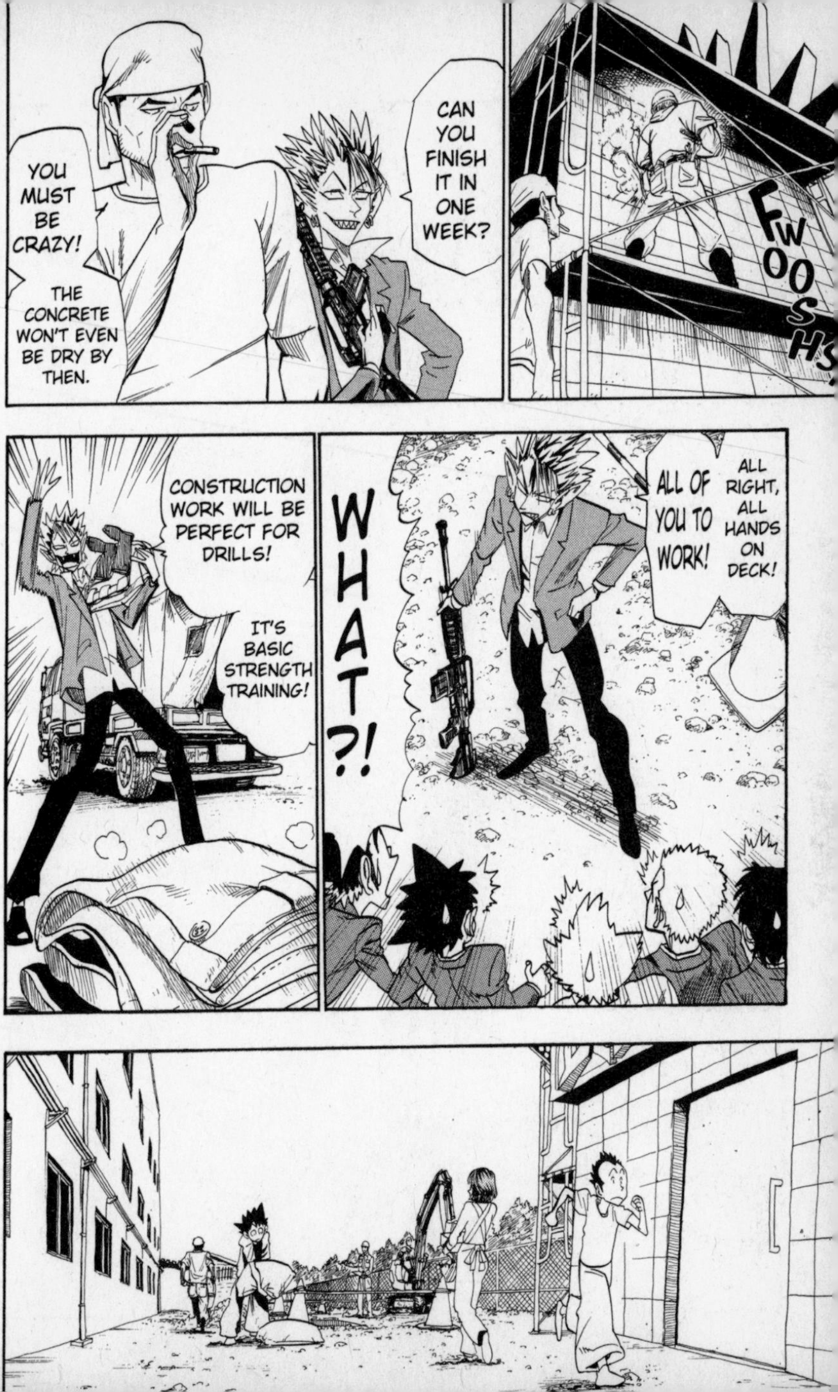
FWOOSH
CAN YOU FINISH IT IN ONE WEEK?
YOU MUST BE CRAZY!
THE CONCRETE WON'T EVEN BE DRY BY THEN.
ALL RIGHT, ALL HANDS ON DECK!
ALL OF YOU TO WORK!
WHAT?!
CONSTRUCTION WORK WILL BE PERFECT FOR DRILLS!
IT'S BASIC STRENGTH TRAINING!

READ THIS WAY

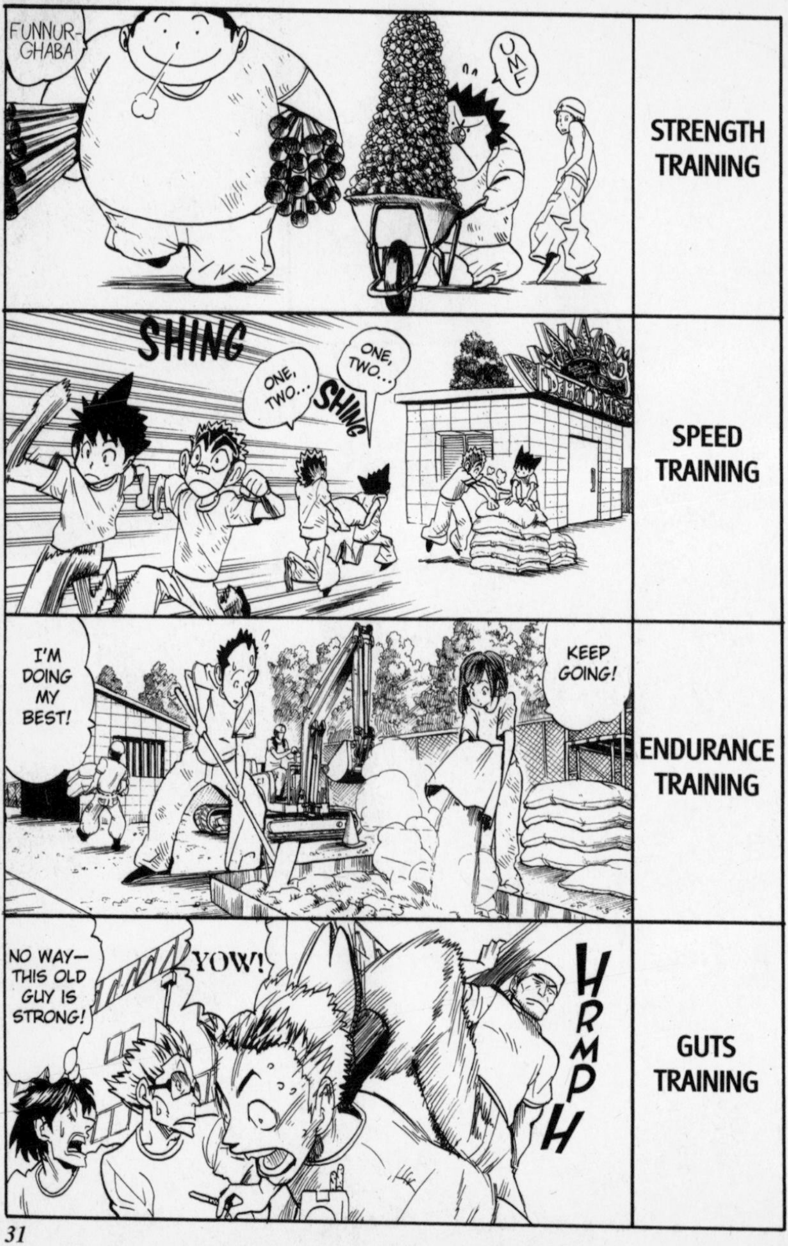
STRENGTH TRAINING
UMF
FUNNURGHABA
SPEED TRAINING
ONE, TWO...
SHING
ONE, TWO...
SHING
ENDURANCE TRAINING
KEEP GOING!
I'M DOING MY BEST!
GUTS TRAINING
HRMPH
YOW!
NO WAY—THIS OLD GUY IS STRONG!

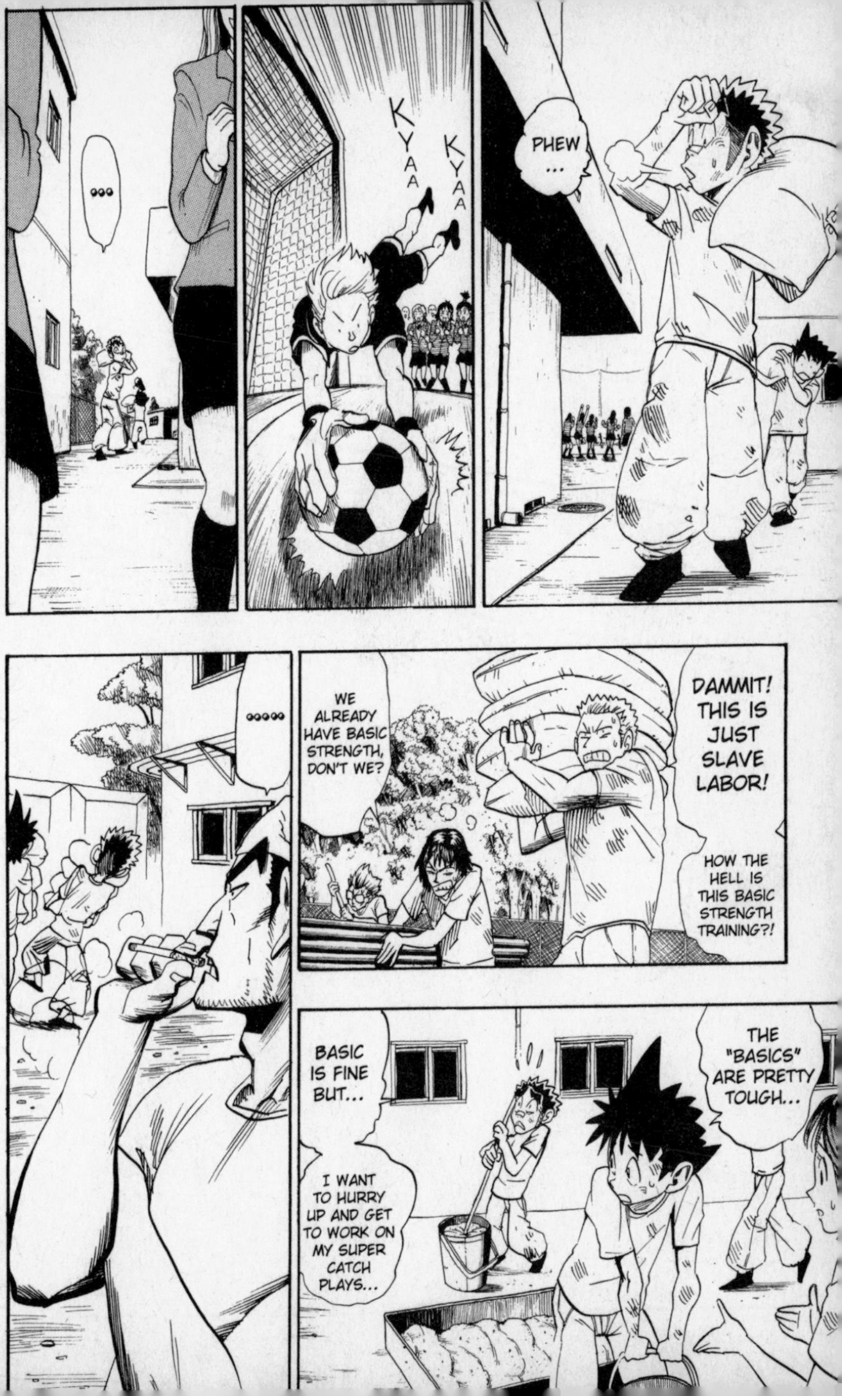
PHEW ...
KYAA
KYAA
...
DAMMIT! THIS IS JUST SLAVE LABOR!
HOW THE HELL IS THIS BASIC STRENGTH TRAINING?!
WE ALREADY HAVE BASIC STRENGTH, DON'T WE?
THE "BASICS" ARE PRETTY TOUGH...
BASIC IS FINE BUT...
I WANT TO HURRY UP AND GET TO WORK ON MY SUPER CATCH PLAYS...
.....

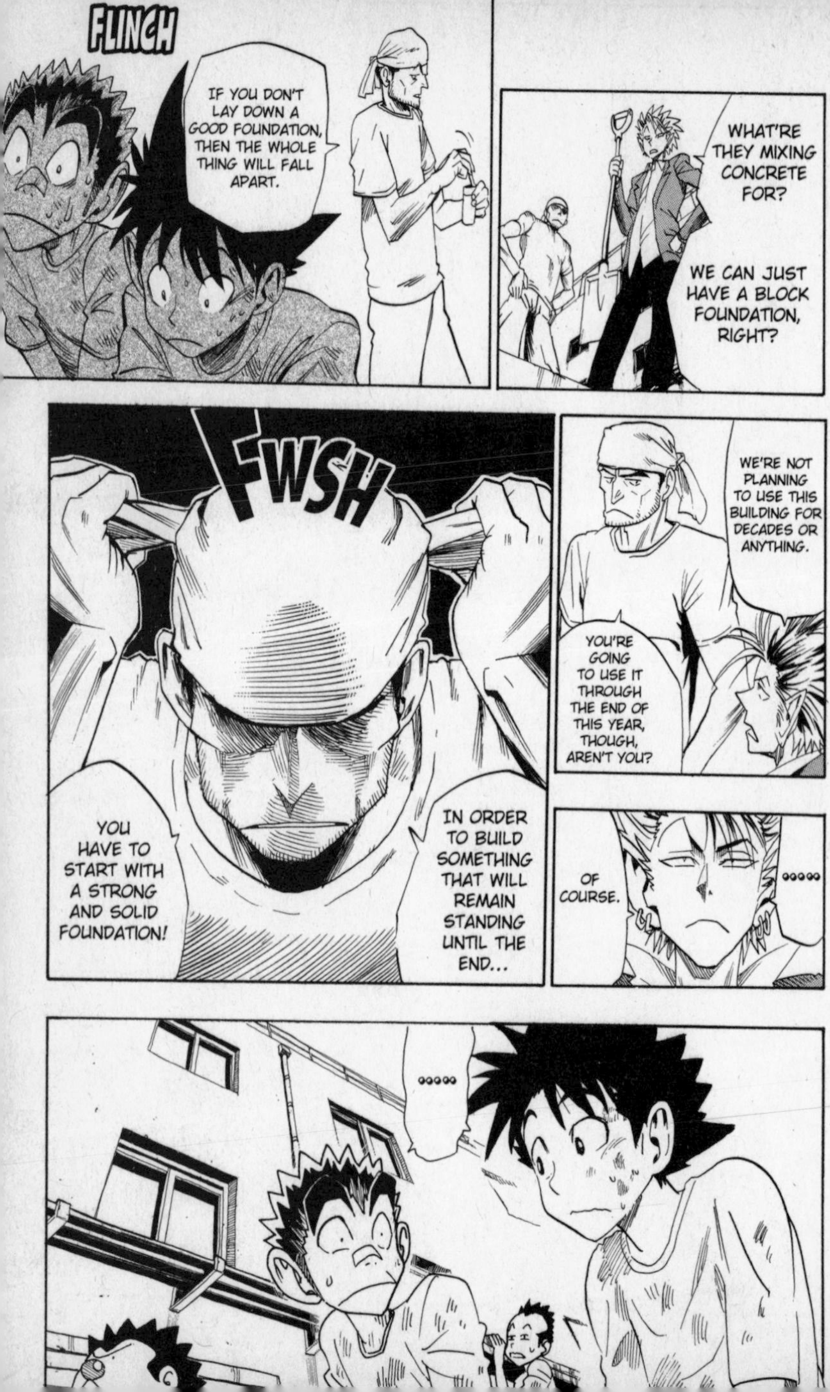
WHAT'RE THEY MIXING CONCRETE FOR?
WE CAN JUST HAVE A BLOCK FOUNDATION, RIGHT?
FLINCH
IF YOU DON'T LAY DOWN A GOOD FOUNDATION, THEN THE WHOLE THING WILL FALL APART.
WE'RE NOT PLANNING TO USE THIS BUILDING FOR DECADES OR ANYTHING.
YOU'RE GOING TO USE IT THROUGH THE END OF THIS YEAR, THOUGH, AREN'T YOU?
.....
OF COURSE.
FWSH
IN ORDER TO BUILD SOMETHING THAT WILL REMAIN STANDING UNTIL THE END...
YOU HAVE TO START WITH A STRONG AND SOLID FOUNDATION!
.....

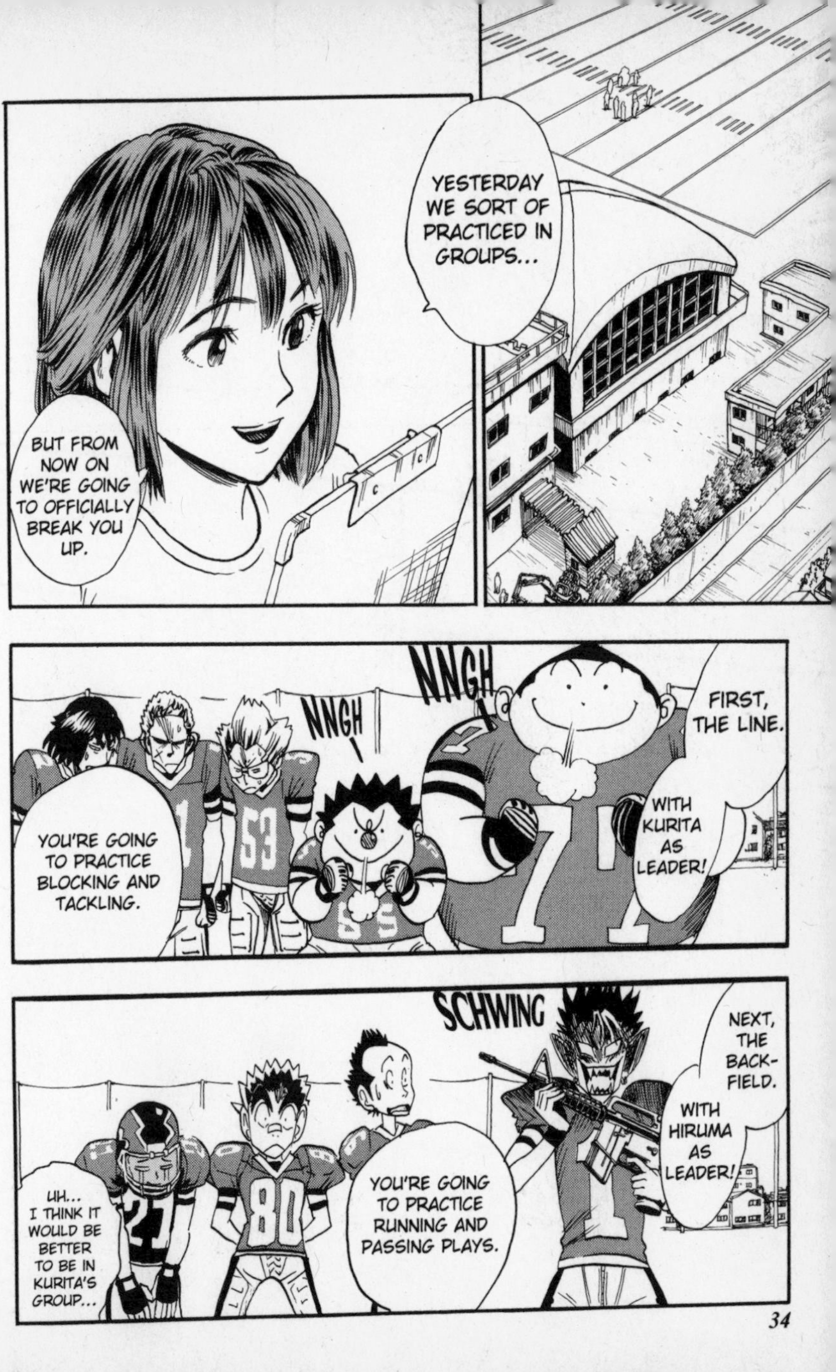
YESTERDAY WE SORT OF PRACTICED IN GROUPS...
BUT FROM NOW ON WE'RE GOING TO OFFICIALLY BREAK YOU UP.
FIRST, THE LINE.
WITH KURITA AS LEADER!
NNGH
NNGH
YOU'RE GOING TO PRACTICE BLOCKING AND TACKLING.
NEXT, THE BACK-FIELD.
WITH HIRUMA AS LEADER!
SCHWING
YOU'RE GOING TO PRACTICE RUNNING AND PASSING PLAYS.
UH... I THINK IT WOULD BE BETTER TO BE IN KURITA'S GROUP...

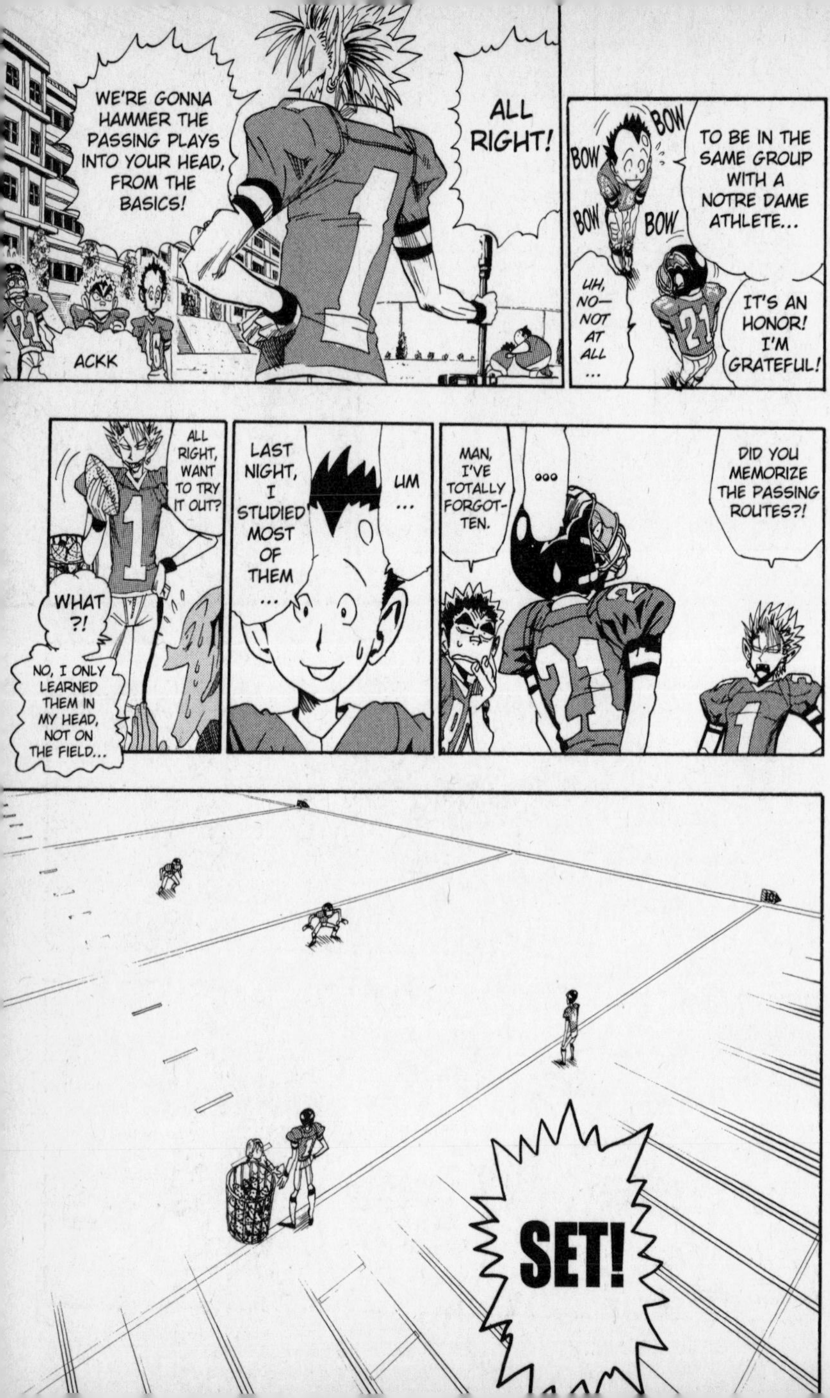
BOW BOW BOW BOW
TO BE IN THE SAME GROUP WITH A NOTRE DAME ATHLETE...
IT'S AN HONOR! I'M GRATEFUL!
UH, NO— NOT AT ALL ...
WE'RE GONNA HAMMER THE PASSING PLAYS INTO YOUR HEAD, FROM THE BASICS!
ALL RIGHT!
ACKK
DID YOU MEMORIZE THE PASSING ROUTES?!
ooo
MAN, I'VE TOTALLY FORGOT-TEN.
UM ...
LAST NIGHT, I STUDIED MOST OF THEM ...
ALL RIGHT, WANT TO TRY IT OUT?
WHAT ?!
NO, I ONLY LEARNED THEM IN MY HEAD, NOT ON THE FIELD...
SET!

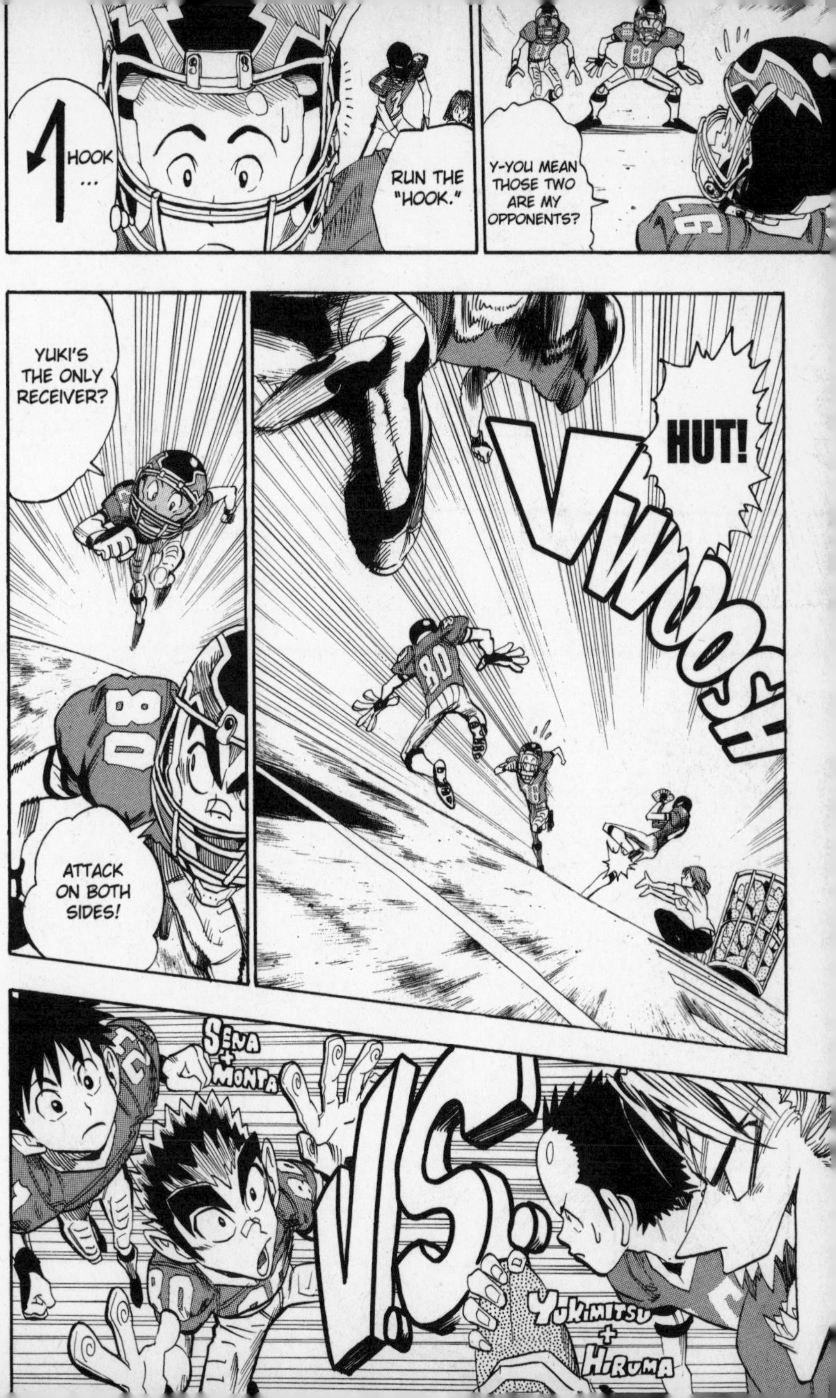
Y-YOU MEAN THOSE TWO ARE MY OPPONENTS?
RUN THE "HOOK."
HOOK ...
HUT!
VWOOSH
YUKI'S THE ONLY RECEIVER?
ATTACK ON BOTH SIDES!
SENA + MONTA
VS.
YUKIMITSU + HIRUMA

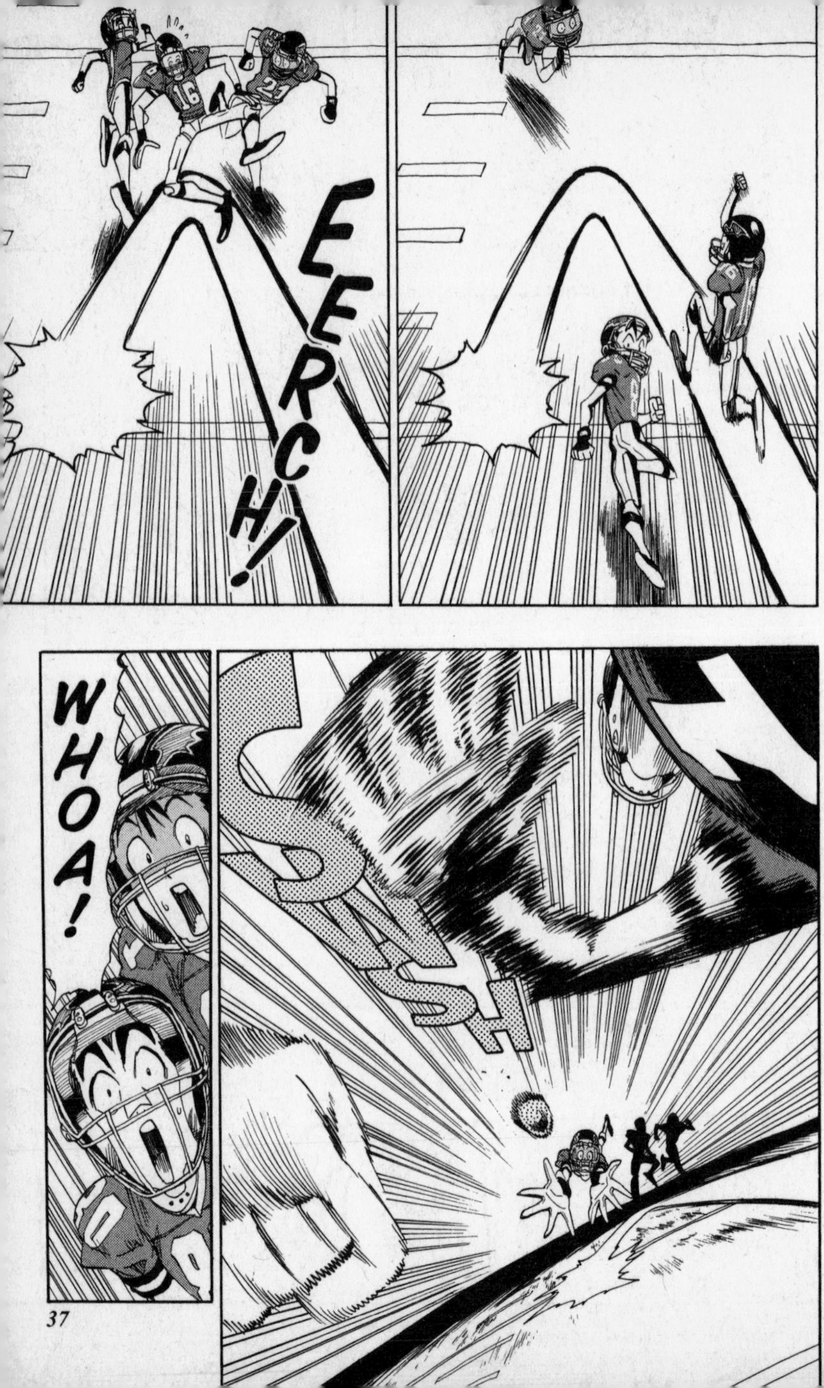
EEERCH!
WHOA!

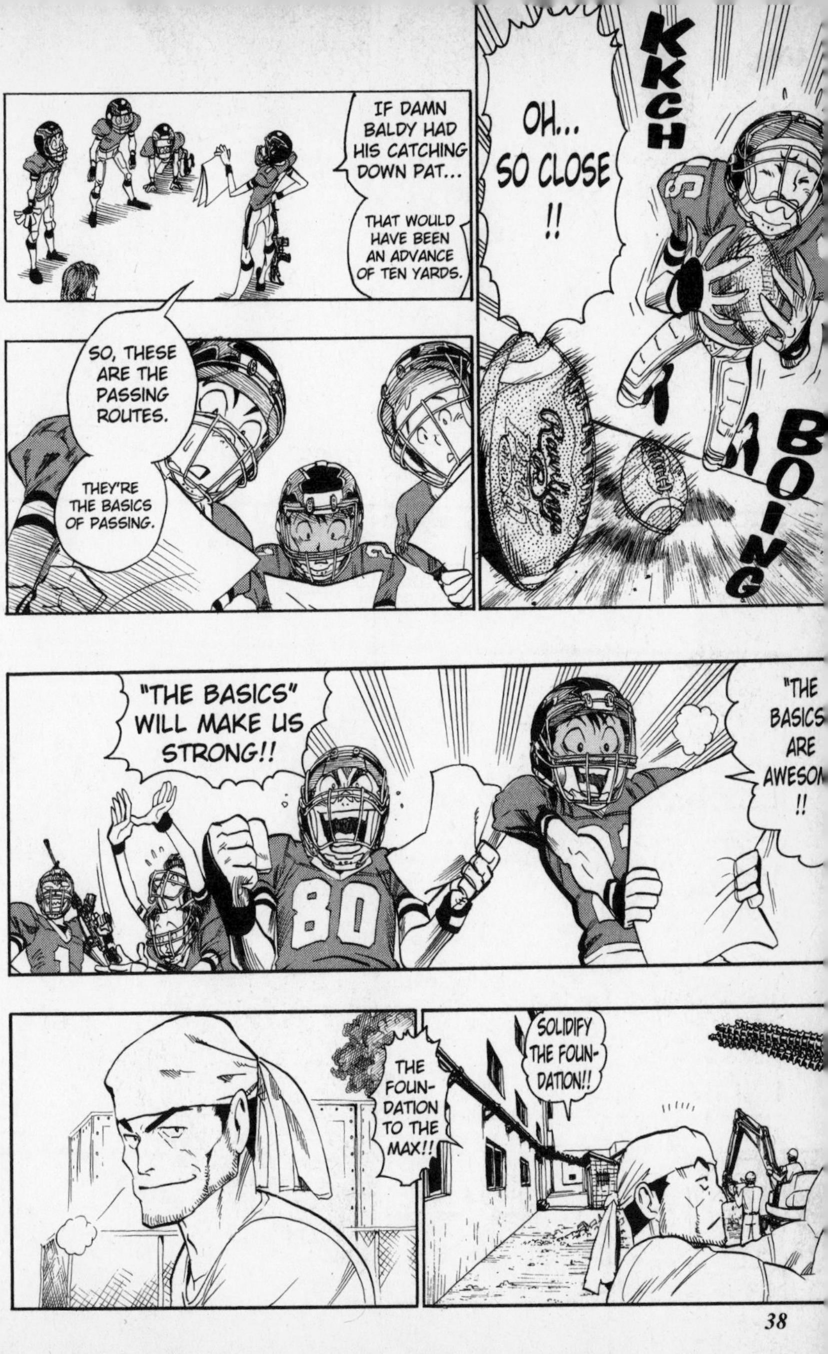
KKCH
OH... SO CLOSE!!
BOING
IF DAMN BALDY HAD HIS CATCHING DOWN PAT...
THAT WOULD HAVE BEEN AN ADVANCE OF TEN YARDS.
SO, THESE ARE THE PASSING ROUTES.
THEY'RE THE BASICS OF PASSING.
"THE BASICS ARE AWESOM!!
"THE BASICS" WILL MAKE US STRONG!!
SOLIDIFY THE FOUNDATION!!
THE FOUNDATION TO THE MAX!!

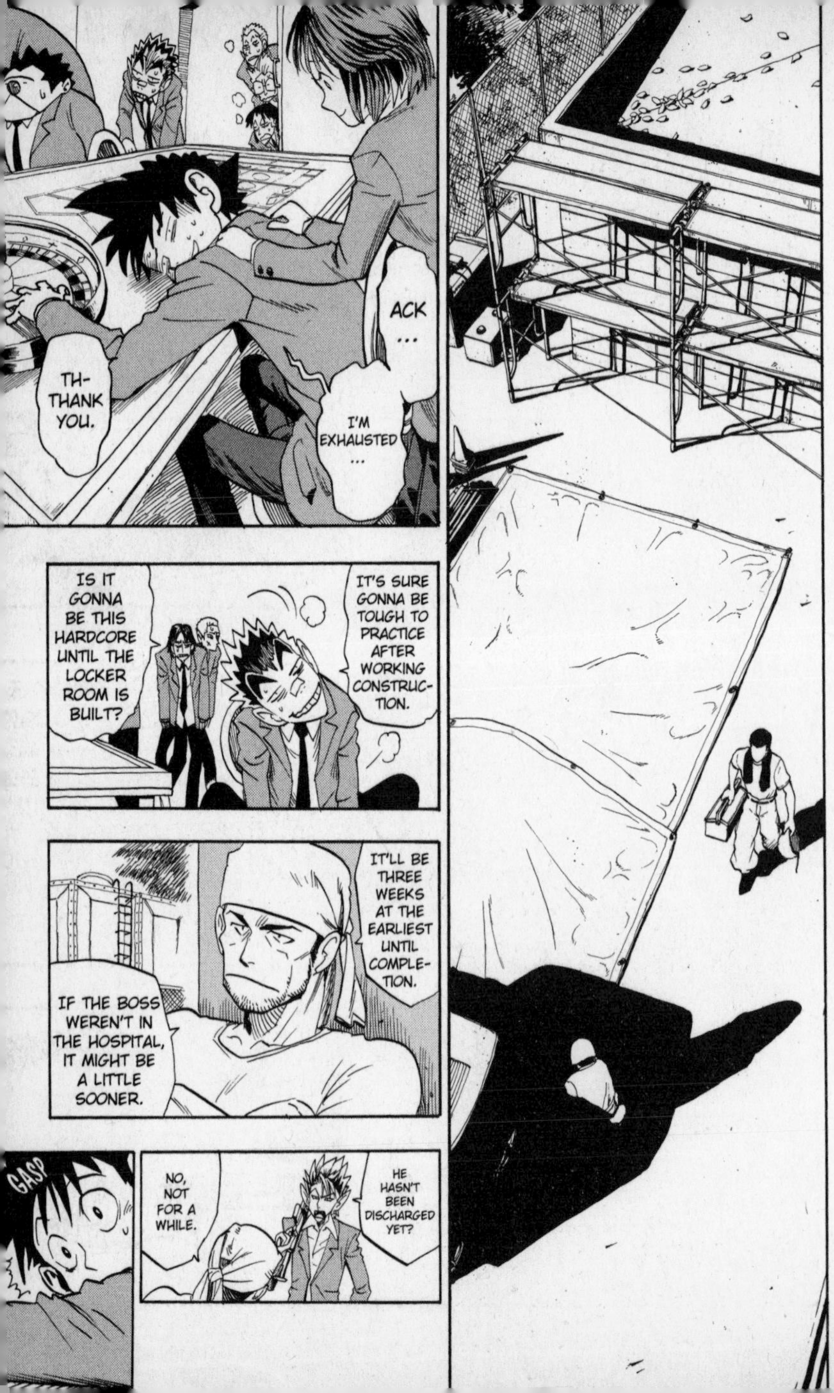
ACK ...
I'M EXHAUSTED ...
TH- THANK YOU.
IT'S SURE GONNA BE TOUGH TO PRACTICE AFTER WORKING CONSTRUCTION.
IS IT GONNA BE THIS HARDCORE UNTIL THE LOCKER ROOM IS BUILT?
IT'LL BE THREE WEEKS AT THE EARLIEST UNTIL COMPLETION.
IF THE BOSS WEREN'T IN THE HOSPITAL, IT MIGHT BE A LITTLE SOONER.
HE HASN'T BEEN DISCHARGED YET?
NO, NOT FOR A WHILE.
GASP

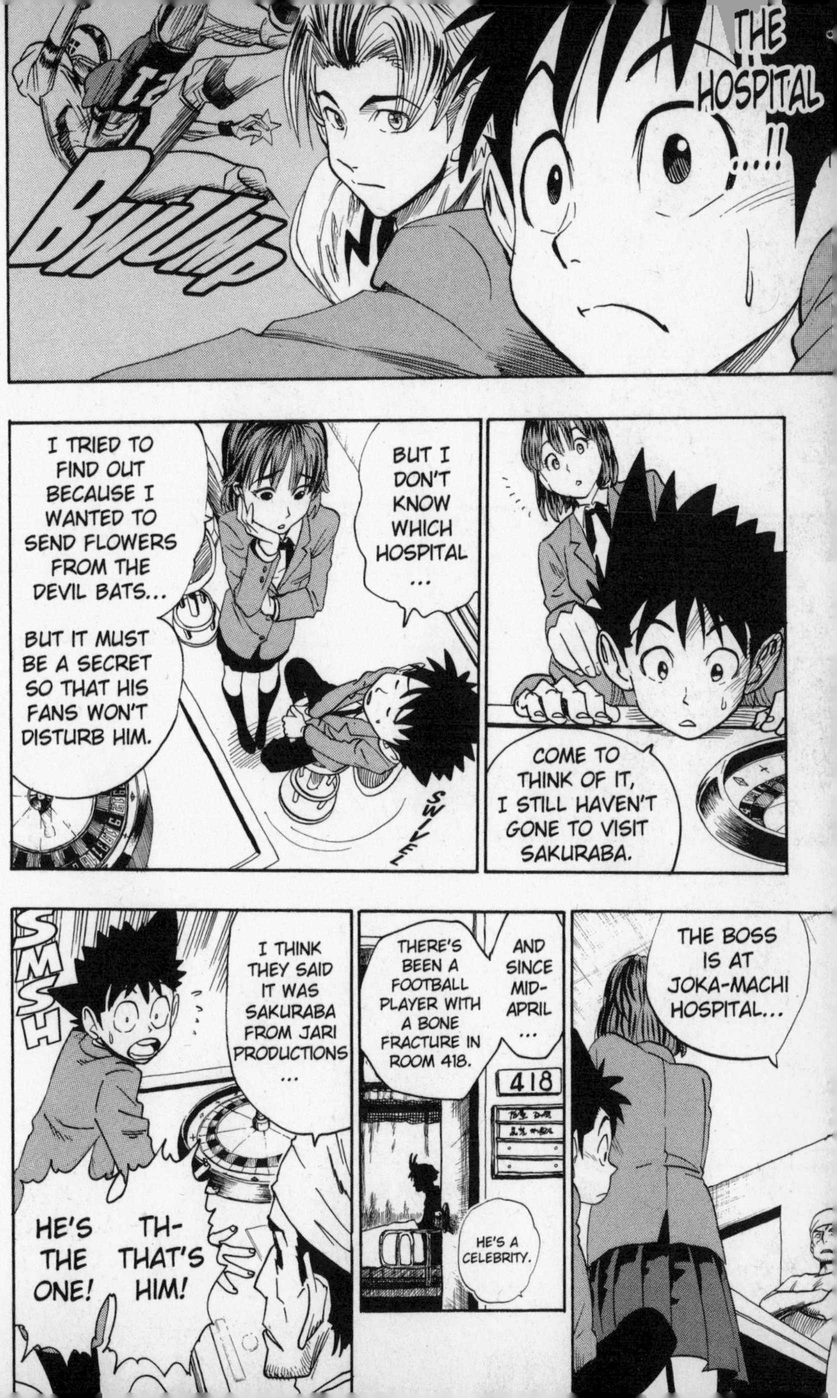
THE HOSPITAL
...!!
COME TO THINK OF IT, I STILL HAVEN'T GONE TO VISIT SAKURABA.
BUT I DON'T KNOW WHICH HOSPITAL ...
I TRIED TO FIND OUT BECAUSE I WANTED TO SEND FLOWERS FROM THE DEVIL BATS...
BUT IT MUST BE A SECRET SO THAT HIS FANS WON'T DISTURB HIM.
SWIVEL
THE BOSS IS AT JOKA-MACHI HOSPITAL...
AND SINCE MID-APRIL ...
THERE'S BEEN A FOOTBALL PLAYER WITH A BONE FRACTURE IN ROOM 418.
418
HE'S A CELEBRITY.
I THINK THEY SAID IT WAS SAKURABA FROM JARI PRODUCTIONS ...
SMSH
TH- THAT'S HIM!
HE'S THE ONE!

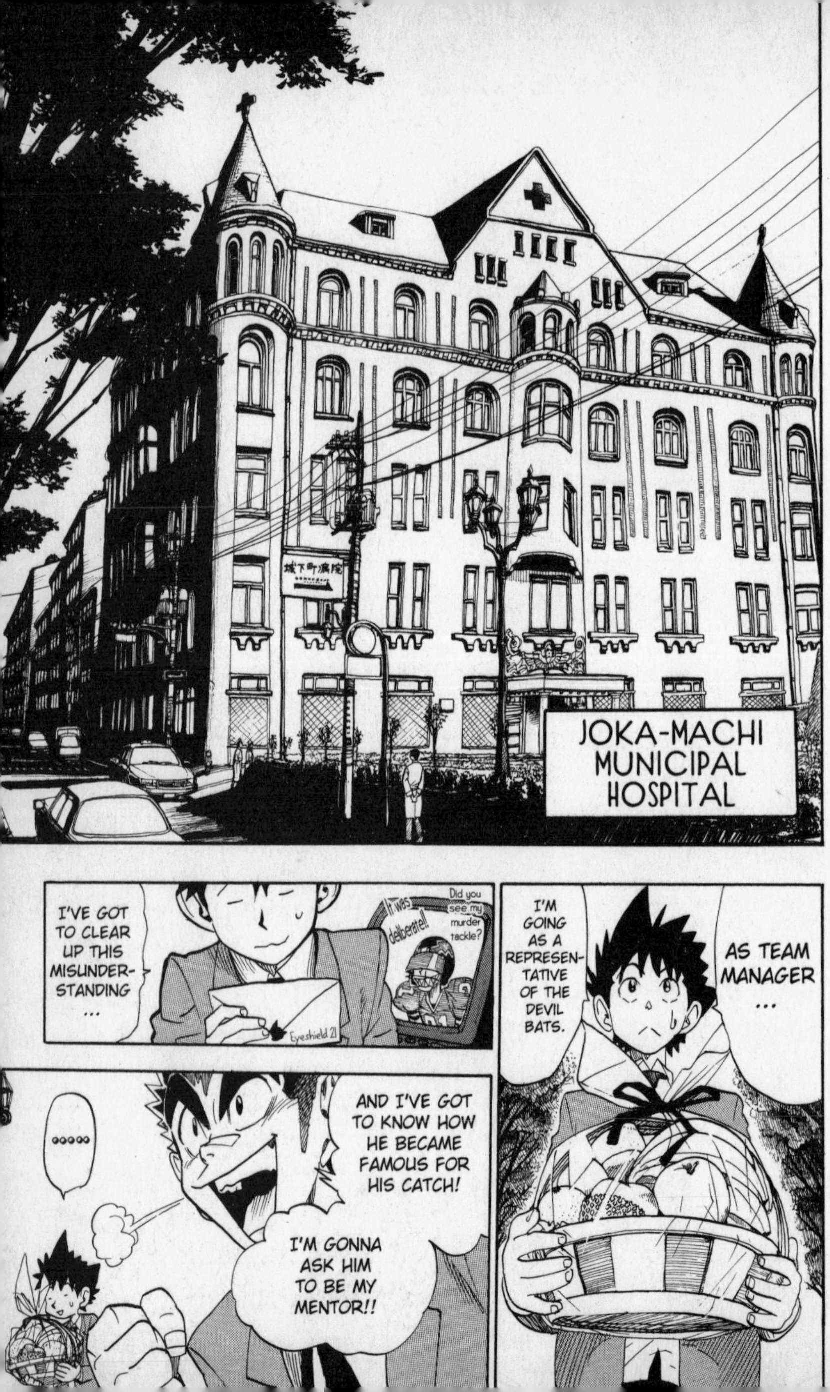
JOKA-MACHI MUNICIPAL HOSPITAL
AS TEAM MANAGER ...
I'M GOING AS A REPRESENTATIVE OF THE DEVIL BATS.
I'VE GOT TO CLEAR UP THIS MISUNDERSTANDING ...
Did you see my murder tackle?
It was deliberate!!
Eyeshield 21
AND I'VE GOT TO KNOW HOW HE BECAME FAMOUS FOR HIS CATCH!
I'M GONNA ASK HIM TO BE MY MENTOR!!
.....

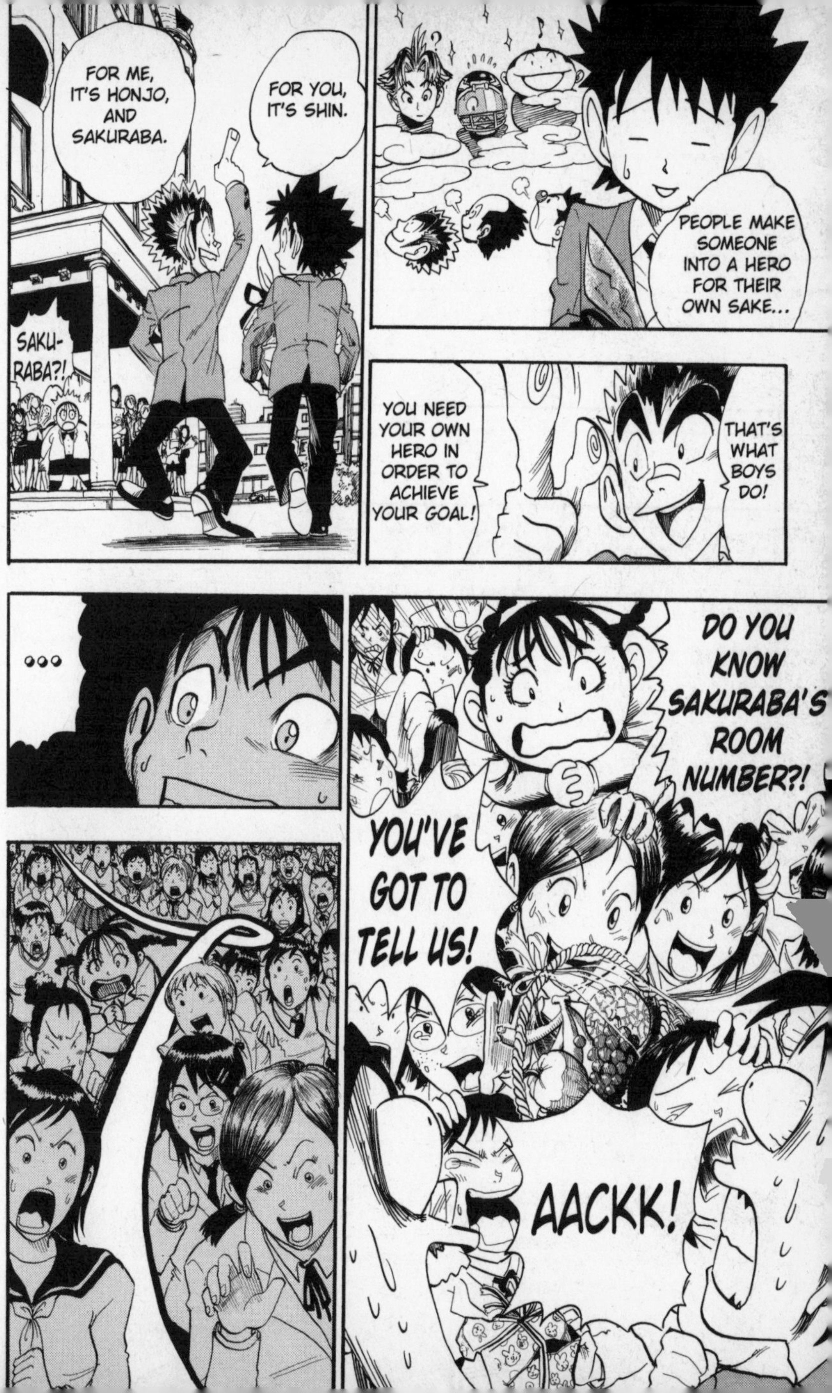
PEOPLE MAKE SOMEONE INTO A HERO FOR THEIR OWN SAKE...
YOU NEED YOUR OWN HERO IN ORDER TO ACHIEVE YOUR GOAL!
THAT'S WHAT BOYS DO!
FOR YOU, IT'S SHIN.
FOR ME, IT'S HONJO, AND SAKURABA.
SAKU-RABA?!
DO YOU KNOW SAKURABA'S ROOM NUMBER?!
YOU'VE GOT TO TELL US!
AACKK!
...

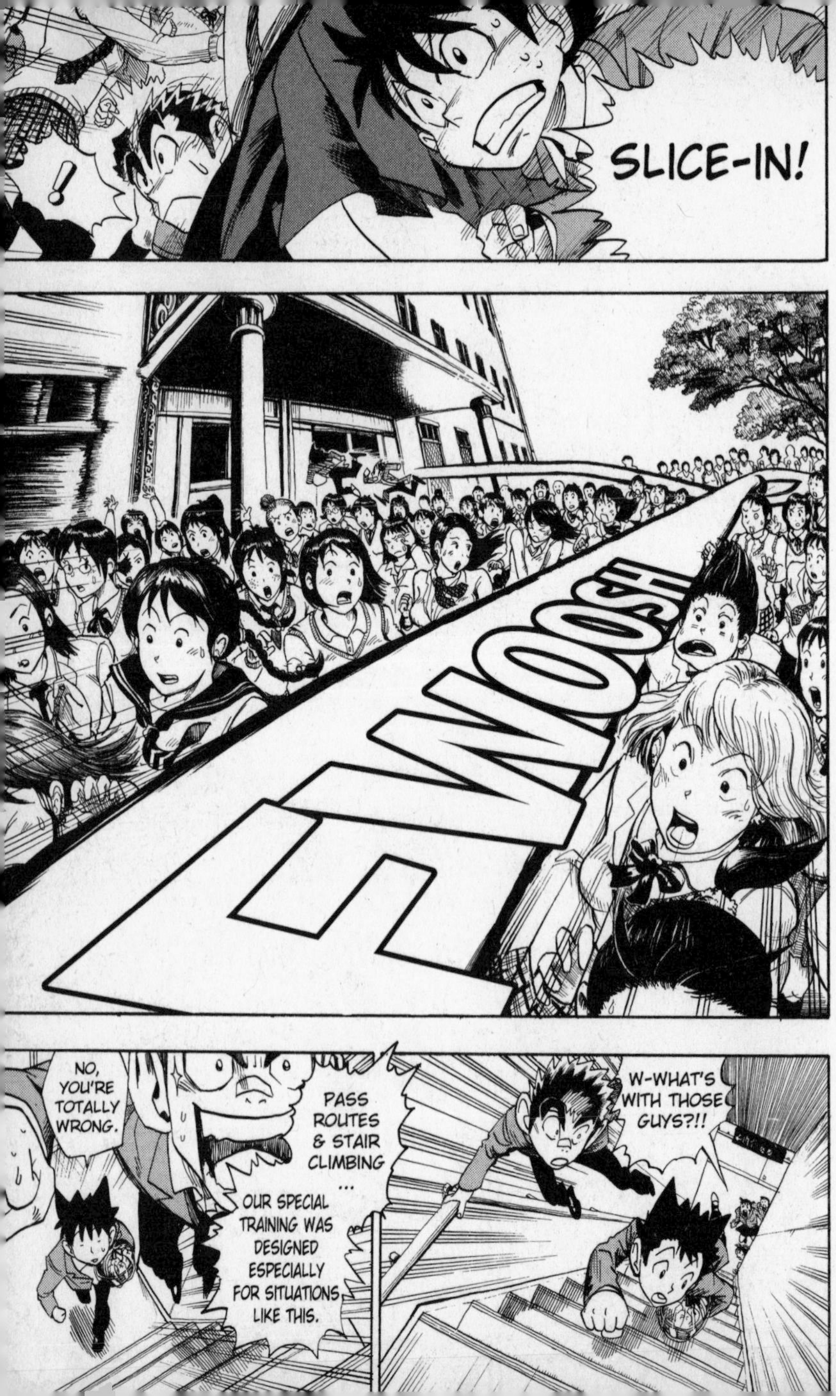
SLICE-IN!
WHOOSH
W-WHAT'S WITH THOSE GUYS?!!
NO, YOU'RE TOTALLY WRONG.
PASS ROUTES & STAIR CLIMBING ...
OUR SPECIAL TRAINING WAS DESIGNED ESPECIALLY FOR SITUATIONS LIKE THIS.

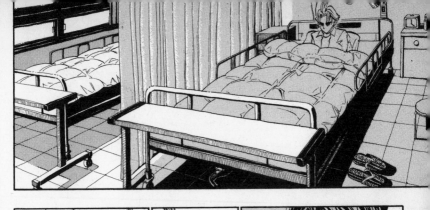

EXCUSE US...

KCHK...

KNOCK KNOCK

...

HEY, SAKURABA! STILL ALIVE?!

BAM

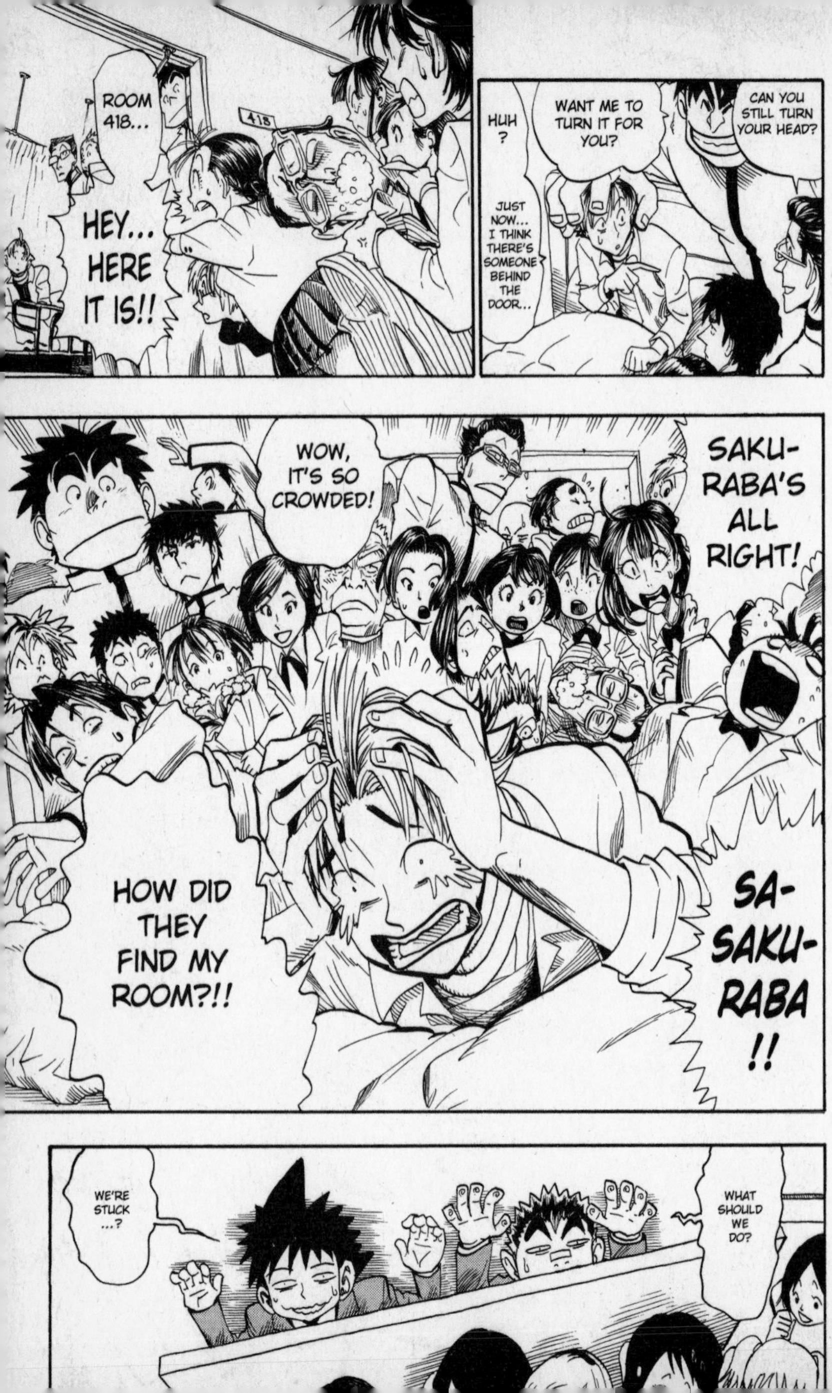
CAN YOU STILL TURN YOUR HEAD?
WANT ME TO TURN IT FOR YOU?
HUH ?
JUST NOW... I THINK THERE'S SOMEONE BEHIND THE DOOR...
ROOM 418...
HEY... HERE IT IS!!
SAKU-RABA'S ALL RIGHT!
SA-SAKU-RABA !!
WOW, IT'S SO CROWDED!
HOW DID THEY FIND MY ROOM?!!
WHAT SHOULD WE DO?
WE'RE STUCK ...?

DEIMON HIGH SCHOOL

SURPRISE SCHOOL BAG INSPECTION

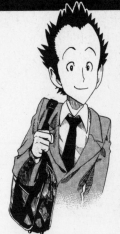

Manabu Yukimitsu

国語辞典
英和辞典
ENGLISH
STUDY
反対語辞典
英文法
受験問題集
四字熟語
慣用辞典
文法
古語例解辞典
国語
物理

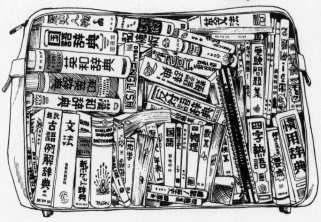

...YOU'RE WELL PREPARED, AREN'T YOU?

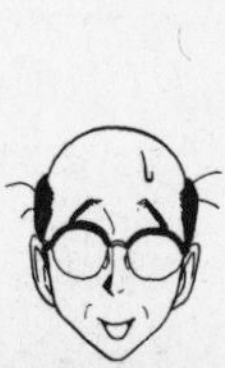

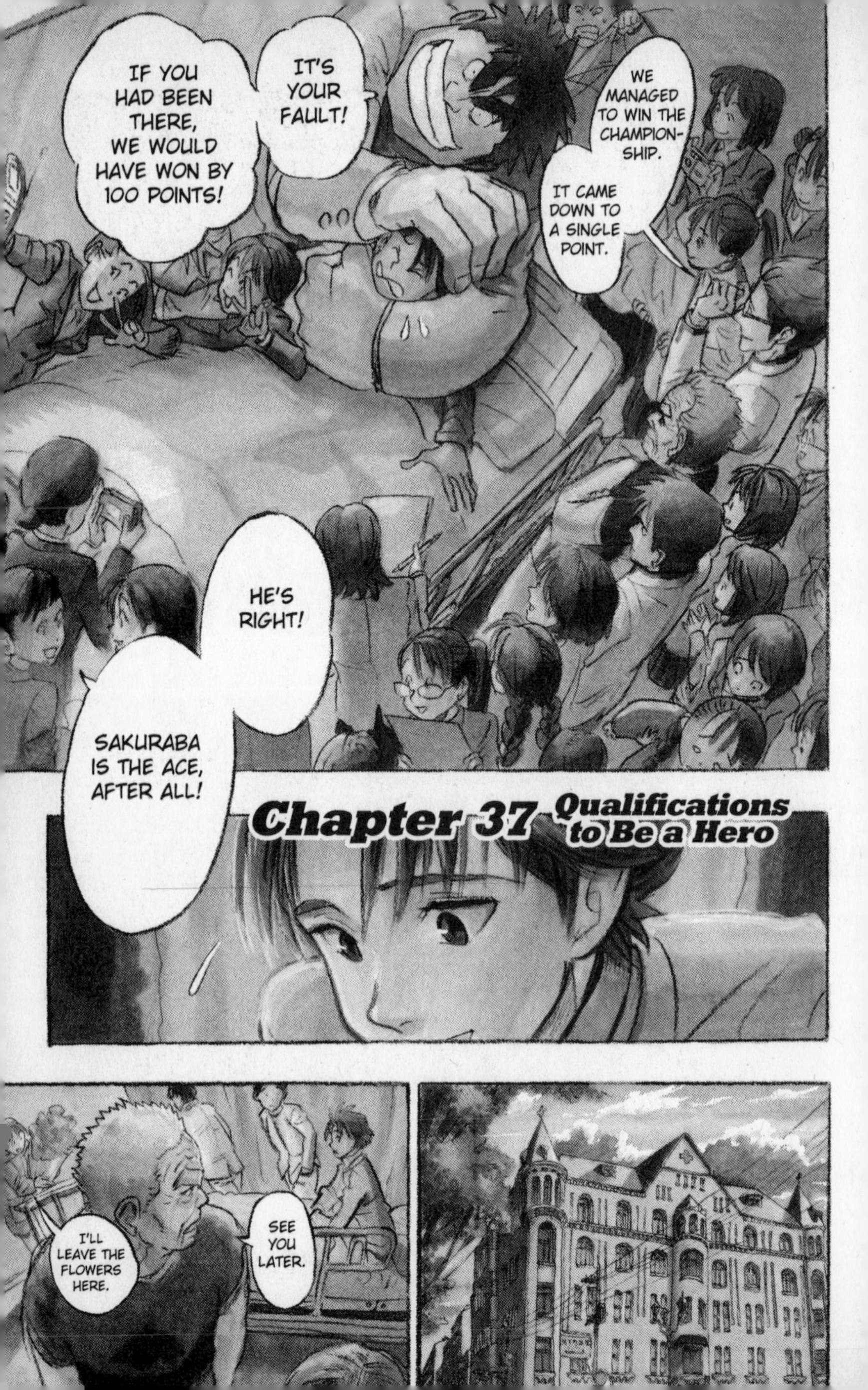
WE MANAGED TO WIN THE CHAMPIONSHIP.
IT CAME DOWN TO A SINGLE POINT.
IT'S YOUR FAULT!
IF YOU HAD BEEN THERE, WE WOULD HAVE WON BY 100 POINTS!
HE'S RIGHT!
SAKURABA IS THE ACE, AFTER ALL!
Chapter 37 Qualifications to Be a Hero
SEE YOU LATER.
I'LL LEAVE THE FLOWERS HERE.

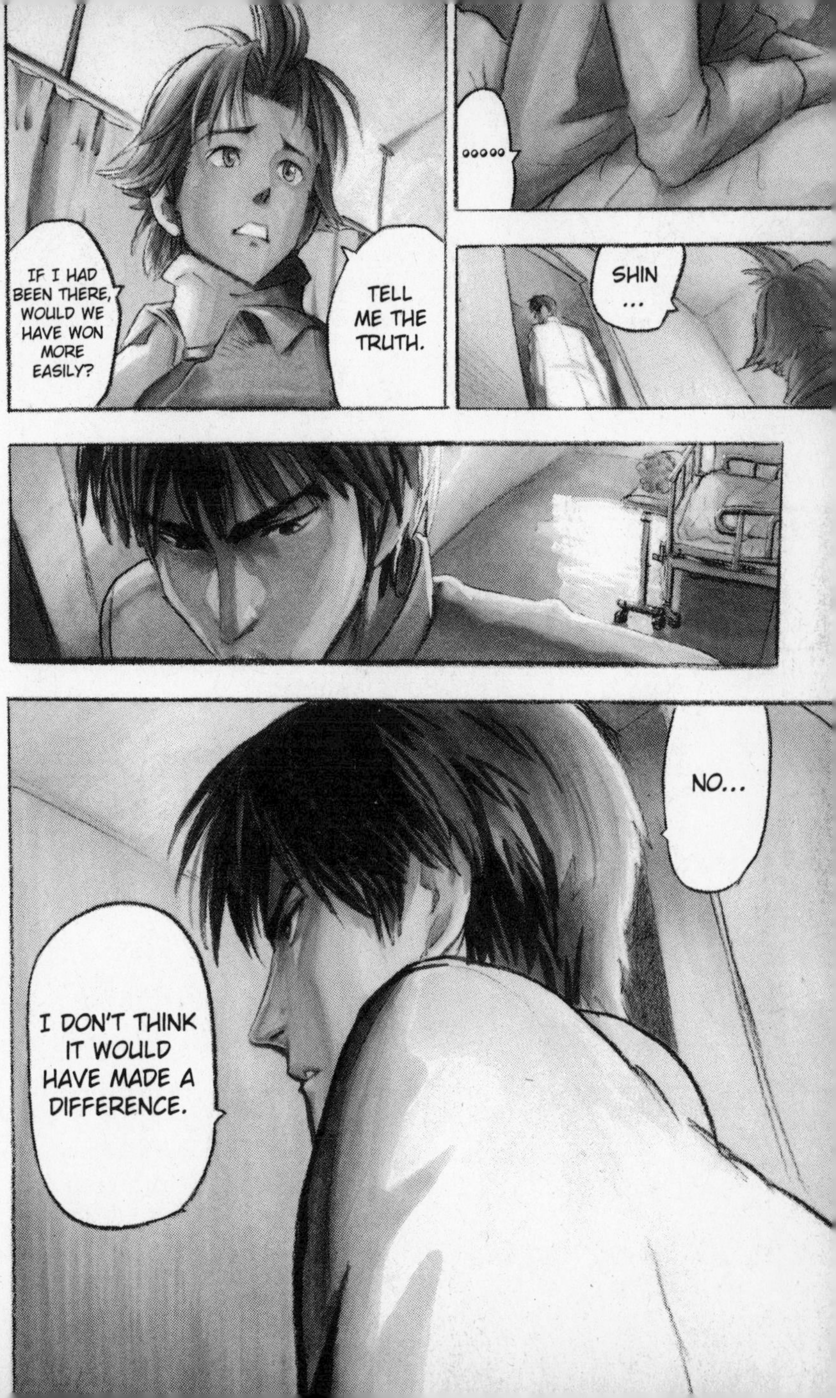
.....
SHIN ...
TELL ME THE TRUTH.
IF I HAD BEEN THERE, WOULD WE HAVE WON MORE EASILY?
NO...
I DON'T THINK IT WOULD HAVE MADE A DIFFERENCE.

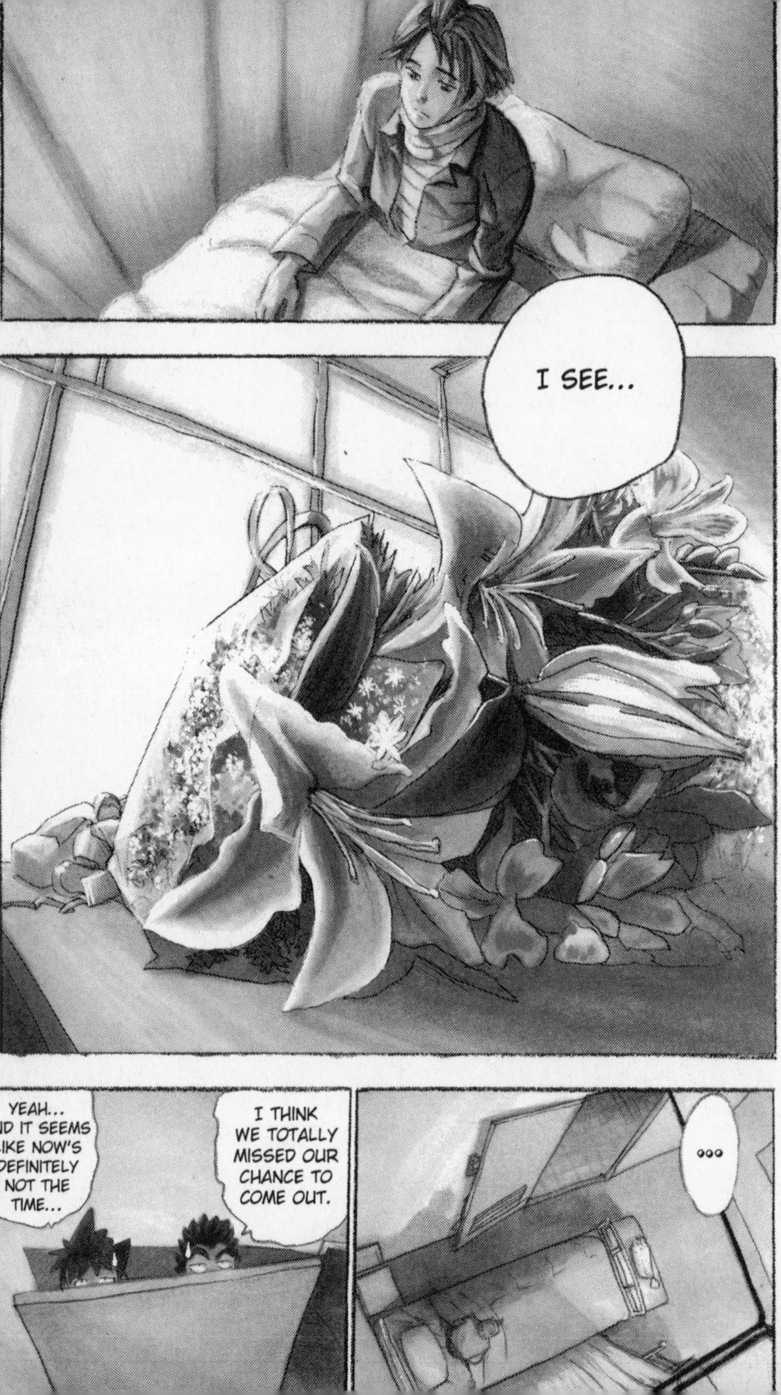
I SEE...
...
I THINK WE TOTALLY MISSED OUR CHANCE TO COME OUT.
YEAH... AND IT SEEMS LIKE NOW'S DEFINITELY NOT THE TIME...

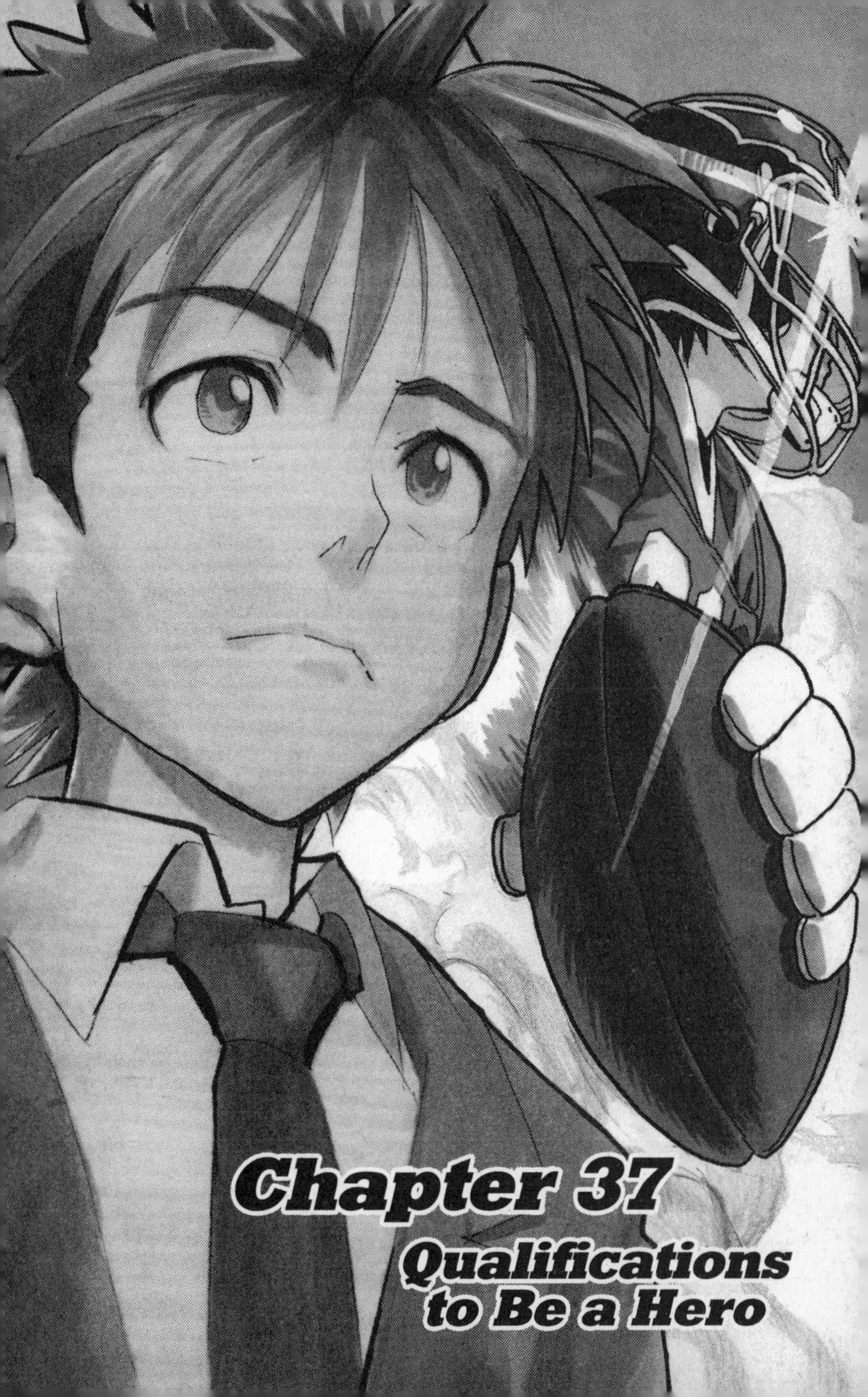
Chapter 37
Qualifications to Be a Hero

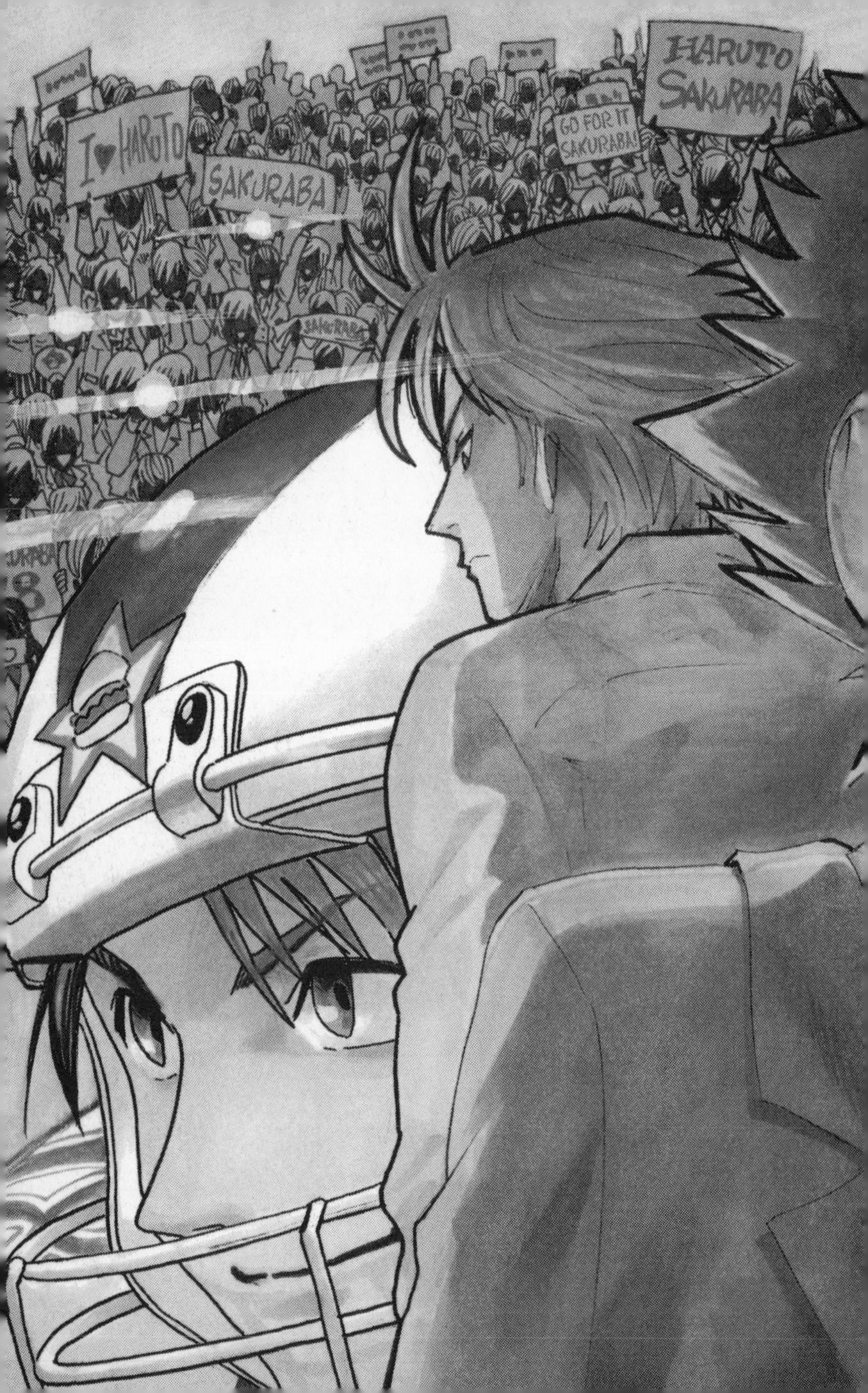
HARUTO SAKURARA
GO FOR IT SAKURABA!
I ♥ HARUTO
SAKURABA

It's a
good thing
they were
already
at the
hospital...

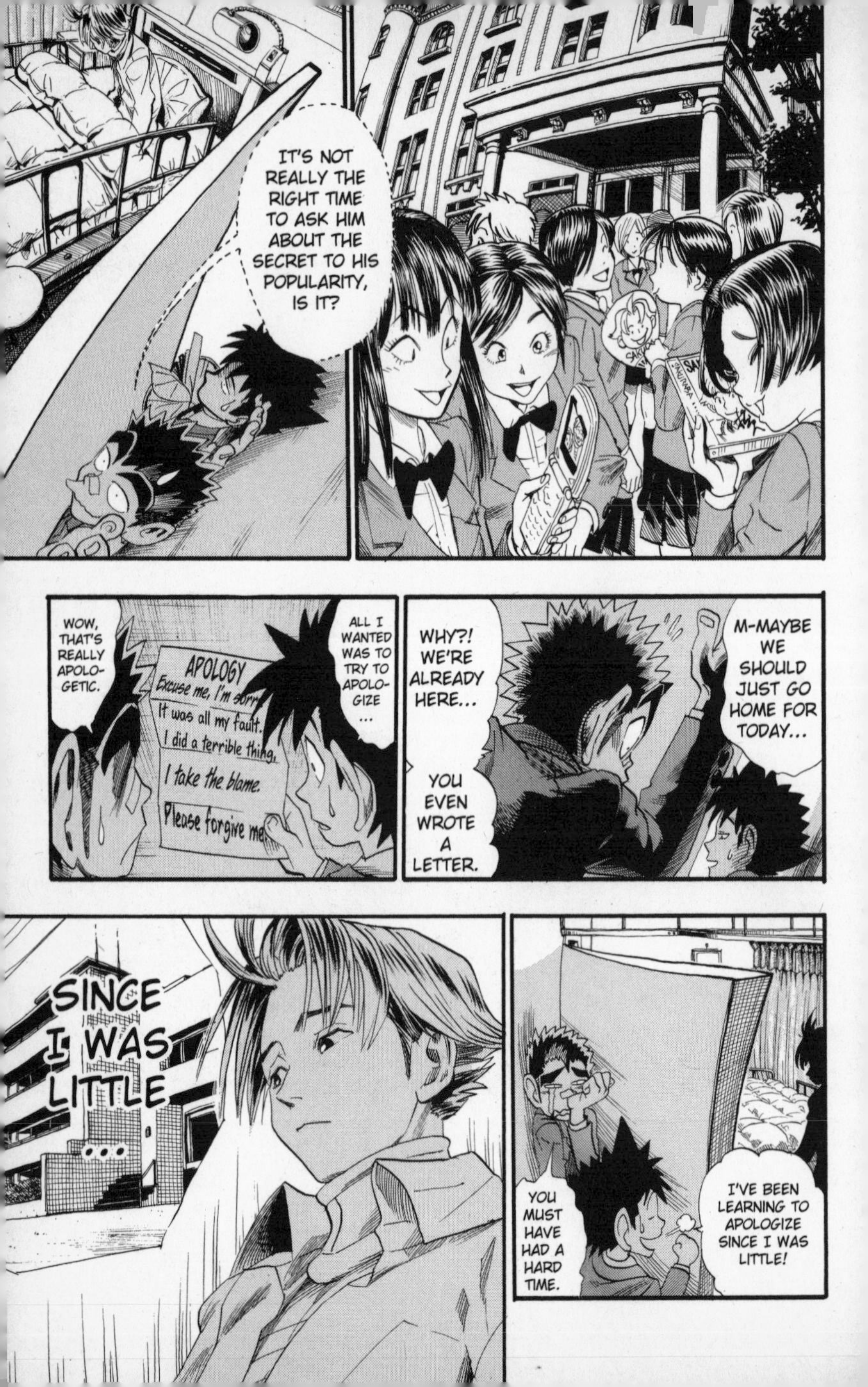
IT'S NOT REALLY THE RIGHT TIME TO ASK HIM ABOUT THE SECRET TO HIS POPULARITY, IS IT?
M-MAYBE WE SHOULD JUST GO HOME FOR TODAY...
WHY?! WE'RE ALREADY HERE...
YOU EVEN WROTE A LETTER.
ALL I WANTED WAS TO TRY TO APOLO-GIZE ...
APOLOGY
Excuse me, I'm sorr
It was all my fault.
I did a terrible thing.
I take the blame.
Please forgive me
WOW, THAT'S REALLY APOLO-GETIC.
I'VE BEEN LEARNING TO APOLOGIZE SINCE I WAS LITTLE!
YOU MUST HAVE HAD A HARD TIME.
SINCE I WAS LITTLE ...

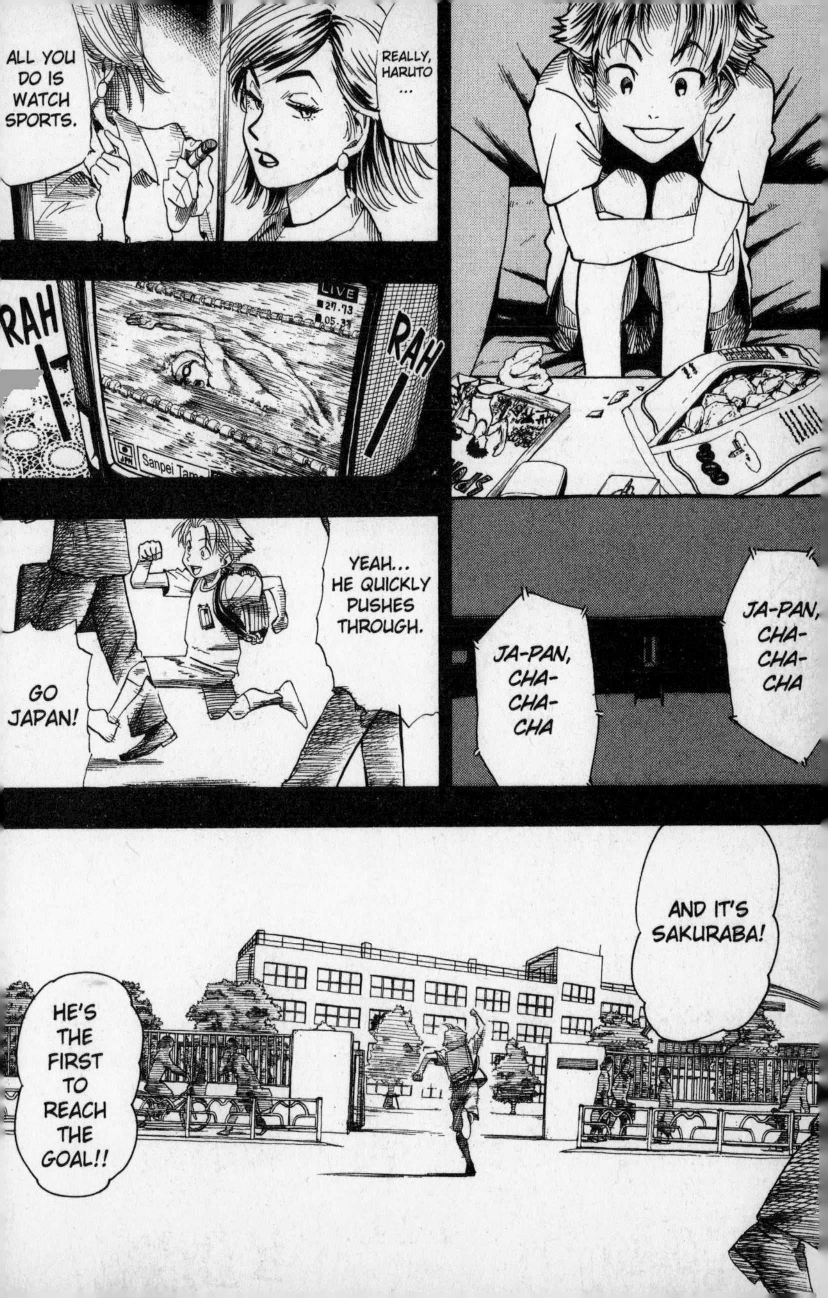
REALLY, HARUTO ...
ALL YOU DO IS WATCH SPORTS.
RAH
RAH
JA-PAN, CHA-CHA-CHA
JA-PAN, CHA-CHA-CHA
YEAH... HE QUICKLY PUSHES THROUGH.
GO JAPAN!
AND IT'S SAKURABA!
HE'S THE FIRST TO REACH THE GOAL!!

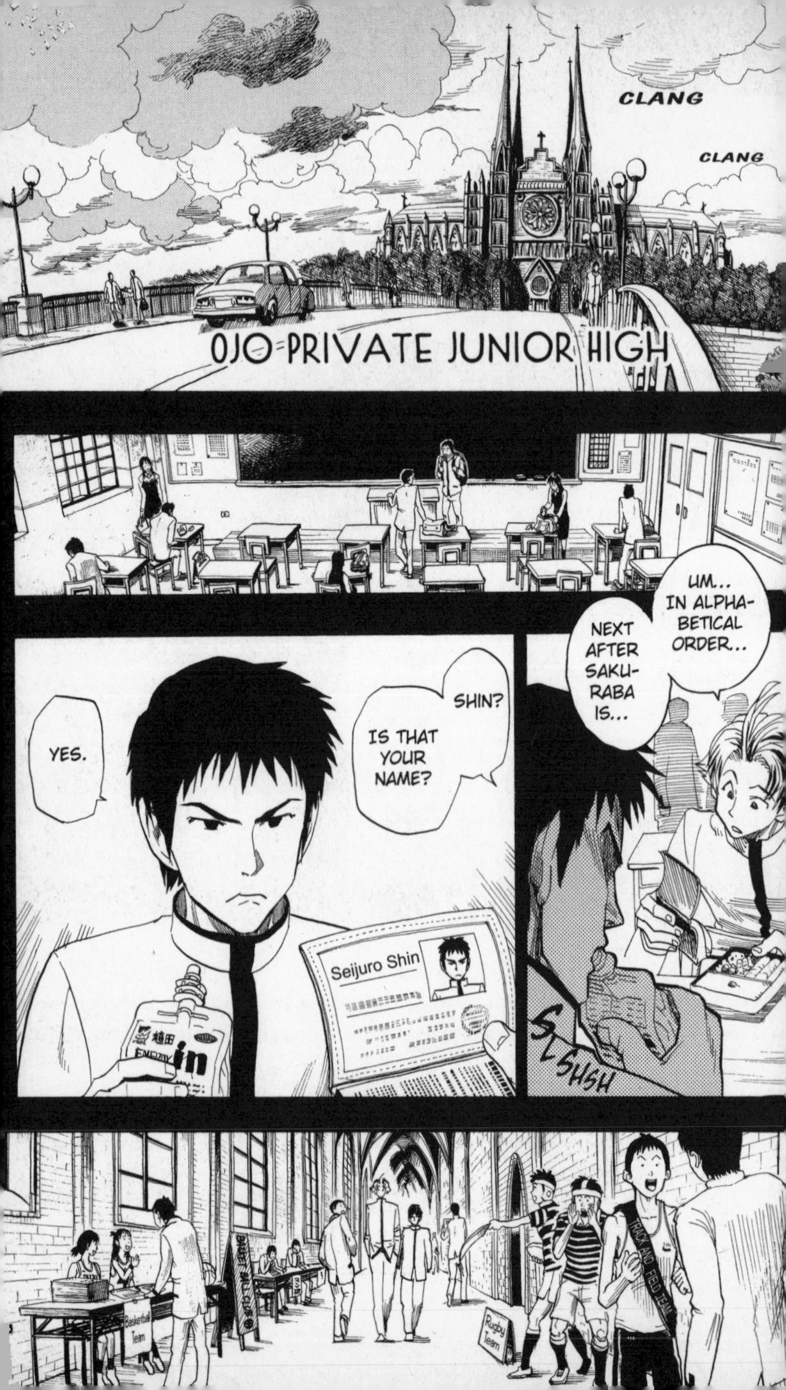

CLANG
CLANG
OJO PRIVATE JUNIOR HIGH
UM... IN ALPHABETICAL ORDER...
NEXT AFTER SAKURABA IS...
SLSHSH
SHIN?
IS THAT YOUR NAME?
YES.
Seijuro Shin
TRACK AND FIELD TEAM
Rugby Team
Basketball Team

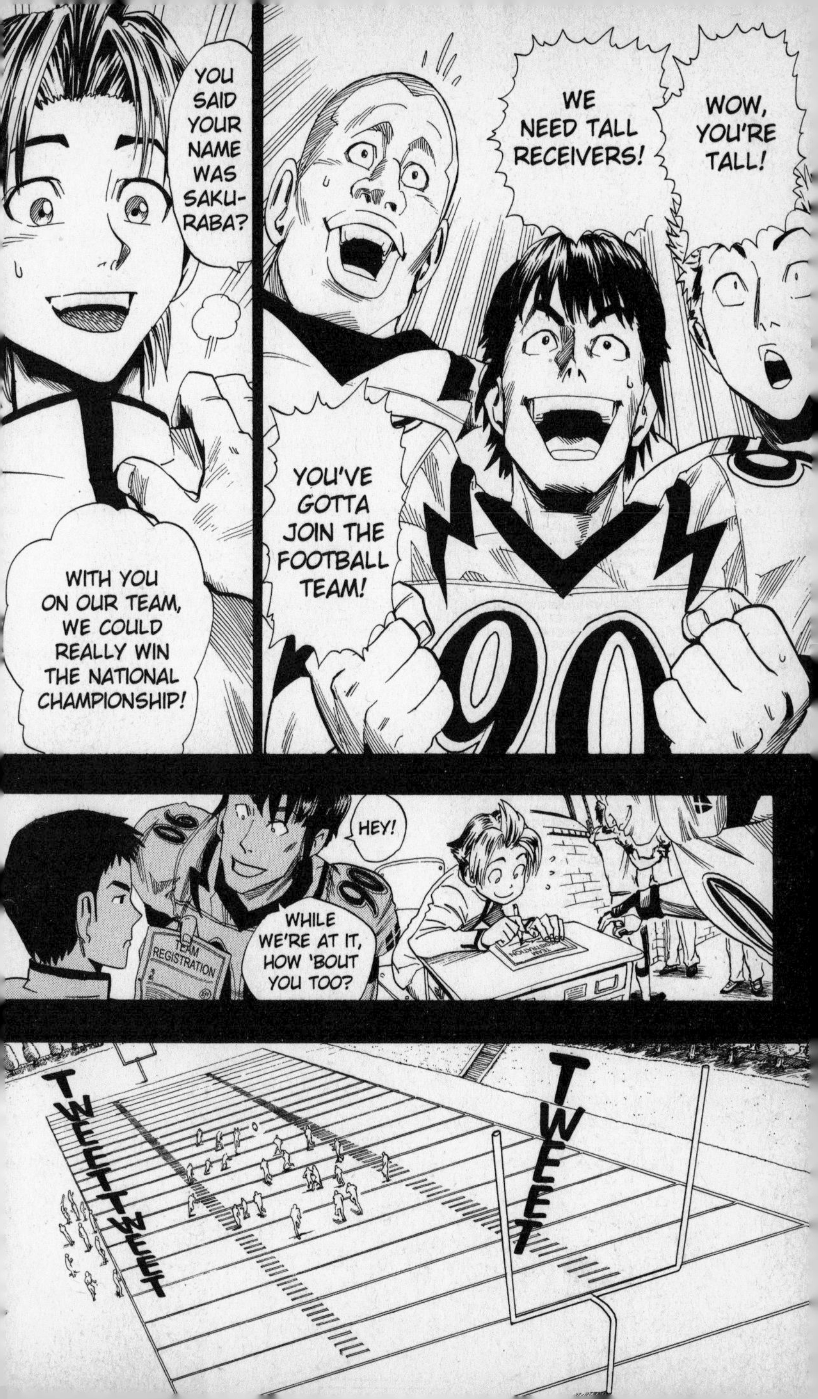
WOW, YOU'RE TALL!
WE NEED TALL RECEIVERS!
YOU'VE GOTTA JOIN THE FOOTBALL TEAM!
YOU SAID YOUR NAME WAS SAKU-RABA?
WITH YOU ON OUR TEAM, WE COULD REALLY WIN THE NATIONAL CHAMPIONSHIP!
TEAM REGISTRATION
HEY!
WHILE WE'RE AT IT, HOW 'BOUT YOU TOO?
TEAM REGISTRATION
TWEET
TWEETTWEET

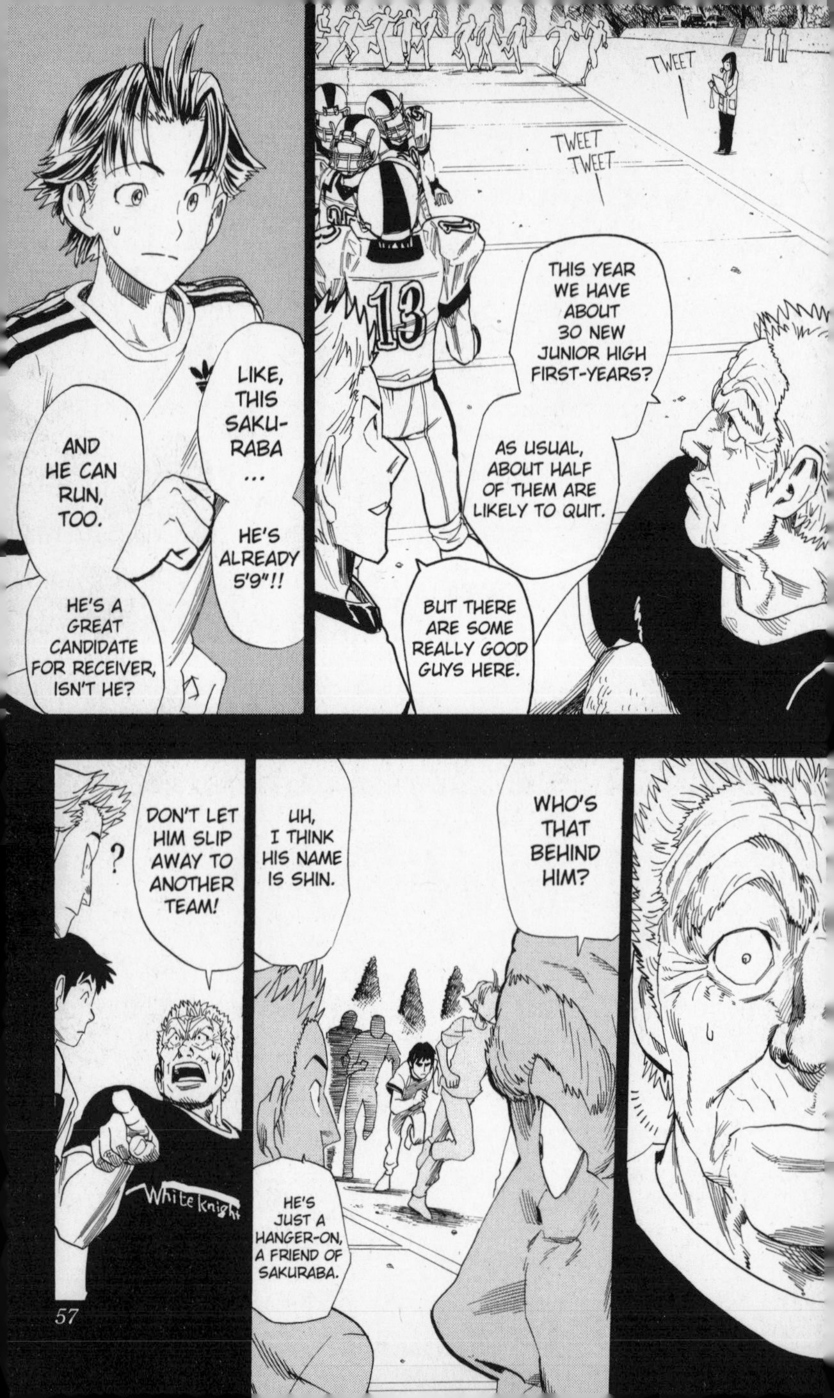
TWEET
TWEET TWEET
THIS YEAR WE HAVE ABOUT 30 NEW JUNIOR HIGH FIRST-YEARS?
AS USUAL, ABOUT HALF OF THEM ARE LIKELY TO QUIT.
BUT THERE ARE SOME REALLY GOOD GUYS HERE.
LIKE, THIS SAKURABA ...
HE'S ALREADY 5'9"!!
AND HE CAN RUN, TOO.
HE'S A GREAT CANDIDATE FOR RECEIVER, ISN'T HE?
WHO'S THAT BEHIND HIM?
UH, I THINK HIS NAME IS SHIN.
HE'S JUST A HANGER-ON, A FRIEND OF SAKURABA.
?
DON'T LET HIM SLIP AWAY TO ANOTHER TEAM!
White knight

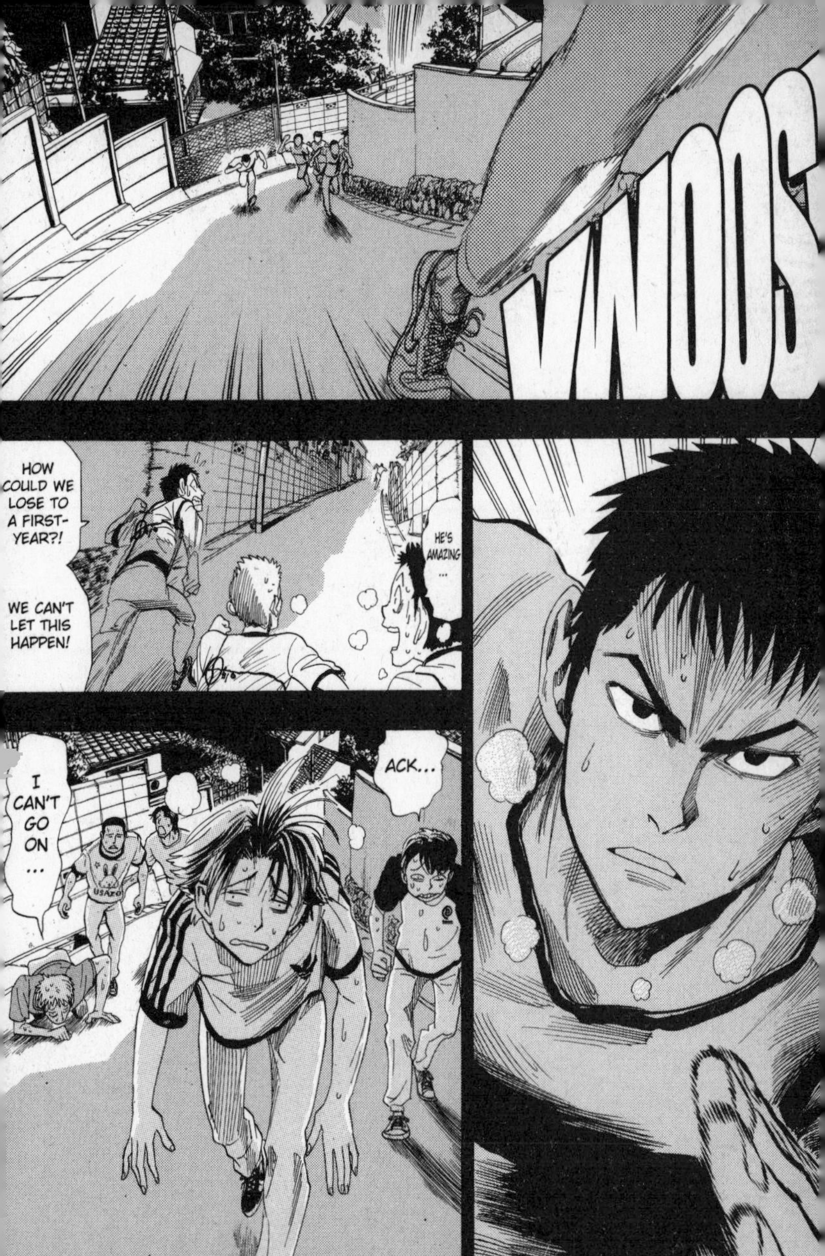
WHOOS
HE'S AMAZING ...
HOW COULD WE LOSE TO A FIRST-YEAR?!
WE CAN'T LET THIS HAPPEN!
ACK...
I CAN'T GO ON ...

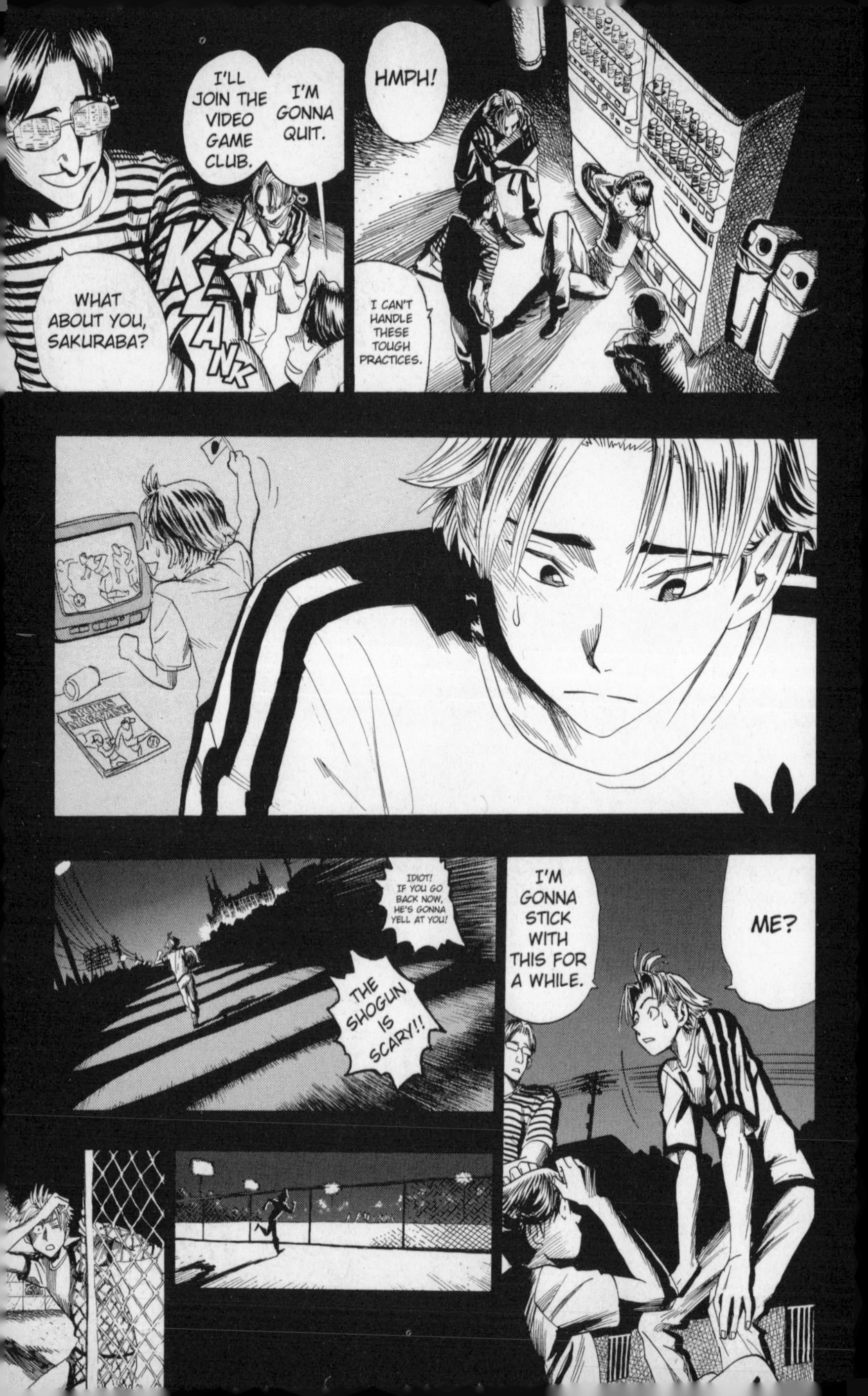
HMPH!
I CAN'T HANDLE THESE TOUGH PRACTICES.
I'M GONNA QUIT.
I'LL JOIN THE VIDEO GAME CLUB.
KLANK
WHAT ABOUT YOU, SAKURABA?
ME?
I'M GONNA STICK WITH THIS FOR A WHILE.
IDIOT! IF YOU GO BACK NOW, HE'S GONNA YELL AT YOU!
THE SHOGUN IS SCARY!!

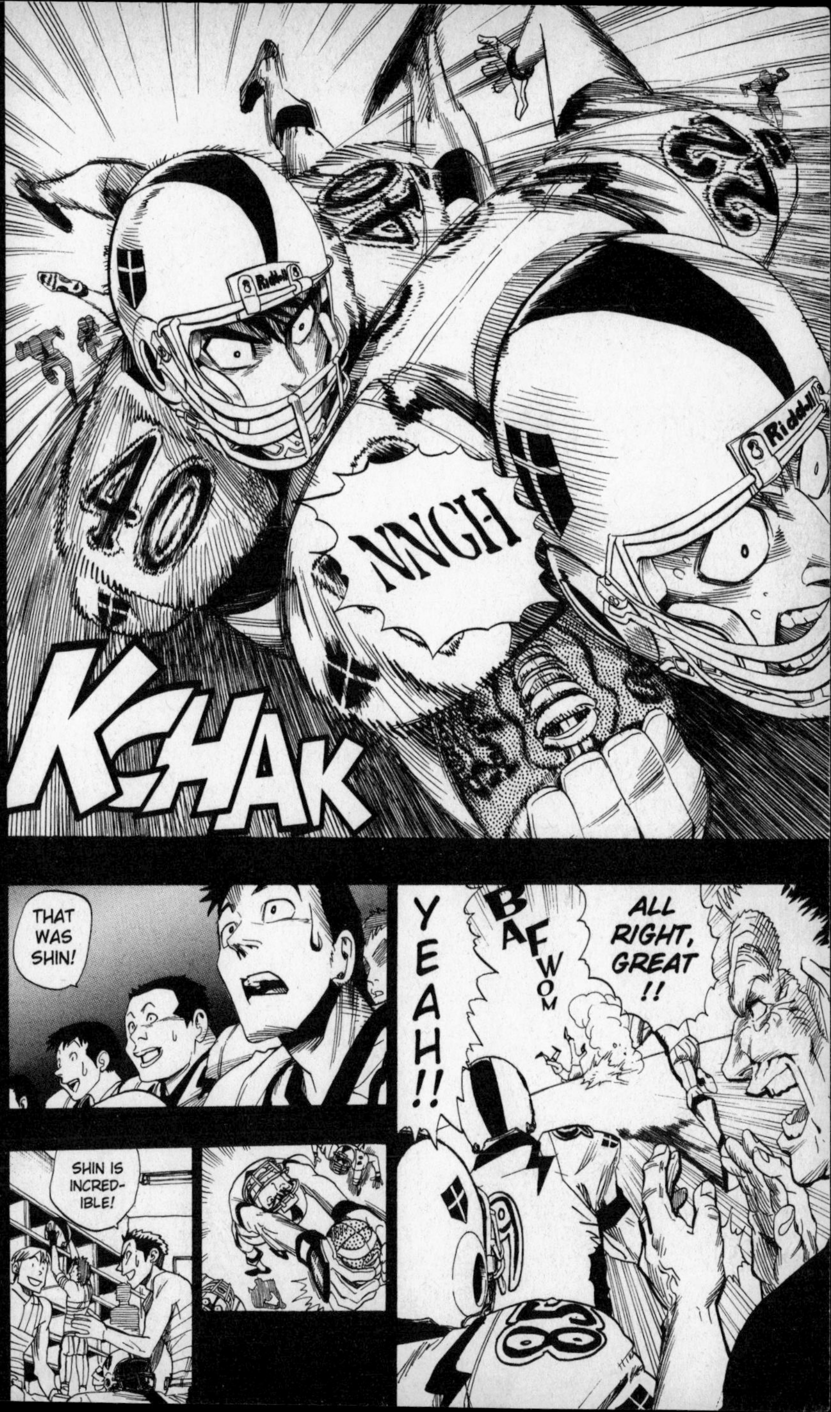
NNGH
K-SHAK
ALL RIGHT, GREAT!!
BAFWOM
YEAH!!
THAT WAS SHIN!
SHIN IS INCREDIBLE!

WHEEZE

WHEEZE

GET YOUR HANDS OUT IN FRONT OF YOU!!

WHAT ARE YOU DOING?!

KKCH

HE'S THE FIRST TO REACH THE GOAL!

IT'S SAKU-RABA!

MAYBE I'LL SKIP THE REST OF PRACTICE TODAY.

ACHE ACHE

IT'S NO GOOD.

ACHE

ACHE ACHE

ACHE ACHE

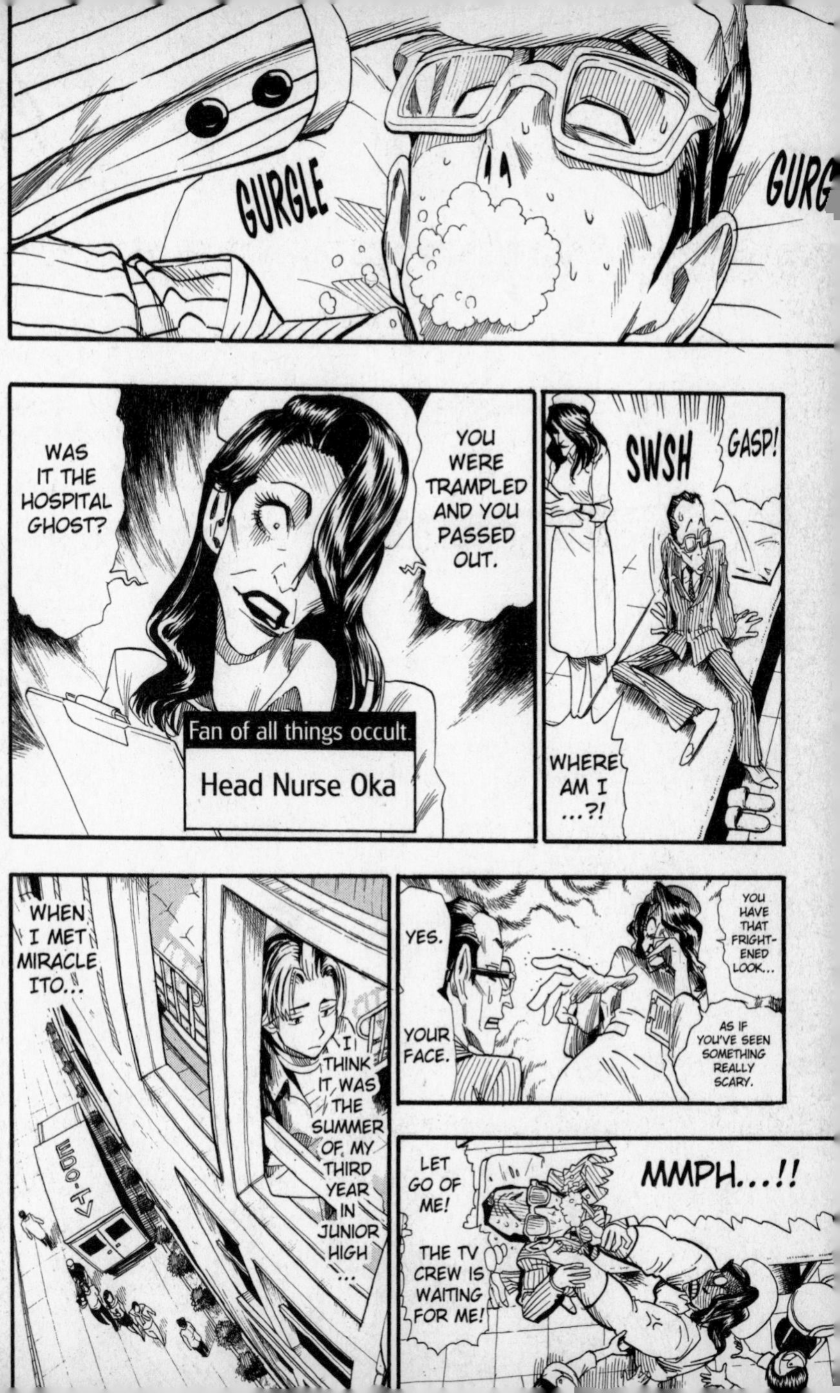
GURG
GURGLE
SWSH
GASP!
WHERE AM I ...?!
YOU WERE TRAMPLED AND YOU PASSED OUT.
WAS IT THE HOSPITAL GHOST?
Fan of all things occult.
Head Nurse Oka
YOU HAVE THAT FRIGHT-ENED LOOK...
AS IF YOU'VE SEEN SOMETHING REALLY SCARY.
YES.
YOUR FACE.
MMPH...!!
LET GO OF ME!
THE TV CREW IS WAITING FOR ME!
I THINK IT WAS THE SUMMER OF MY THIRD YEAR IN JUNIOR HIGH...
WHEN I MET MIRACLE ITO...

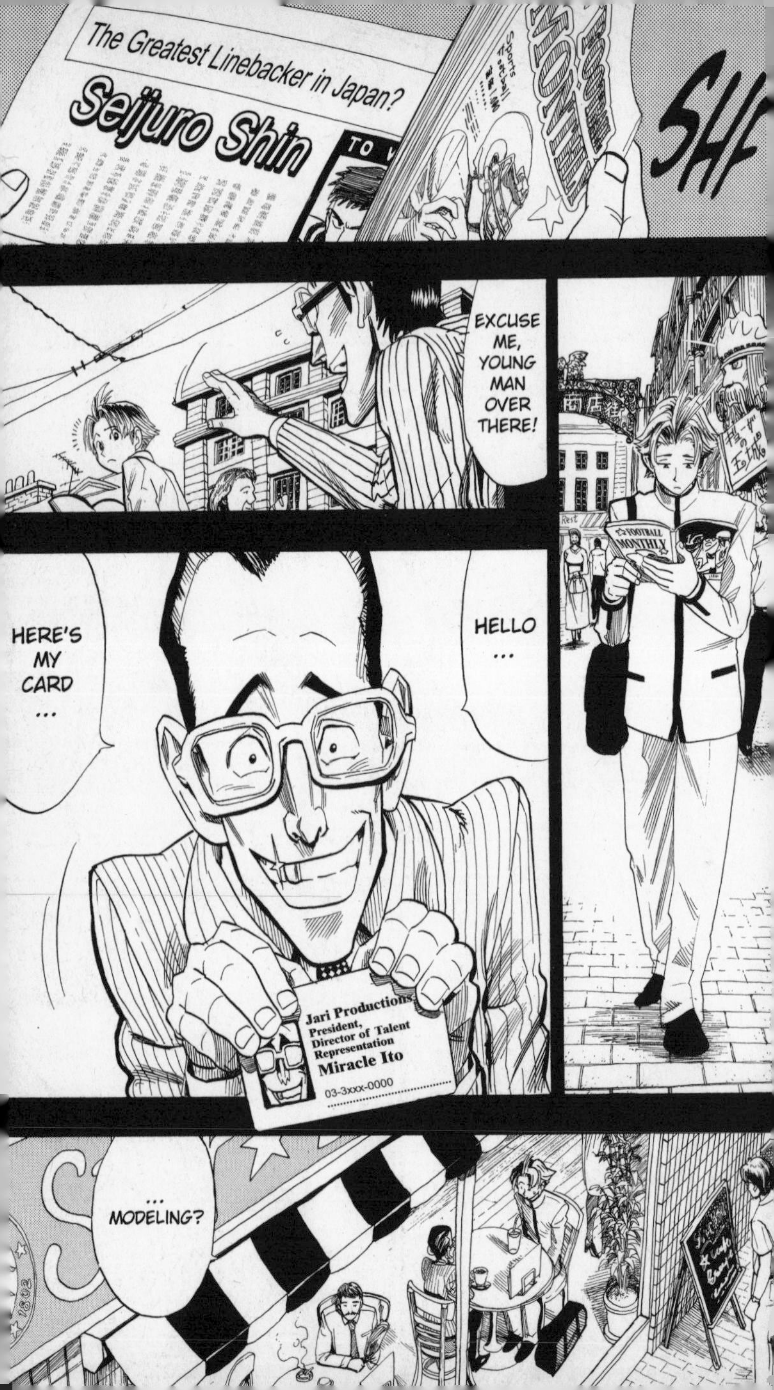
The Greatest Linebacker in Japan?
Seijuro Shin
SHF
FOOTBALL MONTHLY
EXCUSE ME, YOUNG MAN OVER THERE!
HELLO ...
HERE'S MY CARD ...
Jari Productions
President, Director of Talent Representation
Miracle Ito
03-3xxx-0000
... MODELING?

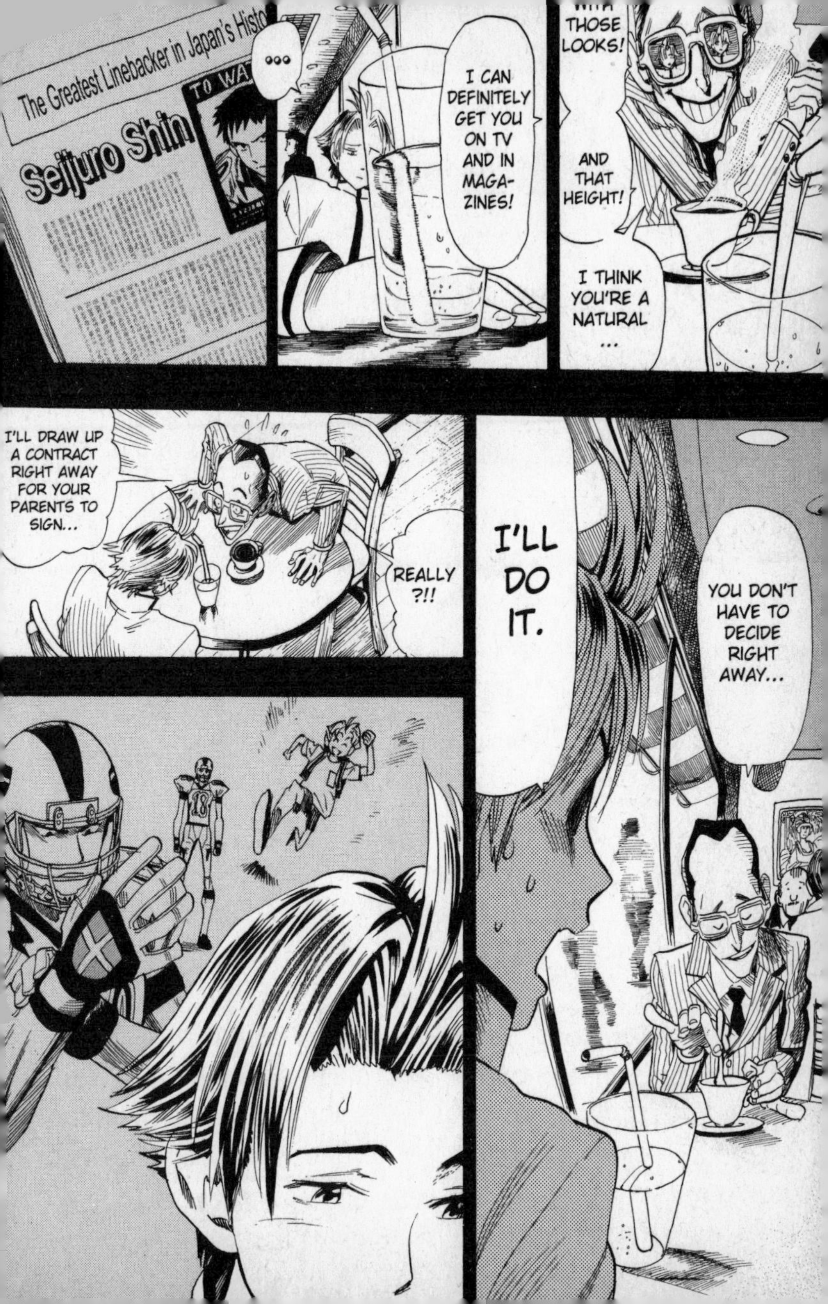

THOSE LOOKS!
AND THAT HEIGHT!
I THINK YOU'RE A NATURAL ...
I CAN DEFINITELY GET YOU ON TV AND IN MAGA-ZINES!
...
The Greatest Linebacker in Japan's Histo
Seijuro Shin
YOU DON'T HAVE TO DECIDE RIGHT AWAY...
I'LL DO IT.
REALLY ?!!
I'LL DRAW UP A CONTRACT RIGHT AWAY FOR YOUR PARENTS TO SIGN...

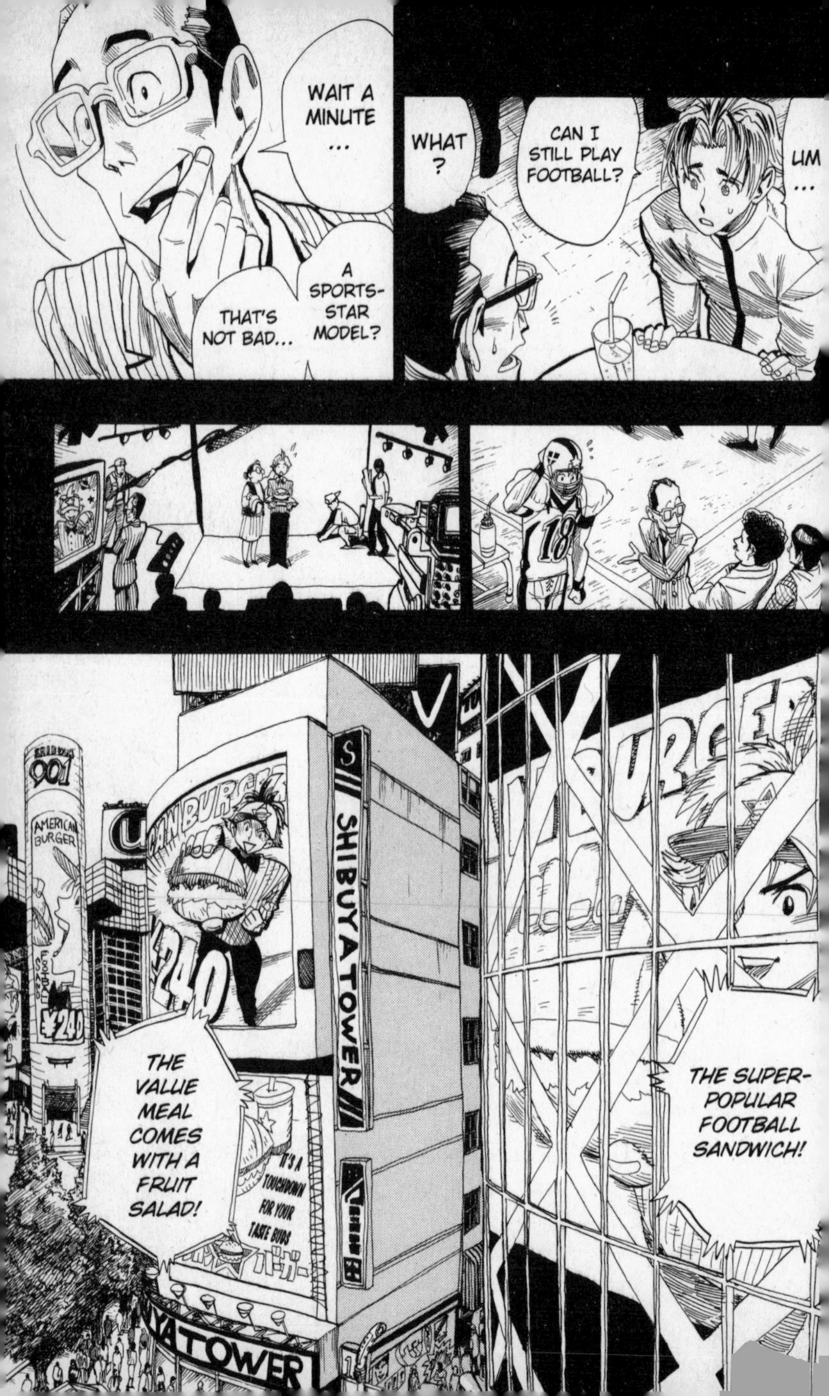
UM ...
CAN I STILL PLAY FOOTBALL?
WHAT?
WAIT A MINUTE ...
A SPORTS-STAR MODEL?
THAT'S NOT BAD...
18
THE SUPER-POPULAR FOOTBALL SANDWICH!
SHIBUYA TOWER
240
901
AMERICAN BURGER
¥240
THE VALUE MEAL COMES WITH A FRUIT SALAD!
IT'S A TOUCHDOWN FOR YOUR TASTE BUDS
バーガー
YATOWER

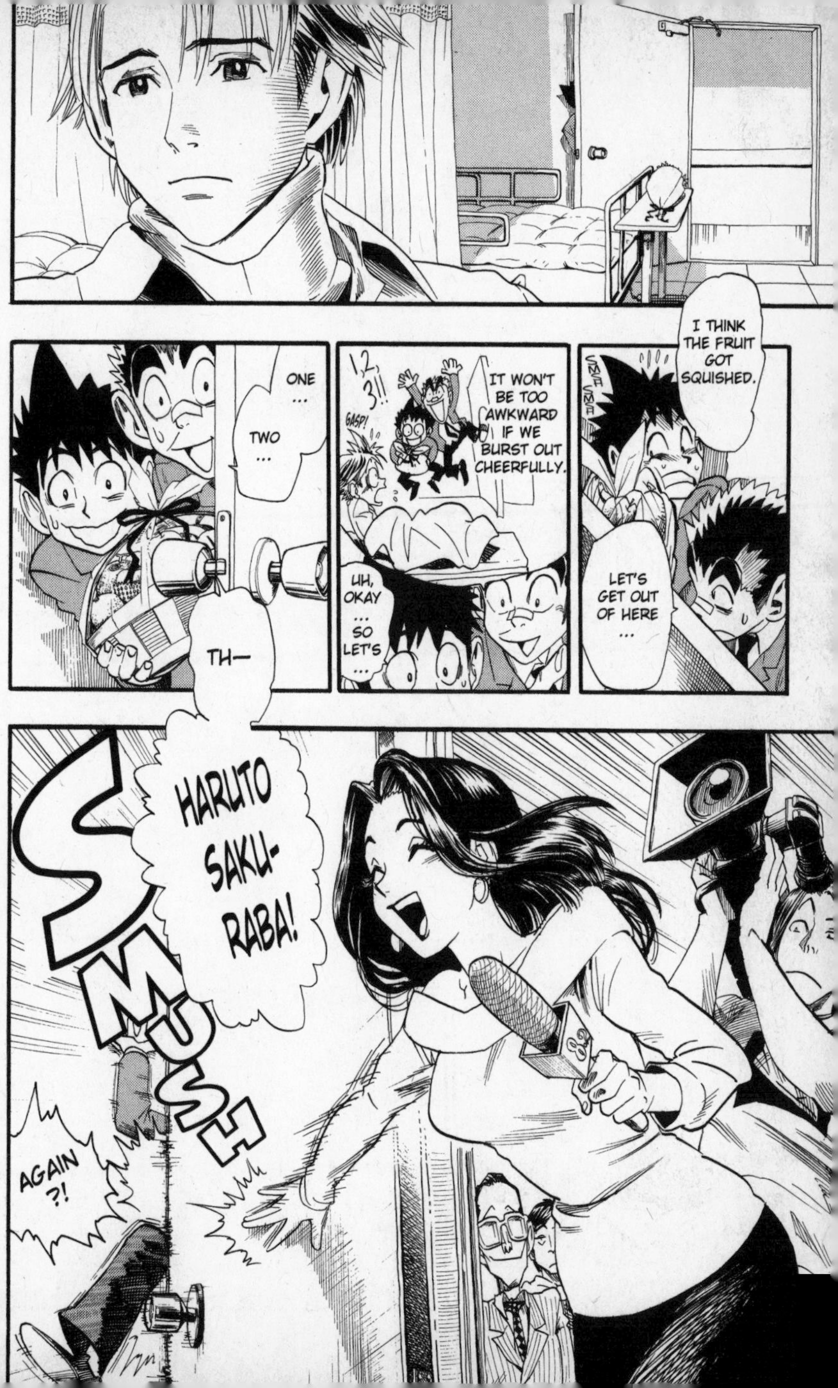
SMA SMA
I THINK THE FRUIT GOT SQUISHED.
LET'S GET OUT OF HERE ...
IT WON'T BE TOO AWKWARD IF WE BURST OUT CHEERFULLY.
1, 2, 3!!
GASP!
UH, OKAY ... SO LET'S ...
ONE ...
TWO ...
TH—
HARUTO SAKU-RABA!
SMUSH
AGAIN ?!

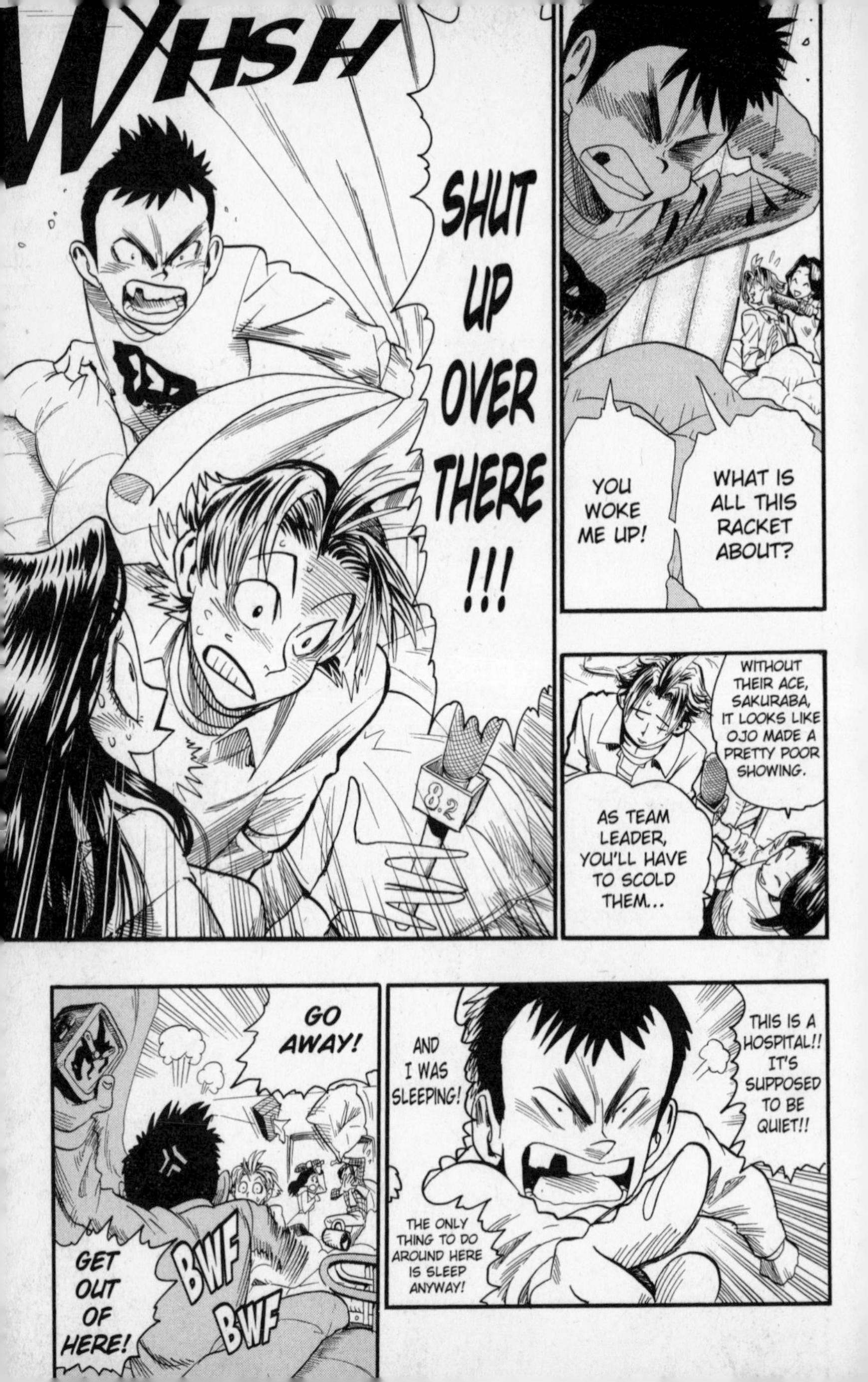
WHAT IS ALL THIS RACKET ABOUT?
YOU WOKE ME UP!
WITHOUT THEIR ACE, SAKURABA, IT LOOKS LIKE OJO MADE A PRETTY POOR SHOWING.
AS TEAM LEADER, YOU'LL HAVE TO SCOLD THEM...
WHSH
SHUT UP OVER THERE!!!
8.2
THIS IS A HOSPITAL!! IT'S SUPPOSED TO BE QUIET!!
AND I WAS SLEEPING!
THE ONLY THING TO DO AROUND HERE IS SLEEP ANYWAY!
GO AWAY!
BWF
BWF
GET OUT OF HERE!

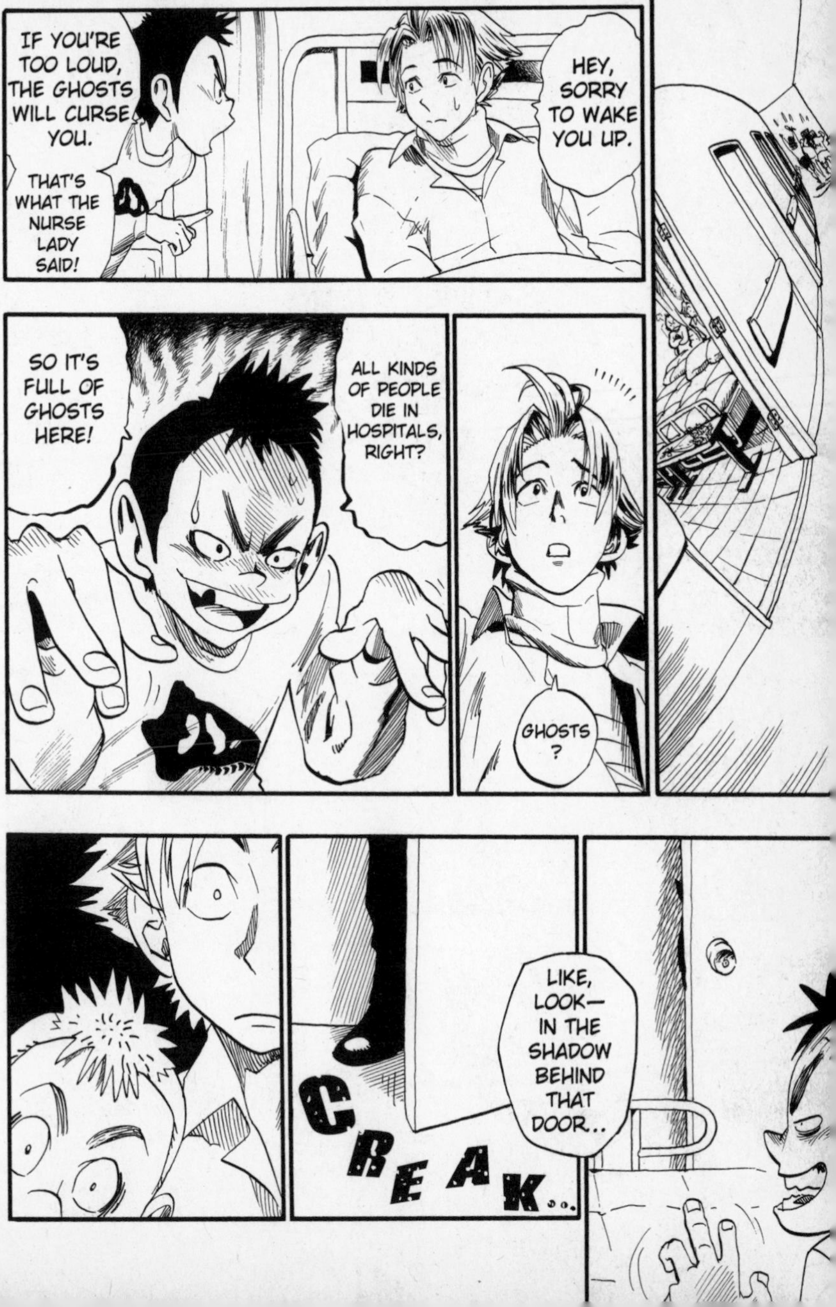
HEY, SORRY TO WAKE YOU UP.
IF YOU'RE TOO LOUD, THE GHOSTS WILL CURSE YOU.
THAT'S WHAT THE NURSE LADY SAID!
GHOSTS?
ALL KINDS OF PEOPLE DIE IN HOSPITALS, RIGHT?
SO IT'S FULL OF GHOSTS HERE!
LIKE, LOOK— IN THE SHADOW BEHIND THAT DOOR...
CREAK...

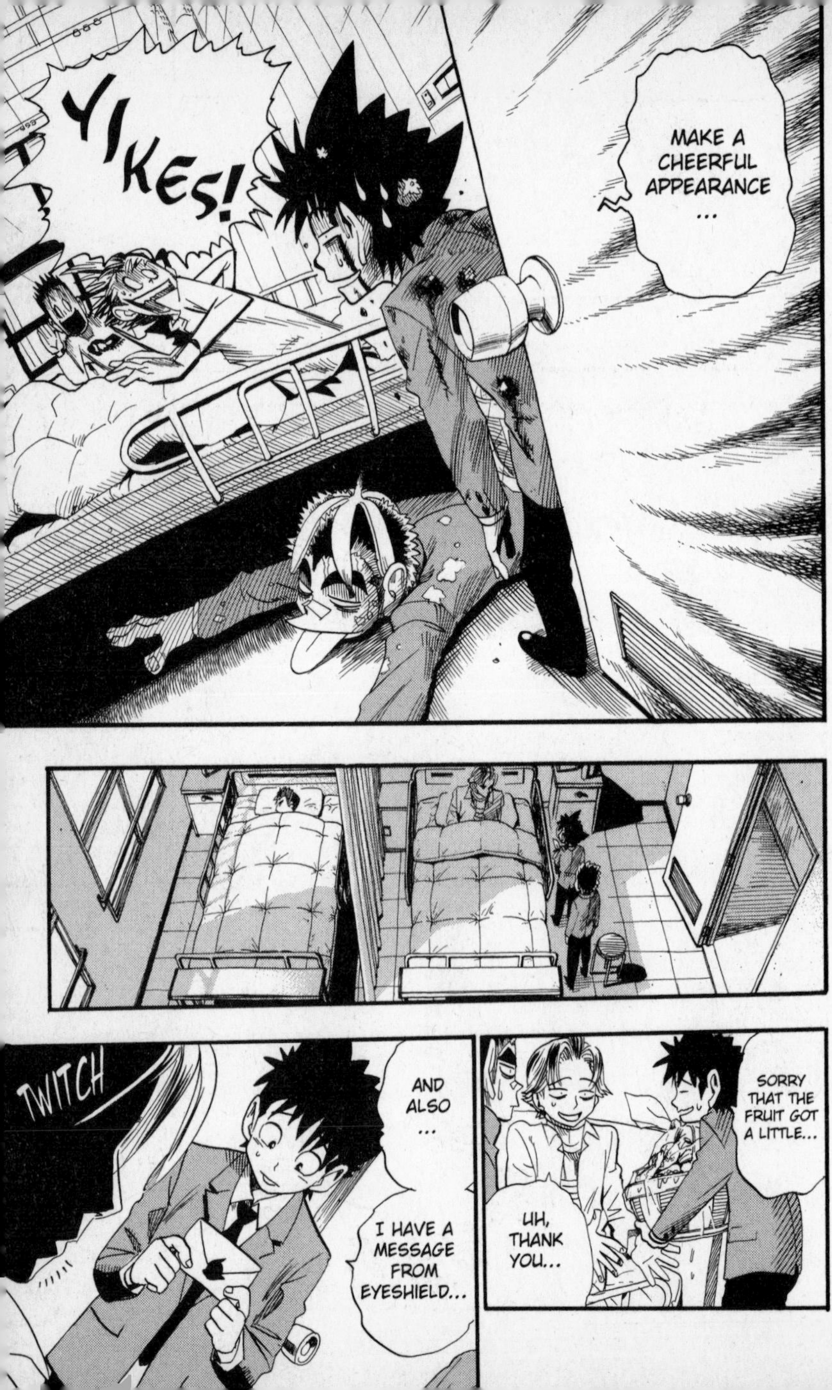
MAKE A CHEERFUL APPEARANCE ...
YIKES!
SORRY THAT THE FRUIT GOT A LITTLE...
UH, THANK YOU...
AND ALSO ...
I HAVE A MESSAGE FROM EYESHIELD...
TWITCH

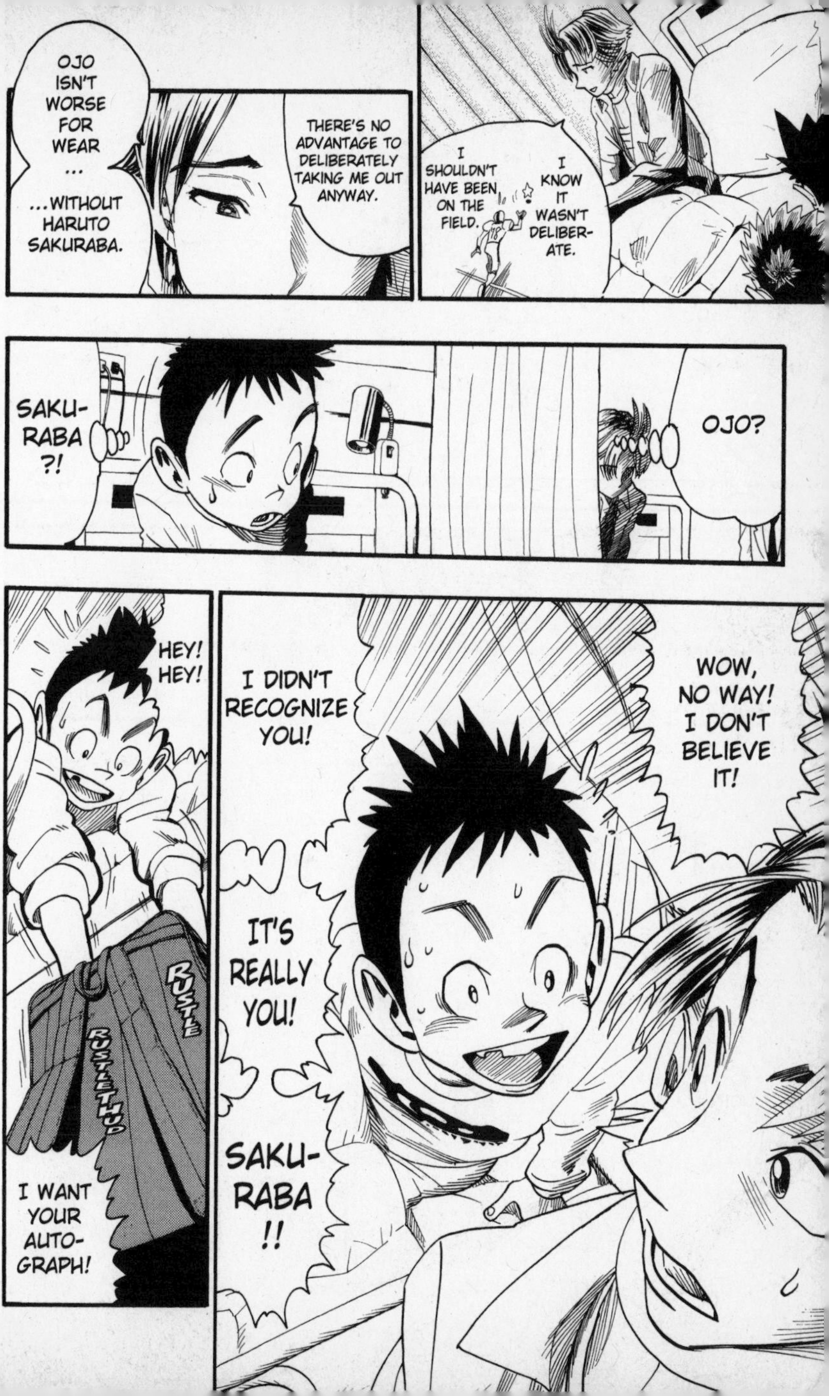
I KNOW IT WASN'T DELIBERATE.
I SHOULDN'T HAVE BEEN ON THE FIELD.
THERE'S NO ADVANTAGE TO DELIBERATELY TAKING ME OUT ANYWAY.
OJO ISN'T WORSE FOR WEAR ...
...WITHOUT HARUTO SAKURABA.
OJO?
SAKU-RABA?!
WOW, NO WAY! I DON'T BELIEVE IT!
I DIDN'T RECOGNIZE YOU!
IT'S REALLY YOU!
SAKU-RABA!!
HEY! HEY!
RUSTLE
RUSTLE THUD
I WANT YOUR AUTO-GRAPH!

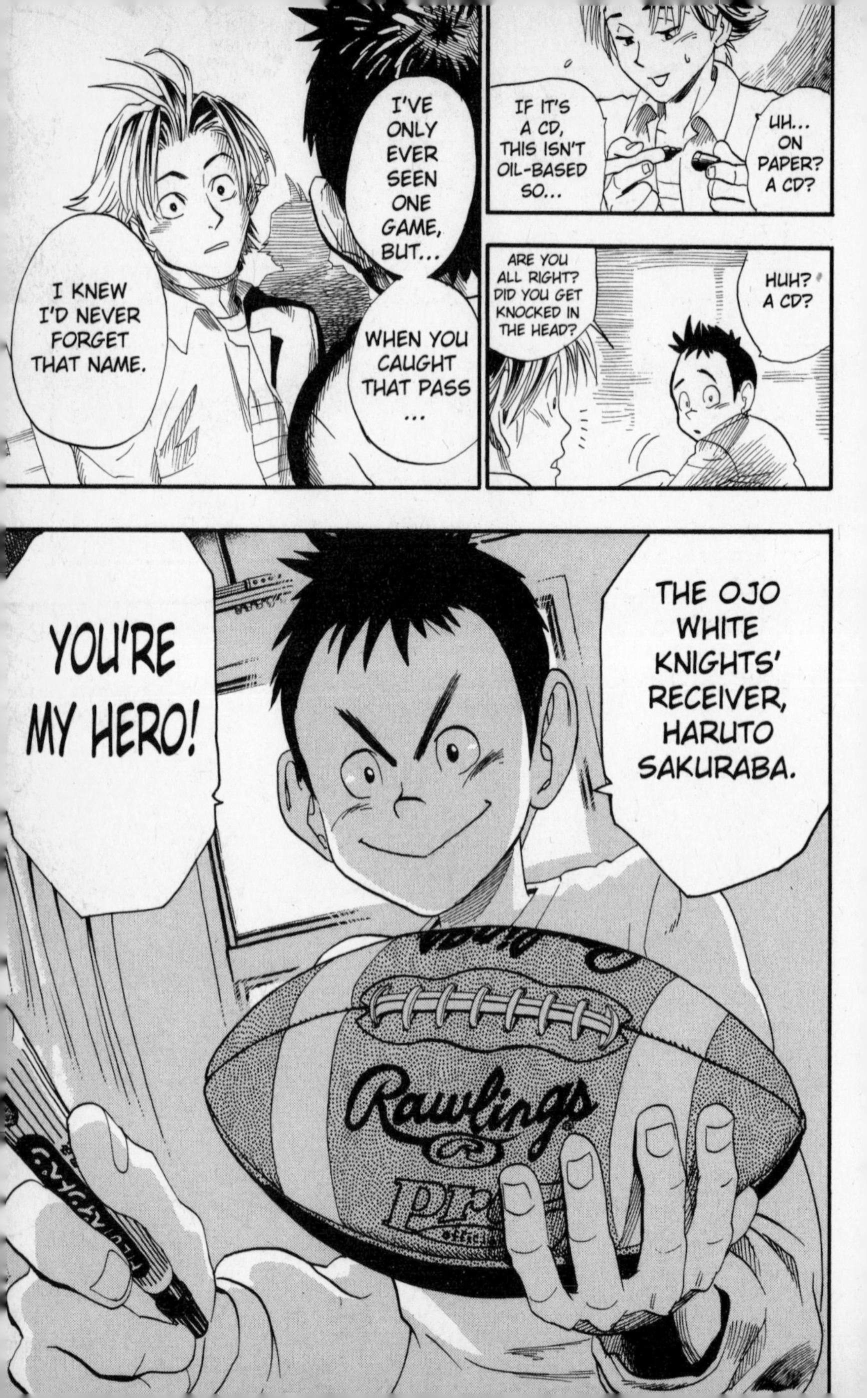
UH... ON PAPER? A CD?
IF IT'S A CD, THIS ISN'T OIL-BASED SO...
HUH? A CD?
ARE YOU ALL RIGHT? DID YOU GET KNOCKED IN THE HEAD?
I'VE ONLY EVER SEEN ONE GAME, BUT...
WHEN YOU CAUGHT THAT PASS...
I KNEW I'D NEVER FORGET THAT NAME.
THE OJO WHITE KNIGHTS' RECEIVER, HARUTO SAKURABA.
YOU'RE MY HERO!
Rawlings

HARUTO SAKURABA PRODUCT CATALOG

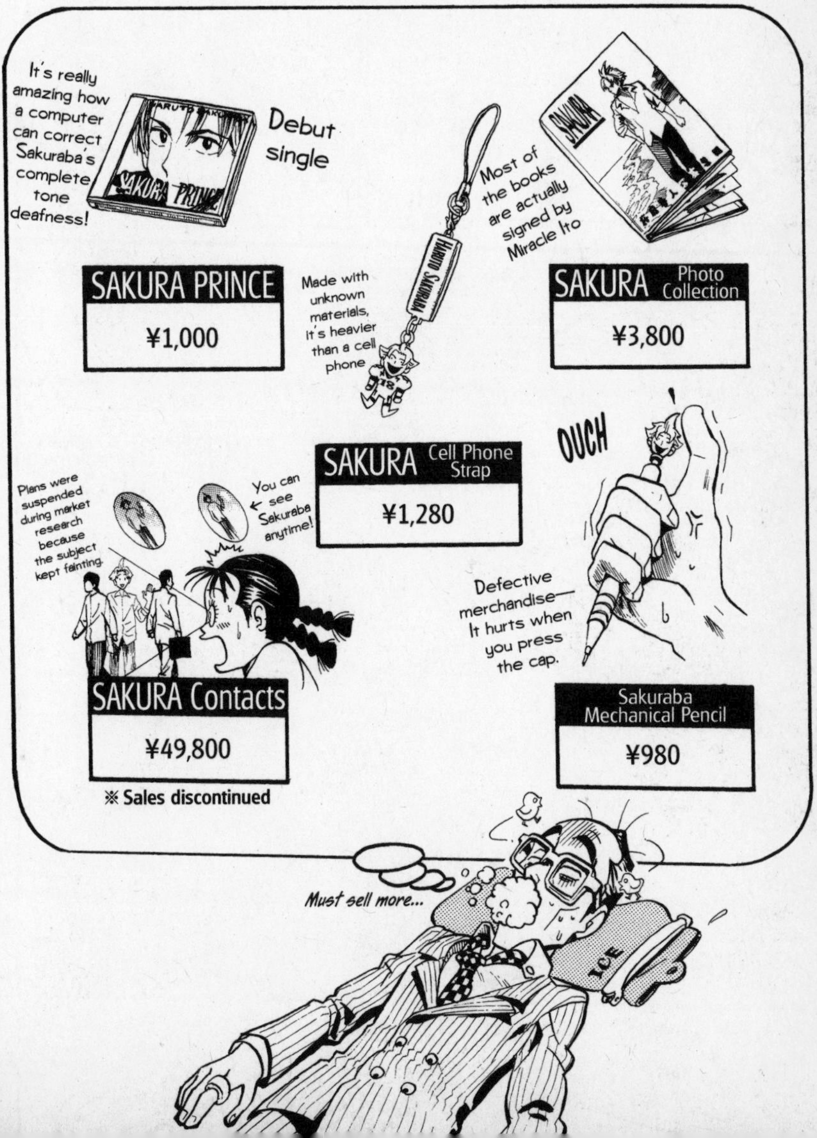

Most of the books are actually signed by Miracle Ito
SAKURA Photo Collection
¥3,800
Made with unknown materials, it's heavier than a cell phone
It's really amazing how a computer can correct Sakuraba's complete tone deafness!
Debut single
SAKURA PRINCE
¥1,000
SAKURA Cell Phone Strap
¥1,280
OUCH
Defective merchandise— It hurts when you press the cap.
Sakuraba Mechanical Pencil
¥980
You can see Sakuraba anytime!
Plans were suspended during market research because the subject kept fainting.
SAKURA Contacts
¥49,800
※ Sales discontinued
Must sell more...
ICE

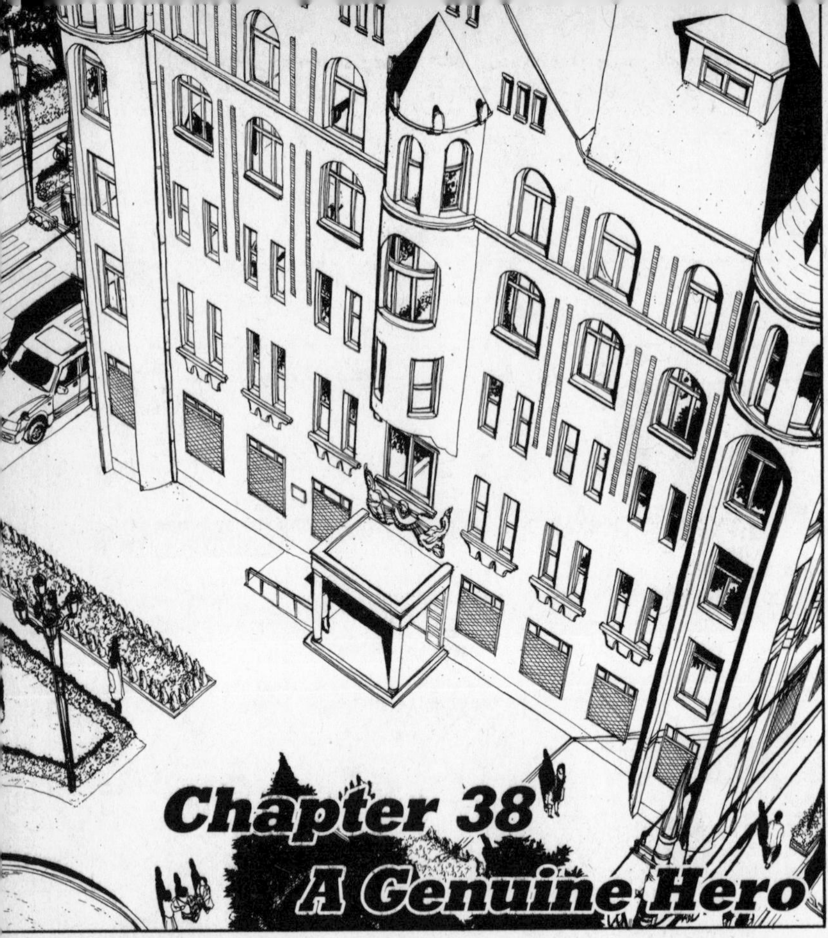
Chapter 38
A Genuine Hero

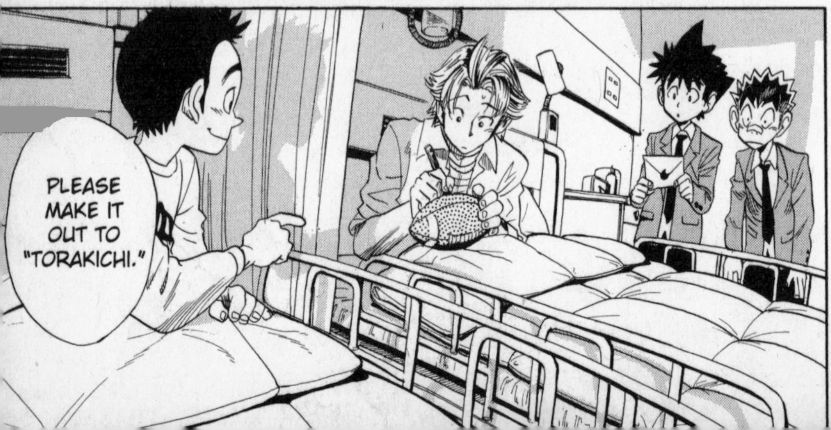
PLEASE MAKE IT OUT TO "TORAKICHI."

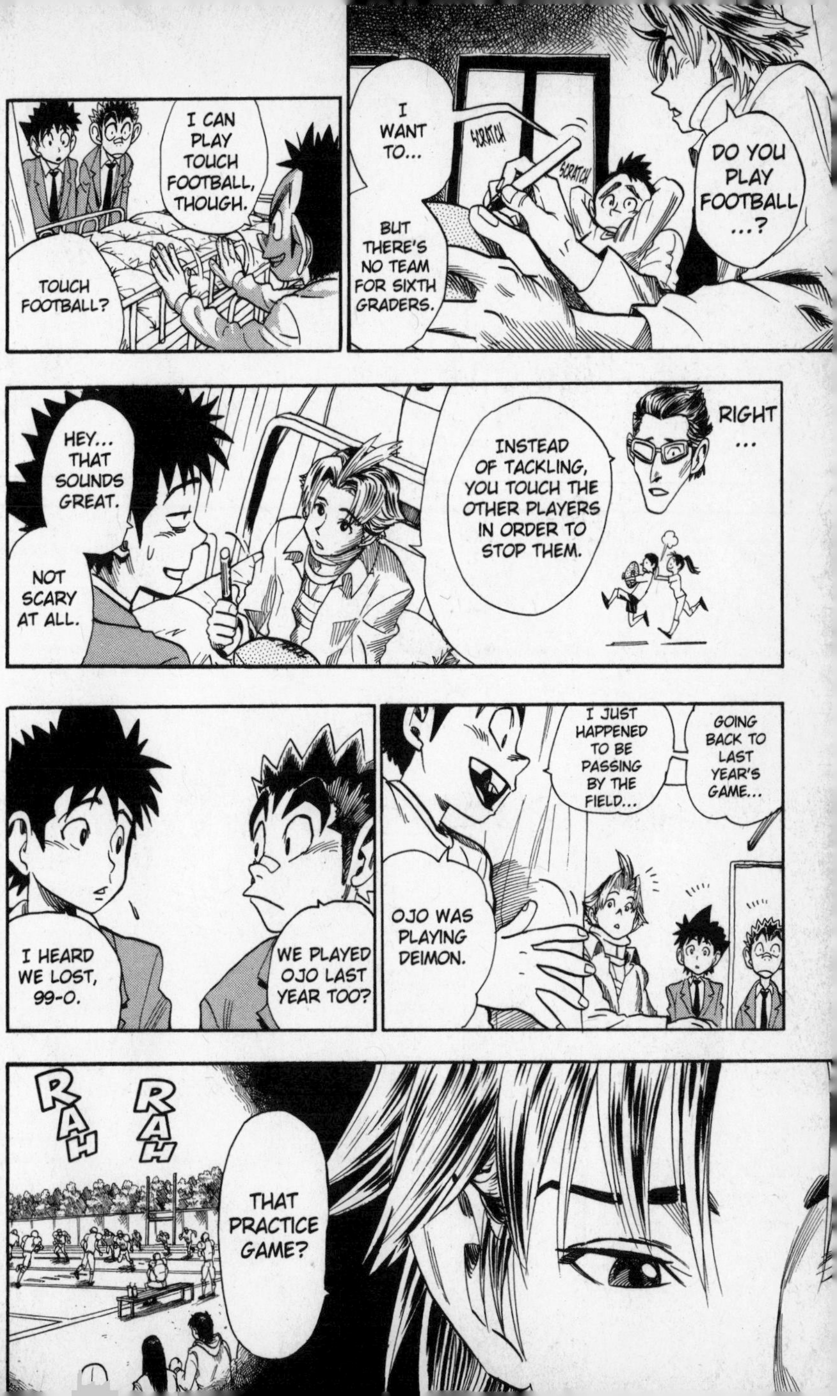
DO YOU PLAY FOOTBALL...?
I WANT TO...
SCRATCH
SCRATCH
BUT THERE'S NO TEAM FOR SIXTH GRADERS.
I CAN PLAY TOUCH FOOTBALL, THOUGH.
TOUCH FOOTBALL?
RIGHT...
INSTEAD OF TACKLING, YOU TOUCH THE OTHER PLAYERS IN ORDER TO STOP THEM.
HEY... THAT SOUNDS GREAT.
NOT SCARY AT ALL.
GOING BACK TO LAST YEAR'S GAME...
I JUST HAPPENED TO BE PASSING BY THE FIELD...
OJO WAS PLAYING DEIMON.
WE PLAYED OJO LAST YEAR TOO?
I HEARD WE LOST, 99-0.
THAT PRACTICE GAME?
RAH RAH
RAH RAH

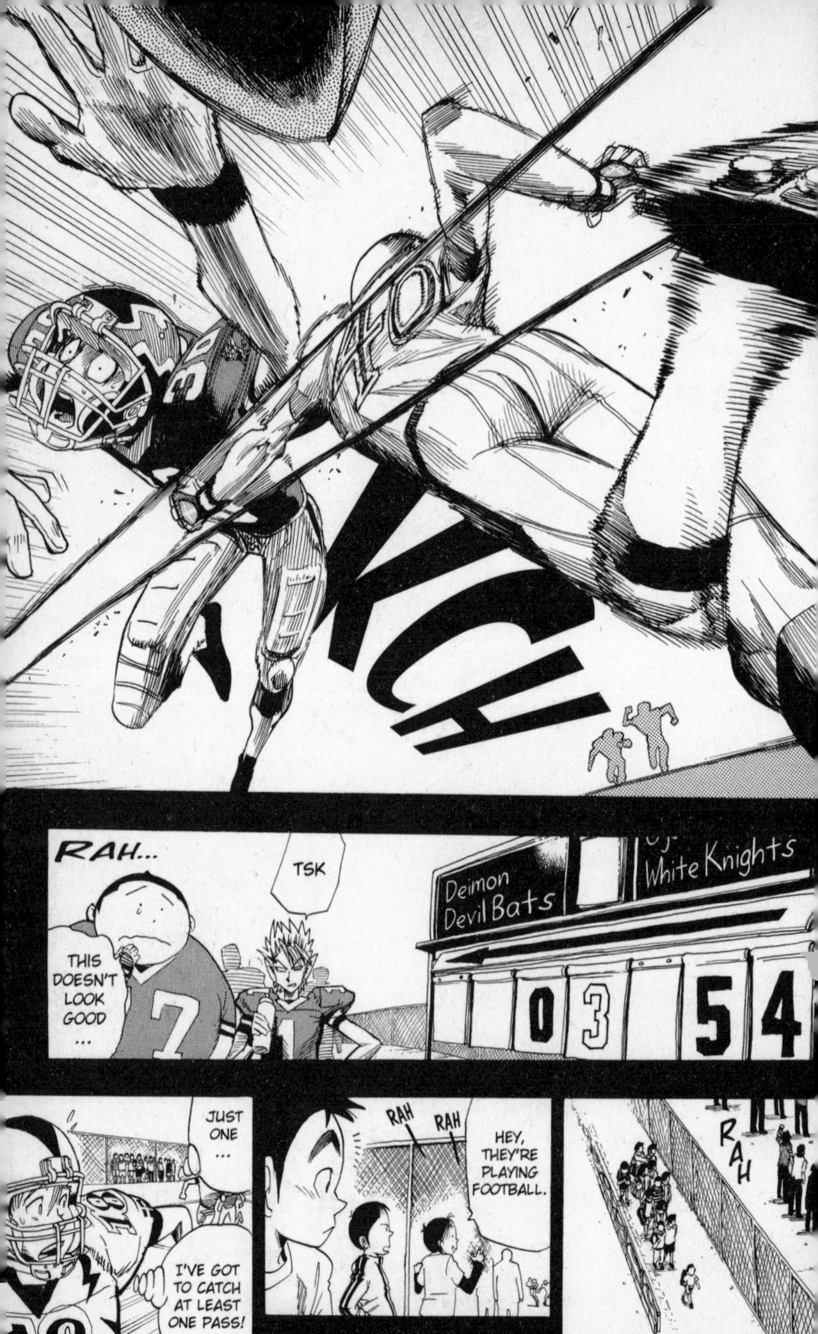
White Knights
Deimon Devil Bats
03
54
TSK
RAH...
THIS DOESN'T LOOK GOOD ...
RAH
RAH
RAH
HEY, THEY'RE PLAYING FOOTBALL.
JUST ONE ...
I'VE GOT TO CATCH AT LEAST ONE PASS!

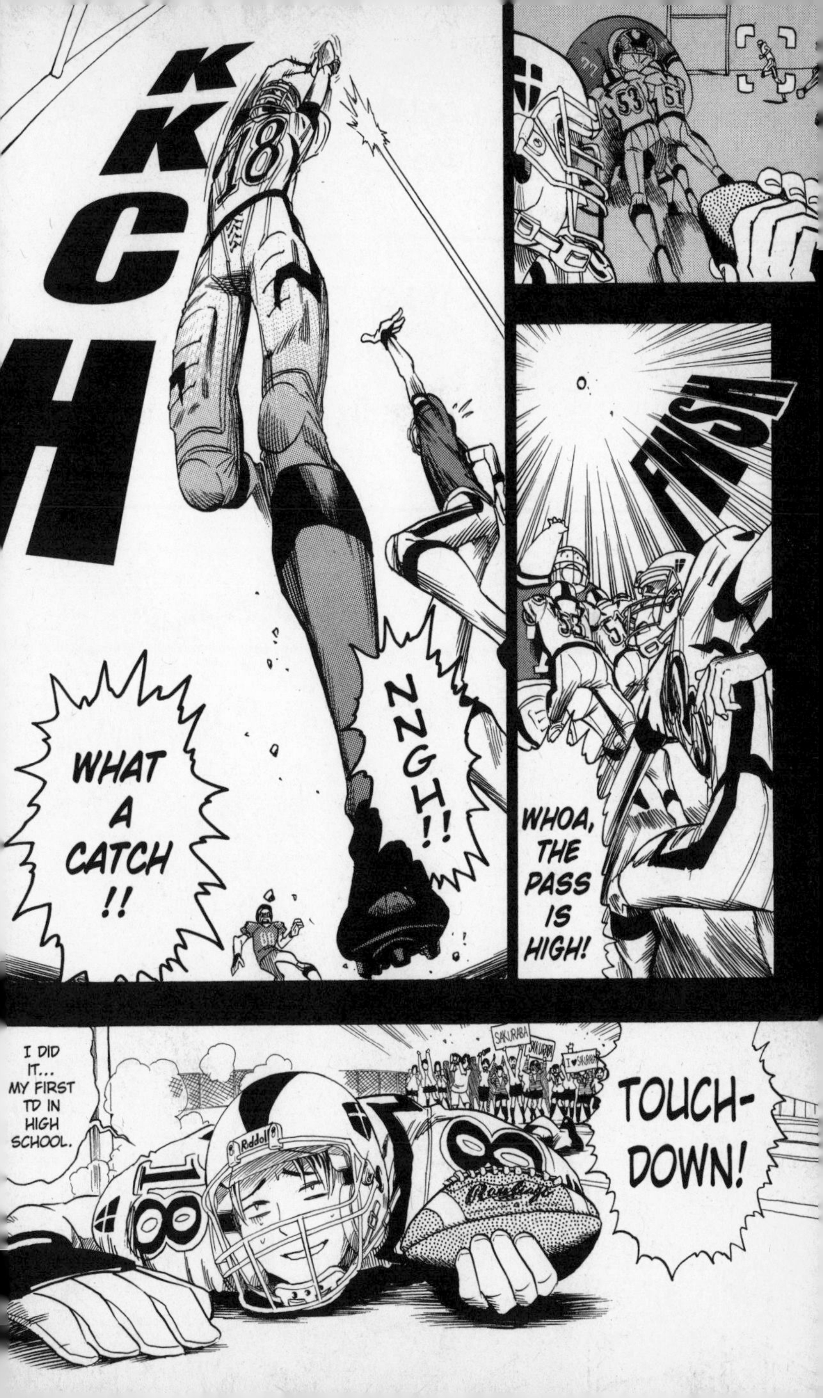
FWSH
WHOA, THE PASS IS HIGH!
KKCH
NNGH!!
WHAT A CATCH!!
TOUCH-DOWN!
SAKURABA
SAKURABA
I ♥ SAKURABA
I DID IT... MY FIRST TD IN HIGH SCHOOL.

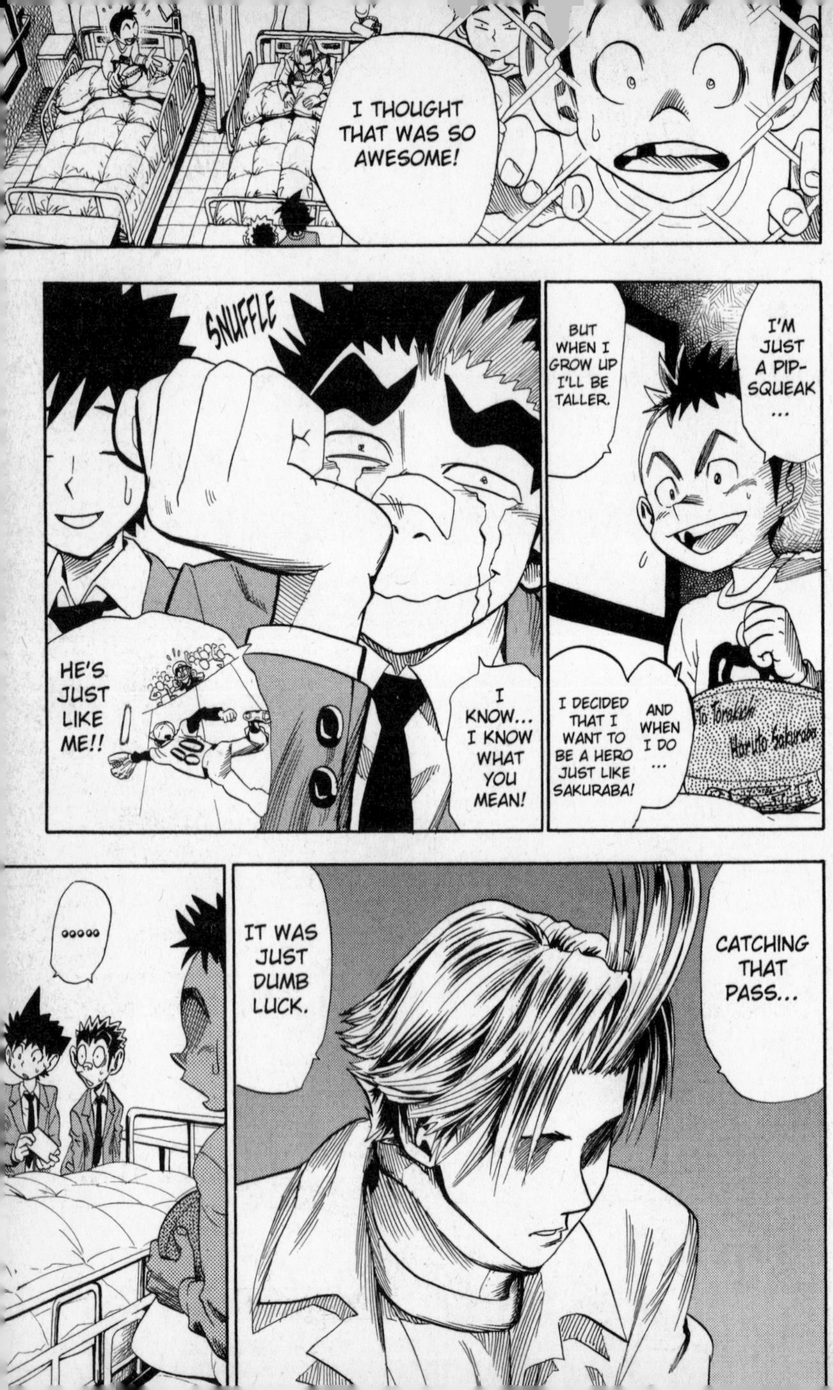
I THOUGHT THAT WAS SO AWESOME!
I'M JUST A PIP-SQUEAK...
BUT WHEN I GROW UP I'LL BE TALLER.
AND WHEN I DO...
I DECIDED THAT I WANT TO BE A HERO JUST LIKE SAKURABA!
To Torakichi Haruto Sakuraba
SNUFFLE
I KNOW... I KNOW WHAT YOU MEAN!
HE'S JUST LIKE ME!!
CATCHING THAT PASS...
IT WAS JUST DUMB LUCK.
.....

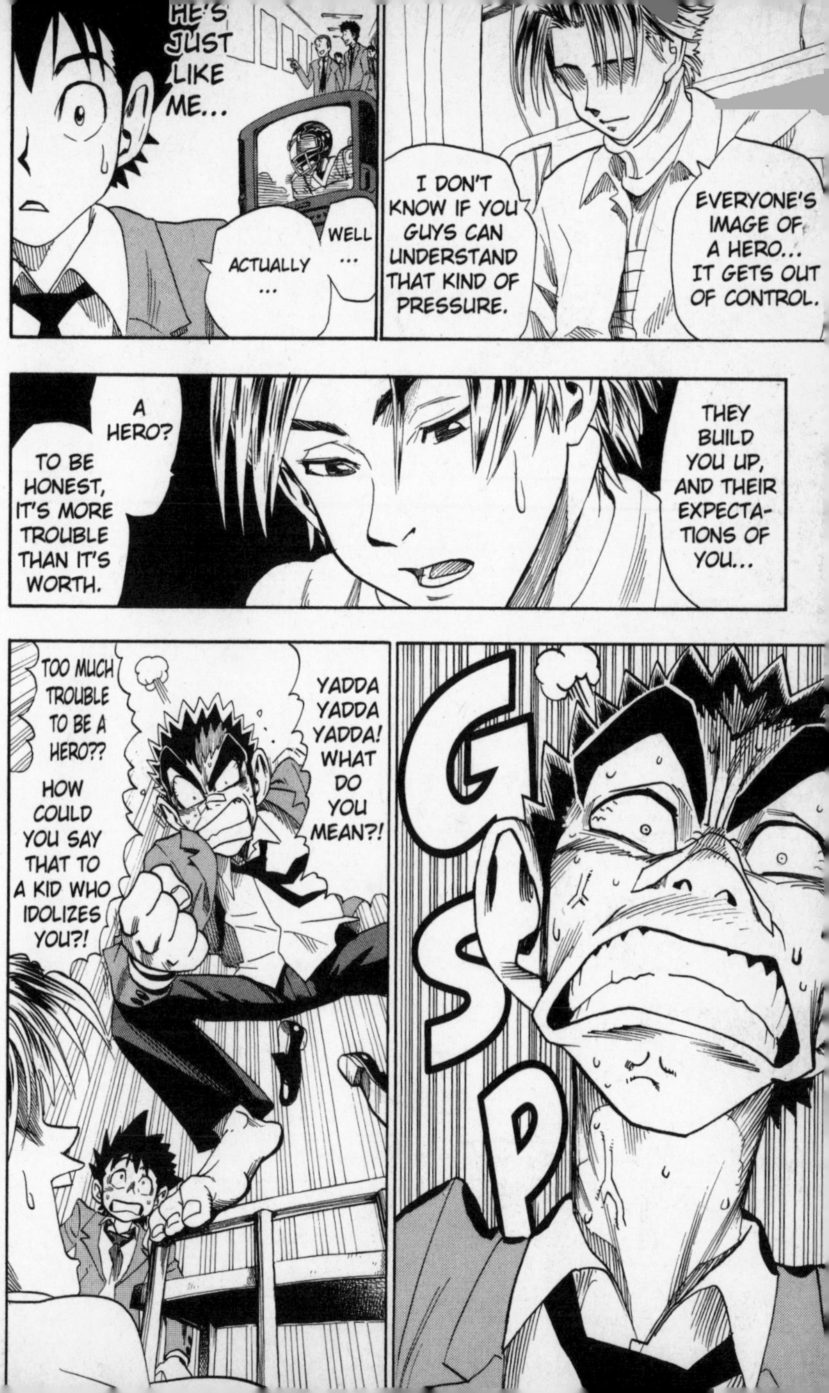
EVERYONE'S IMAGE OF A HERO... IT GETS OUT OF CONTROL.
I DON'T KNOW IF YOU GUYS CAN UNDERSTAND THAT KIND OF PRESSURE.
HE'S JUST LIKE ME...
WELL ...
ACTUALLY ...
THEY BUILD YOU UP, AND THEIR EXPECTA-TIONS OF YOU...
A HERO?
TO BE HONEST, IT'S MORE TROUBLE THAN IT'S WORTH.
GASP
YADDA YADDA YADDA! WHAT DO YOU MEAN?!
TOO MUCH TROUBLE TO BE A HERO??
HOW COULD YOU SAY THAT TO A KID WHO IDOLIZES YOU?!

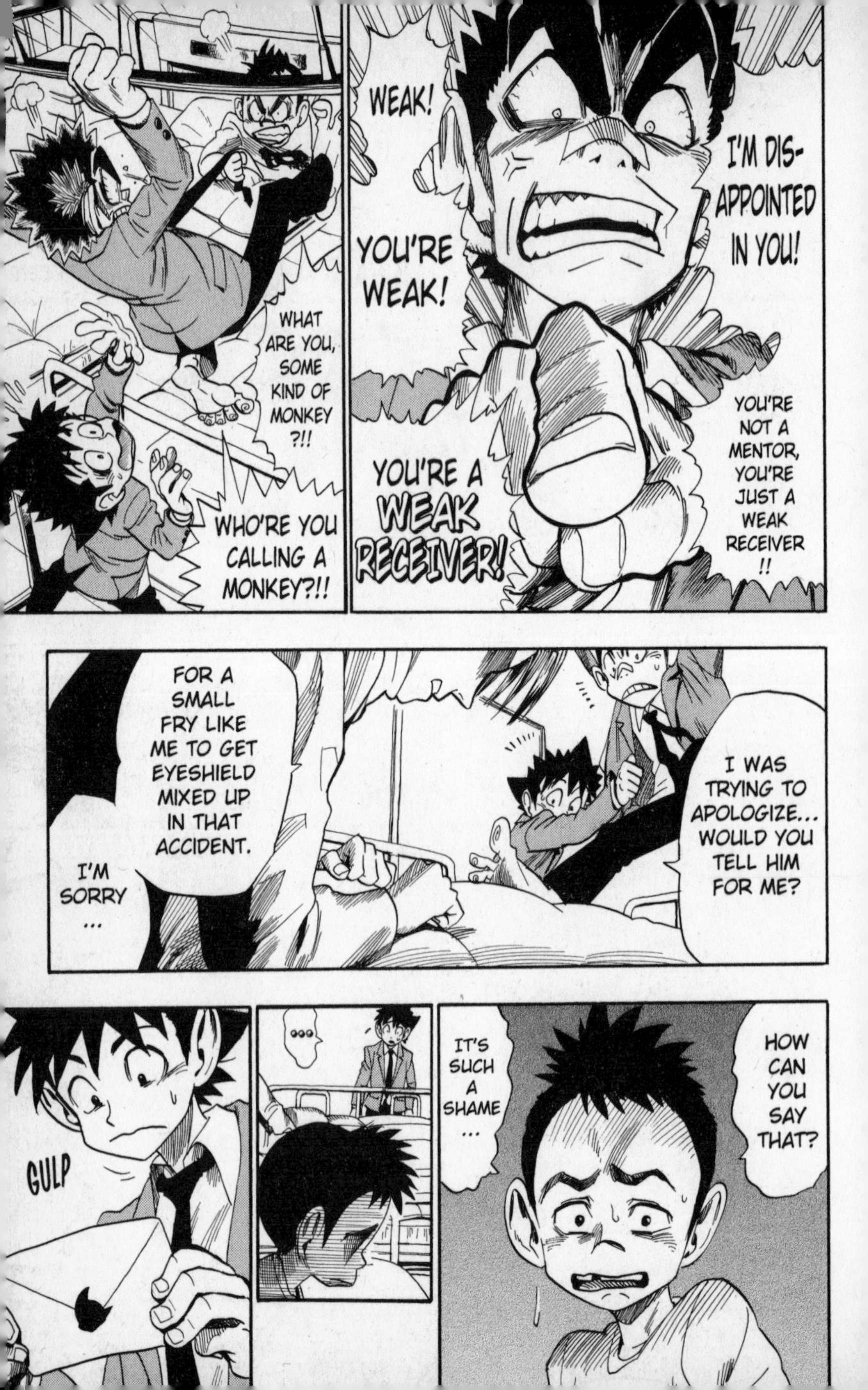
I'M DIS-APPOINTED IN YOU!
WEAK!
YOU'RE WEAK!
YOU'RE NOT A MENTOR, YOU'RE JUST A WEAK RECEIVER!!
YOU'RE A WEAK RECEIVER!
WHAT ARE YOU, SOME KIND OF MONKEY?!!
WHO'RE YOU CALLING A MONKEY?!!
I WAS TRYING TO APOLOGIZE... WOULD YOU TELL HIM FOR ME?
FOR A SMALL FRY LIKE ME TO GET EYESHIELD MIXED UP IN THAT ACCIDENT.
I'M SORRY...
HOW CAN YOU SAY THAT?
IT'S SUCH A SHAME...
...
GULP

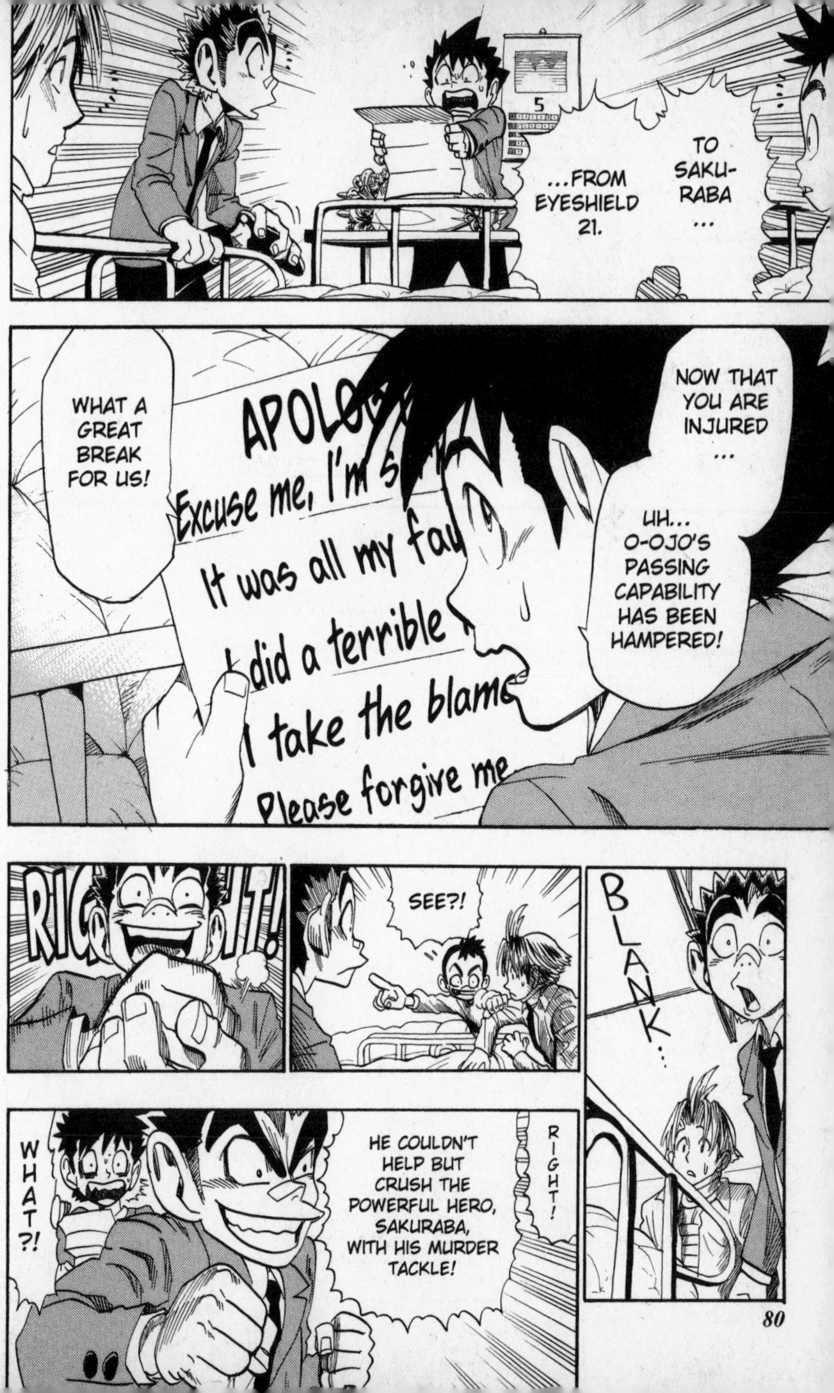
TO SAKU-RABA ...
...FROM EYESHIELD 21.
NOW THAT YOU ARE INJURED ...
UH... O-OJO'S PASSING CAPABILITY HAS BEEN HAMPERED!
WHAT A GREAT BREAK FOR US!
APOLO
Excuse me, I'm s
It was all my fau
I did a terrible
I take the blame
Please forgive me
BLANK...
SEE?!
RIG HT!
RIGHT!
HE COULDN'T HELP BUT CRUSH THE POWERFUL HERO, SAKURABA, WITH HIS MURDER TACKLE!
WHAT?!

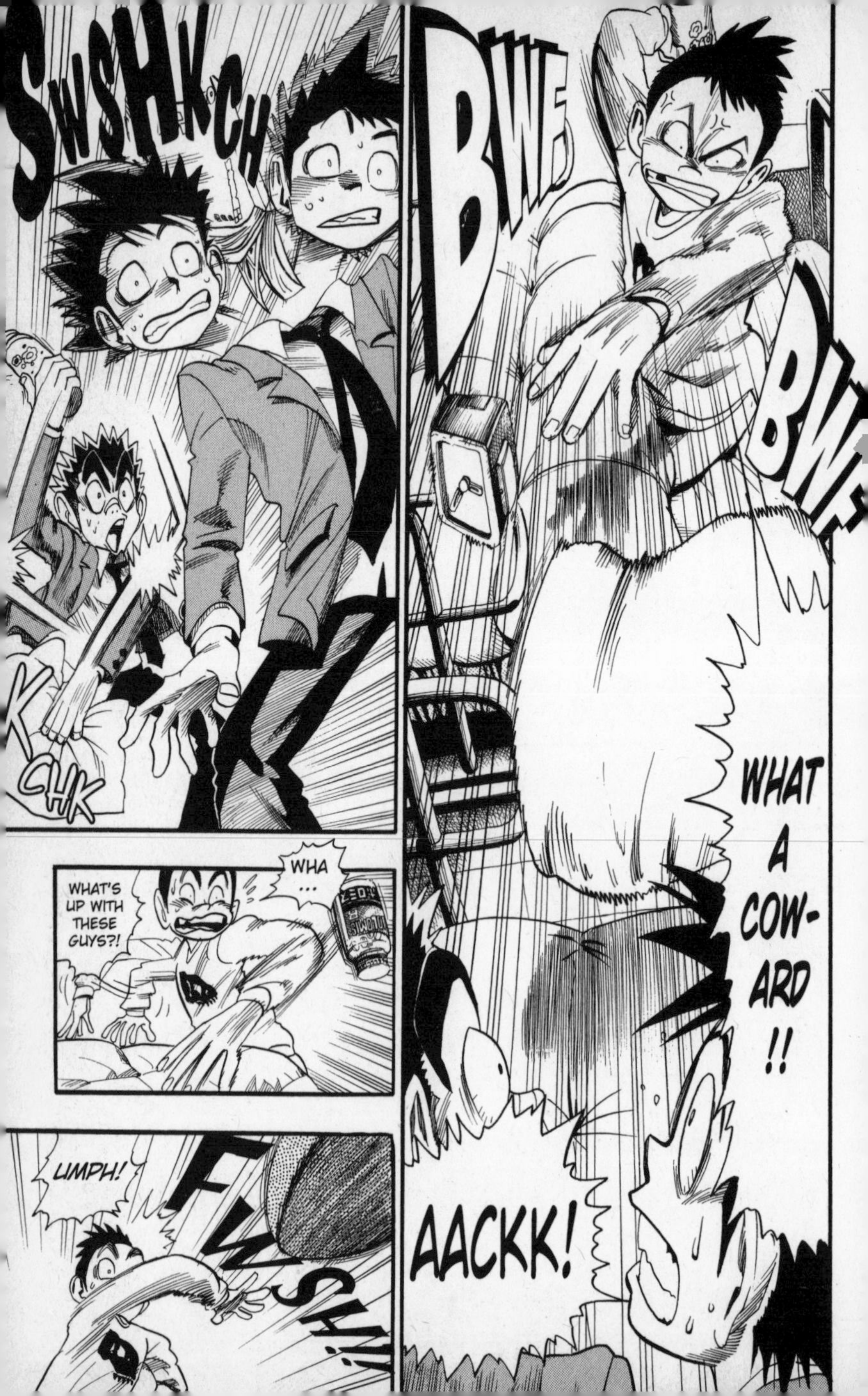
BWF
BWF
WHAT A COW-ARD!!
AACKK!
SWSHKCH
KCHK
WHA ...
WHAT'S UP WITH THESE GUYS?!
UMPH!
FWSH!!

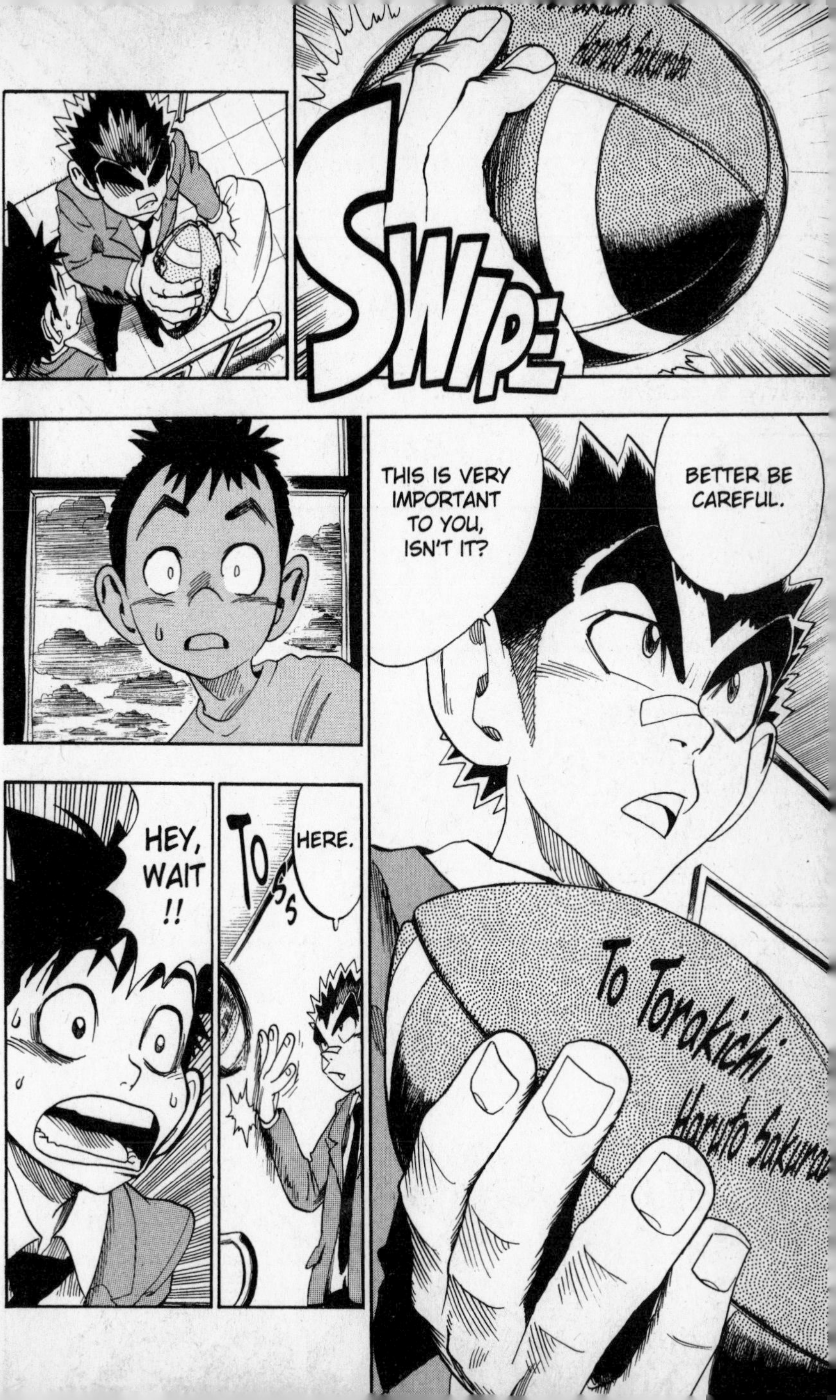
SWIPE
BETTER BE CAREFUL.
THIS IS VERY IMPORTANT TO YOU, ISN'T IT?
To Torakichi
Haruto Sakura
TOSS
HERE.
HEY, WAIT !!

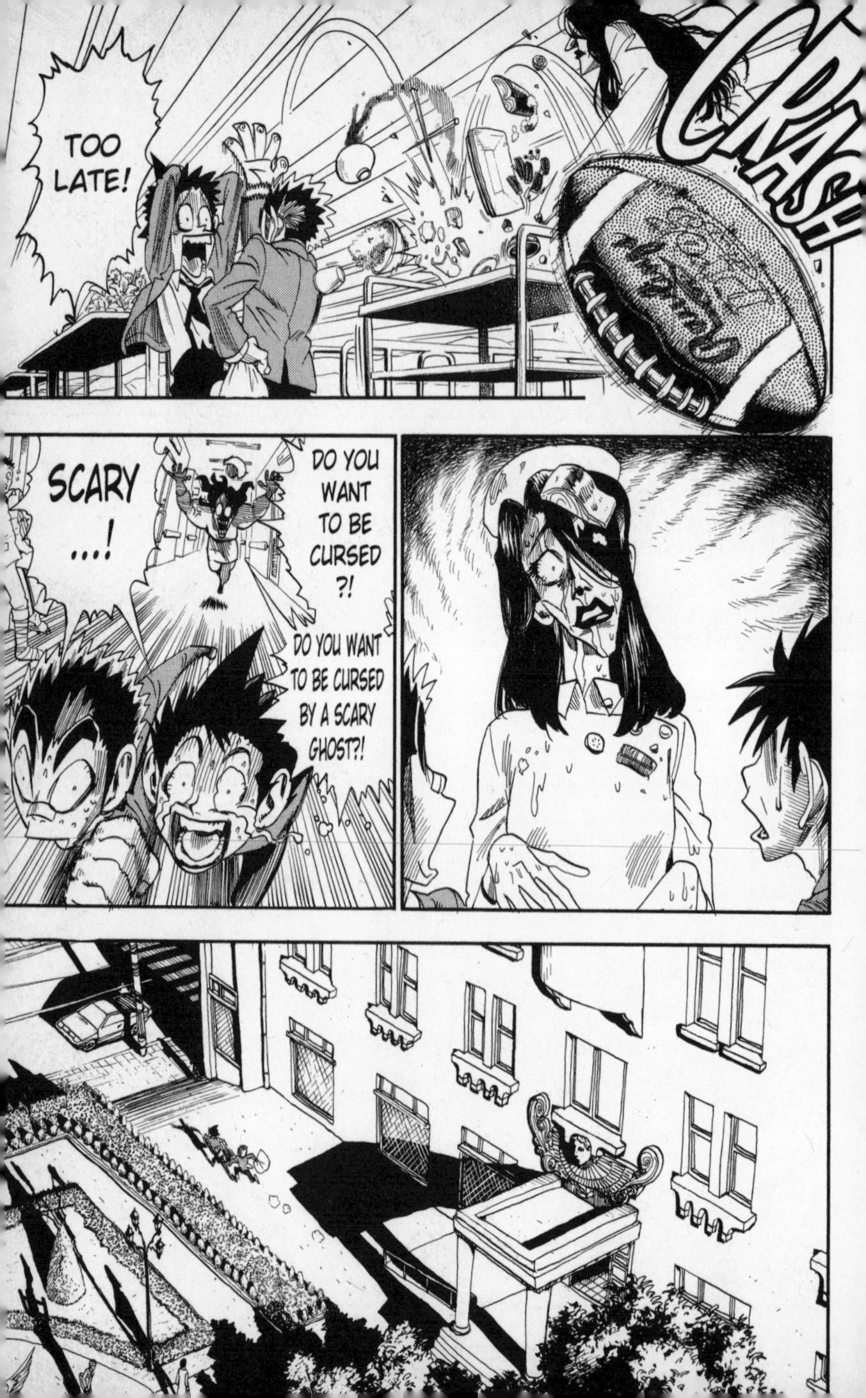
CRASH!
TOO LATE!
DO YOU WANT TO BE CURSED?!
DO YOU WANT TO BE CURSED BY A SCARY GHOST?!
SCARY ...!

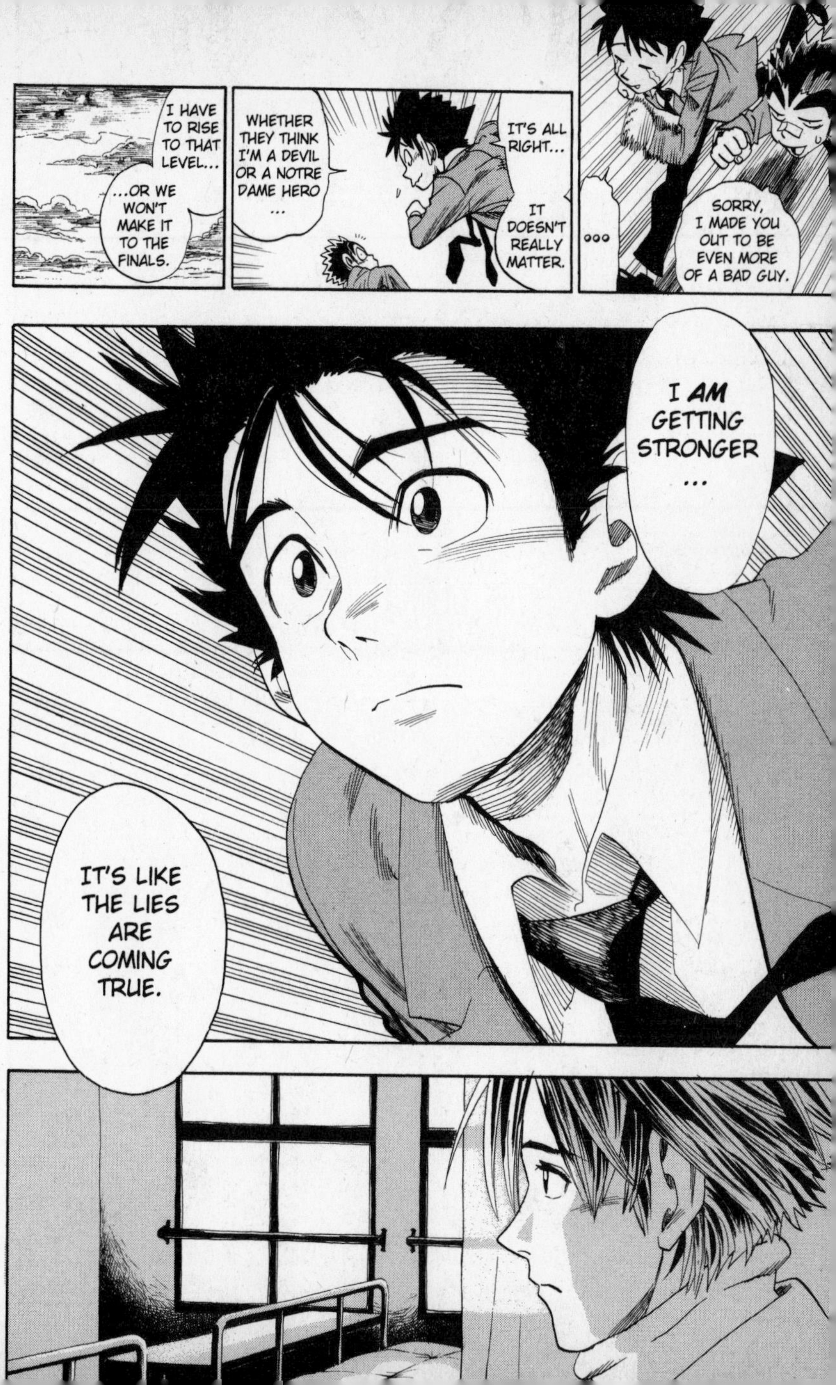
SORRY, I MADE YOU OUT TO BE EVEN MORE OF A BAD GUY.
...
IT'S ALL RIGHT...
IT DOESN'T REALLY MATTER.
WHETHER THEY THINK I'M A DEVIL OR A NOTRE DAME HERO ...
I HAVE TO RISE TO THAT LEVEL...
...OR WE WON'T MAKE IT TO THE FINALS.
I ***AM*** GETTING STRONGER ...
IT'S LIKE THE LIES ARE COMING TRUE.

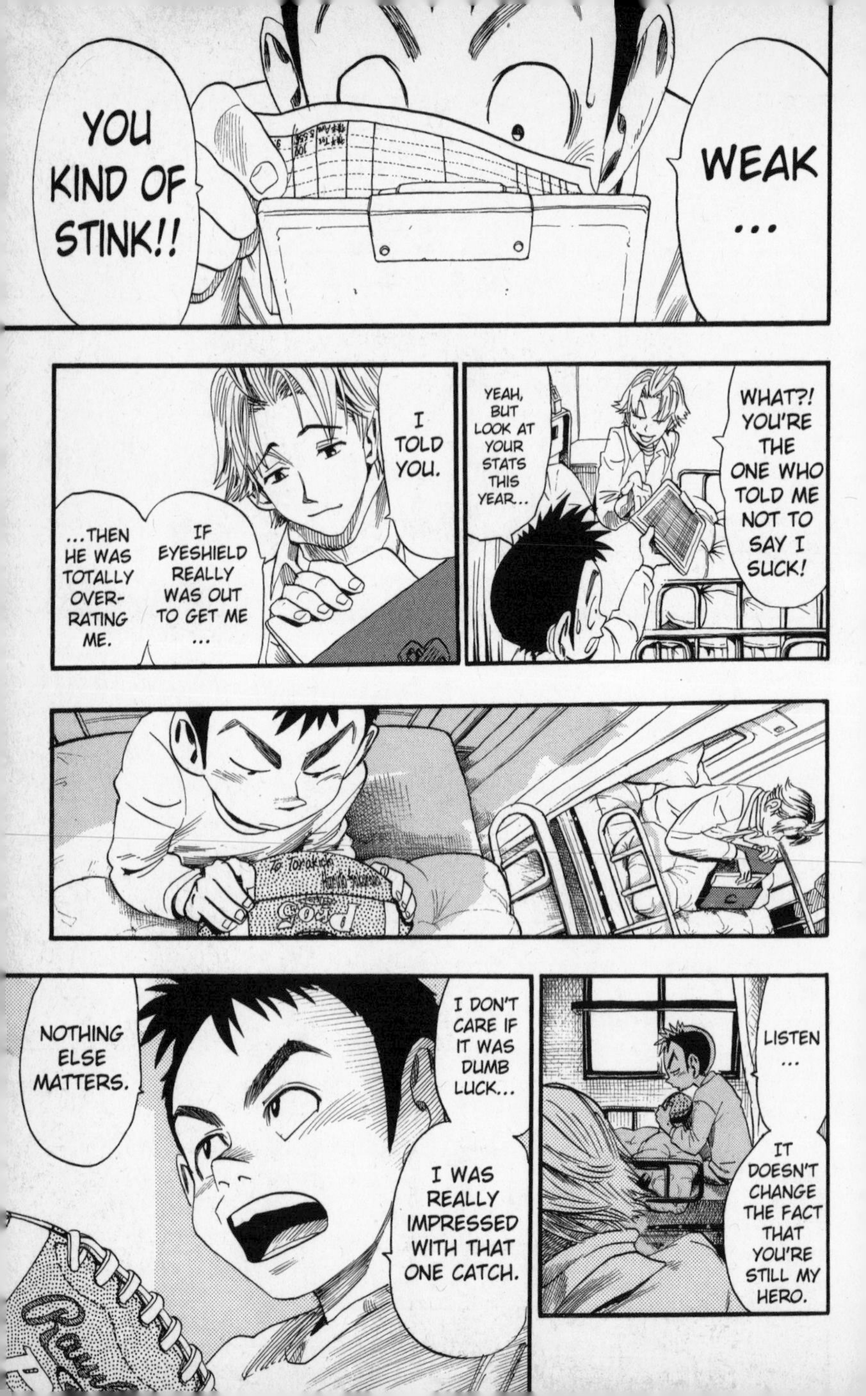
WEAK ...
YOU KIND OF STINK!!
WHAT?! YOU'RE THE ONE WHO TOLD ME NOT TO SAY I SUCK!
YEAH, BUT LOOK AT YOUR STATS THIS YEAR...
I TOLD YOU.
IF EYESHIELD REALLY WAS OUT TO GET ME ...
...THEN HE WAS TOTALLY OVER-RATING ME.
LISTEN ...
IT DOESN'T CHANGE THE FACT THAT YOU'RE STILL MY HERO.
I DON'T CARE IF IT WAS DUMB LUCK...
I WAS REALLY IMPRESSED WITH THAT ONE CATCH.
NOTHING ELSE MATTERS.

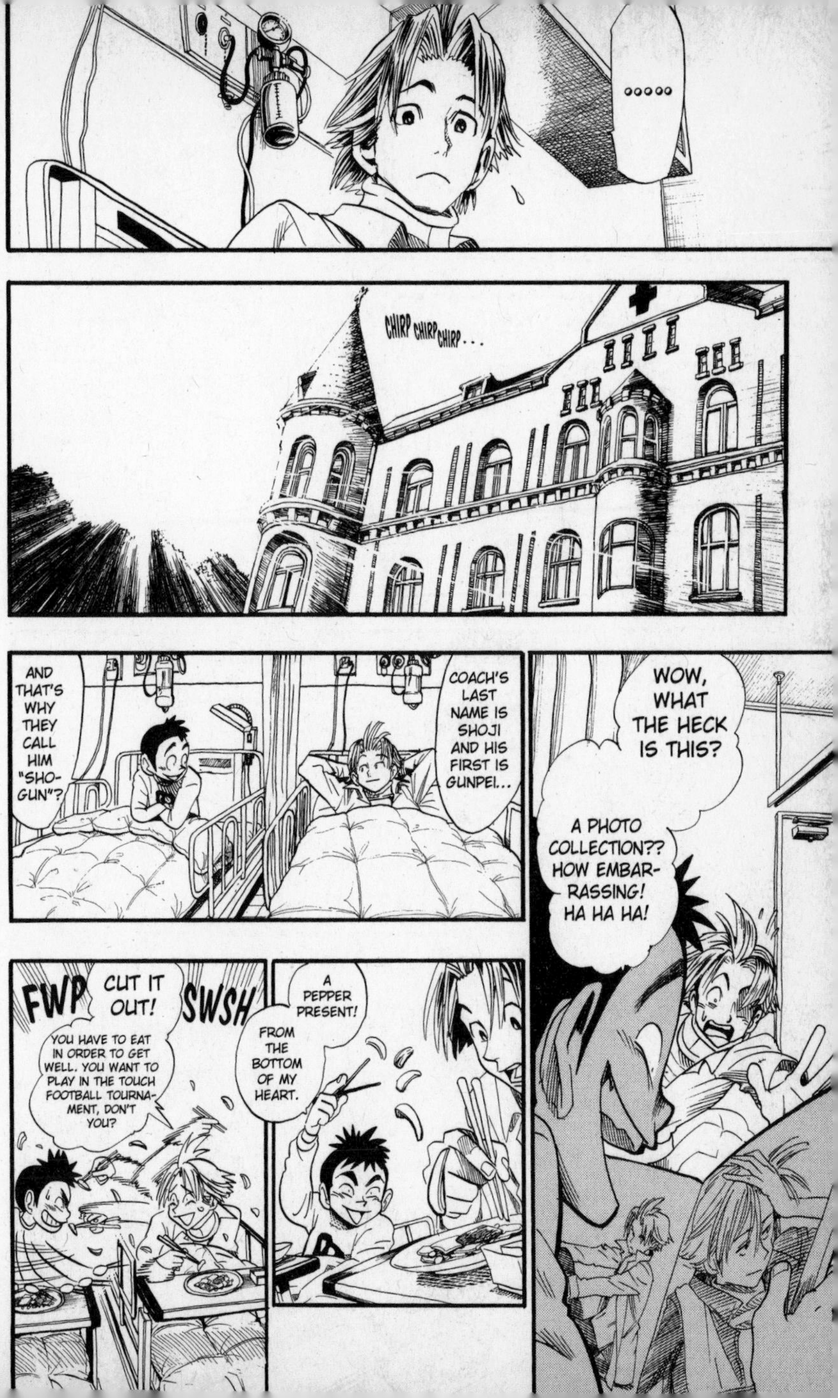
○○○○○
CHIRP CHIRP CHIRP...
WOW, WHAT THE HECK IS THIS?
A PHOTO COLLECTION?? HOW EMBAR-RASSING! HA HA HA!
COACH'S LAST NAME IS SHOJI AND HIS FIRST IS GUNPEI...
AND THAT'S WHY THEY CALL HIM "SHO-GUN"?
A PEPPER PRESENT!
FROM THE BOTTOM OF MY HEART.
SWSH
CUT IT OUT!
FWP
YOU HAVE TO EAT IN ORDER TO GET WELL. YOU WANT TO PLAY IN THE TOUCH FOOTBALL TOURNA-MENT, DON'T YOU?

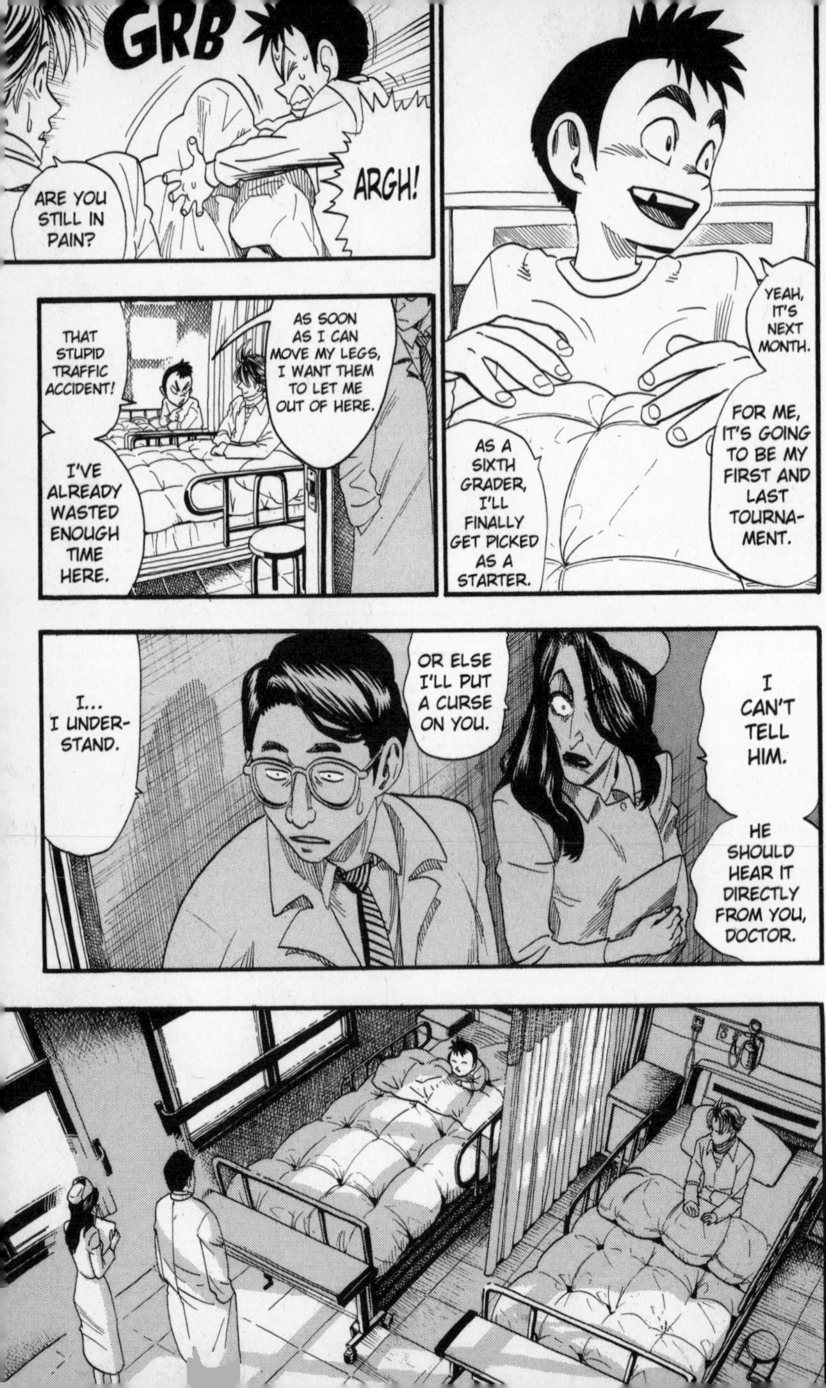
YEAH, IT'S NEXT MONTH.
FOR ME, IT'S GOING TO BE MY FIRST AND LAST TOURNAMENT.
AS A SIXTH GRADER, I'LL FINALLY GET PICKED AS A STARTER.
ARGH!
GRB
ARE YOU STILL IN PAIN?
AS SOON AS I CAN MOVE MY LEGS, I WANT THEM TO LET ME OUT OF HERE.
THAT STUPID TRAFFIC ACCIDENT!
I'VE ALREADY WASTED ENOUGH TIME HERE.
I CAN'T TELL HIM.
HE SHOULD HEAR IT DIRECTLY FROM YOU, DOCTOR.
OR ELSE I'LL PUT A CURSE ON YOU.
I... I UNDERSTAND.

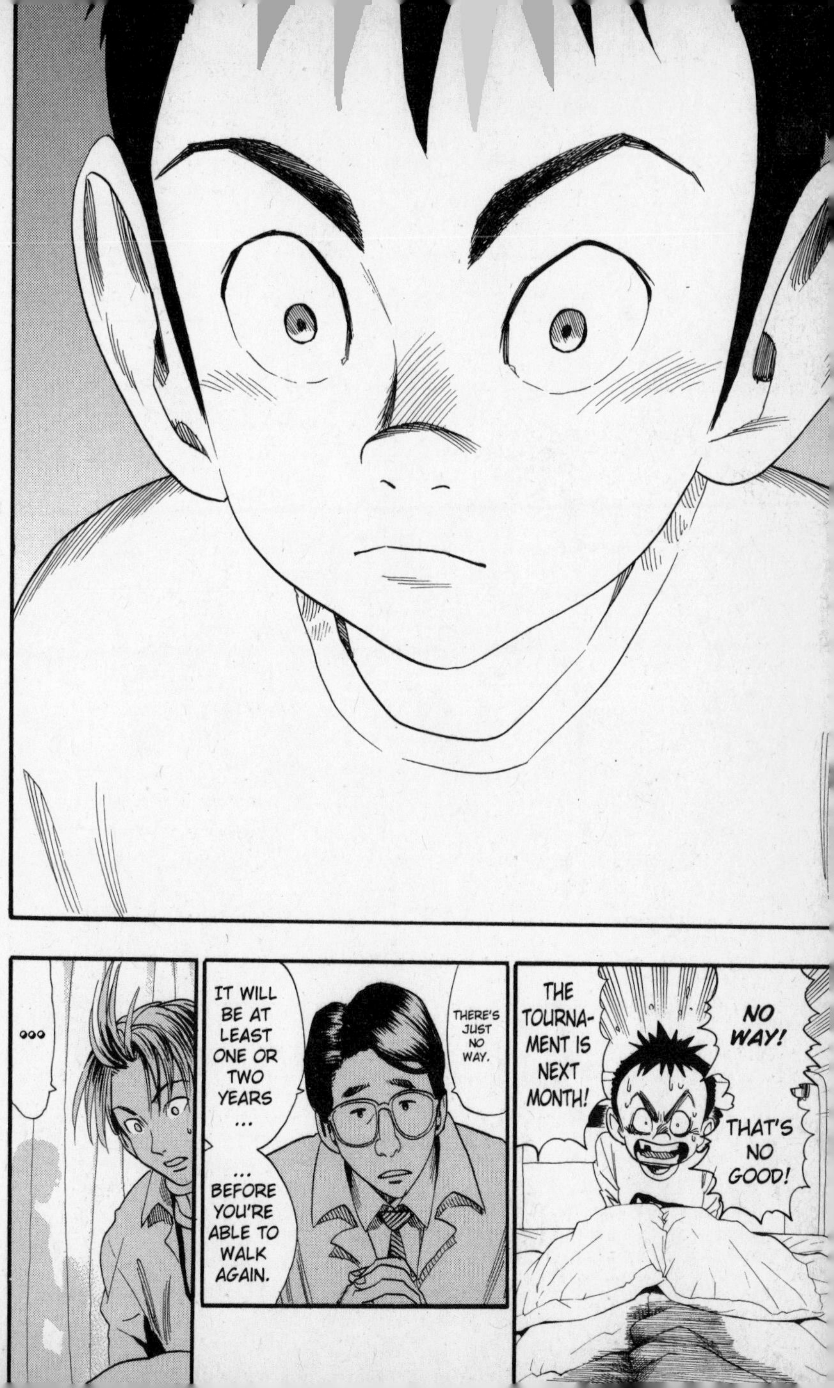
NO WAY!
THE TOURNAMENT IS NEXT MONTH!
THAT'S NO GOOD!
THERE'S JUST NO WAY.
IT WILL BE AT LEAST ONE OR TWO YEARS ...
... BEFORE YOU'RE ABLE TO WALK AGAIN.
...

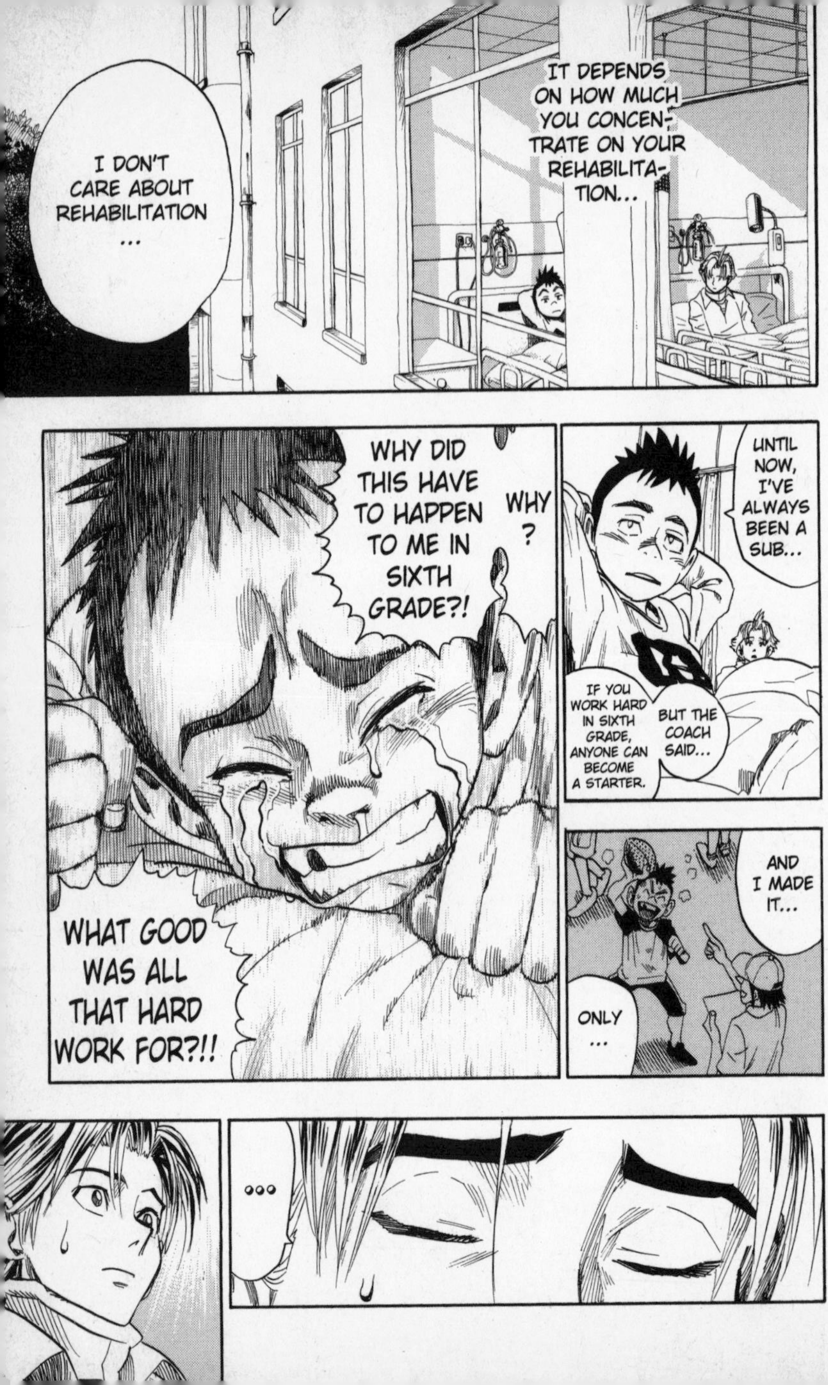
IT DEPENDS ON HOW MUCH YOU CONCEN-TRATE ON YOUR REHABILITA-TION...
I DON'T CARE ABOUT REHABILITATION ...
UNTIL NOW, I'VE ALWAYS BEEN A SUB...
BUT THE COACH SAID...
IF YOU WORK HARD IN SIXTH GRADE, ANYONE CAN BECOME A STARTER.
AND I MADE IT...
ONLY ...
WHY ?
WHY DID THIS HAVE TO HAPPEN TO ME IN SIXTH GRADE?!
WHAT GOOD WAS ALL THAT HARD WORK FOR?!!
...

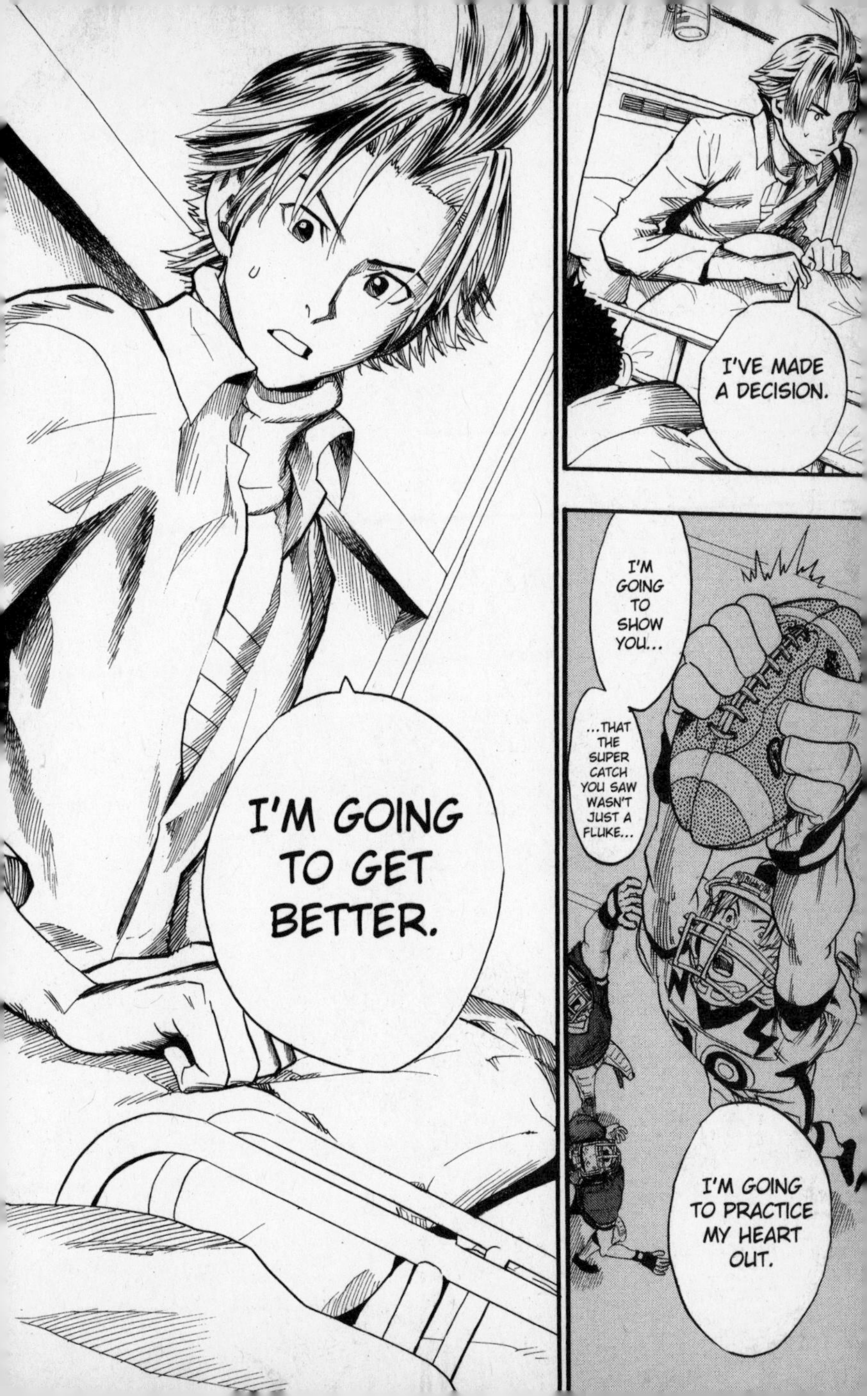
I'VE MADE A DECISION.
I'M GOING TO SHOW YOU...
...THAT THE SUPER CATCH YOU SAW WASN'T JUST A FLUKE...
I'M GOING TO PRACTICE MY HEART OUT.
I'M GOING TO GET BETTER.

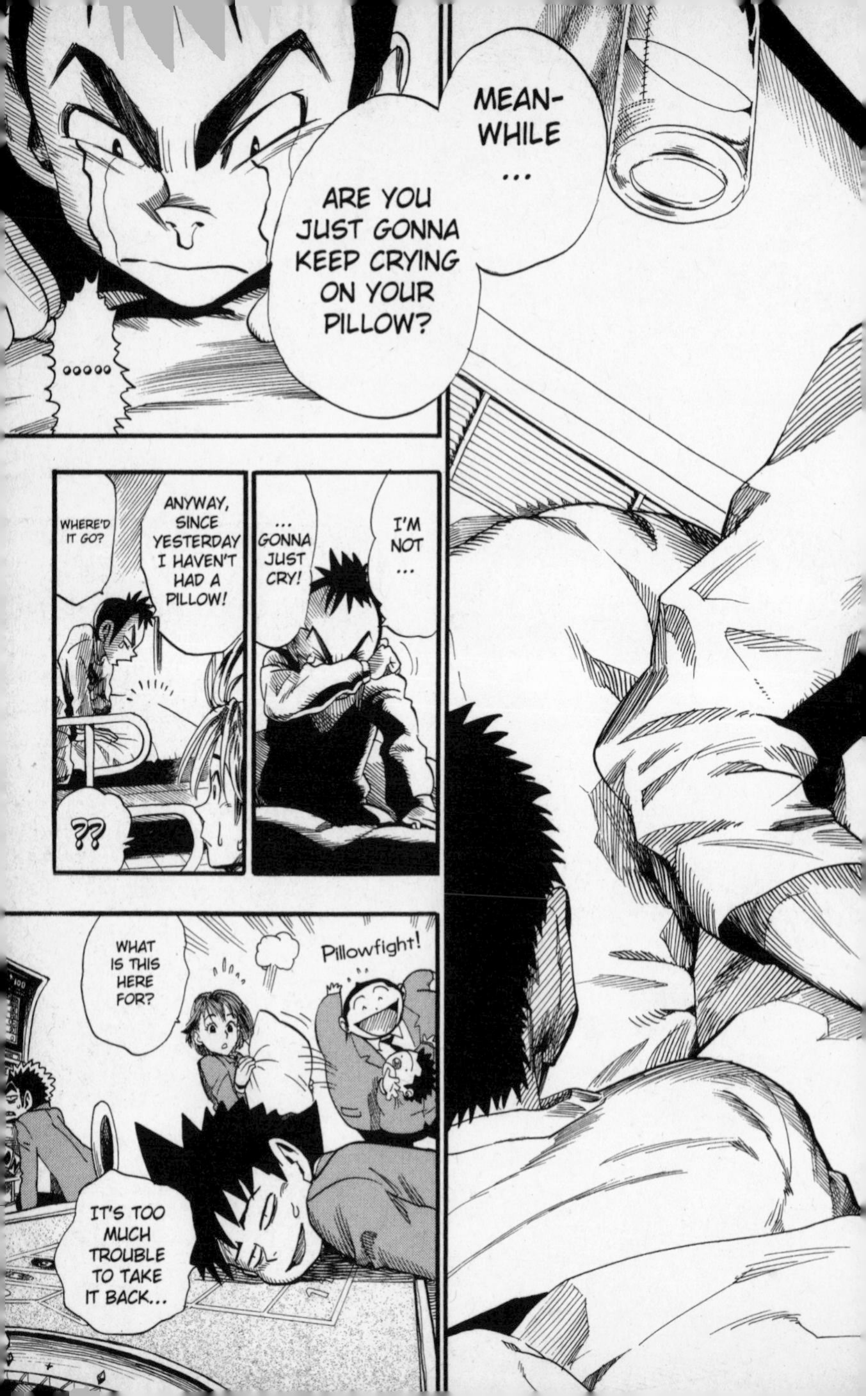
MEAN-WHILE ...
ARE YOU JUST GONNA KEEP CRYING ON YOUR PILLOW?
.....
I'M NOT ...
... GONNA JUST CRY!
ANYWAY, SINCE YESTERDAY I HAVEN'T HAD A PILLOW!
WHERE'D IT GO?
??
Pillowfight!
WHAT IS THIS HERE FOR?
IT'S TOO MUCH TROUBLE TO TAKE IT BACK...

SCARY STORIES THAT REALLY HAPPENED

Told by the Occult-Loving Nurse Oka

Chapter 1: The Missing Pillow

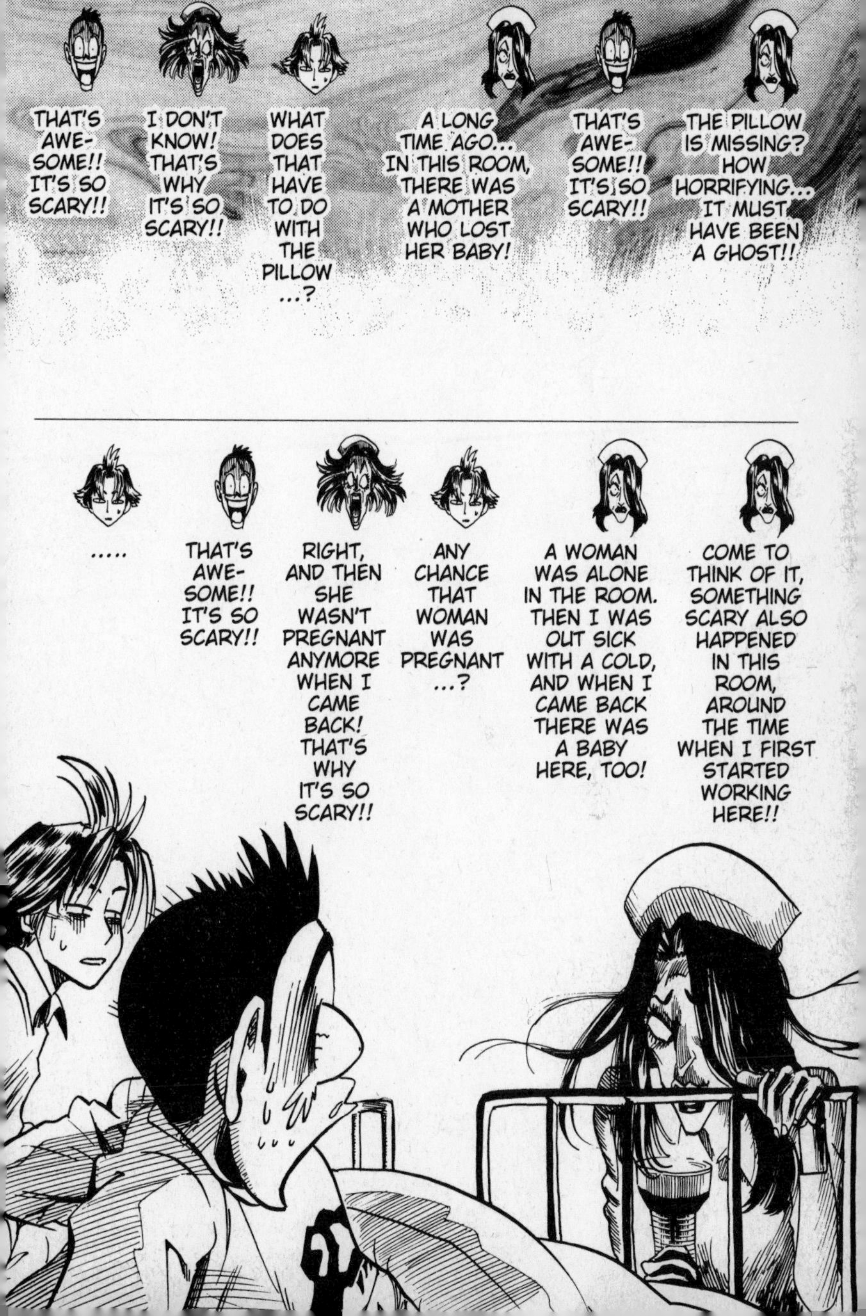
THE PILLOW IS MISSING? HOW HORRIFYING... IT MUST HAVE BEEN A GHOST!!
THAT'S AWE-SOME!! IT'S SO SCARY!!
A LONG TIME AGO... IN THIS ROOM, THERE WAS A MOTHER WHO LOST HER BABY!
WHAT DOES THAT HAVE TO DO WITH THE PILLOW ...?
I DON'T KNOW! THAT'S WHY IT'S SO SCARY!!
THAT'S AWE-SOME!! IT'S SO SCARY!!
COME TO THINK OF IT, SOMETHING SCARY ALSO HAPPENED IN THIS ROOM, AROUND THE TIME WHEN I FIRST STARTED WORKING HERE!!
A WOMAN WAS ALONE IN THE ROOM. THEN I WAS OUT SICK WITH A COLD, AND WHEN I CAME BACK THERE WAS A BABY HERE, TOO!
ANY CHANCE THAT WOMAN WAS PREGNANT ...?
RIGHT, AND THEN SHE WASN'T PREGNANT ANYMORE WHEN I CAME BACK! THAT'S WHY IT'S SO SCARY!!
THAT'S AWE-SOME!! IT'S SO SCARY!!
.....

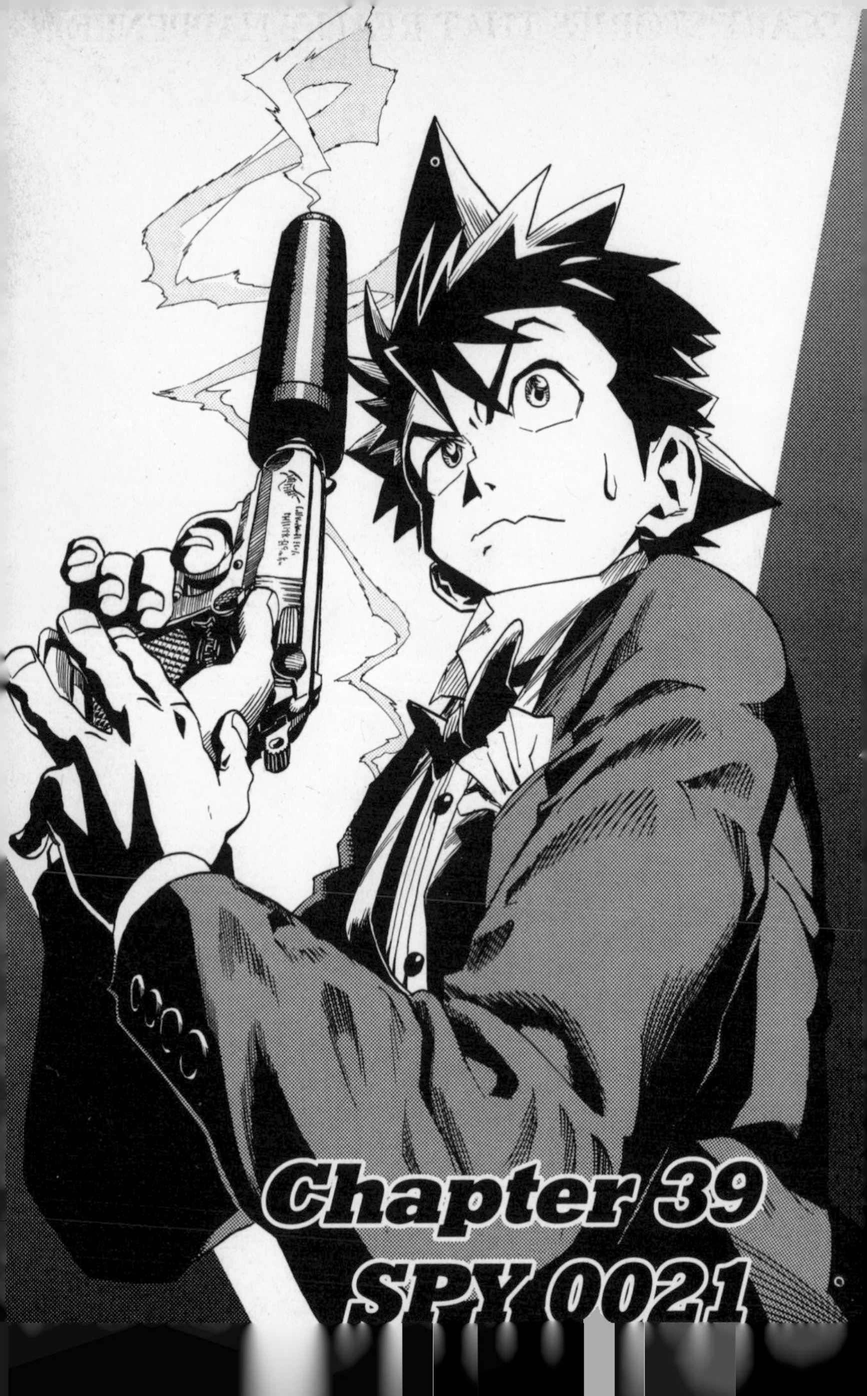
Chapter 39
SPY 0021

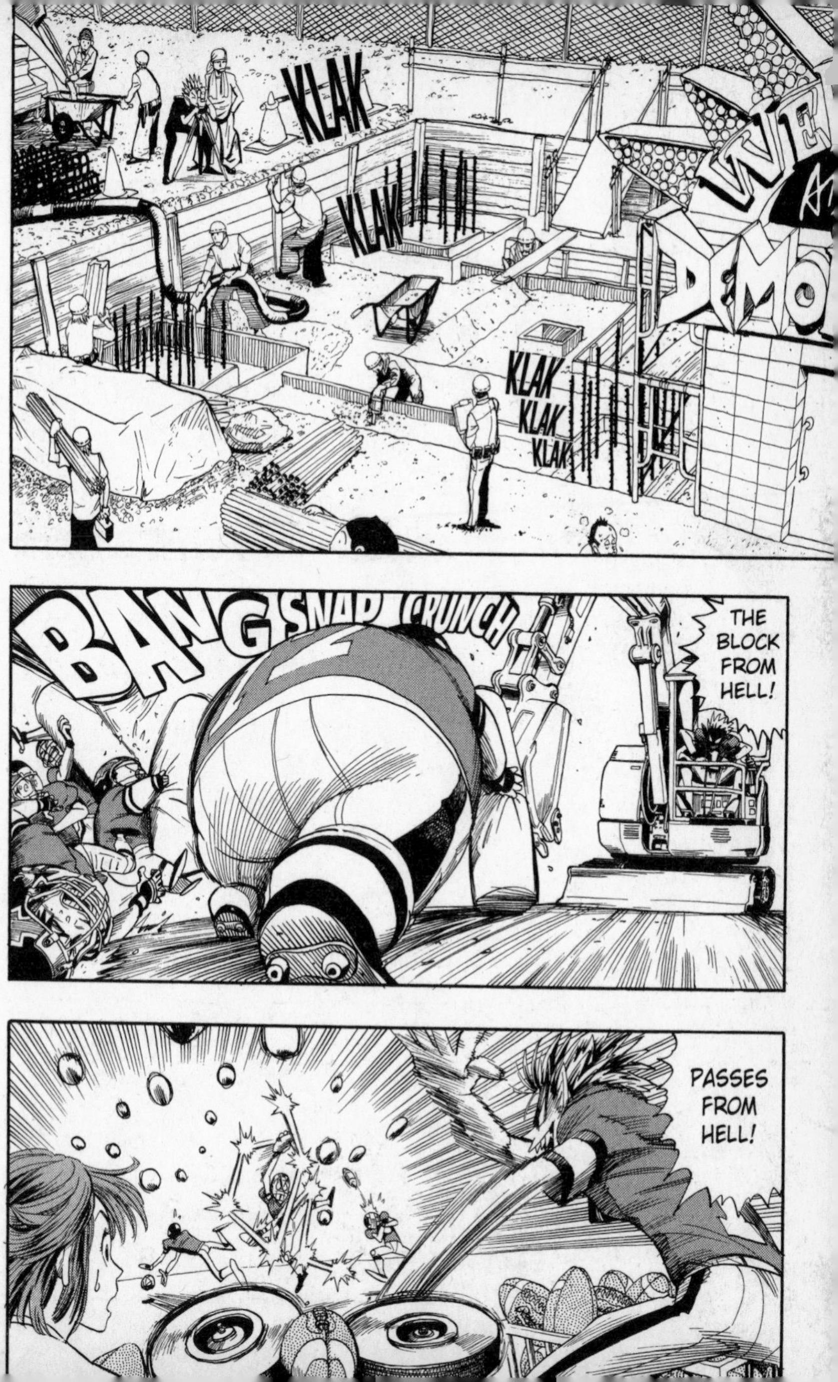
KLAK
KLAK
KLAK
KLAK
KLAK
THE BLOCK FROM HELL!
BANG
SNAP
CRUNCH
PASSES FROM HELL!

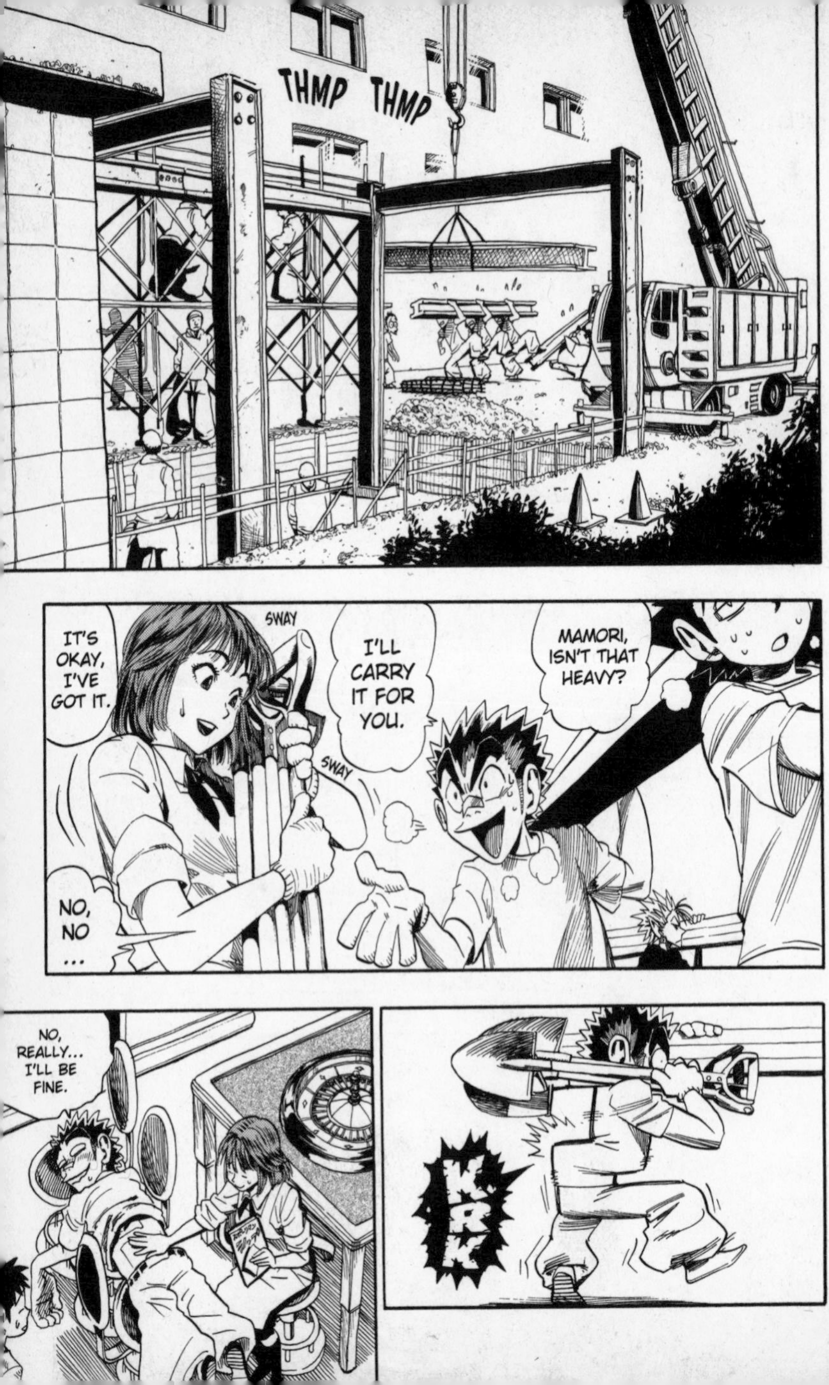
THMP THMP
MAMORI, ISN'T THAT HEAVY?
I'LL CARRY IT FOR YOU.
SWAY
SWAY
IT'S OKAY, I'VE GOT IT.
NO, NO ...
KRK
NO, REALLY... I'LL BE FINE.

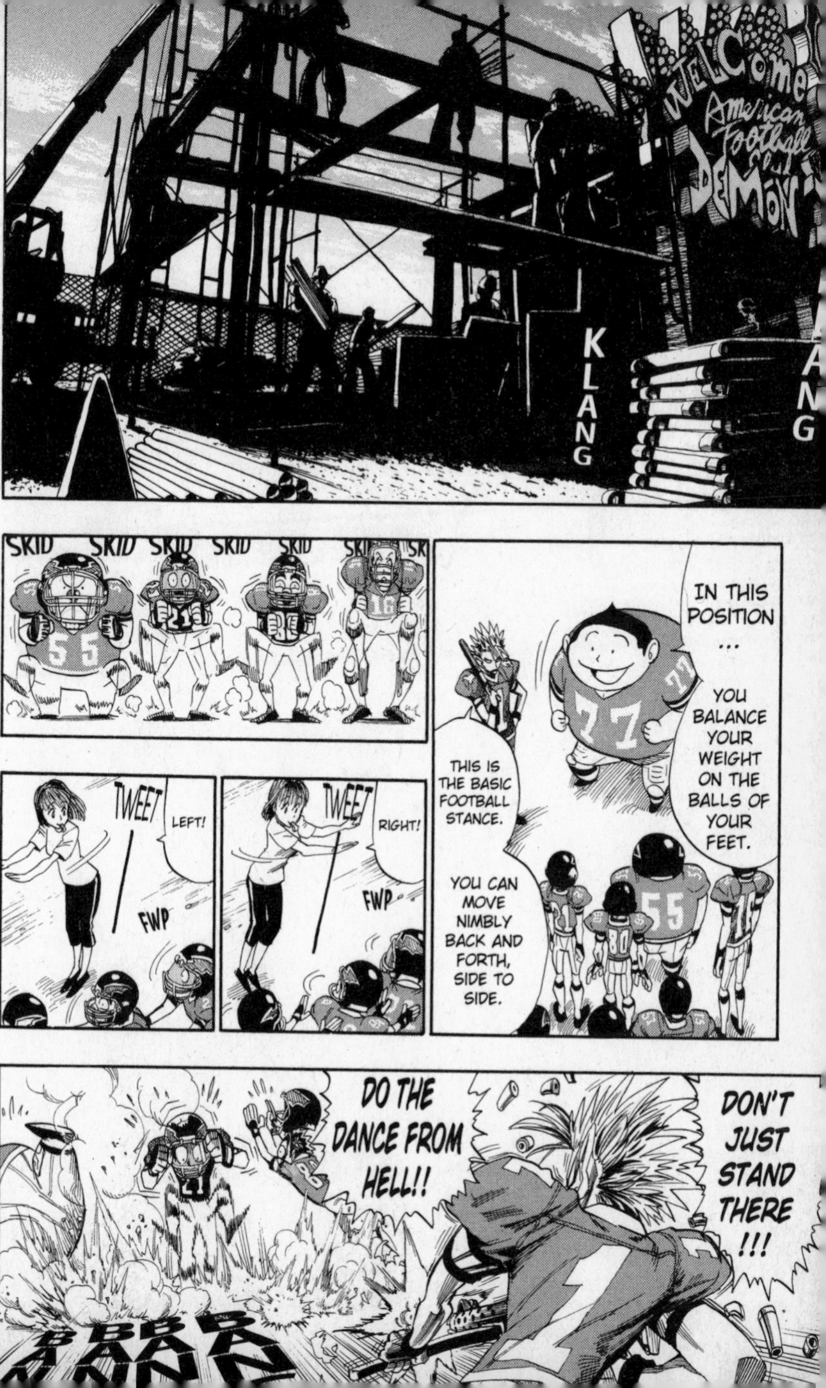

WELCOME
American Football
DEMON
KLANG
IN THIS POSITION ...
YOU BALANCE YOUR WEIGHT ON THE BALLS OF YOUR FEET.
THIS IS THE BASIC FOOTBALL STANCE.
YOU CAN MOVE NIMBLY BACK AND FORTH, SIDE TO SIDE.
SKID SKID SKID SKID SKID
TWEET
RIGHT!
FWP
TWEET
LEFT!
FWP
DON'T JUST STAND THERE!!!
DO THE DANCE FROM HELL!!

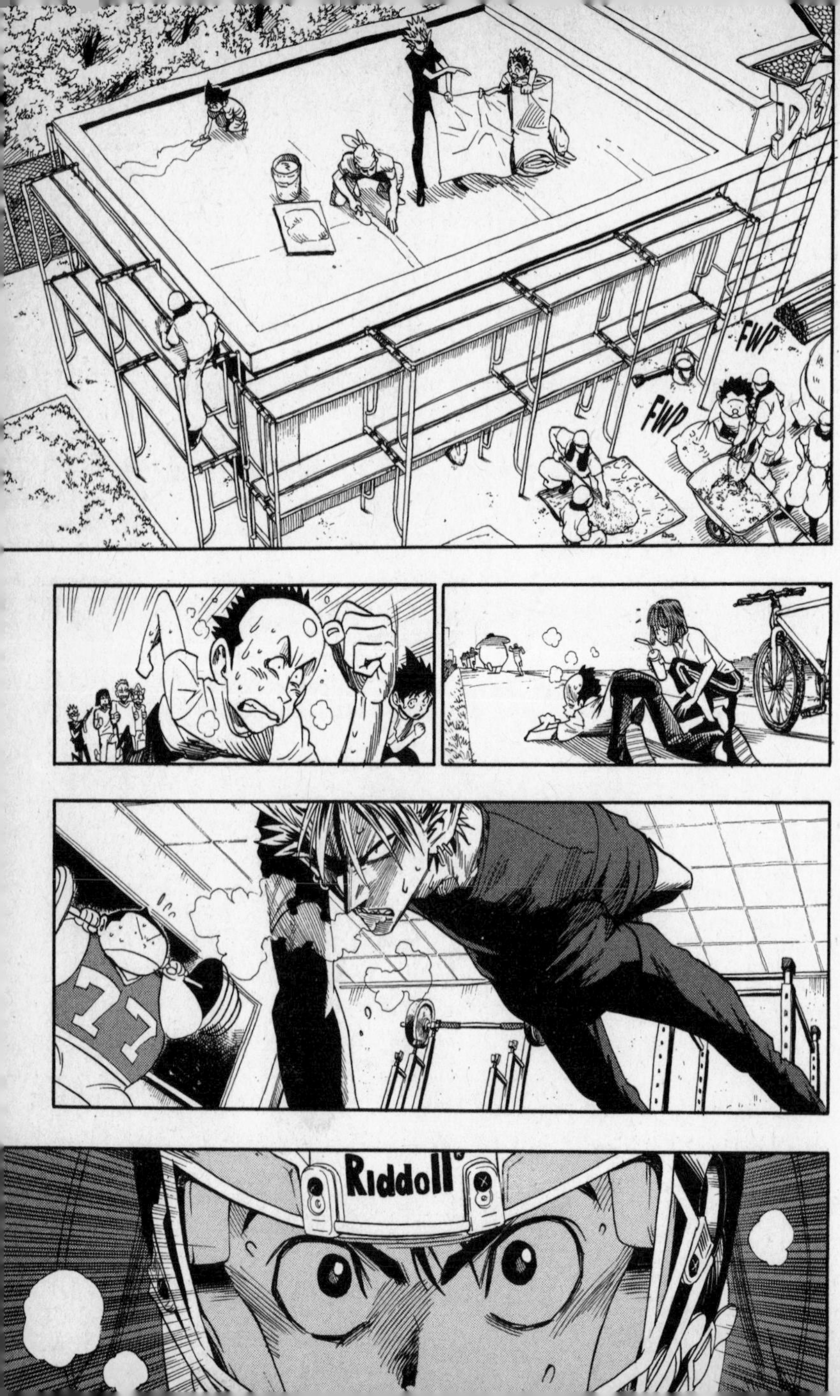
FWP
FWP
Riddoll

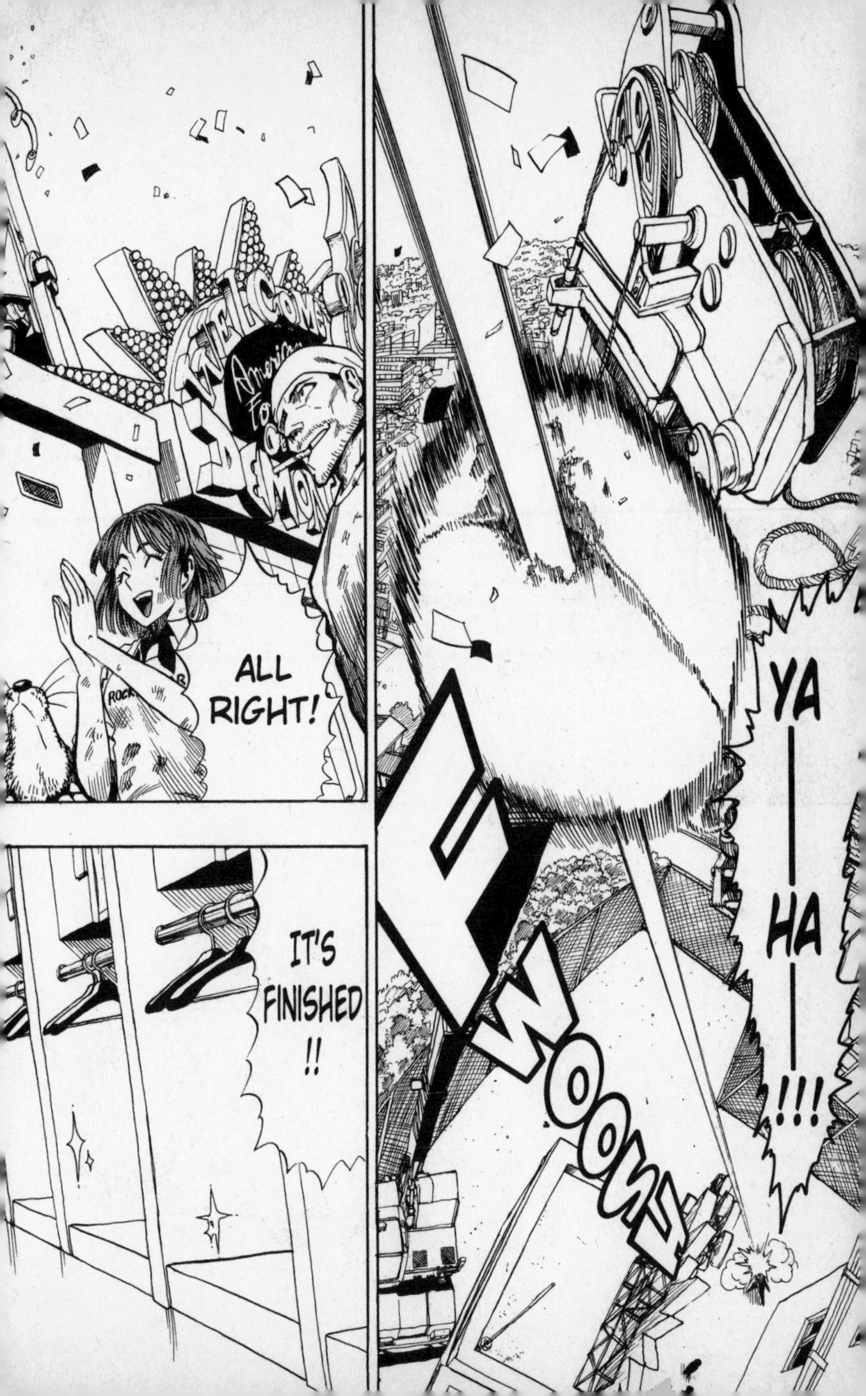

YA—HA——!!!
ZOOOM!
ALL RIGHT!
IT'S FINISHED!!

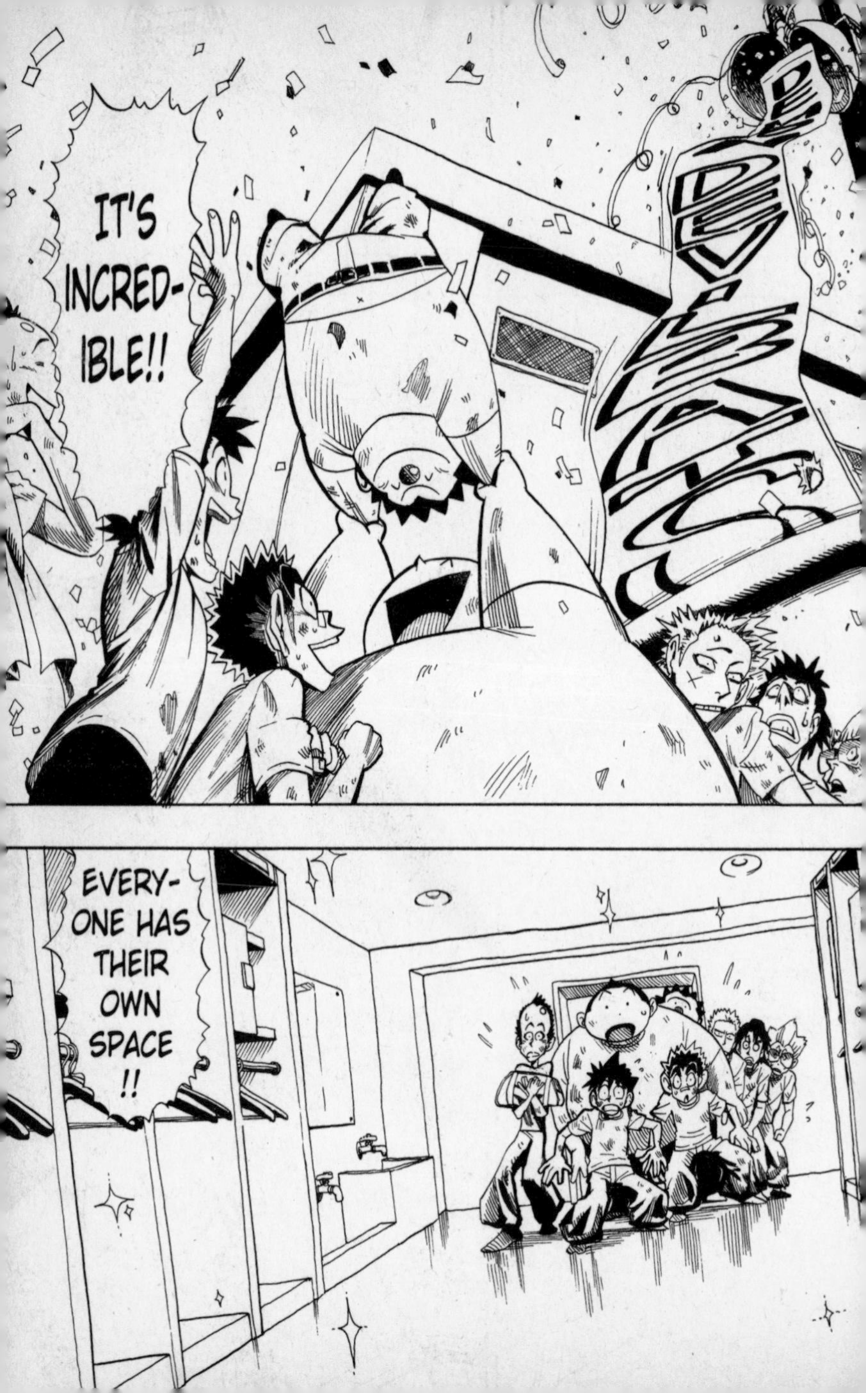
IT'S INCRED-IBLE!!
EVERY-ONE HAS THEIR OWN SPACE!!

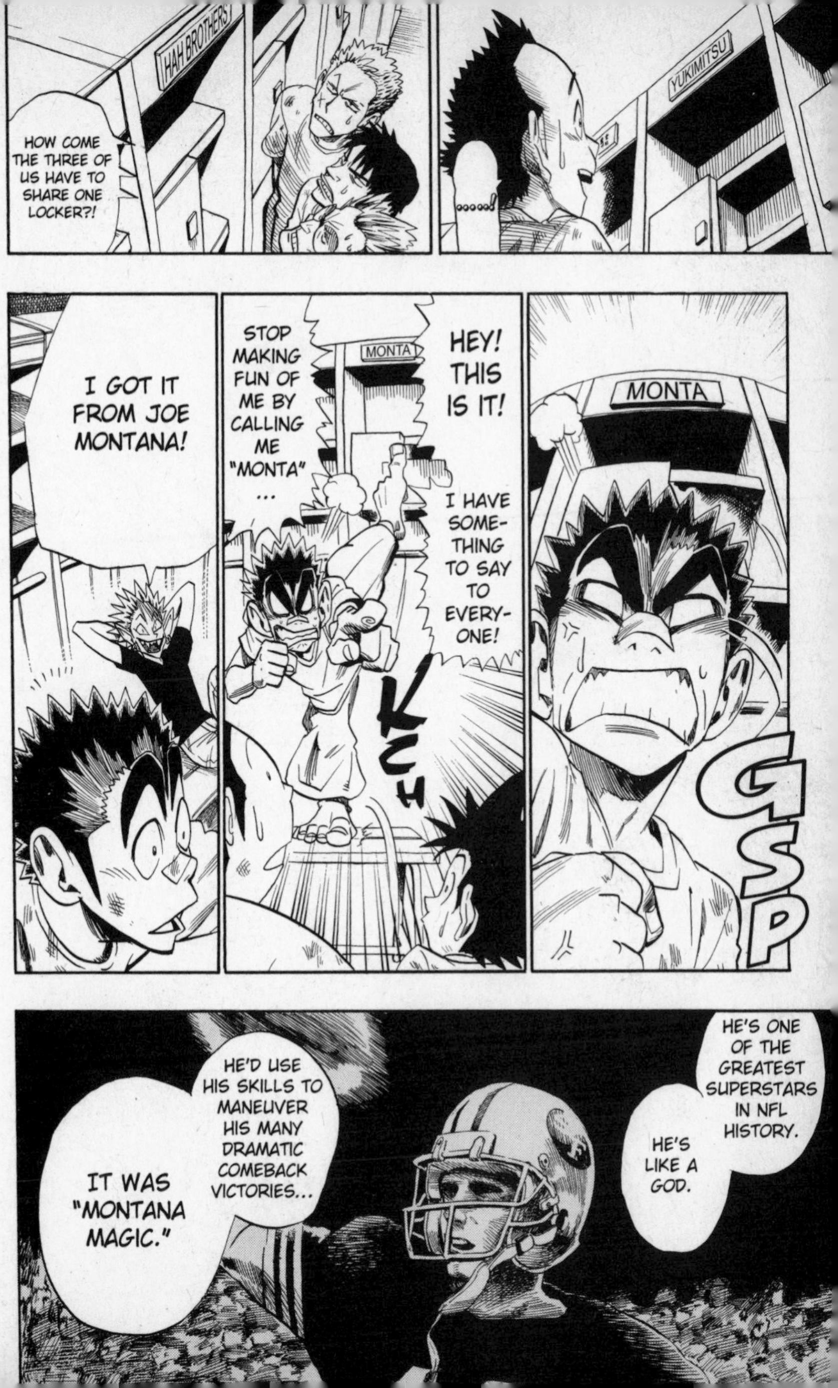
YUKIMITSU
HAH BROTHERS
HOW COME THE THREE OF US HAVE TO SHARE ONE LOCKER?!
MONTA
GSP
HEY! THIS IS IT!
I HAVE SOMETHING TO SAY TO EVERYONE!
MONTA
STOP MAKING FUN OF ME BY CALLING ME "MONTA"...
KCH
I GOT IT FROM JOE MONTANA!
HE'S ONE OF THE GREATEST SUPERSTARS IN NFL HISTORY.
HE'S LIKE A GOD.
HE'D USE HIS SKILLS TO MANEUVER HIS MANY DRAMATIC COMEBACK VICTORIES...
IT WAS "MONTANA MAGIC."

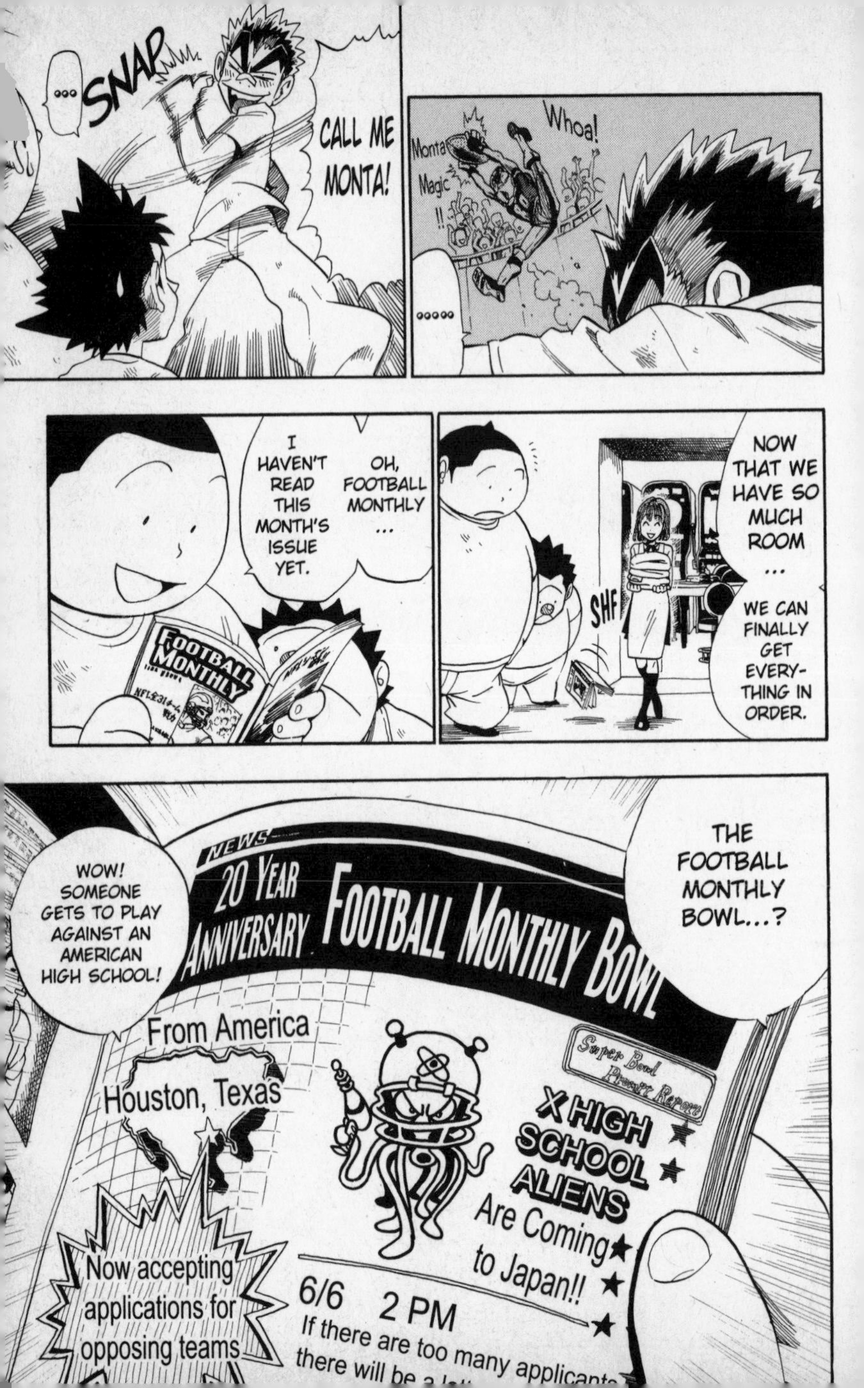

Whoa!
Monta Magic !!
•••••
CALL ME MONTA!
SNAP
•••
NOW THAT WE HAVE SO MUCH ROOM ... WE CAN FINALLY GET EVERYTHING IN ORDER.
SHF
OH, FOOTBALL MONTHLY ...
I HAVEN'T READ THIS MONTH'S ISSUE YET.
FOOTBALL MONTHLY
THE FOOTBALL MONTHLY BOWL...?
WOW! SOMEONE GETS TO PLAY AGAINST AN AMERICAN HIGH SCHOOL!
NEWS
20 YEAR ANNIVERSARY FOOTBALL MONTHLY BOWL
Super Bowl Preview Report
X HIGH SCHOOL ALIENS Are Coming to Japan!!
From America
Houston, Texas
Now accepting applications for opposing teams
6/6 2 PM
If there are too many applicants
there will be a

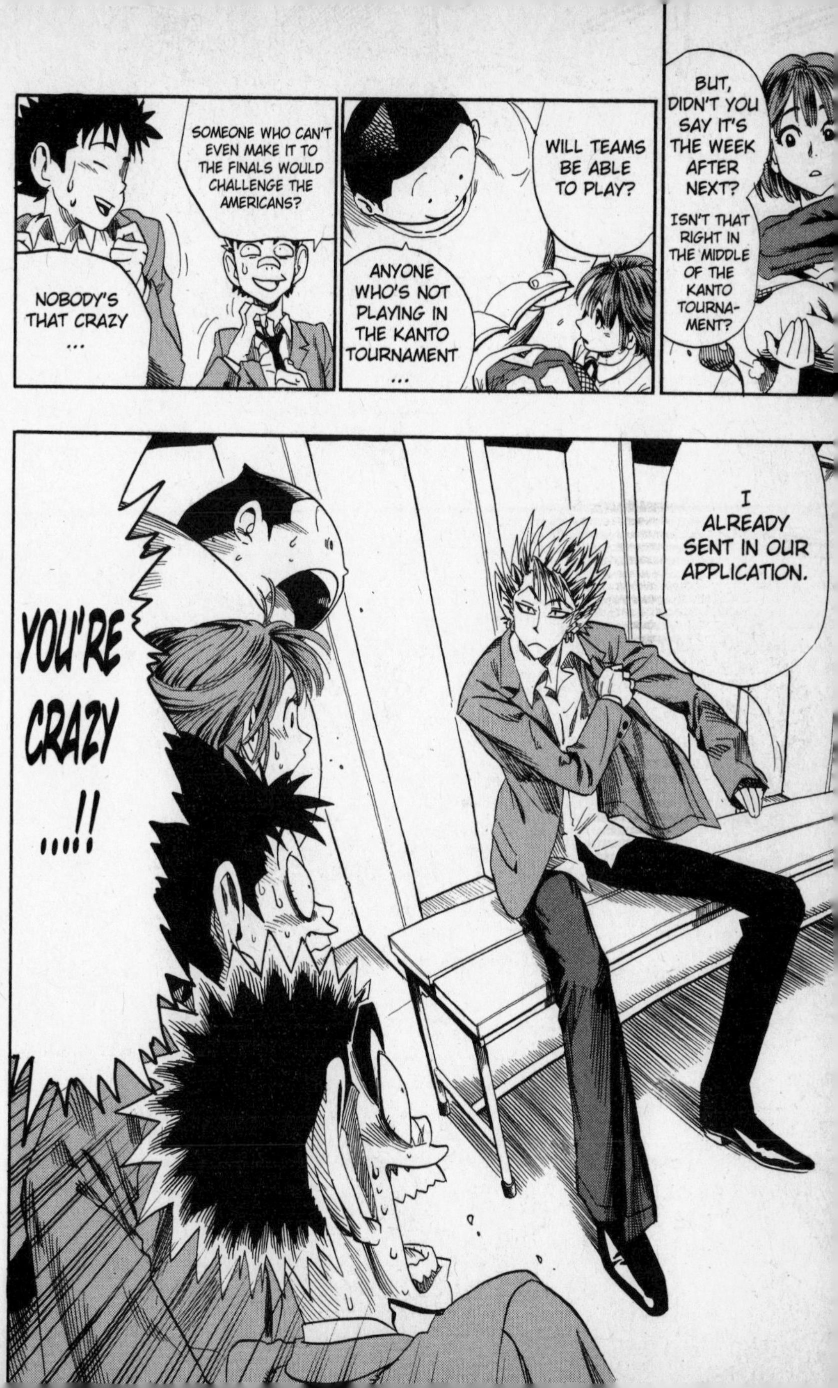

BUT, DIDN'T YOU SAY IT'S THE WEEK AFTER NEXT?
ISN'T THAT RIGHT IN THE MIDDLE OF THE KANTO TOURNAMENT?
WILL TEAMS BE ABLE TO PLAY?
ANYONE WHO'S NOT PLAYING IN THE KANTO TOURNAMENT ...
SOMEONE WHO CAN'T EVEN MAKE IT TO THE FINALS WOULD CHALLENGE THE AMERICANS?
NOBODY'S THAT CRAZY ...
I ALREADY SENT IN OUR APPLICATION.
YOU'RE CRAZY ...!!

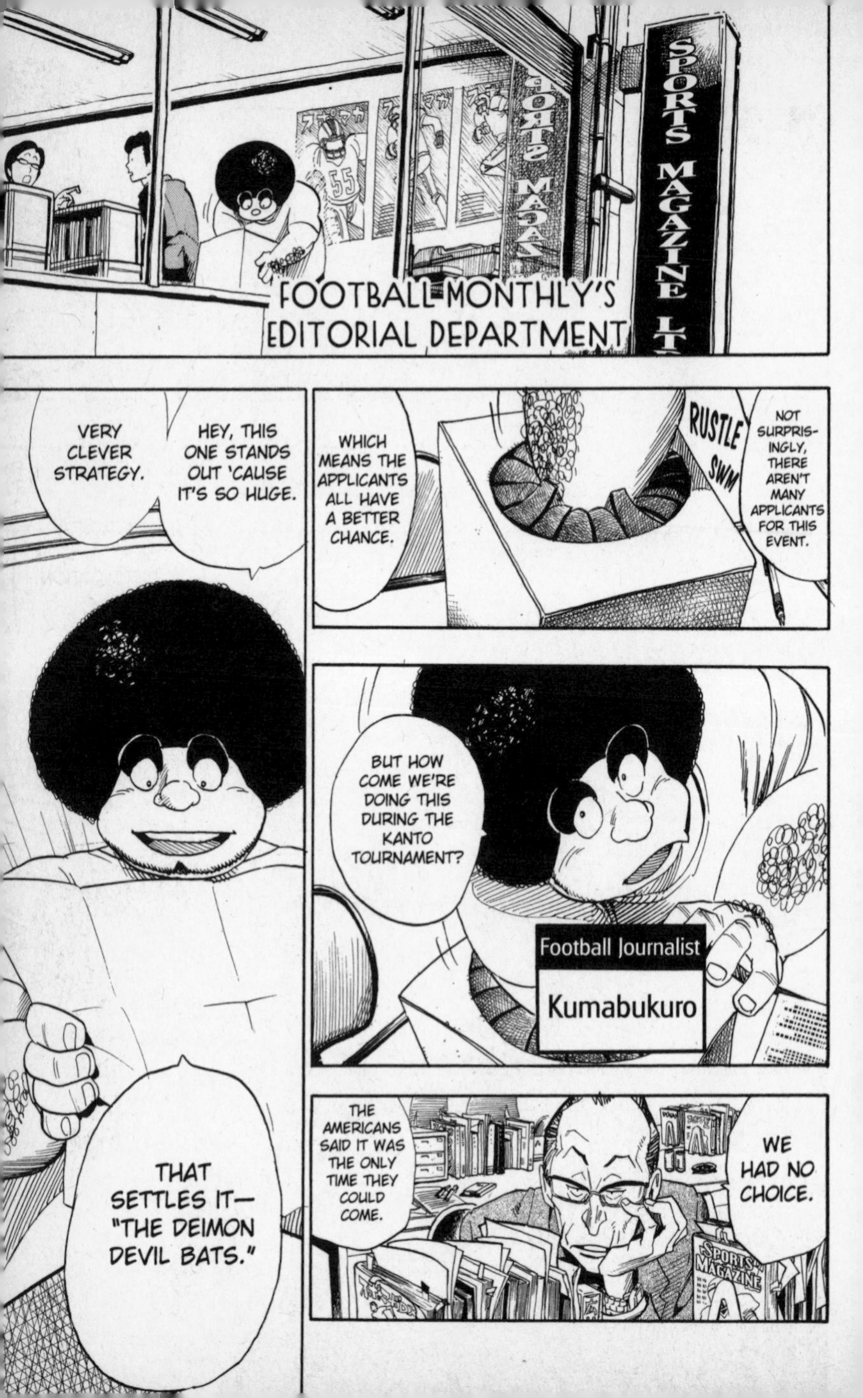
SPORTS MAGAZINE
FOOTBALL MONTHLY'S EDITORIAL DEPARTMENT
RUSTLE
SWM
NOT SURPRISINGLY, THERE AREN'T MANY APPLICANTS FOR THIS EVENT.
WHICH MEANS THE APPLICANTS ALL HAVE A BETTER CHANCE.
BUT HOW COME WE'RE DOING THIS DURING THE KANTO TOURNAMENT?
Football Journalist
Kumabukuro
WE HAD NO CHOICE.
THE AMERICANS SAID IT WAS THE ONLY TIME THEY COULD COME.
SPORTS MAGAZINE
HEY, THIS ONE STANDS OUT 'CAUSE IT'S SO HUGE.
VERY CLEVER STRATEGY.
THAT SETTLES IT— "THE DEIMON DEVIL BATS."

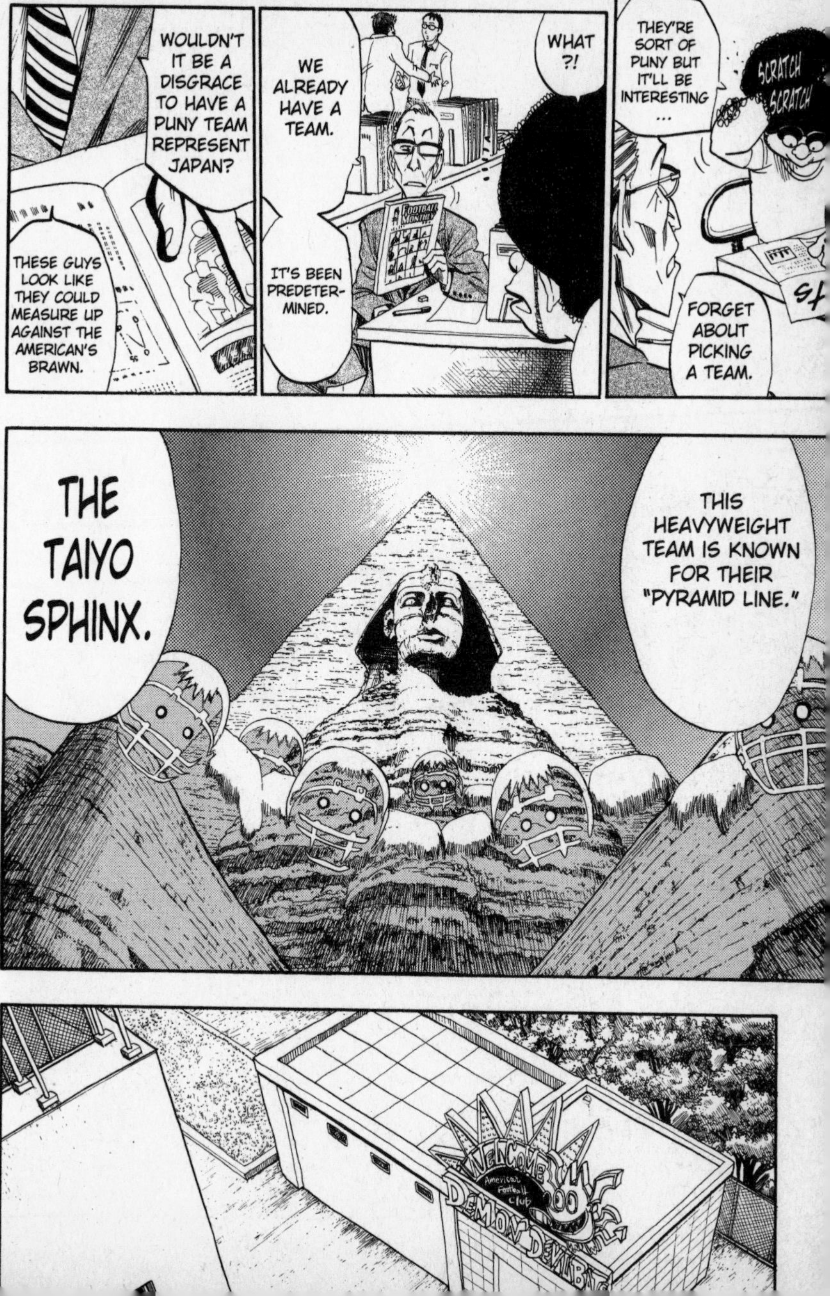
THEY'RE SORT OF PUNY BUT IT'LL BE INTERESTING ...
SCRATCH SCRATCH
FORGET ABOUT PICKING A TEAM.
WHAT ?!
WE ALREADY HAVE A TEAM.
IT'S BEEN PREDETERMINED.
WOULDN'T IT BE A DISGRACE TO HAVE A PUNY TEAM REPRESENT JAPAN?
THESE GUYS LOOK LIKE THEY COULD MEASURE UP AGAINST THE AMERICAN'S BRAWN.
THIS HEAVYWEIGHT TEAM IS KNOWN FOR THEIR "PYRAMID LINE."
THE TAIYO SPHINX.
WELCOME
American Football club

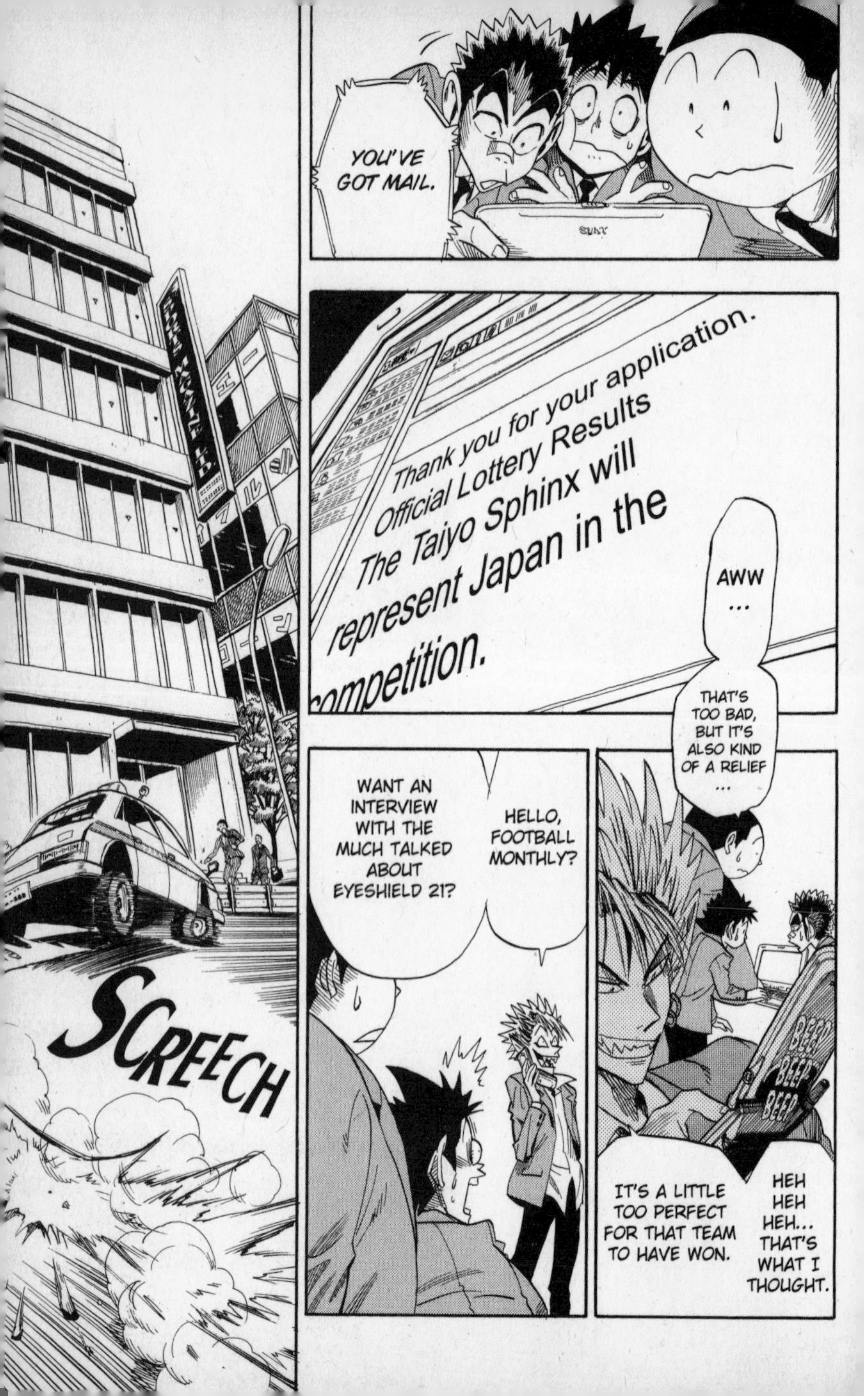

YOU'VE GOT MAIL.
Thank you for your application.
Official Lottery Results
The Taiyo Sphinx will represent Japan in the competition.
AWW ...
THAT'S TOO BAD, BUT IT'S ALSO KIND OF A RELIEF ...
BEEP BEEP BEEP
HEH HEH HEH... THAT'S WHAT I THOUGHT.
IT'S A LITTLE TOO PERFECT FOR THAT TEAM TO HAVE WON.
HELLO, FOOTBALL MONTHLY?
WANT AN INTERVIEW WITH THE MUCH TALKED ABOUT EYESHIELD 21?
SCREECH

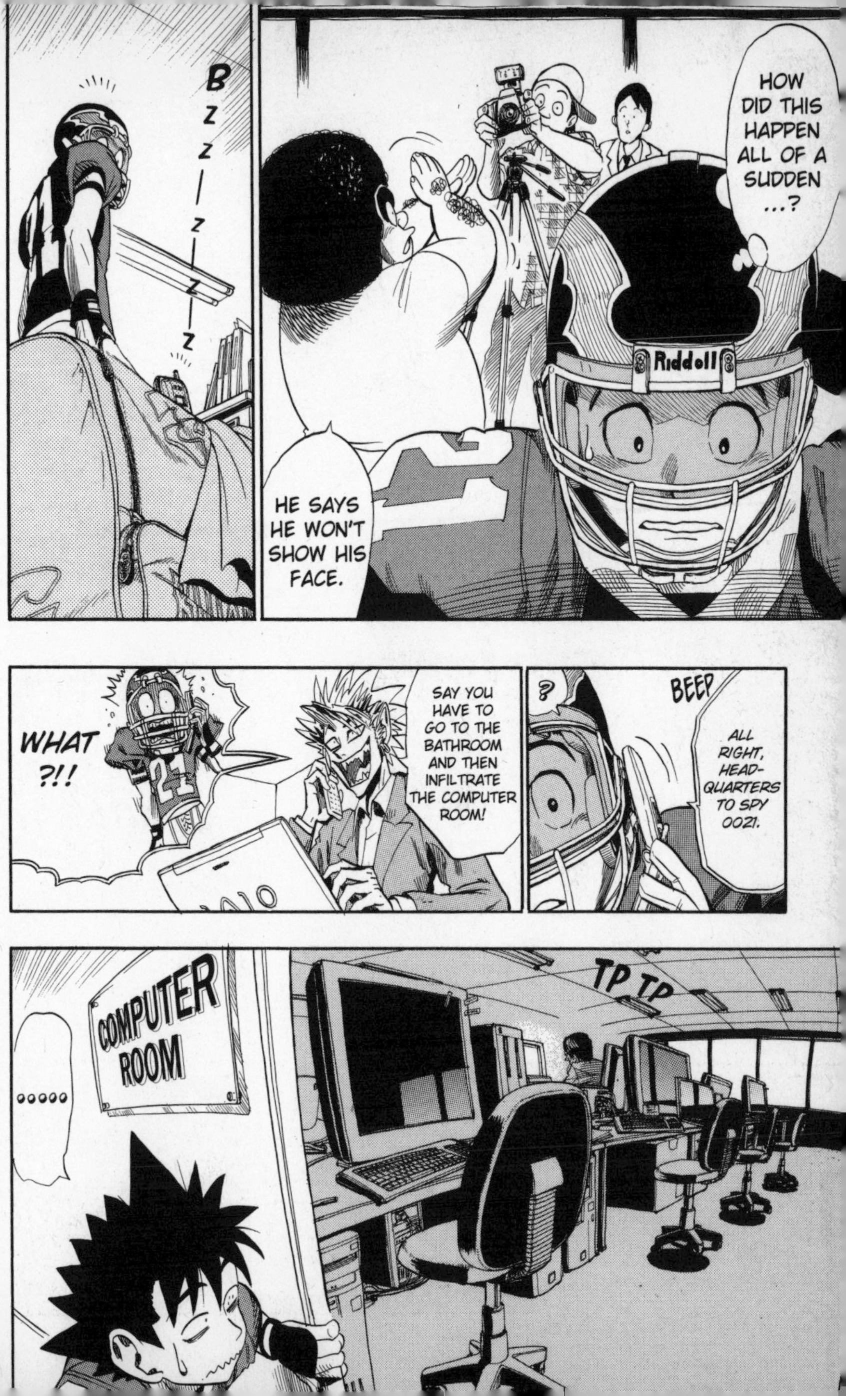
HOW DID THIS HAPPEN ALL OF A SUDDEN ...?
HE SAYS HE WON'T SHOW HIS FACE.
BZZZZZ
?
BEEP
ALL RIGHT, HEAD-QUARTERS TO SPY 0021.
SAY YOU HAVE TO GO TO THE BATHROOM AND THEN INFILTRATE THE COMPUTER ROOM!
WHAT ?!!
TP TP
COMPUTER ROOM
.....

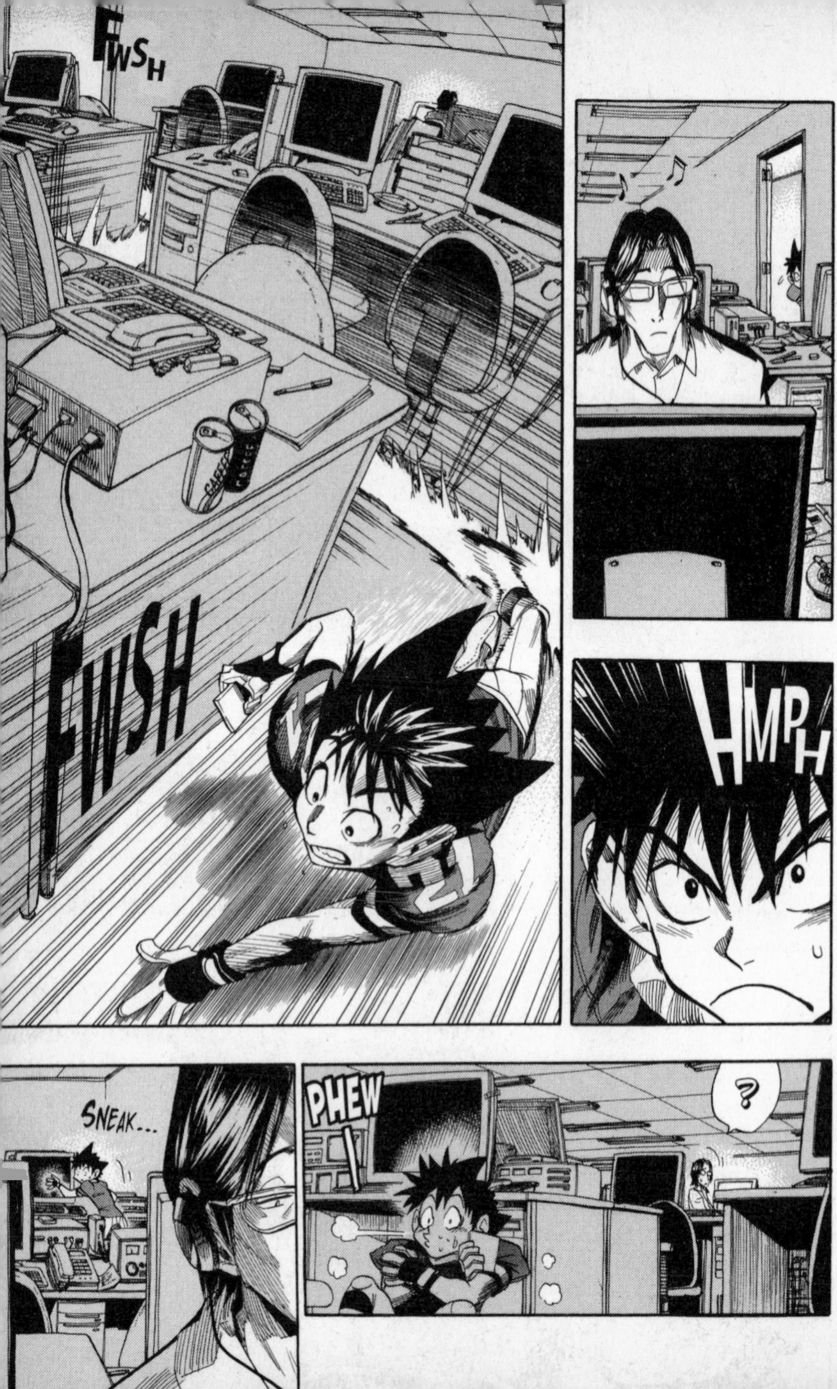
HMPH
FWSH
FWSH
?
PHEW
SNEAK...

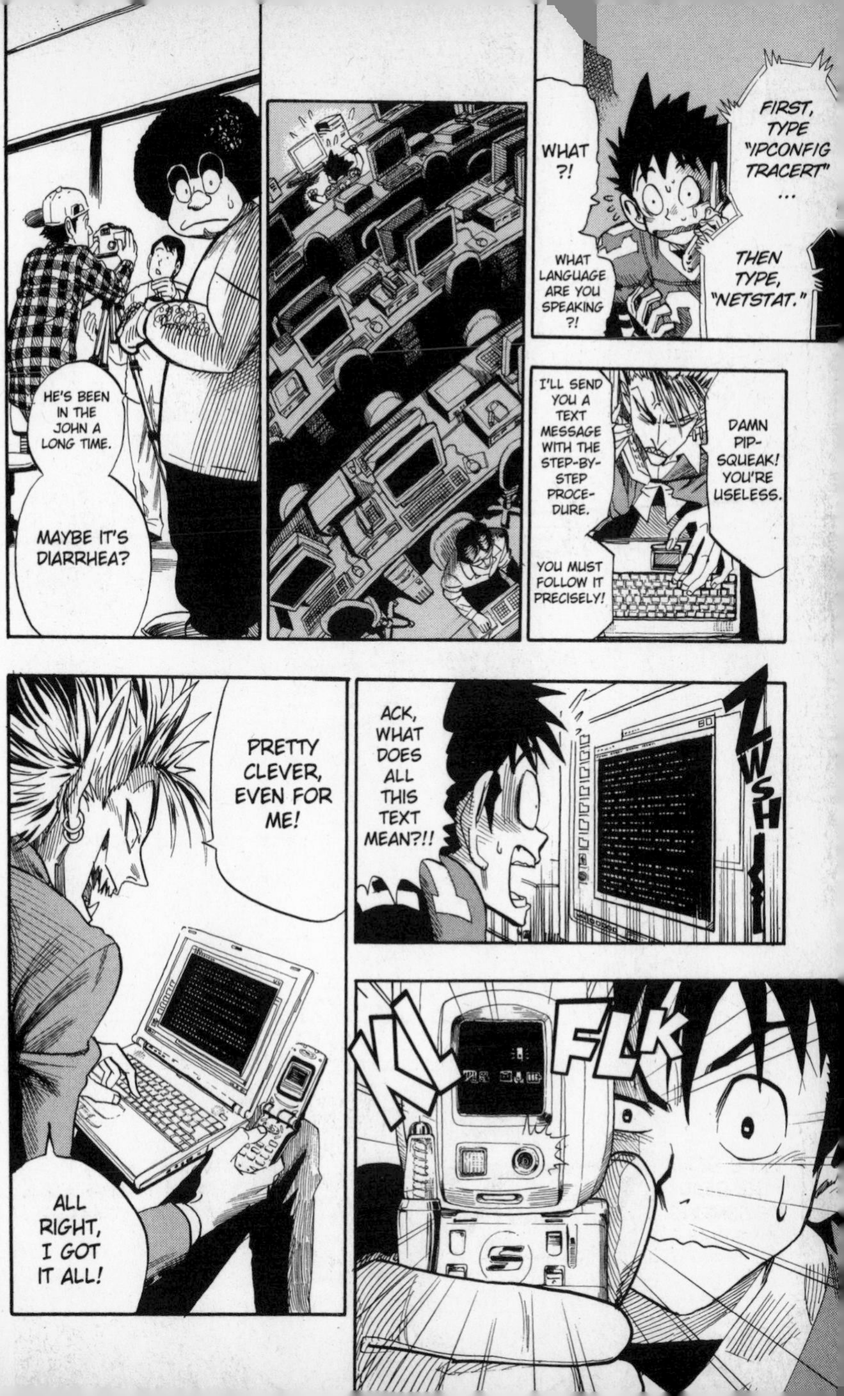
FIRST, TYPE "IPCONFIG TRACERT" ...
WHAT ?!
THEN TYPE, "NETSTAT."
WHAT LANGUAGE ARE YOU SPEAKING ?!
DAMN PIP-SQUEAK! YOU'RE USELESS.
I'LL SEND YOU A TEXT MESSAGE WITH THE STEP-BY-STEP PROCE-DURE.
YOU MUST FOLLOW IT PRECISELY!
HE'S BEEN IN THE JOHN A LONG TIME.
MAYBE IT'S DIARRHEA?
ZWSH
ACK, WHAT DOES ALL THIS TEXT MEAN?!!
KLFLK
PRETTY CLEVER, EVEN FOR ME!
ALL RIGHT, I GOT IT ALL!

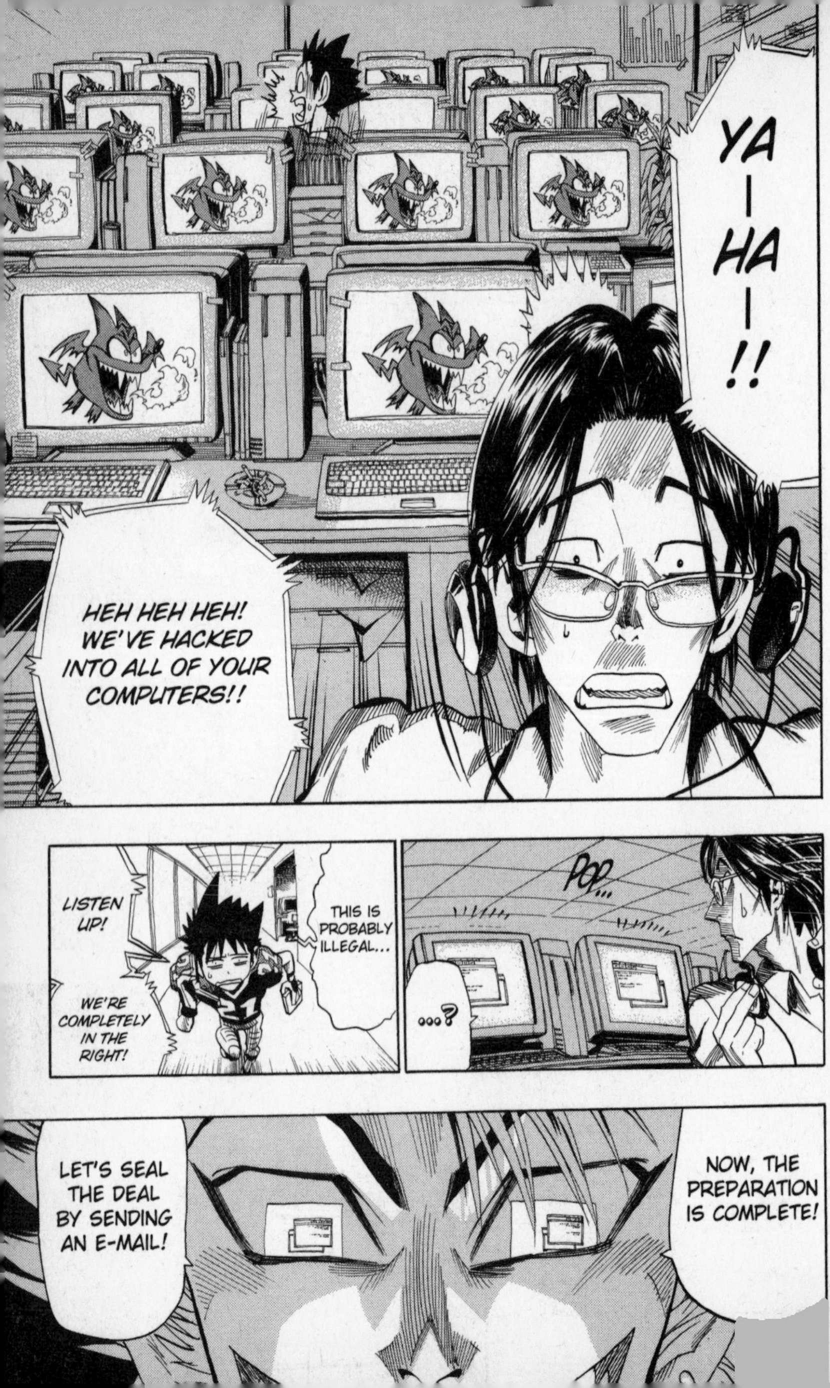
YA-HA-!!
HEH HEH HEH! WE'VE HACKED INTO ALL OF YOUR COMPUTERS!!
POP...
...?
THIS IS PROBABLY ILLEGAL...
LISTEN UP!
WE'RE COMPLETELY IN THE RIGHT!
NOW, THE PREPARATION IS COMPLETE!
LET'S SEAL THE DEAL BY SENDING AN E-MAIL!

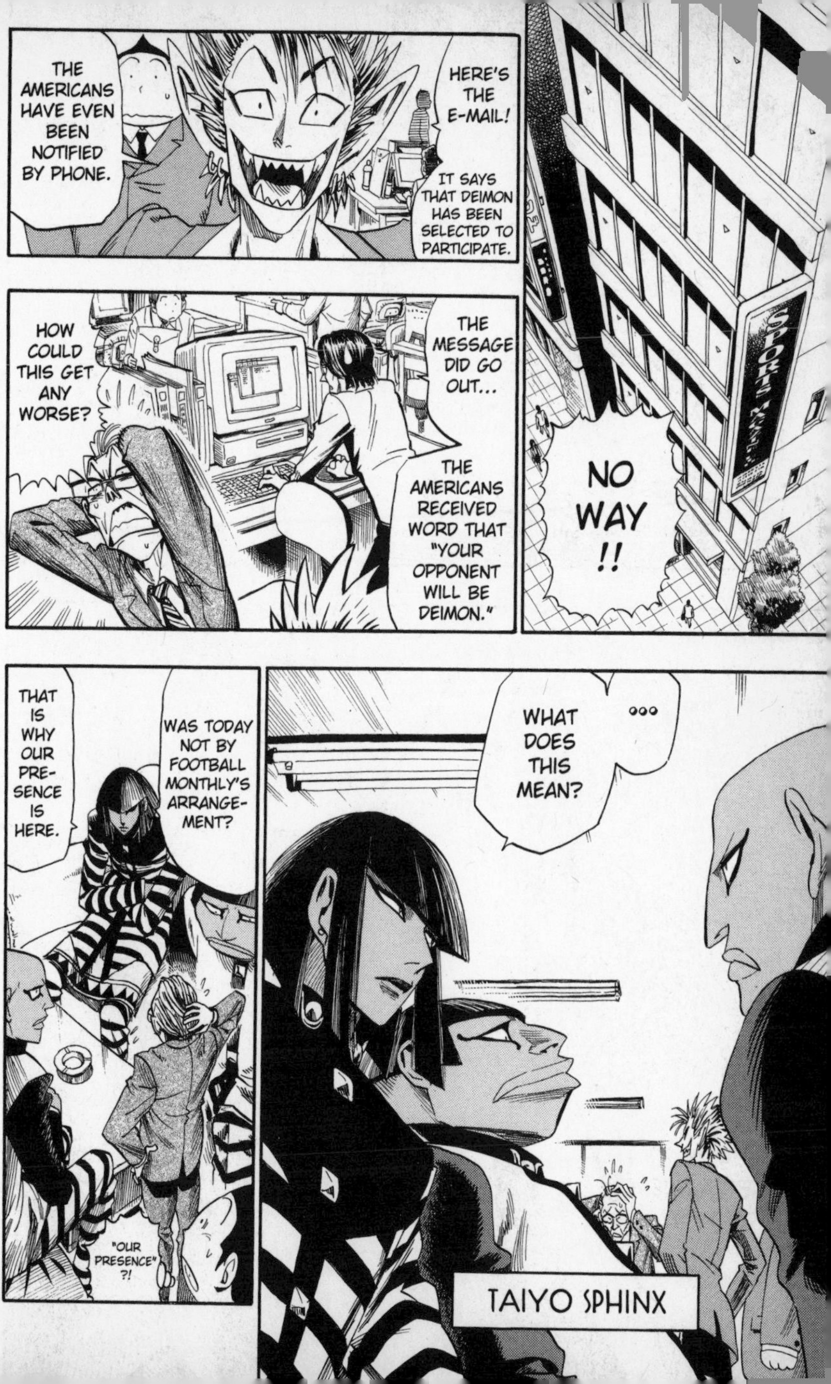
NO WAY !!
HERE'S THE E-MAIL!
IT SAYS THAT DEIMON HAS BEEN SELECTED TO PARTICIPATE.
THE AMERICANS HAVE EVEN BEEN NOTIFIED BY PHONE.
THE MESSAGE DID GO OUT...
THE AMERICANS RECEIVED WORD THAT "YOUR OPPONENT WILL BE DEIMON."
HOW COULD THIS GET ANY WORSE?
...
WHAT DOES THIS MEAN?
TAIYO SPHINX
WAS TODAY NOT BY FOOTBALL MONTHLY'S ARRANGE-MENT?
THAT IS WHY OUR PRE-SENCE IS HERE.
"OUR PRESENCE"?!

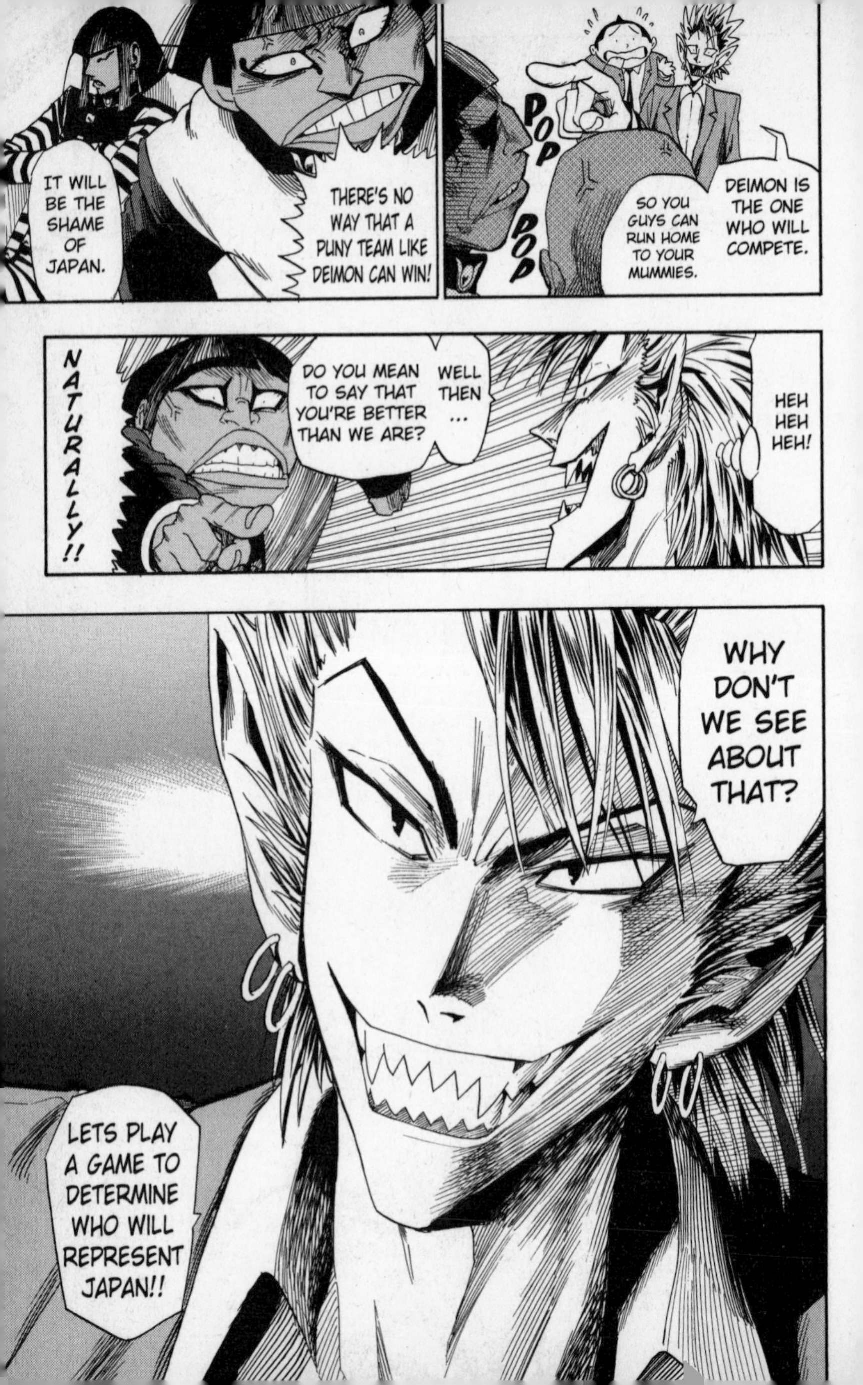
DEIMON IS THE ONE WHO WILL COMPETE.
SO YOU GUYS CAN RUN HOME TO YOUR MUMMIES.
POP
POP
THERE'S NO WAY THAT A PUNY TEAM LIKE DEIMON CAN WIN!
IT WILL BE THE SHAME OF JAPAN.
HEH HEH HEH!
WELL THEN ...
DO YOU MEAN TO SAY THAT YOU'RE BETTER THAN WE ARE?
NATURALLY!!
WHY DON'T WE SEE ABOUT THAT?
LETS PLAY A GAME TO DETERMINE WHO WILL REPRESENT JAPAN!!

DEIMON HIGH SCHOOL
SURPRISE SCHOOL BAG INSPECTION

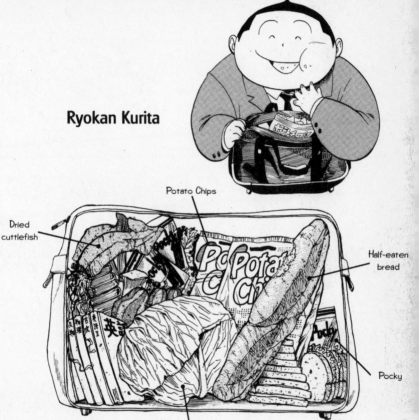

Ryokan Kurita

Potato Chips

Dried cuttlefish

Half-eaten bread

Pocky

Cabbage

UM... SINCE IT'S SUMMERTIME, YOU SHOULD BE ESPECIALLY CAREFUL ABOUT FOOD GOING BAD...

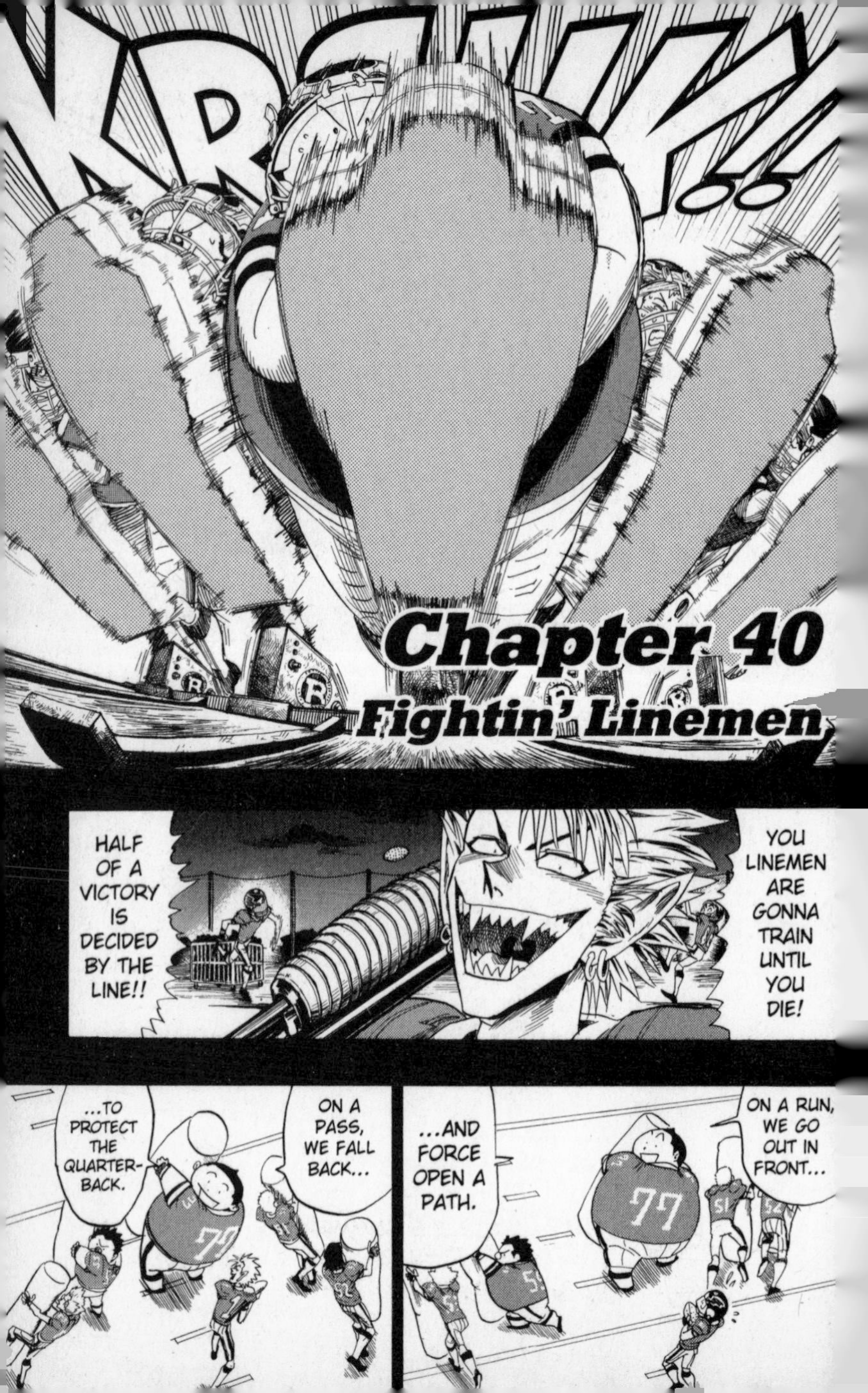
Chapter 40
Fightin' Linemen
YOU LINEMEN ARE GONNA TRAIN UNTIL YOU DIE!
HALF OF A VICTORY IS DECIDED BY THE LINE!!
ON A RUN, WE GO OUT IN FRONT...
...AND FORCE OPEN A PATH.
ON A PASS, WE FALL BACK...
...TO PROTECT THE QUARTER-BACK.

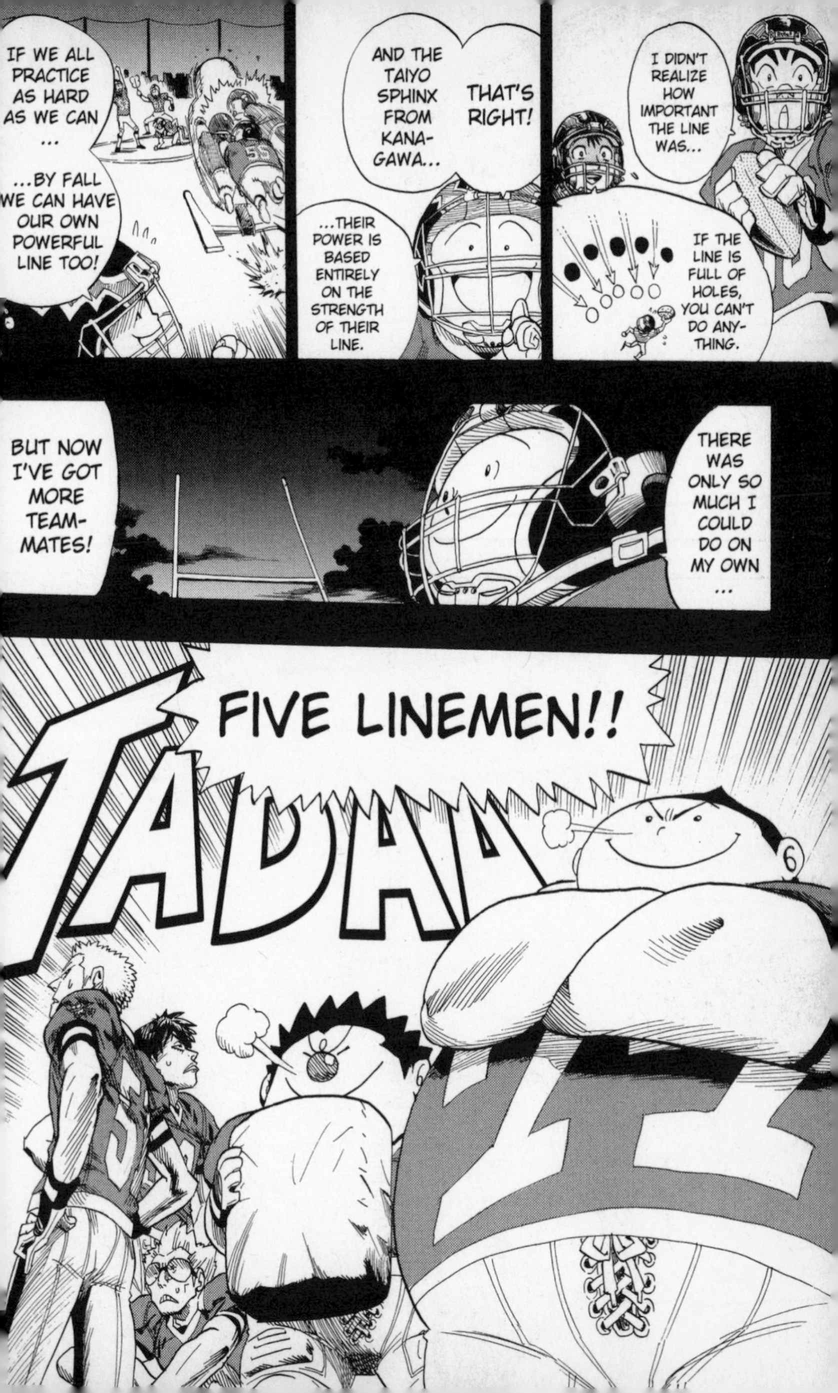
I DIDN'T REALIZE HOW IMPORTANT THE LINE WAS...
IF THE LINE IS FULL OF HOLES, YOU CAN'T DO ANY-THING.
THAT'S RIGHT!
AND THE TAIYO SPHINX FROM KANA-GAWA...
...THEIR POWER IS BASED ENTIRELY ON THE STRENGTH OF THEIR LINE.
IF WE ALL PRACTICE AS HARD AS WE CAN ...
...BY FALL WE CAN HAVE OUR OWN POWERFUL LINE TOO!
THERE WAS ONLY SO MUCH I COULD DO ON MY OWN ...
BUT NOW I'VE GOT MORE TEAM-MATES!
FIVE LINEMEN!!
TADAA

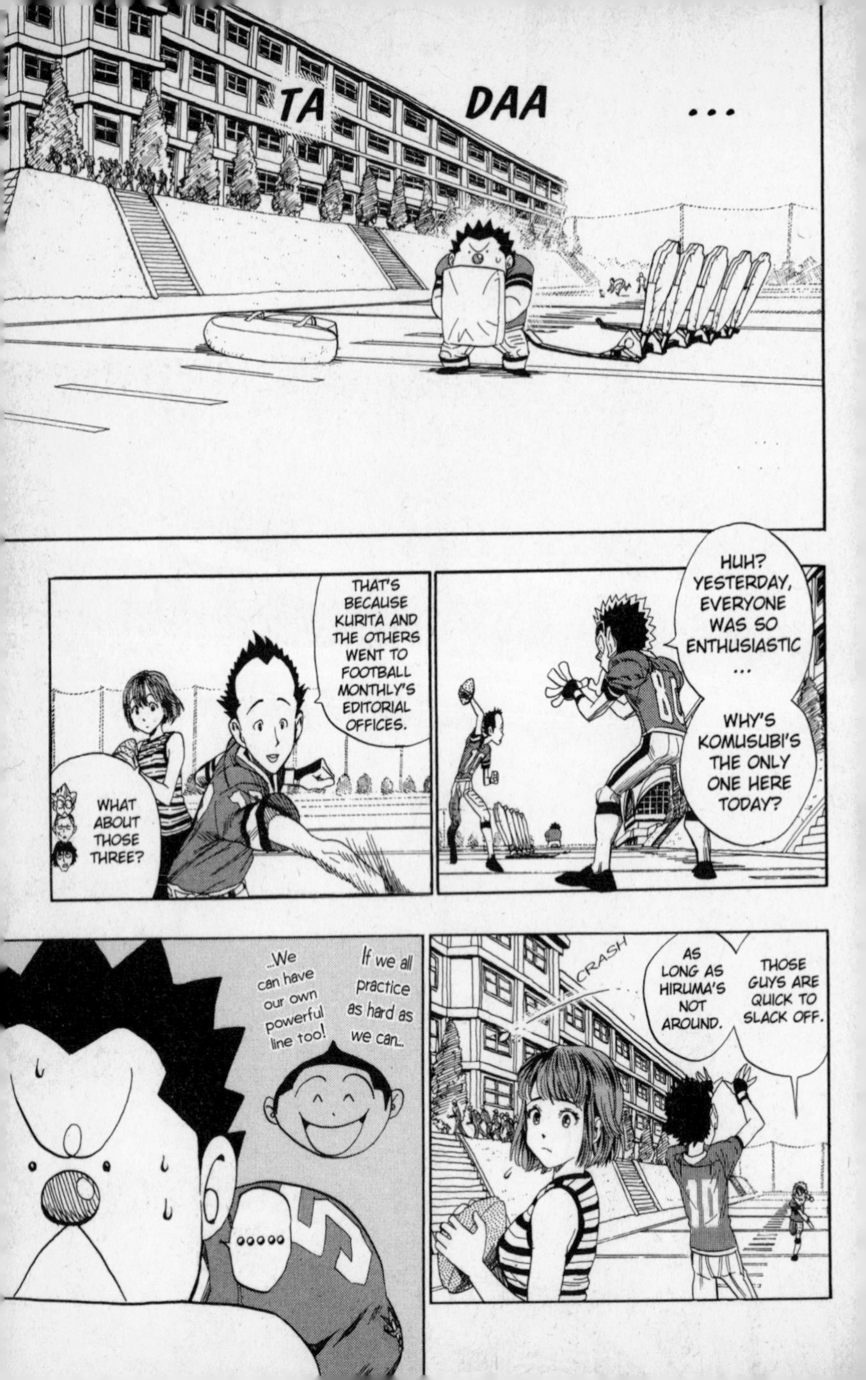
TA DAA ...
HUH? YESTERDAY, EVERYONE WAS SO ENTHUSIASTIC ...
WHY'S KOMUSUBI'S THE ONLY ONE HERE TODAY?
THAT'S BECAUSE KURITA AND THE OTHERS WENT TO FOOTBALL MONTHLY'S EDITORIAL OFFICES.
WHAT ABOUT THOSE THREE?
CRASH
THOSE GUYS ARE QUICK TO SLACK OFF.
AS LONG AS HIRUMA'S NOT AROUND.
If we all practice as hard as we can..
..We can have our own powerful line too!
.....

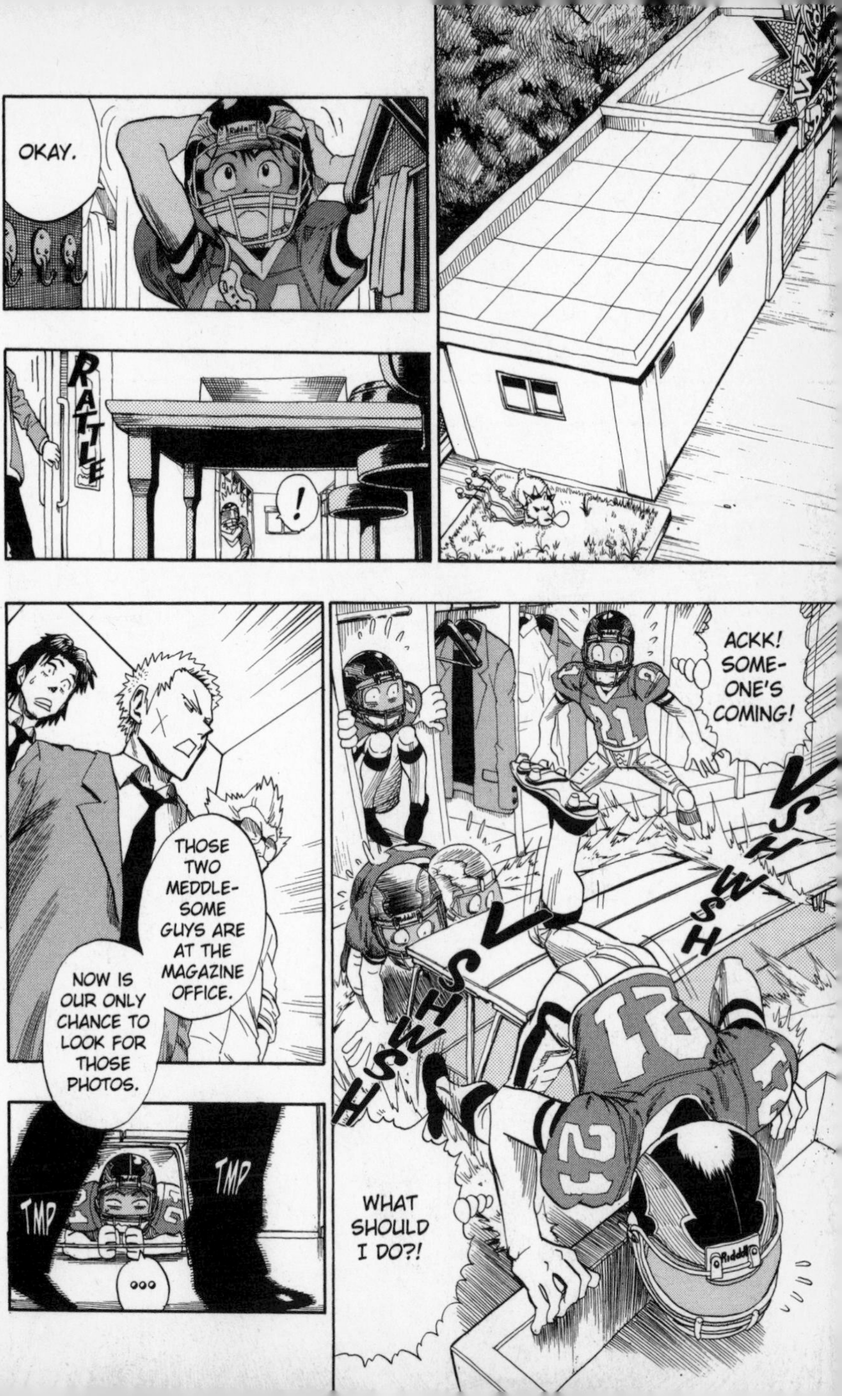
OKAY.
RATTLE
!
ACKK! SOME-ONE'S COMING!
VSHWSH
SHWSH
WHAT SHOULD I DO?!
THOSE TWO MEDDLE-SOME GUYS ARE AT THE MAGAZINE OFFICE.
NOW IS OUR ONLY CHANCE TO LOOK FOR THOSE PHOTOS.
TMP
TMP
...

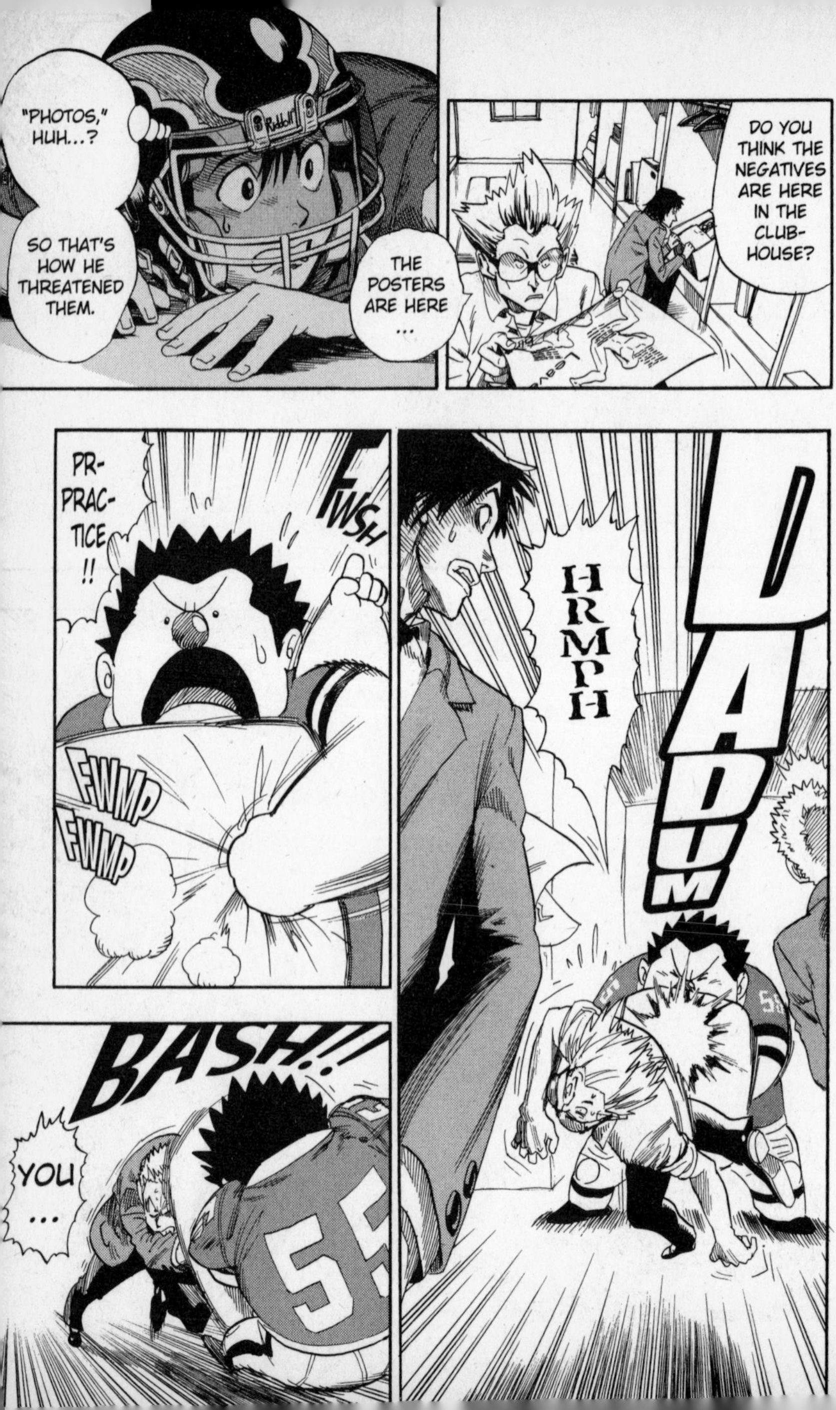
DO YOU THINK THE NEGATIVES ARE HERE IN THE CLUB-HOUSE?
THE POSTERS ARE HERE ...
"PHOTOS," HUH...?
SO THAT'S HOW HE THREATENED THEM.
DADUM
HRMPH
FWSH
PR-PRAC-TICE!!
FWMP FWMP
BASH!!
YOU ...

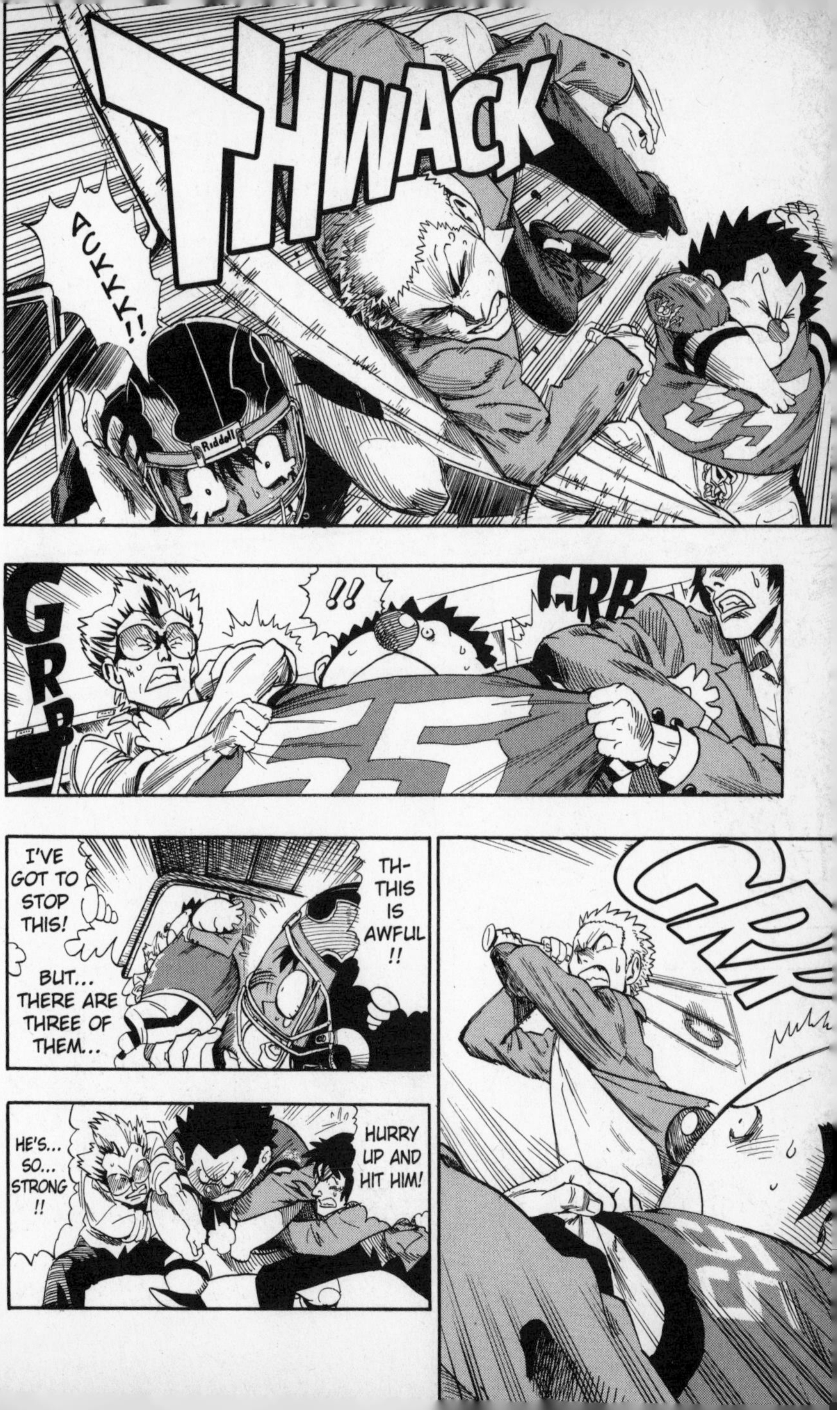
THWACK
AUKKKK!!
GRB
!!
GRB
CRR
TH- THIS IS AWFUL !!
I'VE GOT TO STOP THIS!
BUT... THERE ARE THREE OF THEM...
HURRY UP AND HIT HIM!
HE'S... SO... STRONG !!

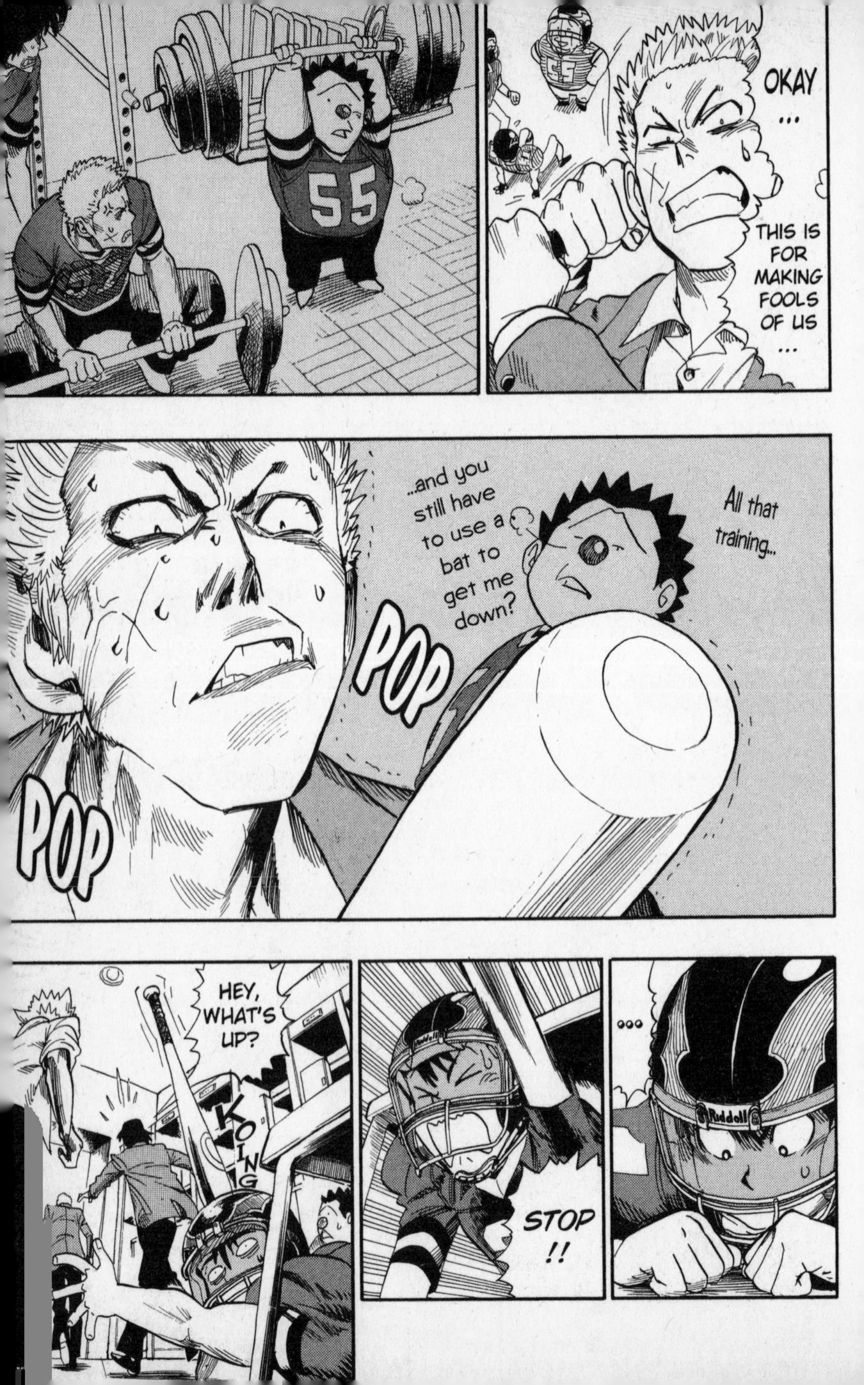
OKAY ...
THIS IS FOR MAKING FOOLS OF US ...
All that training...
...and you still have to use a bat to get me down?
POP
POP
...
STOP !!
HEY, WHAT'S UP?
KOING

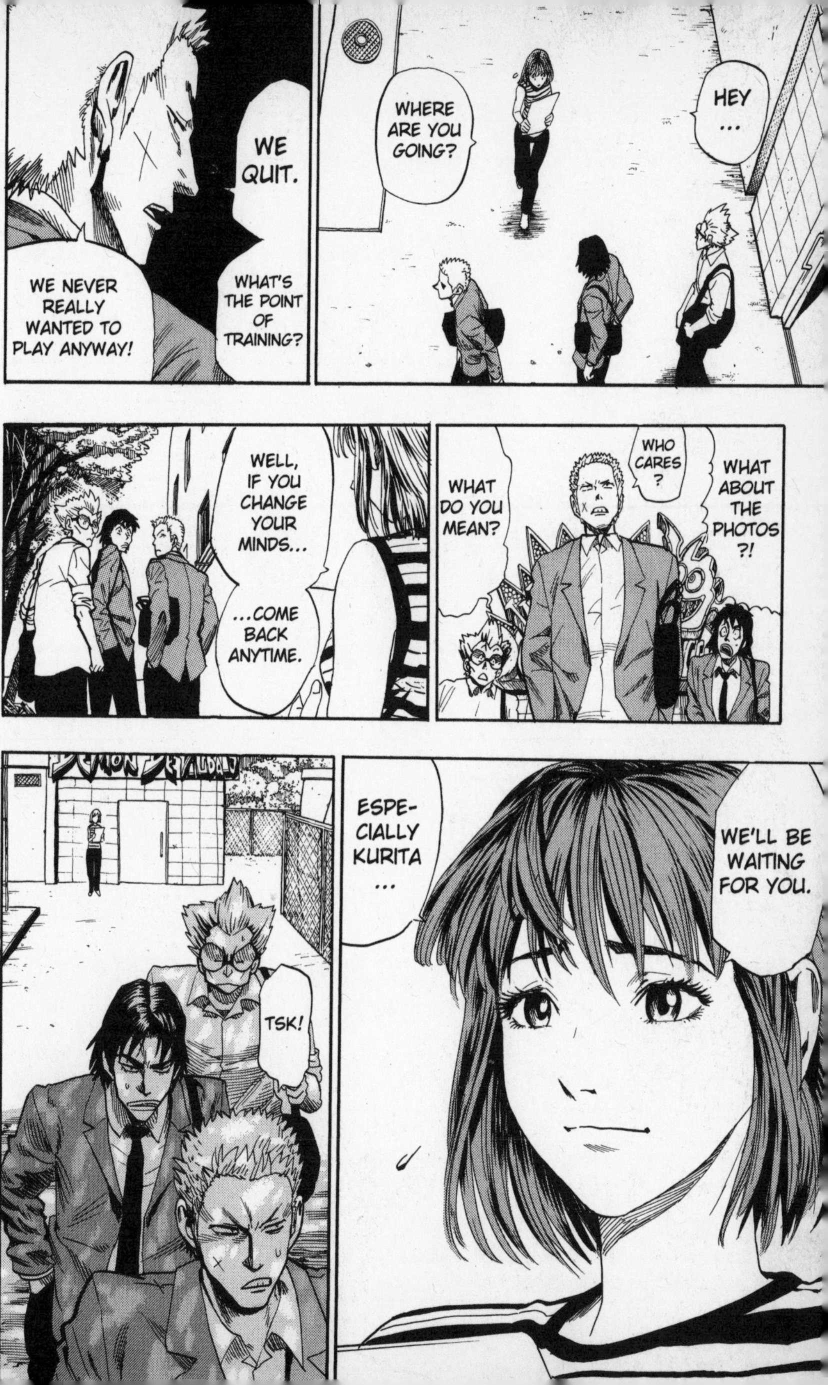
HEY ...
WHERE ARE YOU GOING?
WE QUIT.
WHAT'S THE POINT OF TRAINING?
WE NEVER REALLY WANTED TO PLAY ANYWAY!
WHAT ABOUT THE PHOTOS ?!
WHO CARES ?
WHAT DO YOU MEAN?
WELL, IF YOU CHANGE YOUR MINDS...
...COME BACK ANYTIME.
WE'LL BE WAITING FOR YOU.
ESPE- CIALLY KURITA ...
TSK!

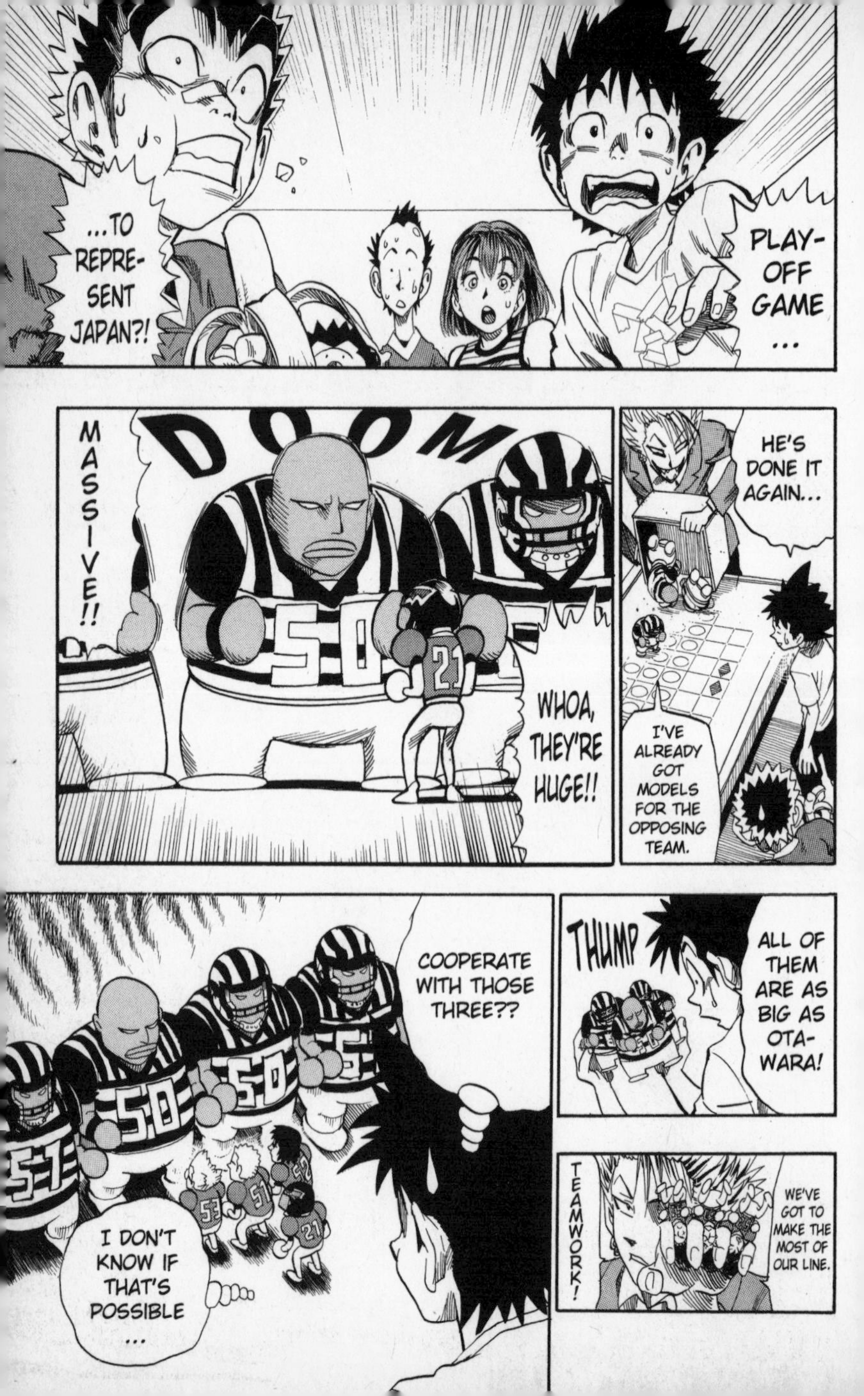
PLAY-OFF GAME ...
...TO REPRESENT JAPAN?!
HE'S DONE IT AGAIN...
I'VE ALREADY GOT MODELS FOR THE OPPOSING TEAM.
DOOM
WHOA, THEY'RE HUGE!!
MASSIVE!!
THUMP
ALL OF THEM ARE AS BIG AS OTAWARA!
WE'VE GOT TO MAKE THE MOST OF OUR LINE.
TEAMWORK!
COOPERATE WITH THOSE THREE??
I DON'T KNOW IF THAT'S POSSIBLE ...

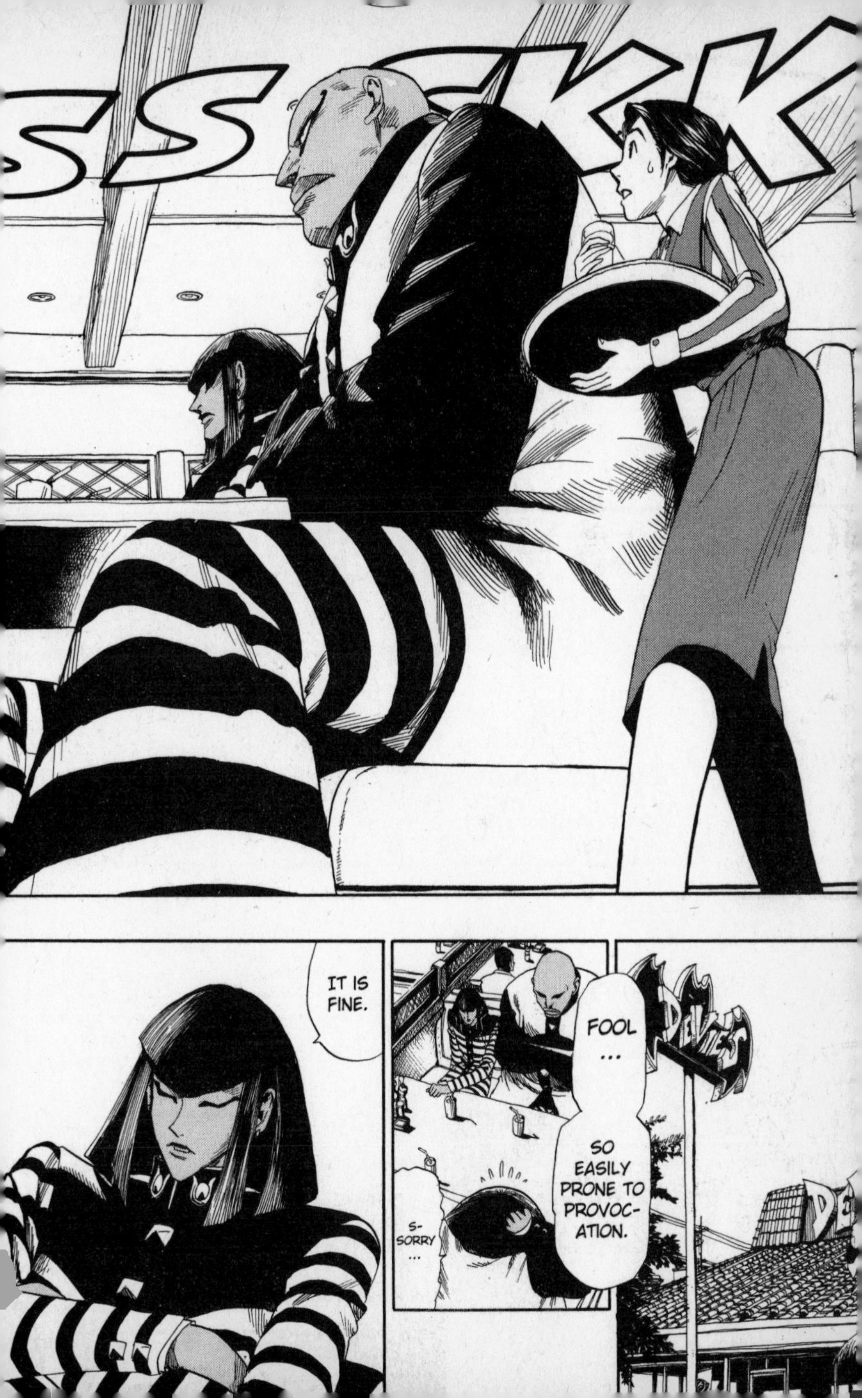
SSCKK
FOOL...
SO EASILY PRONE TO PROVOC-ATION.
S-SORRY...
IT IS FINE.

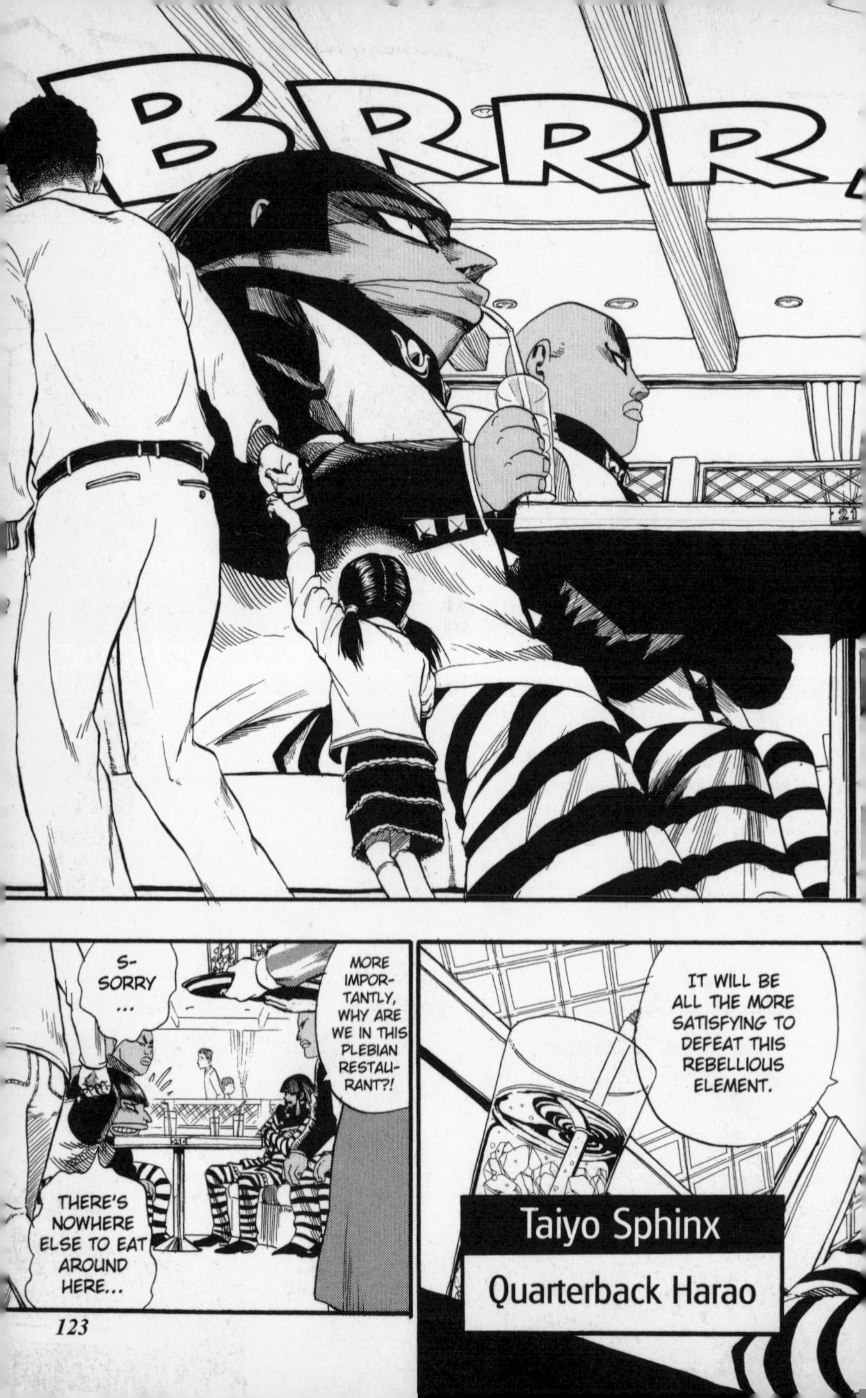
BRRR
IT WILL BE ALL THE MORE SATISFYING TO DEFEAT THIS REBELLIOUS ELEMENT.
Taiyo Sphinx
Quarterback Harao
MORE IMPORTANTLY, WHY ARE WE IN THIS PLEBIAN RESTAURANT?!
S-SORRY...
THERE'S NOWHERE ELSE TO EAT AROUND HERE...

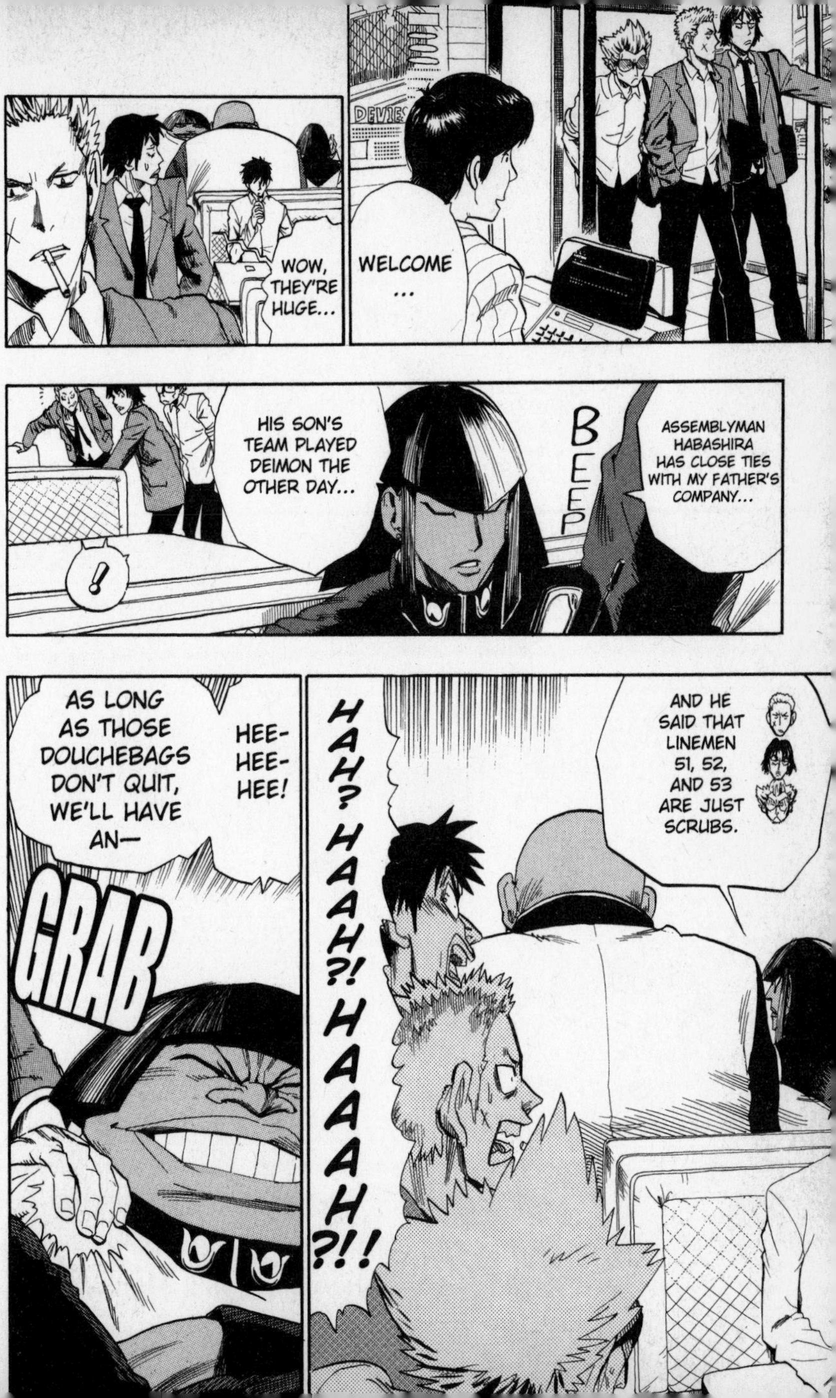
WELCOME ...
WOW, THEY'RE HUGE...
ASSEMBLYMAN HABASHIRA HAS CLOSE TIES WITH MY FATHER'S COMPANY...
BEEP
HIS SON'S TEAM PLAYED DEIMON THE OTHER DAY...
!
AND HE SAID THAT LINEMEN 51, 52, AND 53 ARE JUST SCRUBS.
HAH? HAAAH?! HAAAAAH?!!
HEE-HEE-HEE!
AS LONG AS THOSE DOUCHEBAGS DON'T QUIT, WE'LL HAVE AN—
GRAB

READ THIS WAY

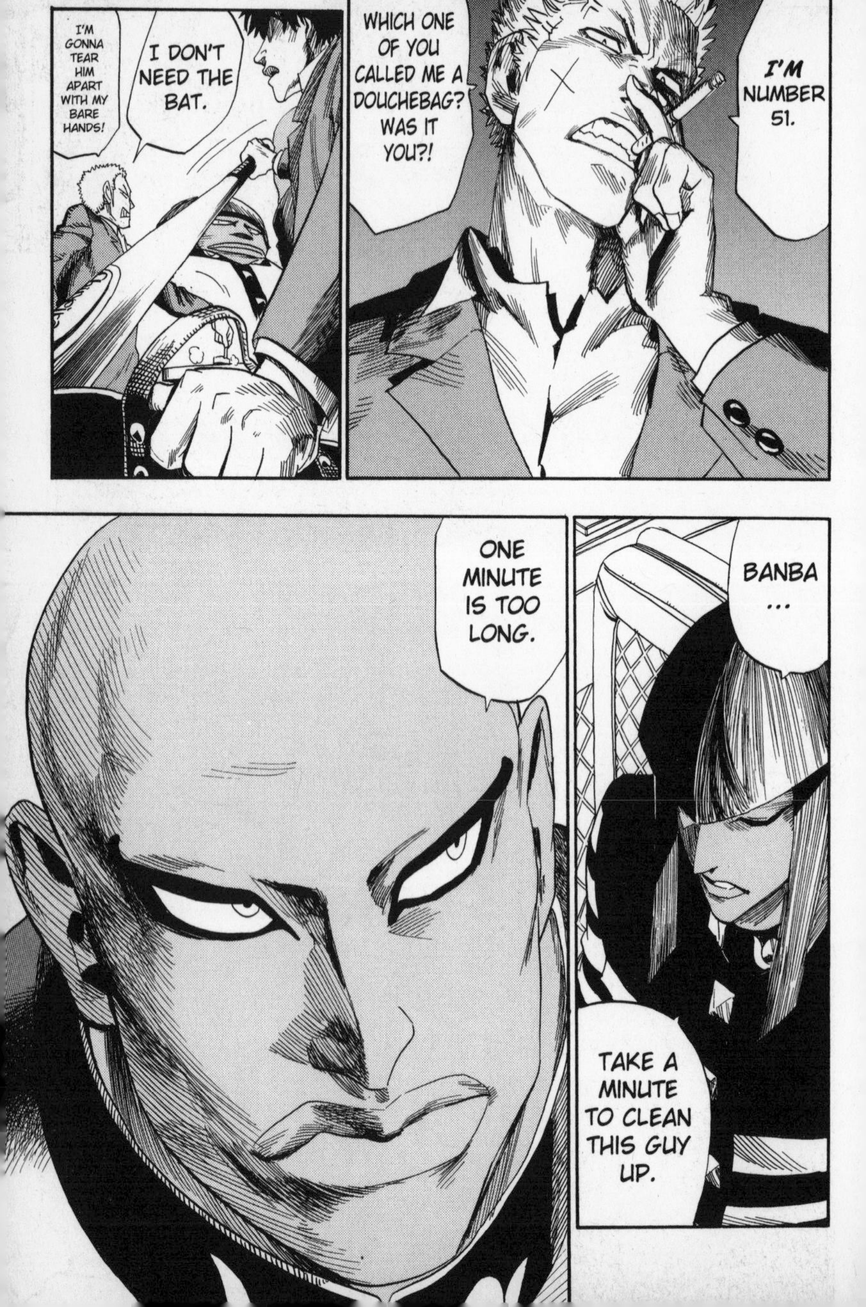

I'M NUMBER 51.
WHICH ONE OF YOU CALLED ME A DOUCHEBAG? WAS IT YOU?!
I DON'T NEED THE BAT.
I'M GONNA TEAR HIM APART WITH MY BARE HANDS!
BANBA ...
TAKE A MINUTE TO CLEAN THIS GUY UP.
ONE MINUTE IS TOO LONG.

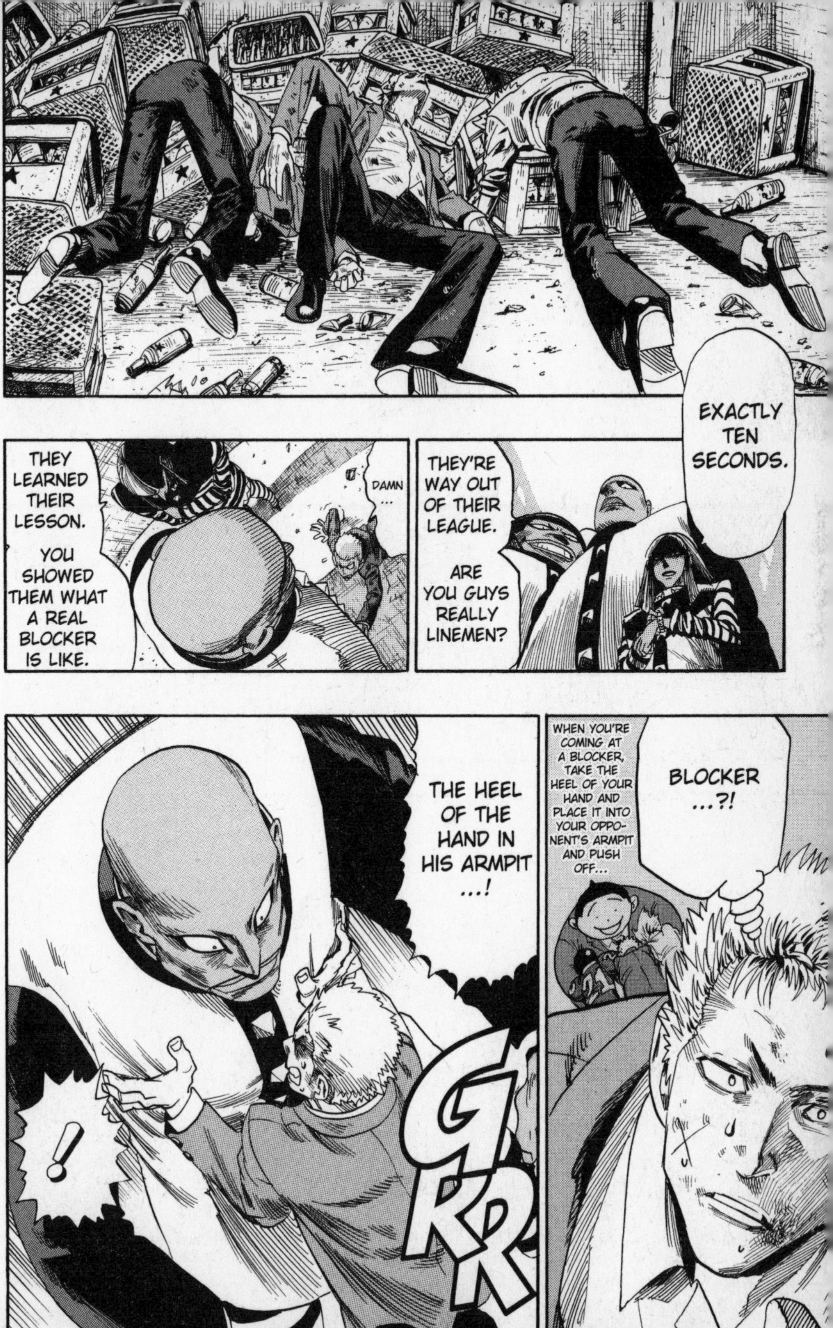

EXACTLY TEN SECONDS.
THEY'RE WAY OUT OF THEIR LEAGUE.
ARE YOU GUYS REALLY LINEMEN?
DAMN...
THEY LEARNED THEIR LESSON.
YOU SHOWED THEM WHAT A REAL BLOCKER IS LIKE.
BLOCKER...?!
WHEN YOU'RE COMING AT A BLOCKER, TAKE THE HEEL OF YOUR HAND AND PLACE IT INTO YOUR OPPONENT'S ARMPIT AND PUSH OFF...
THE HEEL OF THE HAND IN HIS ARMPIT...!
GRR
!

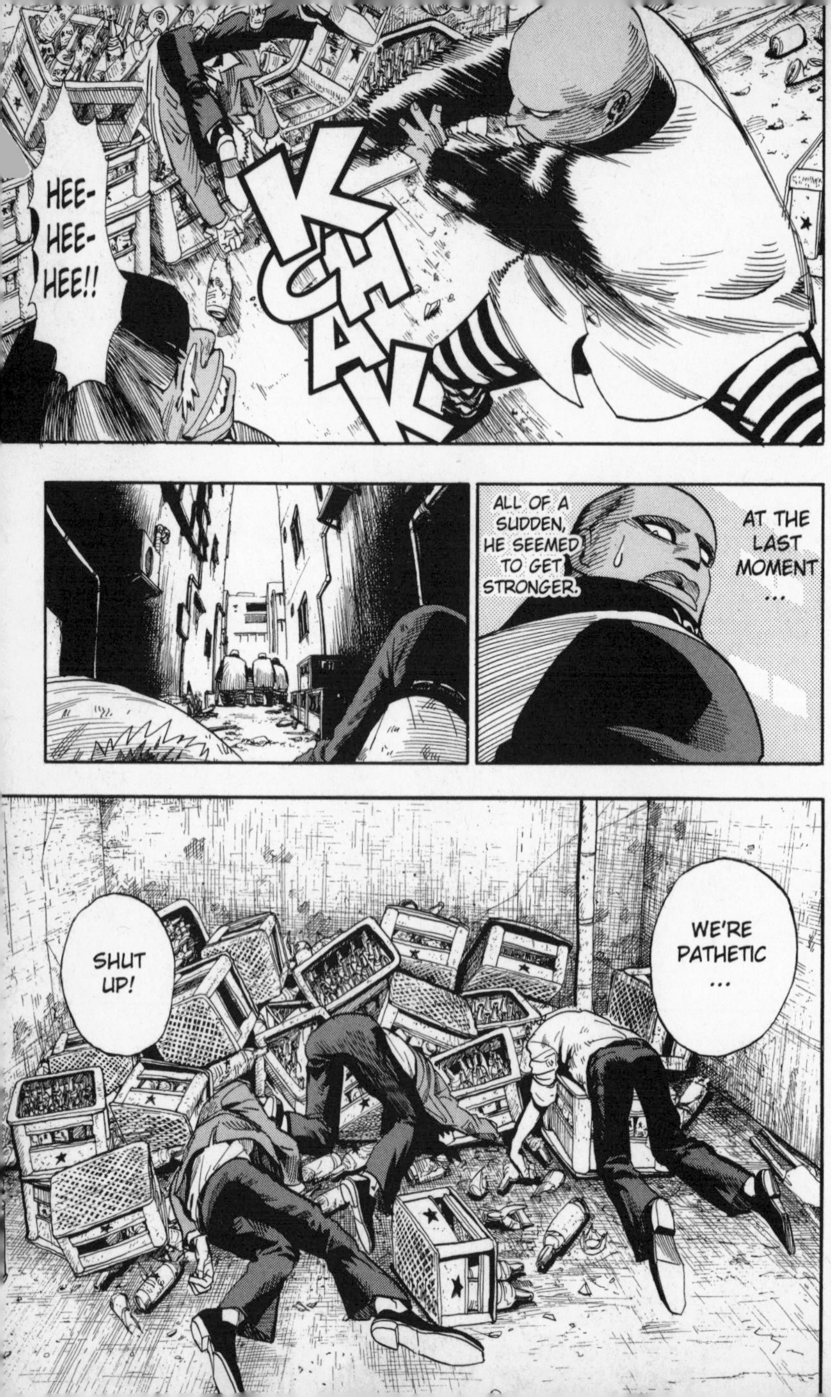
KCHAK
HEE-HEE-HEE!!
AT THE LAST MOMENT...
ALL OF A SUDDEN, HE SEEMED TO GET STRONGER.
WE'RE PATHETIC...
SHUT UP!

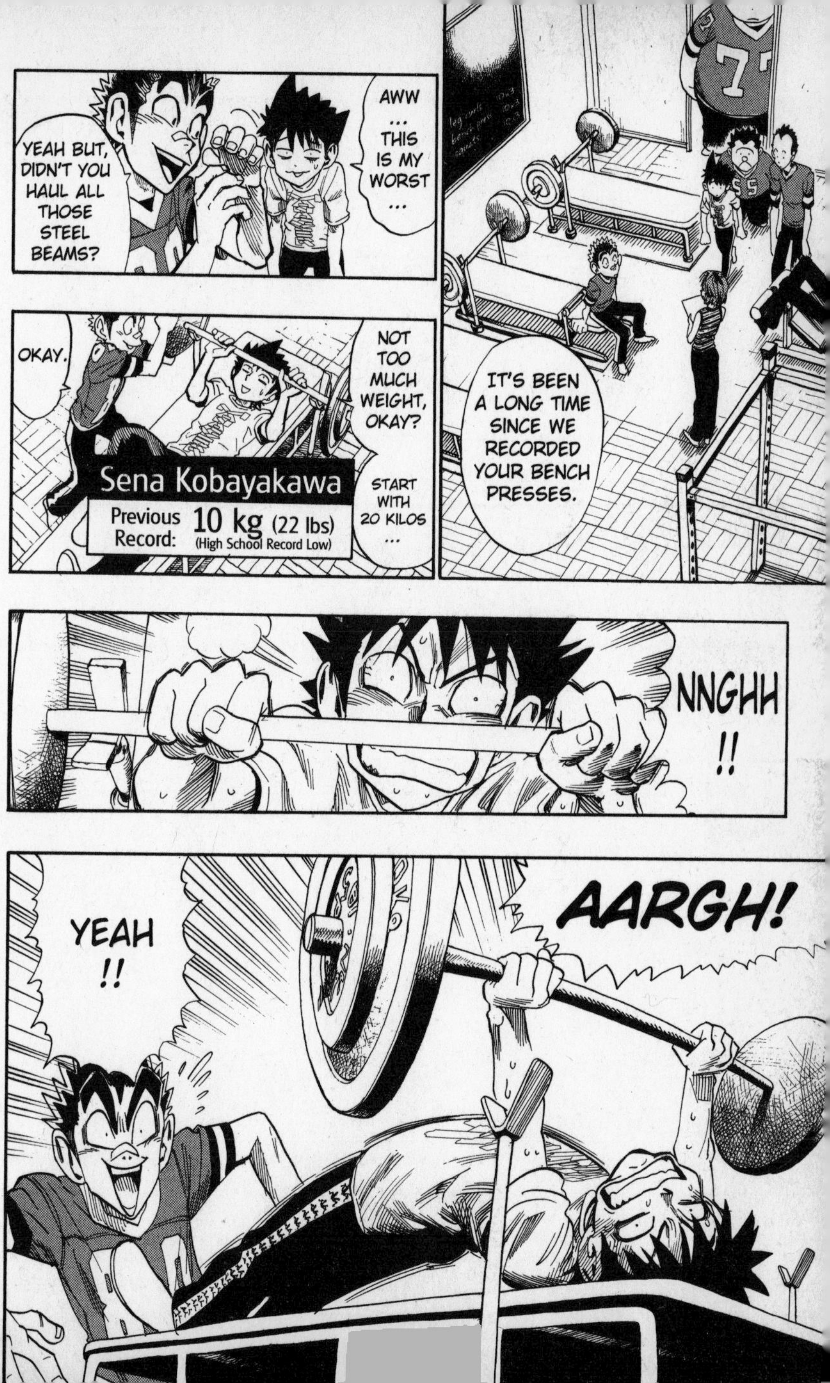
IT'S BEEN A LONG TIME SINCE WE RECORDED YOUR BENCH PRESSES.
AWW ... THIS IS MY WORST ...
YEAH BUT, DIDN'T YOU HAUL ALL THOSE STEEL BEAMS?
NOT TOO MUCH WEIGHT, OKAY?
START WITH 20 KILOS ...
OKAY.
Sena Kobayakawa
Previous Record: 10 kg (22 lbs) (High School Record Low)
NNGHH !!
AARGH!
YEAH !!

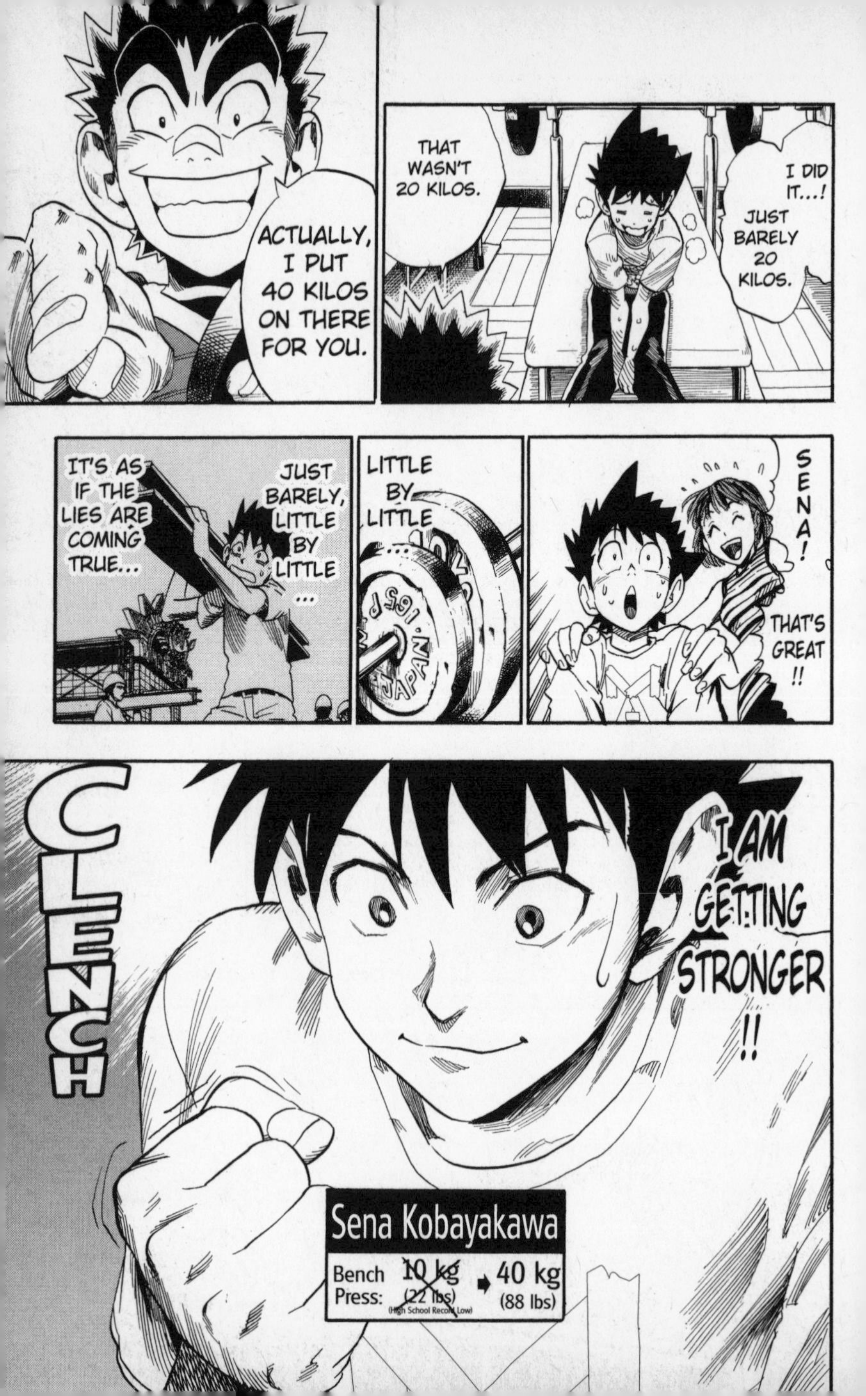
I DID IT...! JUST BARELY 20 KILOS.
THAT WASN'T 20 KILOS.
ACTUALLY, I PUT 40 KILOS ON THERE FOR YOU.
SENA!
THAT'S GREAT!!
LITTLE BY LITTLE ...
JUST BARELY, LITTLE BY LITTLE ...
IT'S AS IF THE LIES ARE COMING TRUE...
I AM GETTING STRONGER!!
CLENCH
Sena Kobayakawa
Bench Press: ~~10 kg (22 lbs) (High School Record Low)~~ ➡ 40 kg (88 lbs)

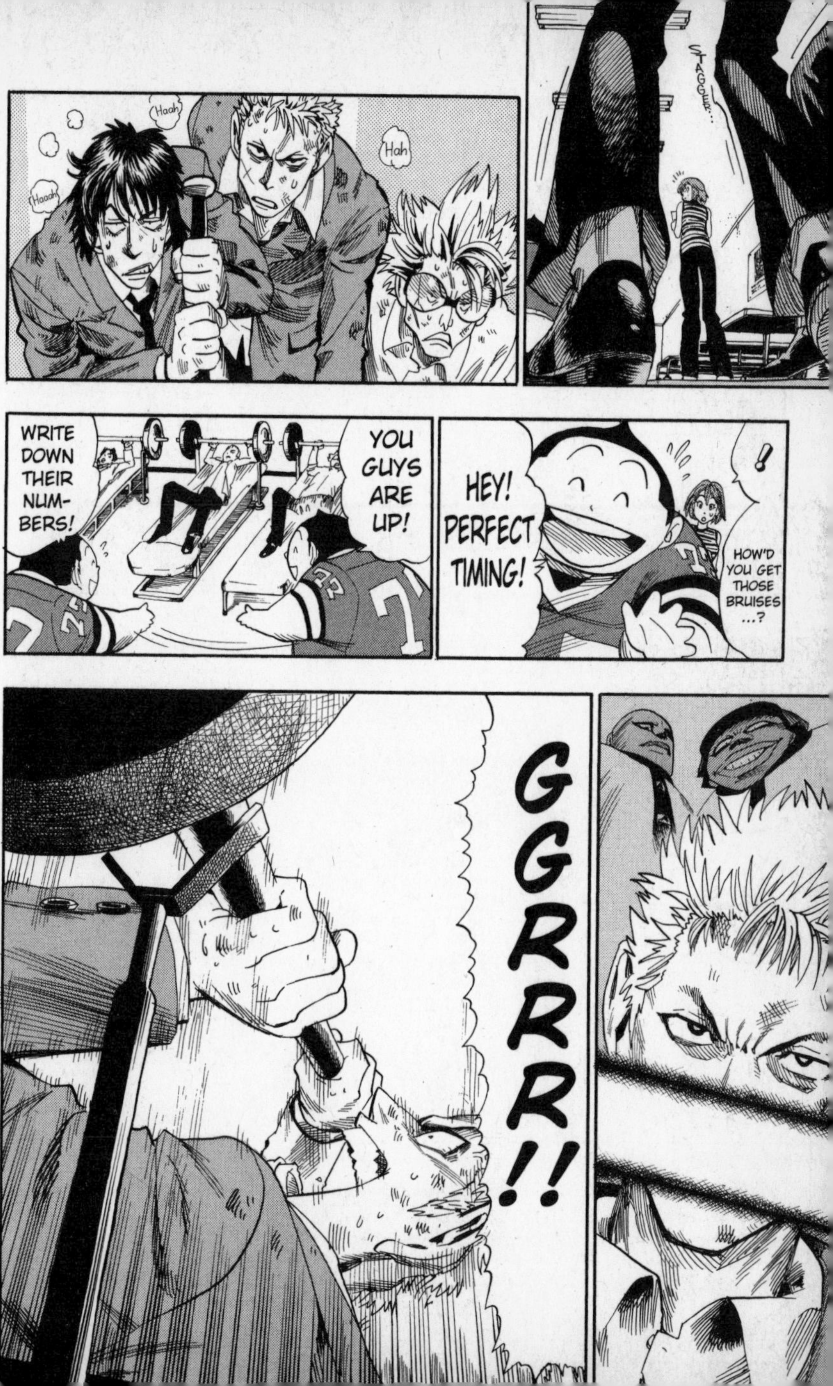
STAGGER...
Haah
Hah
Haaah
!
HEY! PERFECT TIMING!
HOW'D YOU GET THOSE BRUISES ...?
YOU GUYS ARE UP!
WRITE DOWN THEIR NUM-BERS!
GGRRR!!

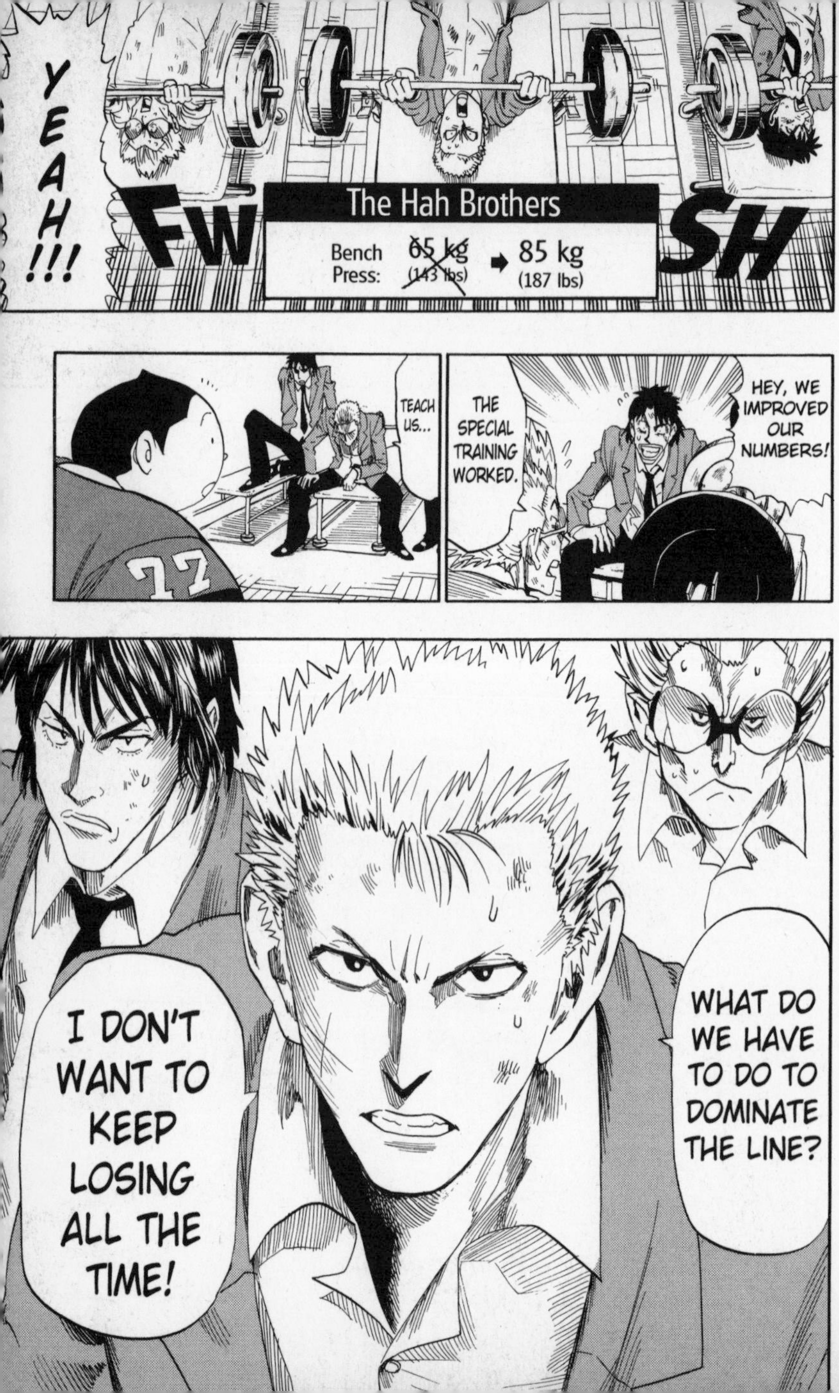
FW SH
The Hah Brothers
Bench Press: 65 kg (143 lbs) → 85 kg (187 lbs)
YEAH!!!
HEY, WE IMPROVED OUR NUMBERS!
THE SPECIAL TRAINING WORKED.
TEACH US...
WHAT DO WE HAVE TO DO TO DOMINATE THE LINE?
I DON'T WANT TO KEEP LOSING ALL THE TIME!

DEIMON HIGH SCHOOL
SURPRISE SCHOOL BAG INSPECTION

Mamori Anezaki

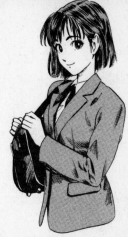

Umbrella for Sena
Lunchbox for Sena & Honeyed lemons for football team
Sena
ENGLISH
Math I
WORLD HISTORY
Physics
Japanese-English Dictionary
Handkerchief for Sena
Sewing Kit
Band Aids
Patches

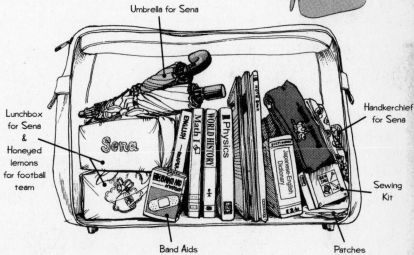

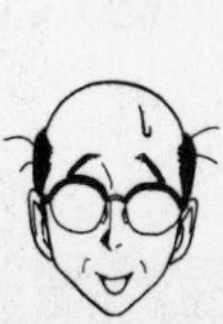

UH... VERY MOTHERLY...

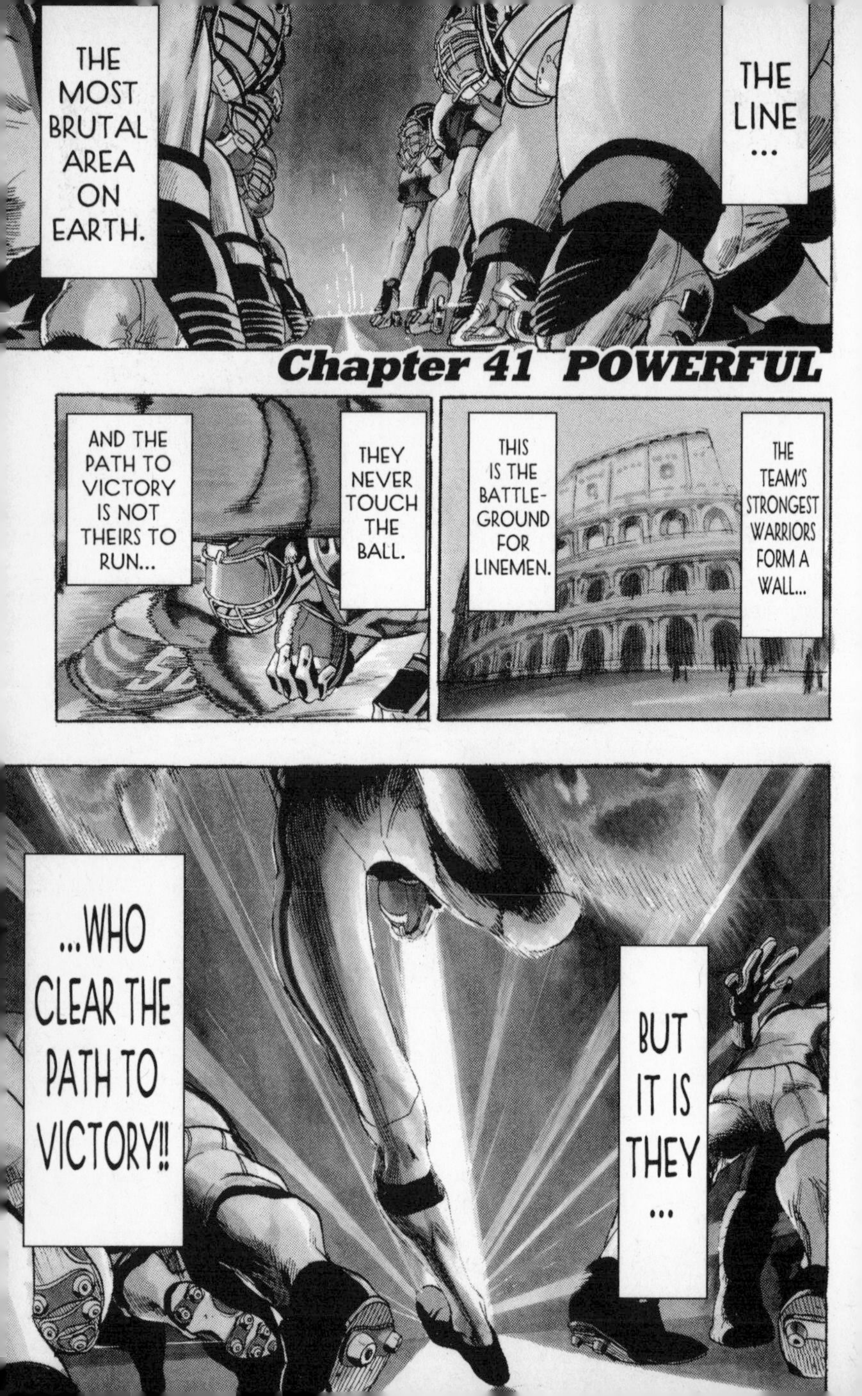
THE LINE...
THE MOST BRUTAL AREA ON EARTH.
Chapter 41 POWERFUL
THE TEAM'S STRONGEST WARRIORS FORM A WALL...
THIS IS THE BATTLE-GROUND FOR LINEMEN.
THEY NEVER TOUCH THE BALL.
AND THE PATH TO VICTORY IS NOT THEIRS TO RUN...
BUT IT IS THEY...
...WHO CLEAR THE PATH TO VICTORY!!

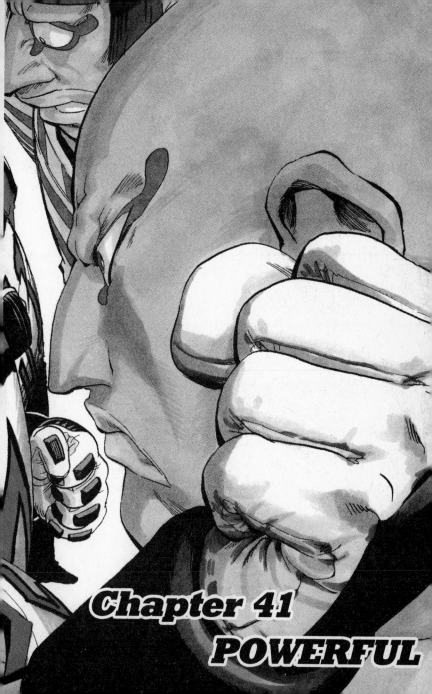

Chapter 41
POWERFUL

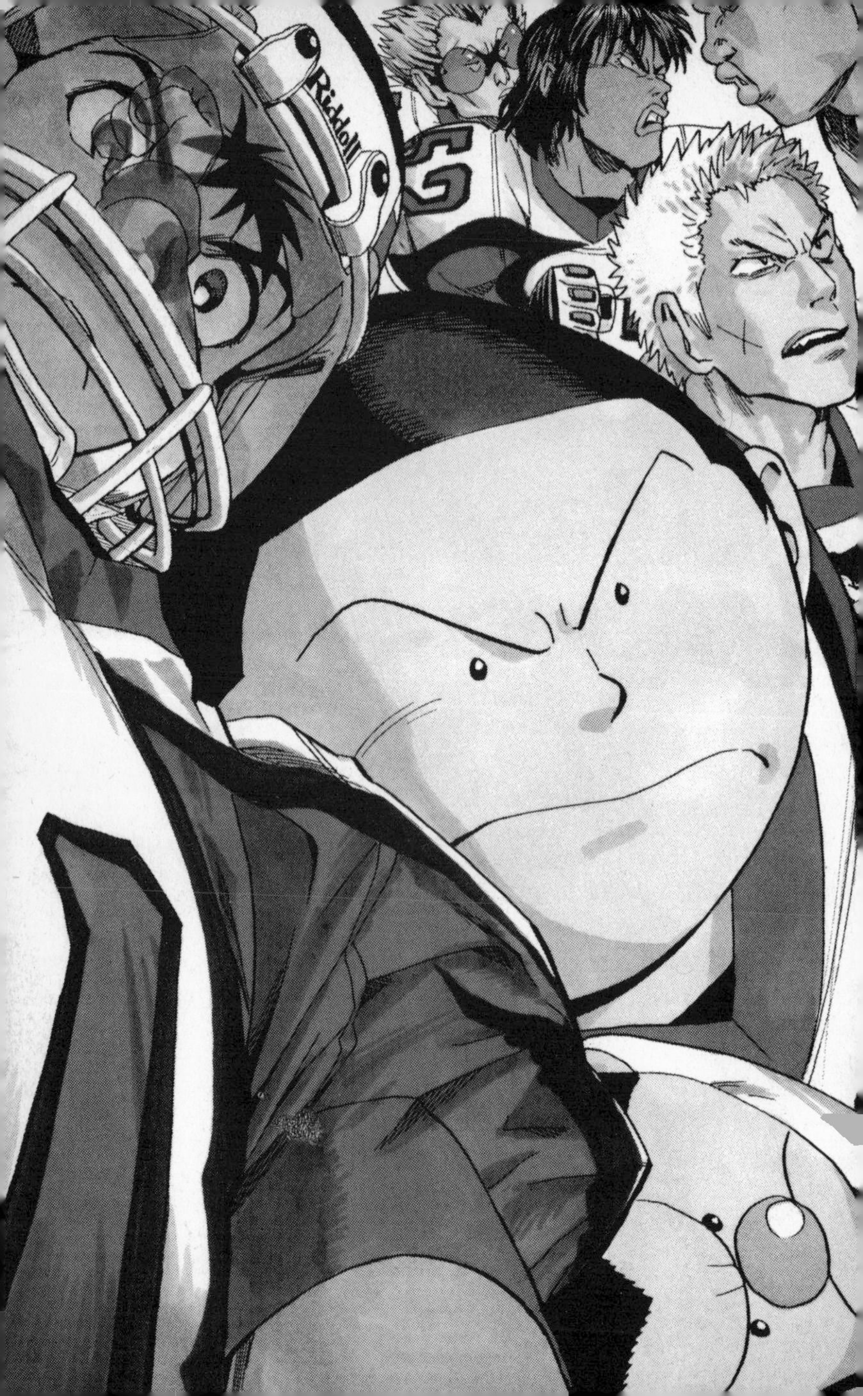
Riddell

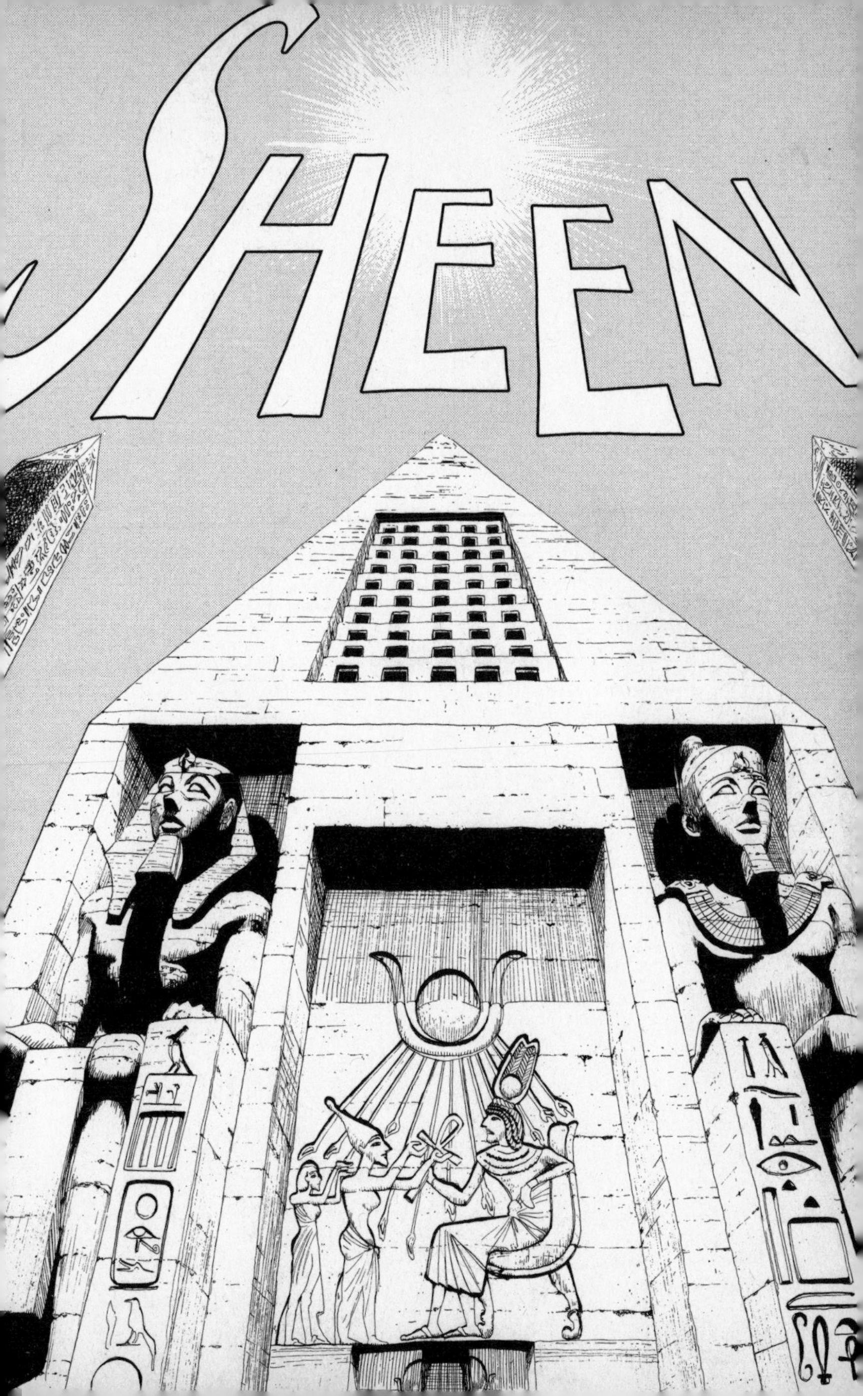
SHEEN

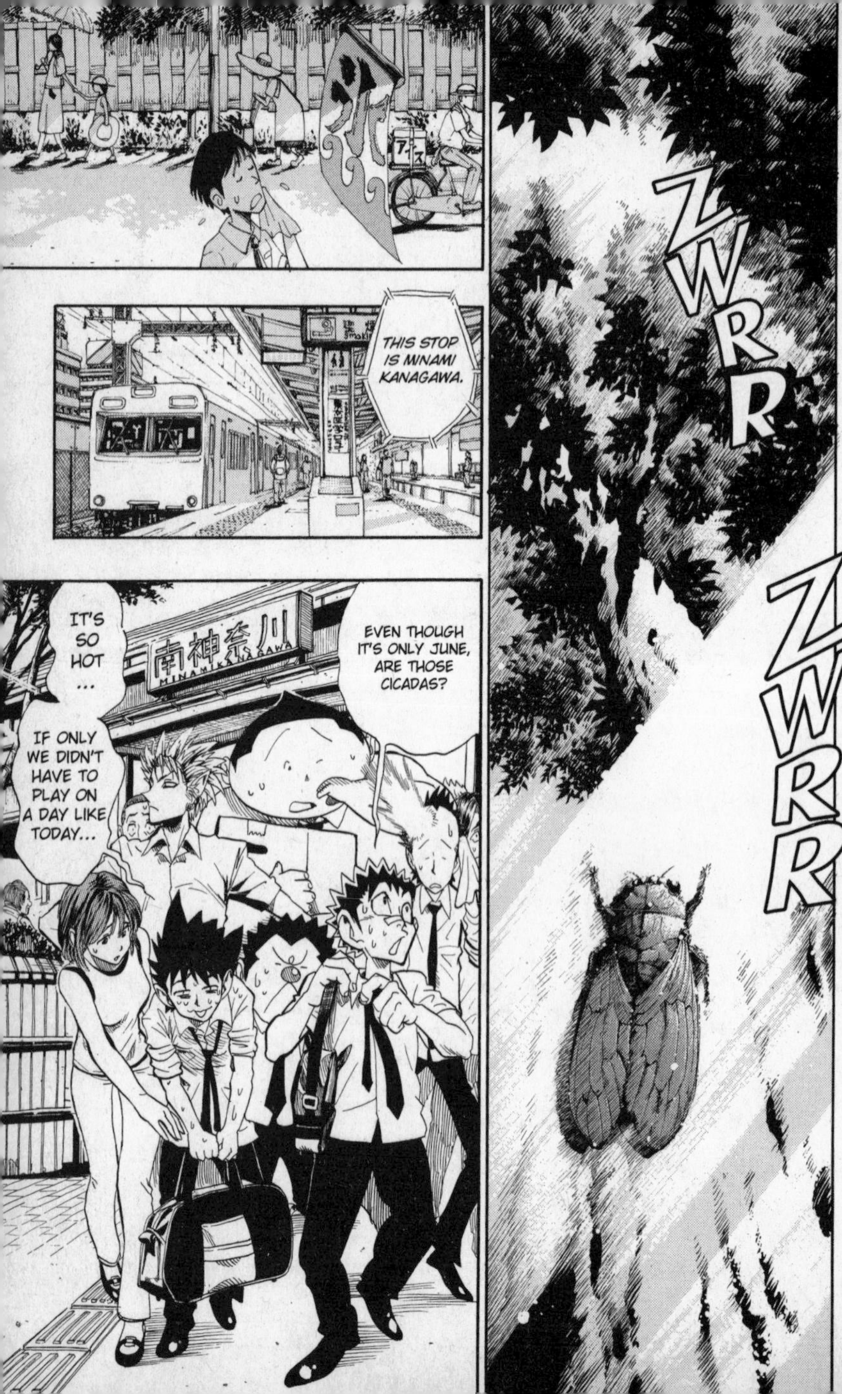
ZWRR
ZWRR
アイス
THIS STOP IS MINAMI KANAGAWA.
南神奈川 MINAMIKANAGAWA
EVEN THOUGH IT'S ONLY JUNE, ARE THOSE CICADAS?
IT'S SO HOT...
IF ONLY WE DIDN'T HAVE TO PLAY ON A DAY LIKE TODAY...

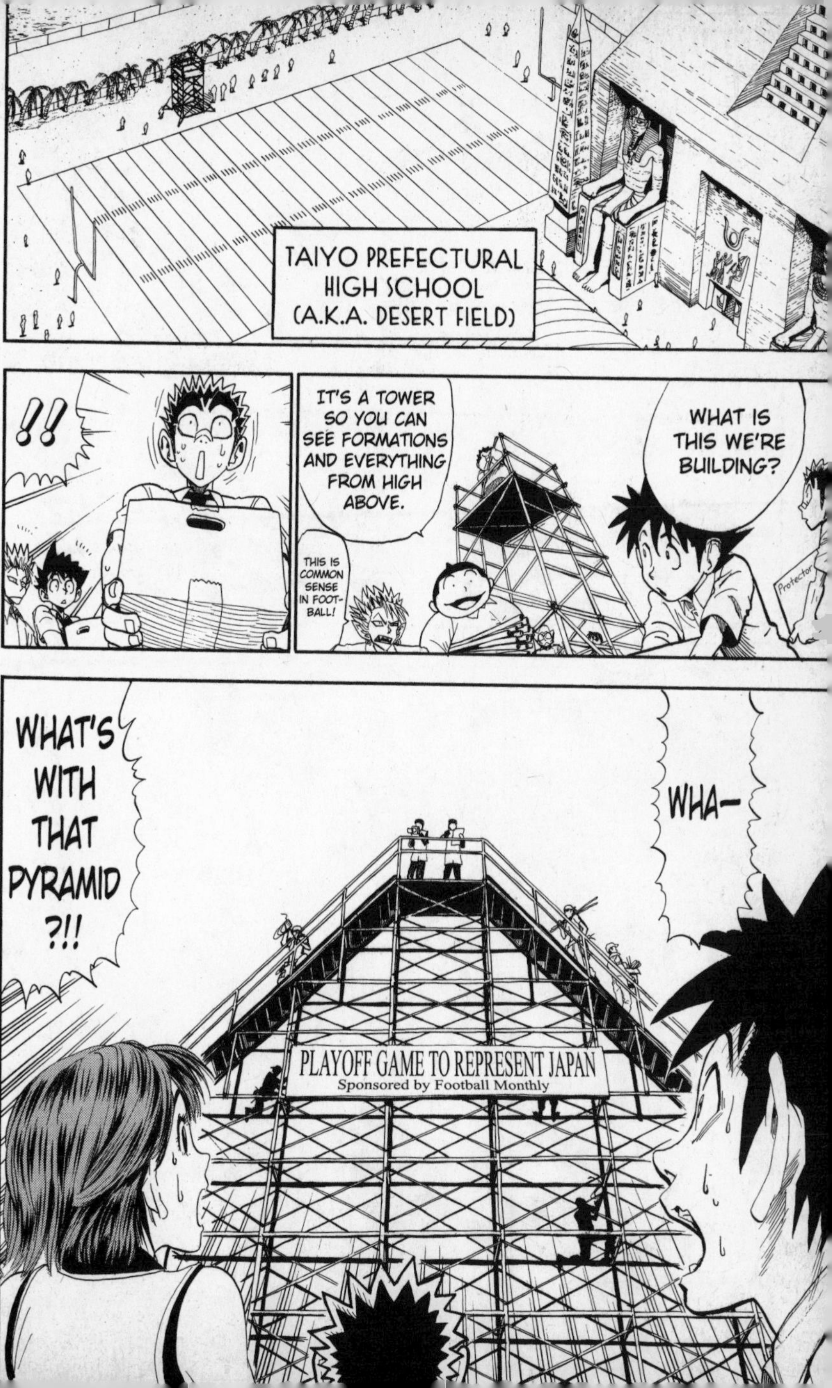
TAIYO PREFECTURAL HIGH SCHOOL (A.K.A. DESERT FIELD)
WHAT IS THIS WE'RE BUILDING?
Protector
IT'S A TOWER SO YOU CAN SEE FORMATIONS AND EVERYTHING FROM HIGH ABOVE.
THIS IS COMMON SENSE IN FOOTBALL!
!!
WHA-
WHAT'S WITH THAT PYRAMID ?!!
PLAYOFF GAME TO REPRESENT JAPAN
Sponsored by Football Monthly

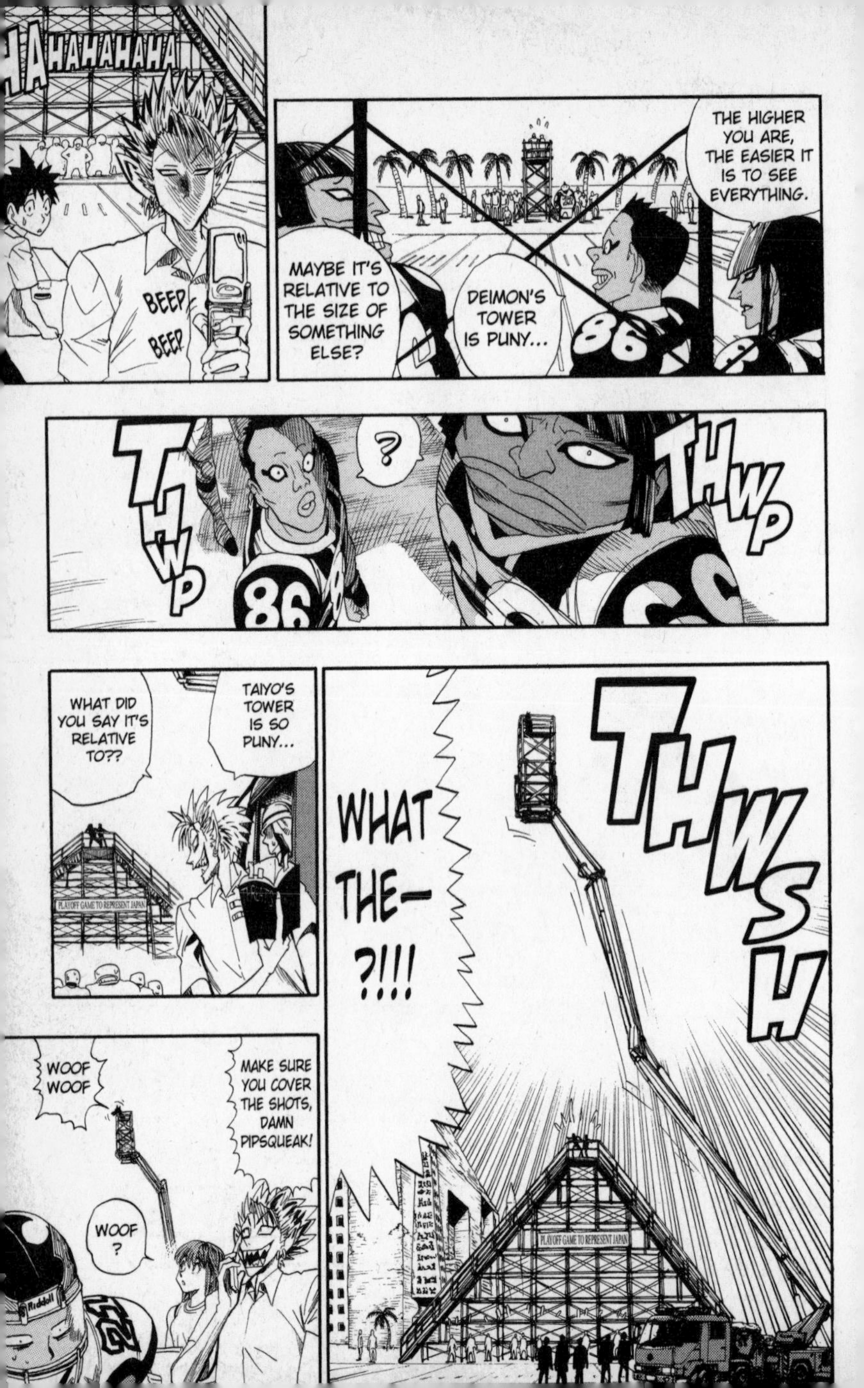
THE HIGHER YOU ARE, THE EASIER IT IS TO SEE EVERYTHING.
DEIMON'S TOWER IS PUNY...
MAYBE IT'S RELATIVE TO THE SIZE OF SOMETHING ELSE?
HAHAHAHAHA
BEEP BEEP
THWP
?
THWP
THWSH
WHAT THE—?!!!
PLAYOFF GAME TO REPRESENT JAPAN
TAIYO'S TOWER IS SO PUNY...
WHAT DID YOU SAY IT'S RELATIVE TO??
PLAYOFF GAME TO REPRESENT JAPAN
MAKE SURE YOU COVER THE SHOTS, DAMN PIPSQUEAK!
WOOF WOOF
WOOF ?

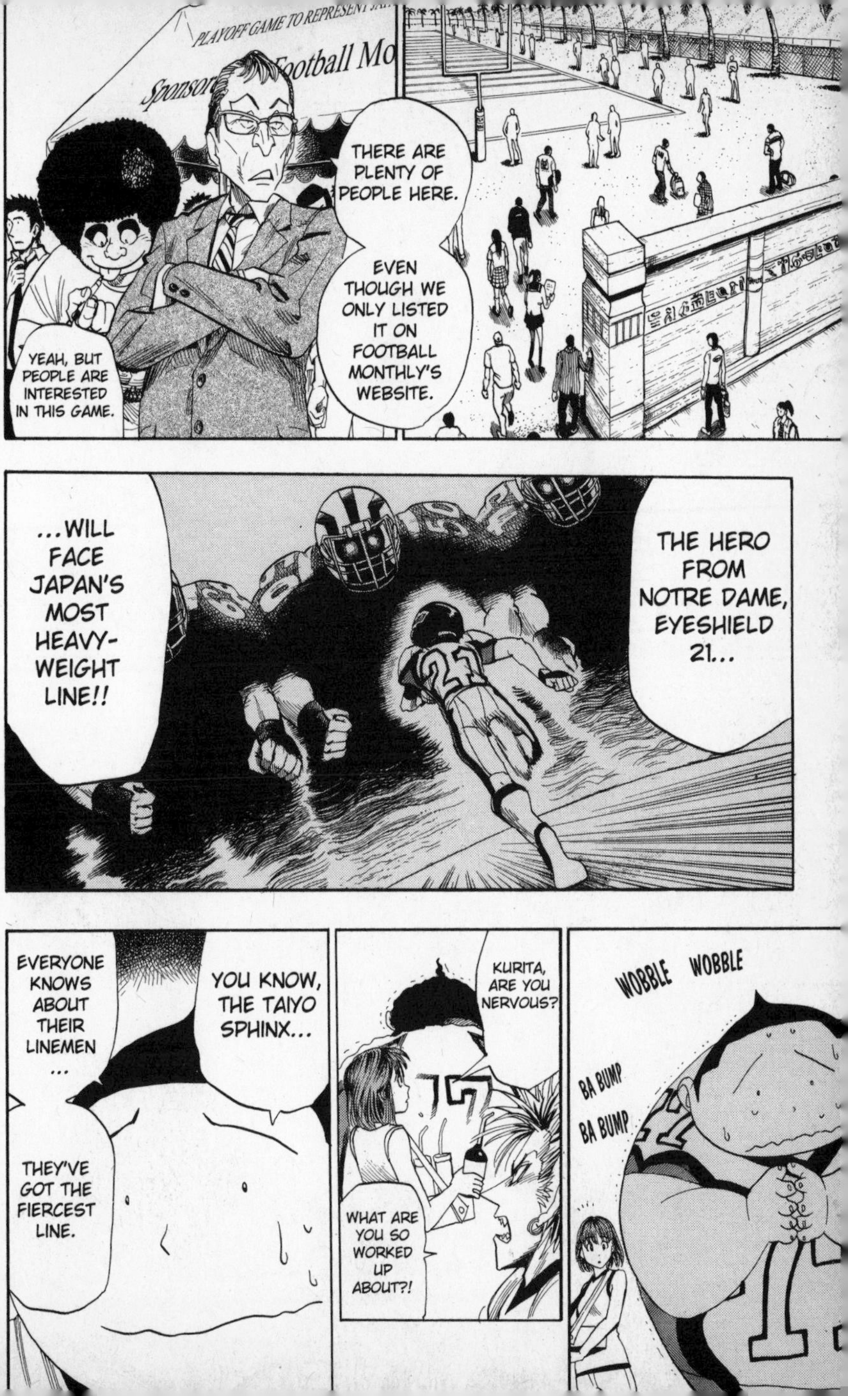
THERE ARE PLENTY OF PEOPLE HERE.
EVEN THOUGH WE ONLY LISTED IT ON FOOTBALL MONTHLY'S WEBSITE.
YEAH, BUT PEOPLE ARE INTERESTED IN THIS GAME.
THE HERO FROM NOTRE DAME, EYESHIELD 21...
...WILL FACE JAPAN'S MOST HEAVY-WEIGHT LINE!!
WOBBLE WOBBLE
BA BUMP
BA BUMP
KURITA, ARE YOU NERVOUS?
WHAT ARE YOU SO WORKED UP ABOUT?!
YOU KNOW, THE TAIYO SPHINX...
EVERYONE KNOWS ABOUT THEIR LINEMEN...
THEY'VE GOT THE FIERCEST LINE.

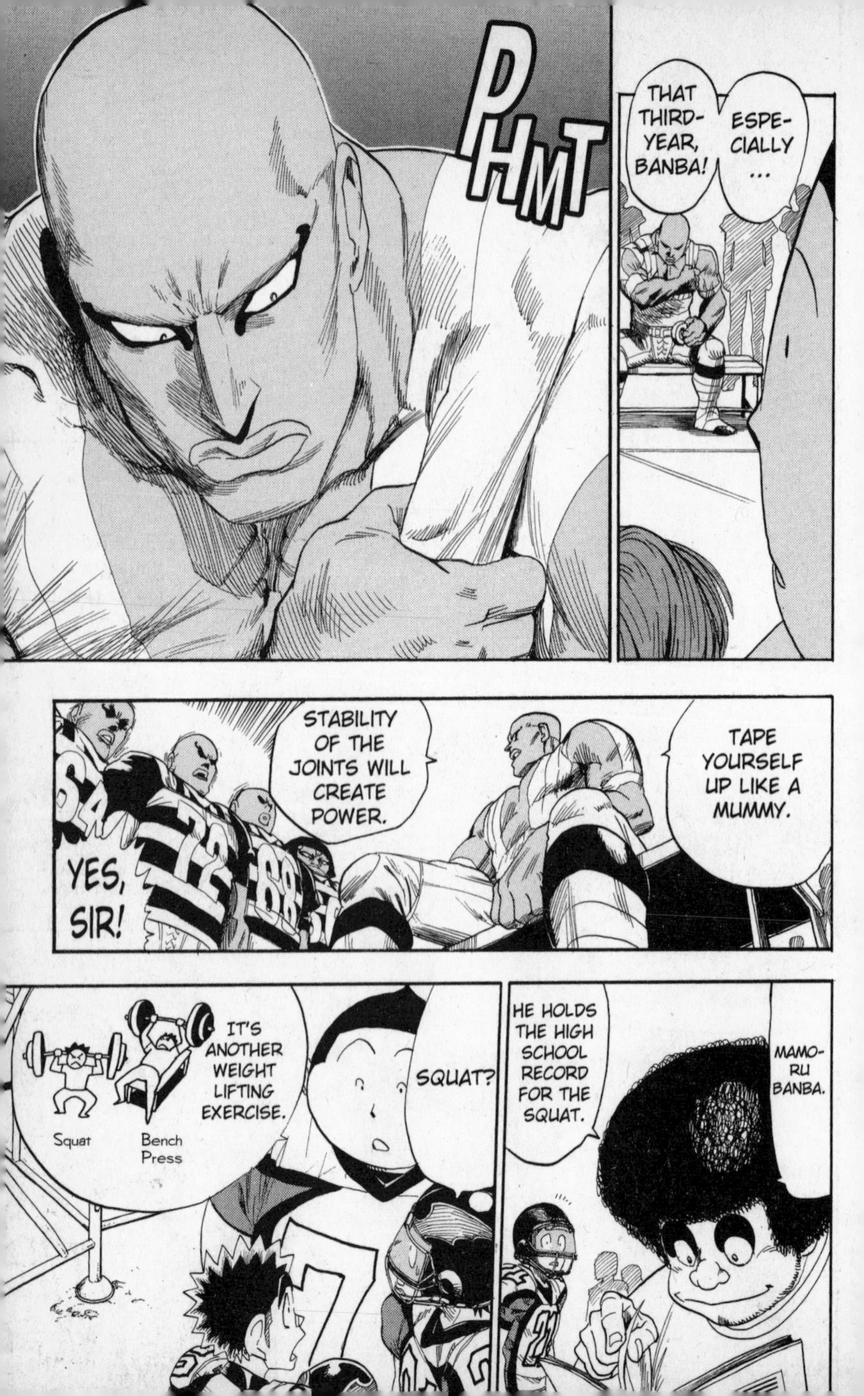
ESPE-CIALLY ...
THAT THIRD-YEAR, BANBA!
PHMT
TAPE YOURSELF UP LIKE A MUMMY.
STABILITY OF THE JOINTS WILL CREATE POWER.
YES, SIR!
MAMO-RU BANBA.
HE HOLDS THE HIGH SCHOOL RECORD FOR THE SQUAT.
SQUAT?
IT'S ANOTHER WEIGHT LIFTING EXERCISE.
Squat
Bench Press

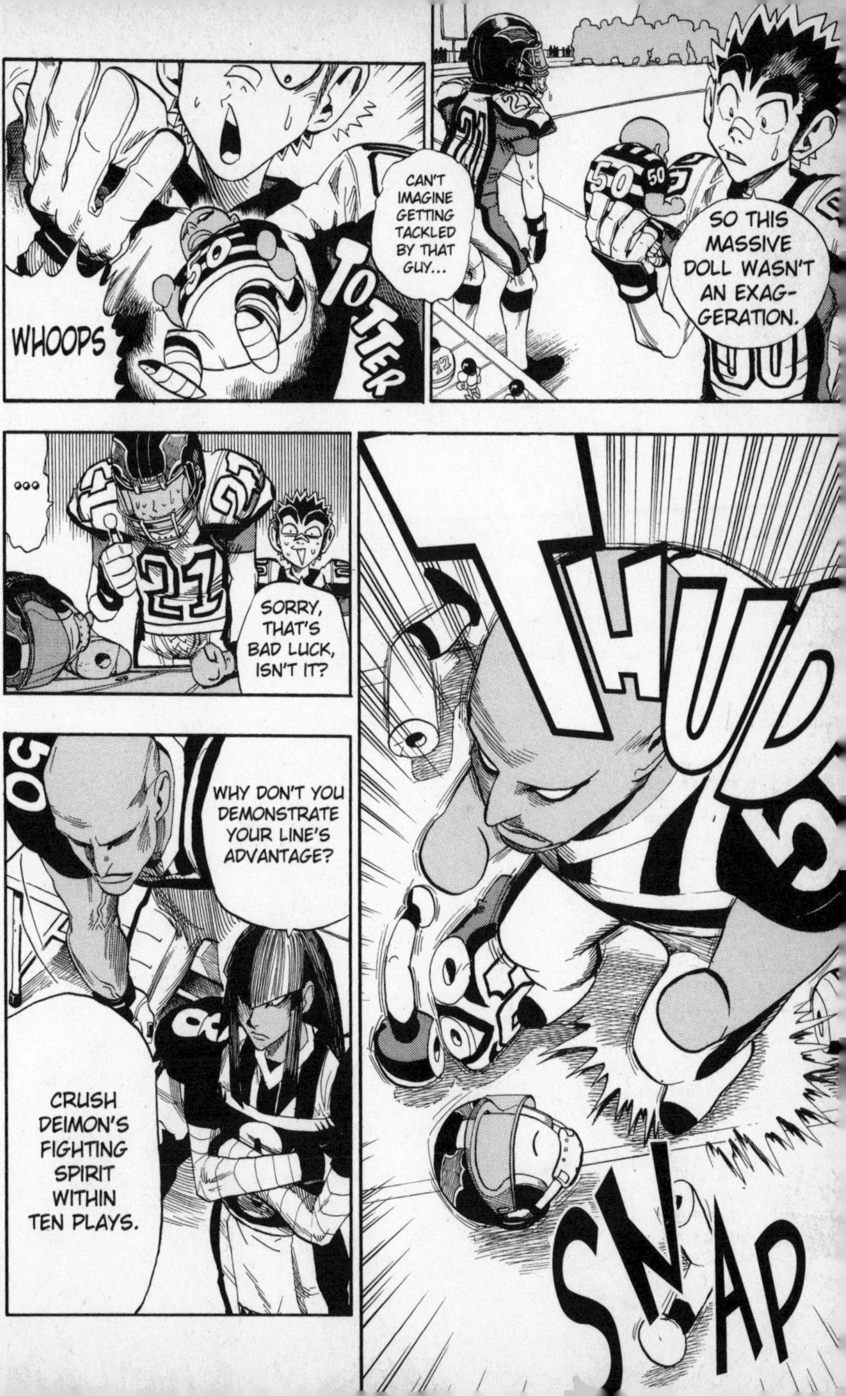
SO THIS MASSIVE DOLL WASN'T AN EXAG- GERATION.
CAN'T IMAGINE GETTING TACKLED BY THAT GUY...
TOTTER
WHOOPS
THUD
SNAP
...
SORRY, THAT'S BAD LUCK, ISN'T IT?
WHY DON'T YOU DEMONSTRATE YOUR LINE'S ADVANTAGE?
CRUSH DEIMON'S FIGHTING SPIRIT WITHIN TEN PLAYS.

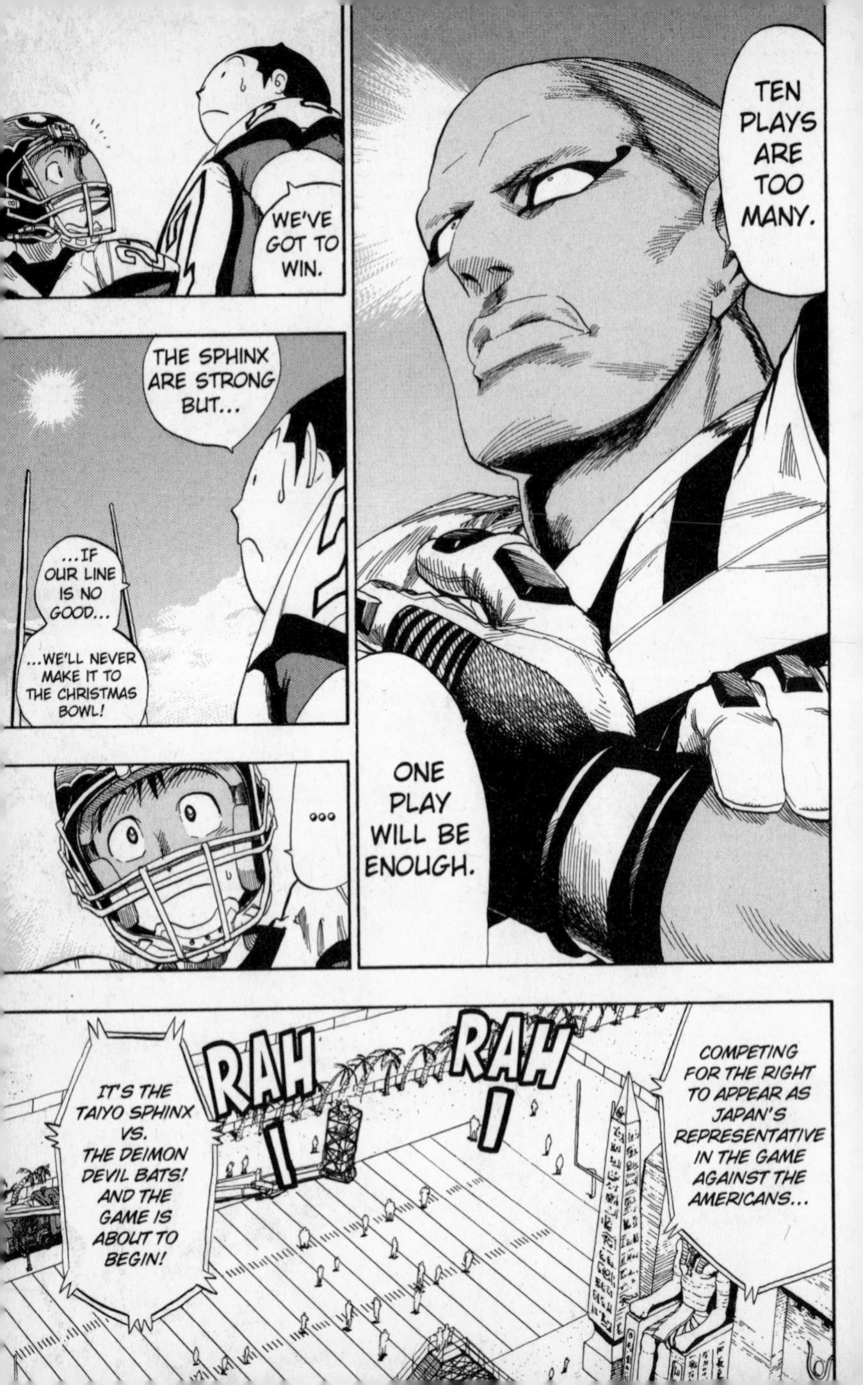
TEN PLAYS ARE TOO MANY.
ONE PLAY WILL BE ENOUGH.
WE'VE GOT TO WIN.
THE SPHINX ARE STRONG BUT...
...IF OUR LINE IS NO GOOD...
...WE'LL NEVER MAKE IT TO THE CHRISTMAS BOWL!
...
COMPETING FOR THE RIGHT TO APPEAR AS JAPAN'S REPRESENTATIVE IN THE GAME AGAINST THE AMERICANS...
RAH I
RAH I
IT'S THE TAIYO SPHINX VS. THE DEIMON DEVIL BATS! AND THE GAME IS ABOUT TO BEGIN!

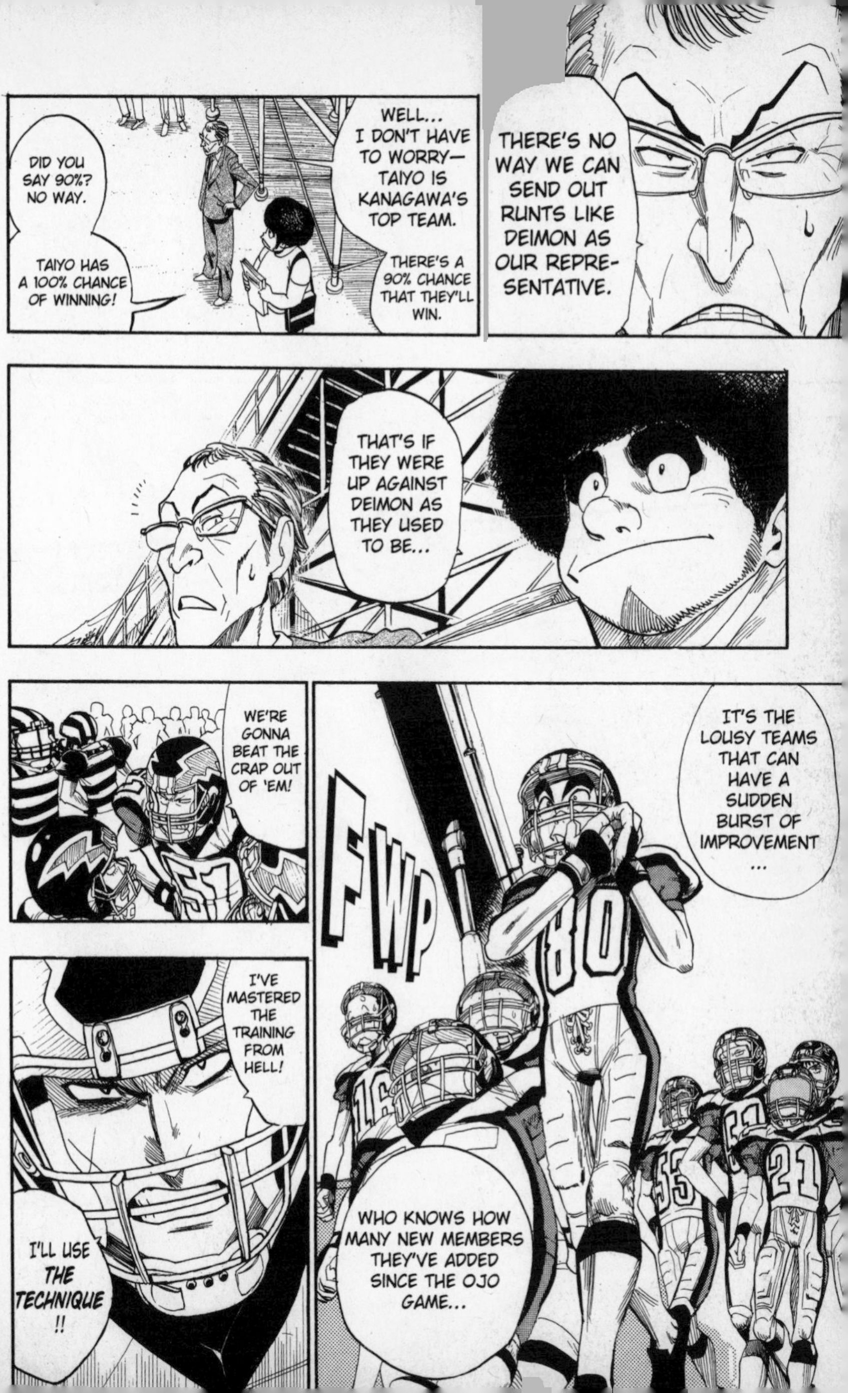
THERE'S NO WAY WE CAN SEND OUT RUNTS LIKE DEIMON AS OUR REPRESENTATIVE.
WELL... I DON'T HAVE TO WORRY— TAIYO IS KANAGAWA'S TOP TEAM.
THERE'S A 90% CHANCE THAT THEY'LL WIN.
DID YOU SAY 90%? NO WAY.
TAIYO HAS A 100% CHANCE OF WINNING!
THAT'S IF THEY WERE UP AGAINST DEIMON AS THEY USED TO BE...
IT'S THE LOUSY TEAMS THAT CAN HAVE A SUDDEN BURST OF IMPROVEMENT ...
FWP
WHO KNOWS HOW MANY NEW MEMBERS THEY'VE ADDED SINCE THE OJO GAME...
WE'RE GONNA BEAT THE CRAP OUT OF 'EM!
I'VE MASTERED THE TRAINING FROM HELL!
I'LL USE *THE TECHNIQUE* !!

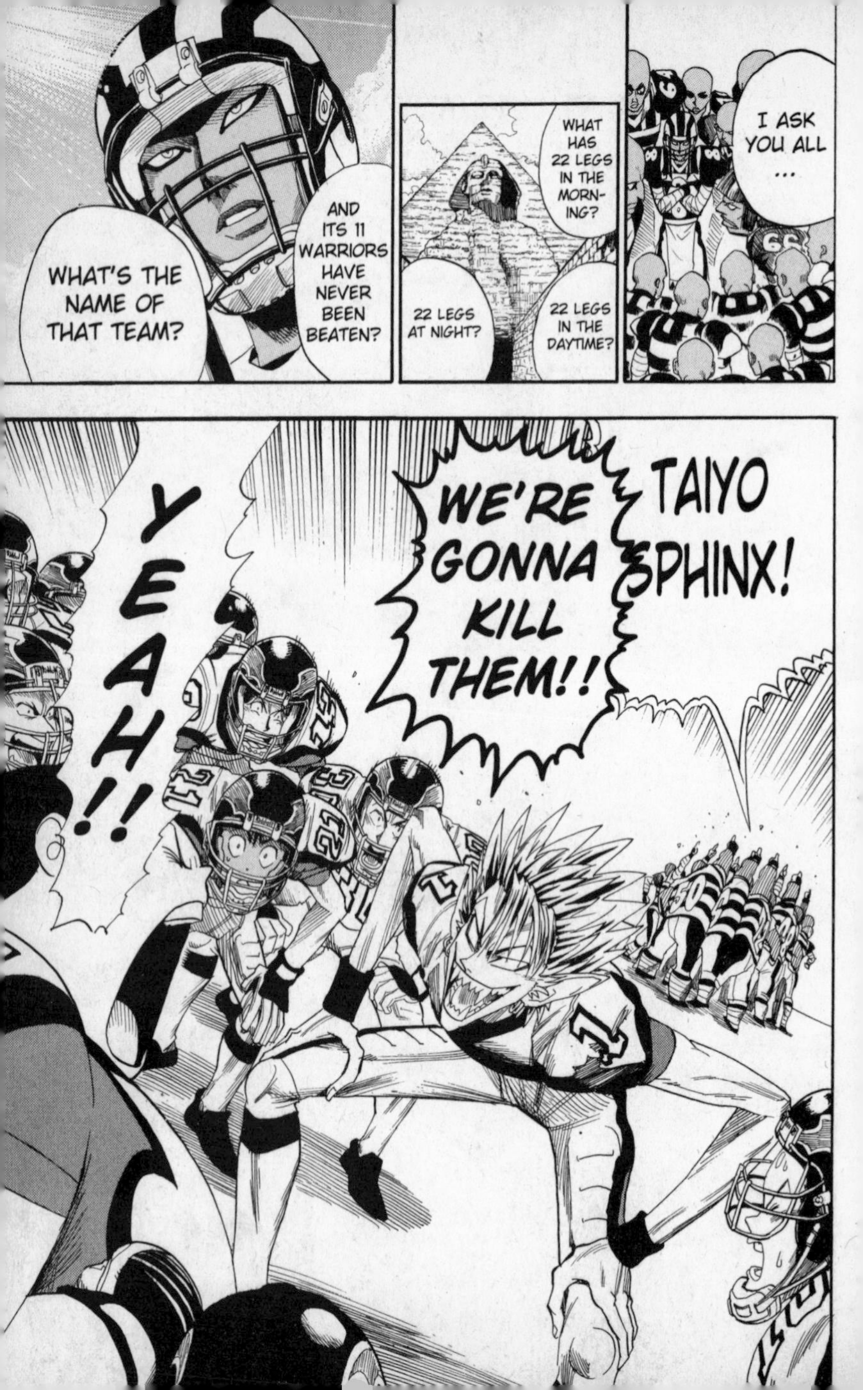
I ASK YOU ALL ...
WHAT HAS 22 LEGS IN THE MORNING?
22 LEGS IN THE DAYTIME?
22 LEGS AT NIGHT?
AND ITS 11 WARRIORS HAVE NEVER BEEN BEATEN?
WHAT'S THE NAME OF THAT TEAM?
TAIYO SPHINX!
WE'RE GONNA KILL THEM!!
YEAH!!

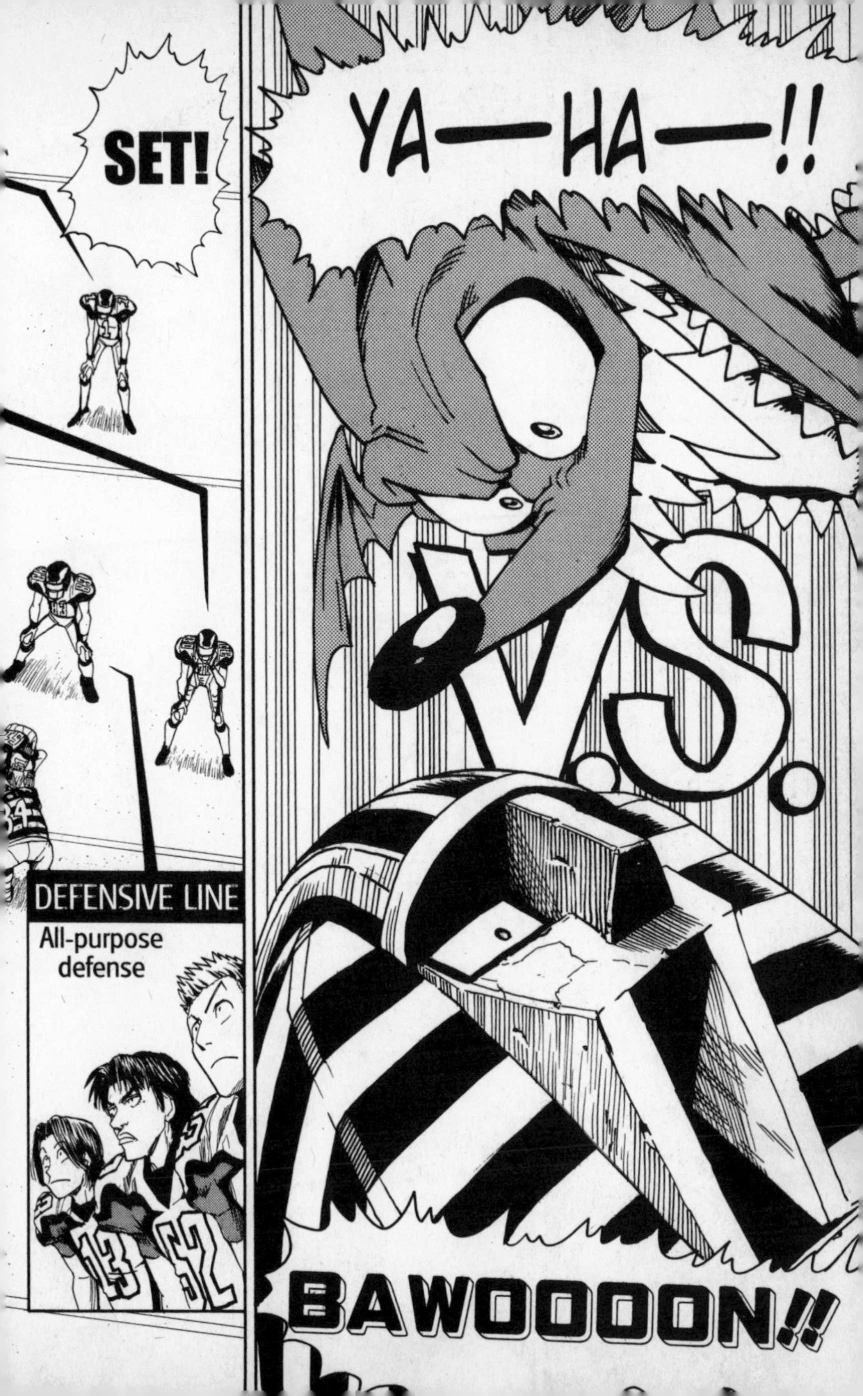
YA—HA—!!
V.S.!
BAWOOOON!!
SET!
DEFENSIVE LINE
All-purpose defense

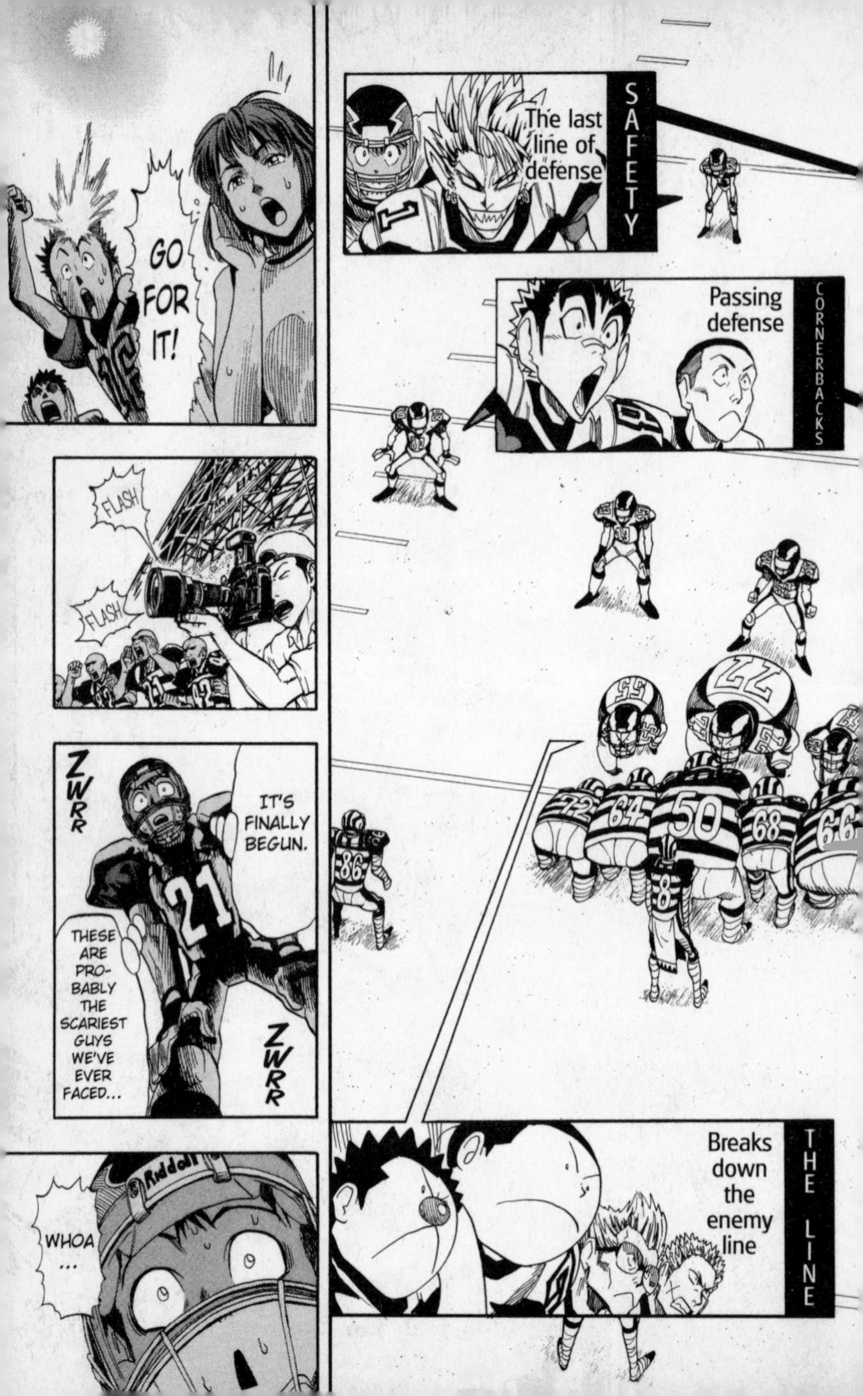
SAFETY
The last line of defense
CORNERBACKS
Passing defense
THE LINE
Breaks down the enemy line
GO FOR IT!
FLASH
FLASH
ZWRR
IT'S FINALLY BEGUN.
THESE ARE PROBABLY THE SCARIEST GUYS WE'VE EVER FACED...
ZWRR
WHOA...

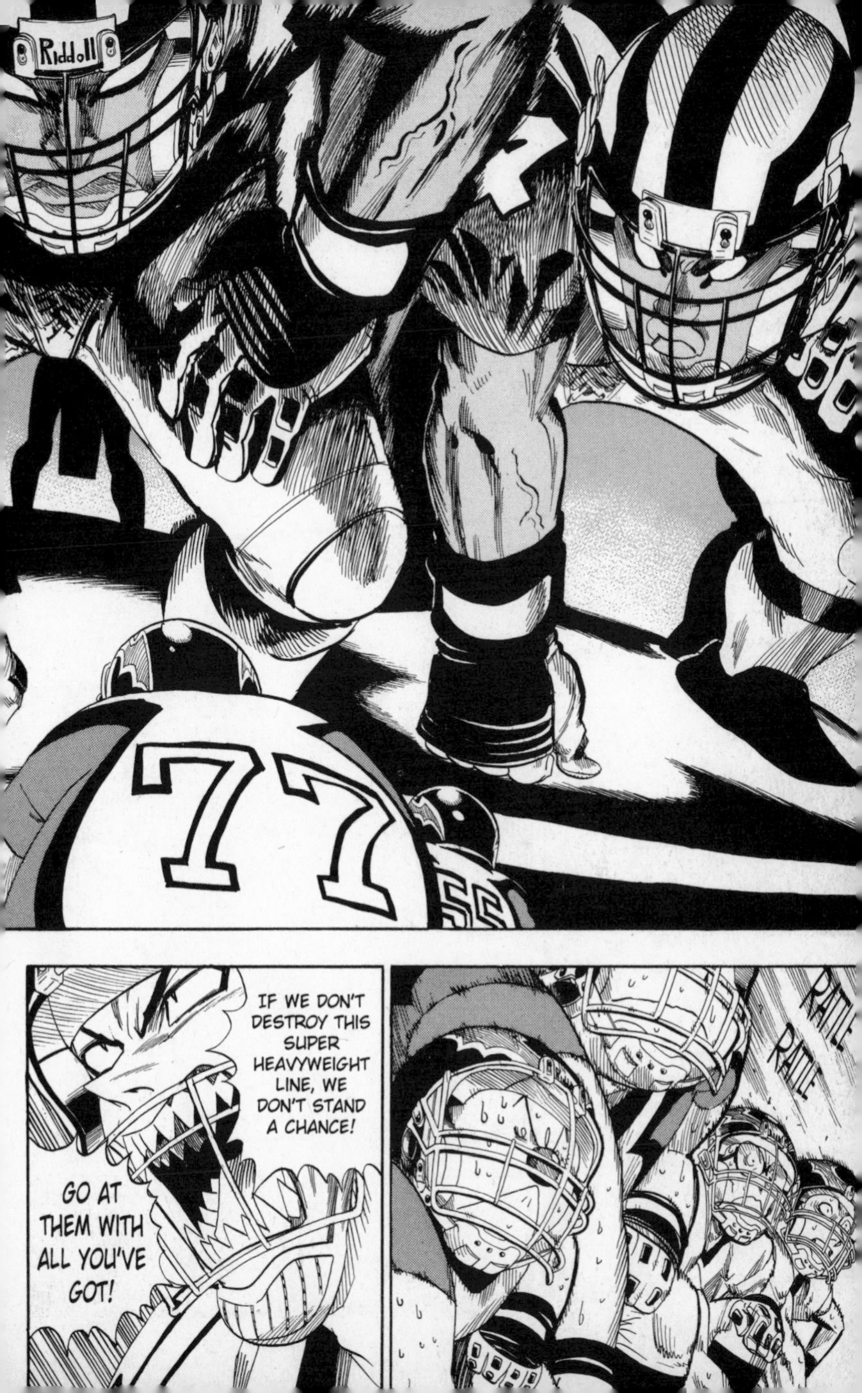
RATTLE
RATTLE
IF WE DON'T DESTROY THIS SUPER HEAVYWEIGHT LINE, WE DON'T STAND A CHANCE!
GO AT THEM WITH ALL YOU'VE GOT!

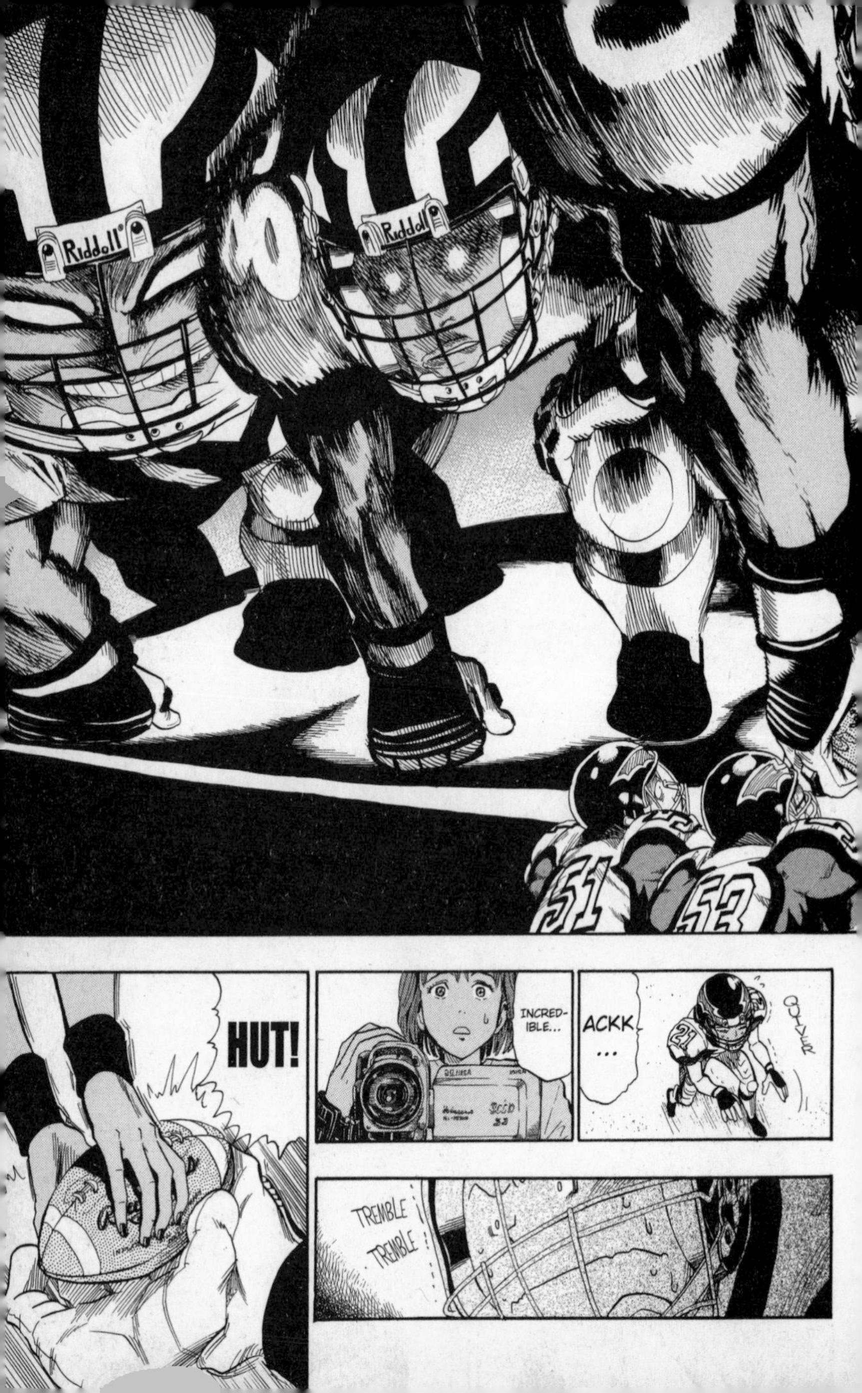
ACKK...
QUIVER
INCRED-IBLE...
TREMBLE TREMBLE
HUT!

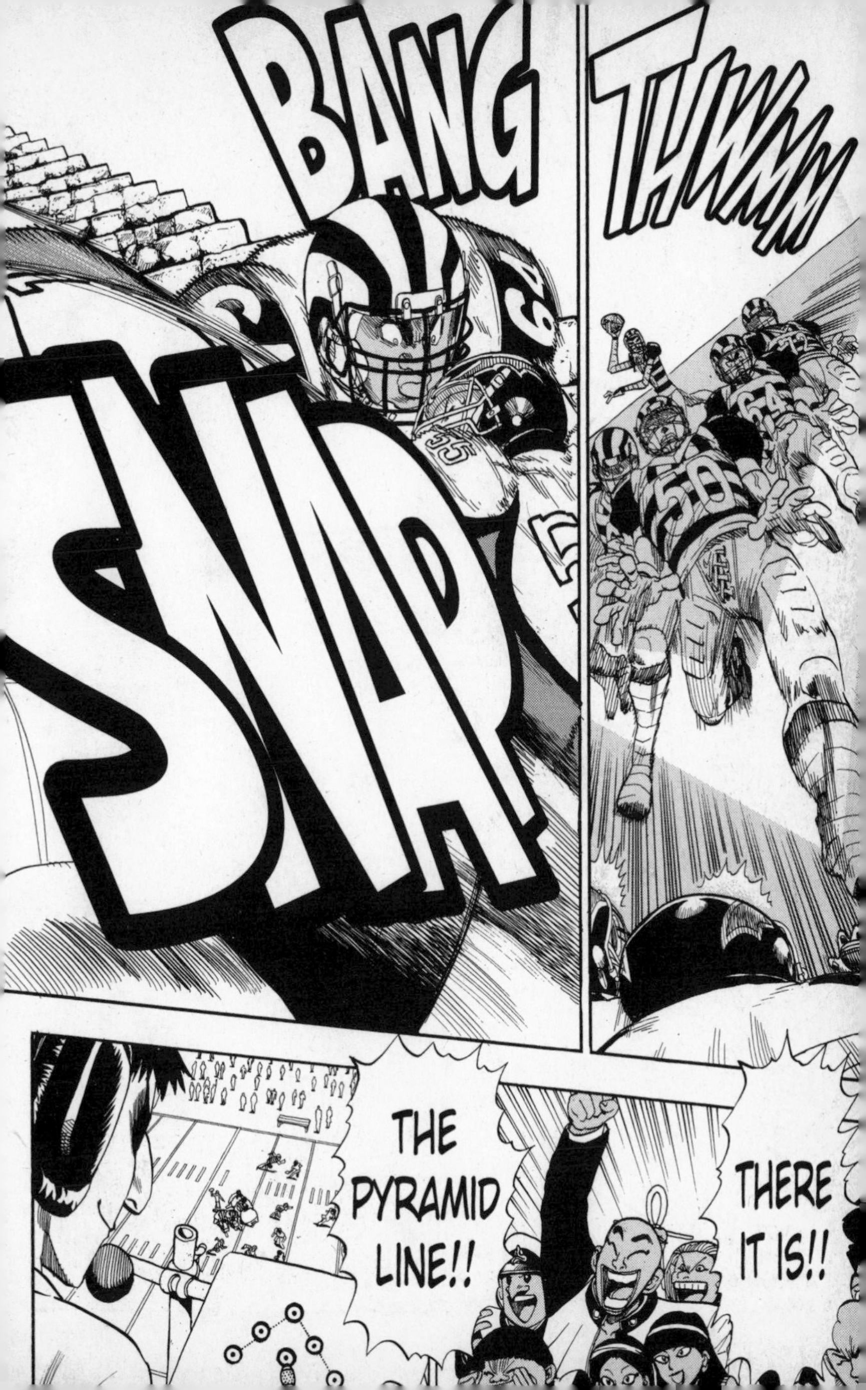
BANG
SNAP
THERE IT IS!!
THE PYRAMID LINE!!

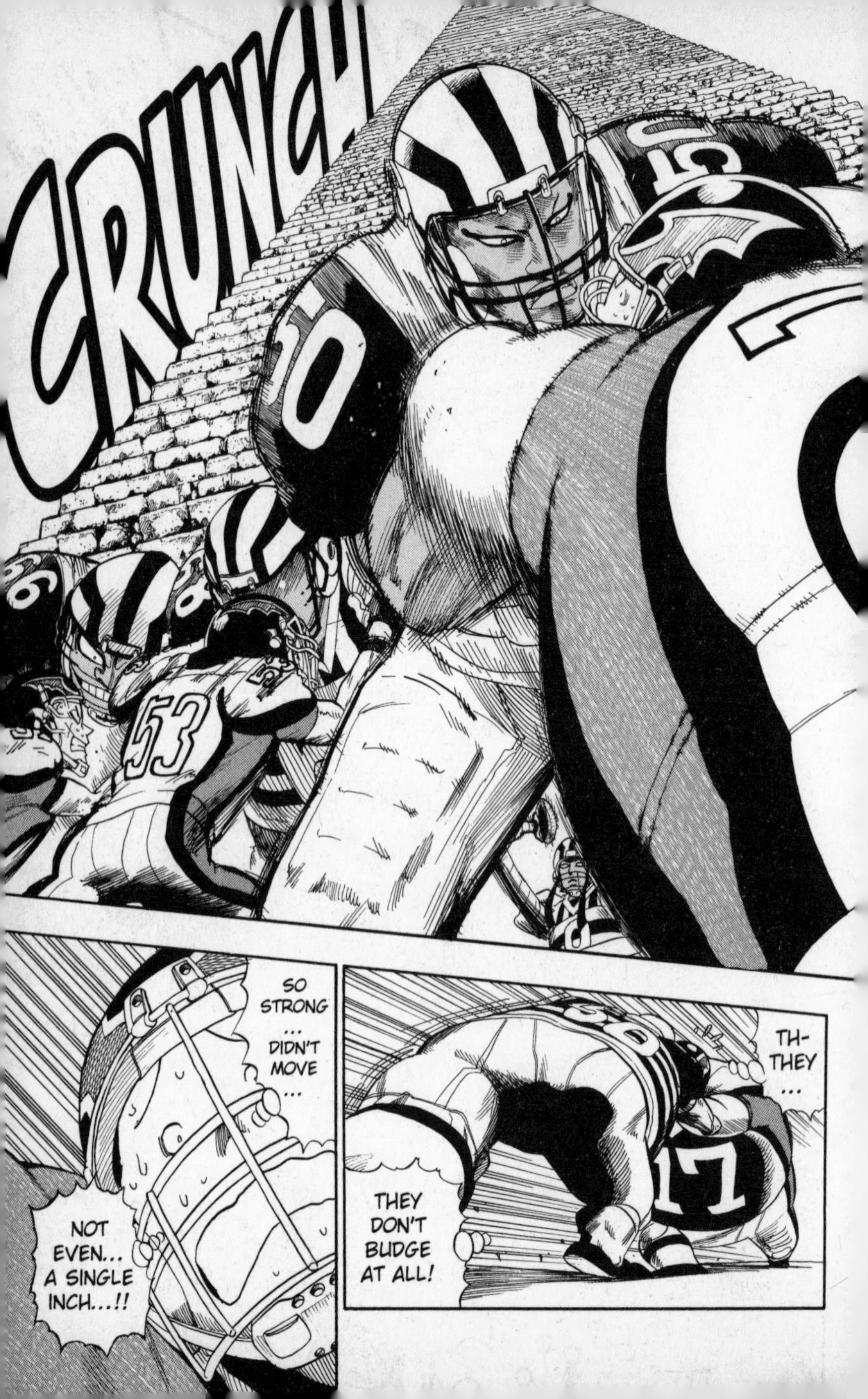
CRUNG!!
TH-THEY ...
THEY DON'T BUDGE AT ALL!
SO STRONG ... DIDN'T MOVE ...
NOT EVEN... A SINGLE INCH...!!

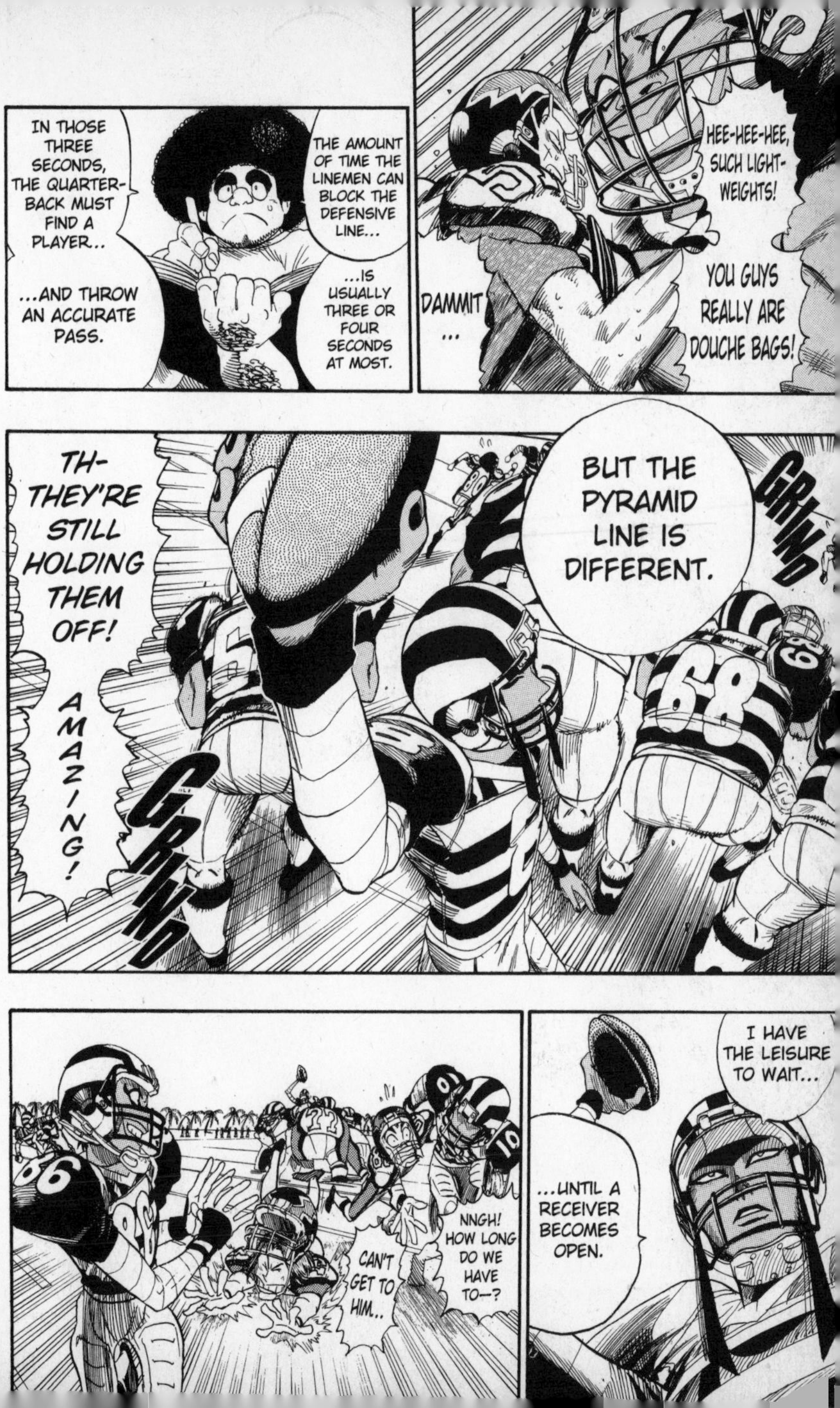
HEE-HEE-HEE, SUCH LIGHT-WEIGHTS!
YOU GUYS REALLY ARE DOUCHE BAGS!
DAMMIT...
THE AMOUNT OF TIME THE LINEMEN CAN BLOCK THE DEFENSIVE LINE...
...IS USUALLY THREE OR FOUR SECONDS AT MOST.
IN THOSE THREE SECONDS, THE QUARTER-BACK MUST FIND A PLAYER...
...AND THROW AN ACCURATE PASS.
GRIND
BUT THE PYRAMID LINE IS DIFFERENT.
TH- THEY'RE STILL HOLDING THEM OFF!
AMAZING!
GRIND
I HAVE THE LEISURE TO WAIT...
...UNTIL A RECEIVER BECOMES OPEN.
NNGH! HOW LONG DO WE HAVE TO—?
CAN'T GET TO HIM...

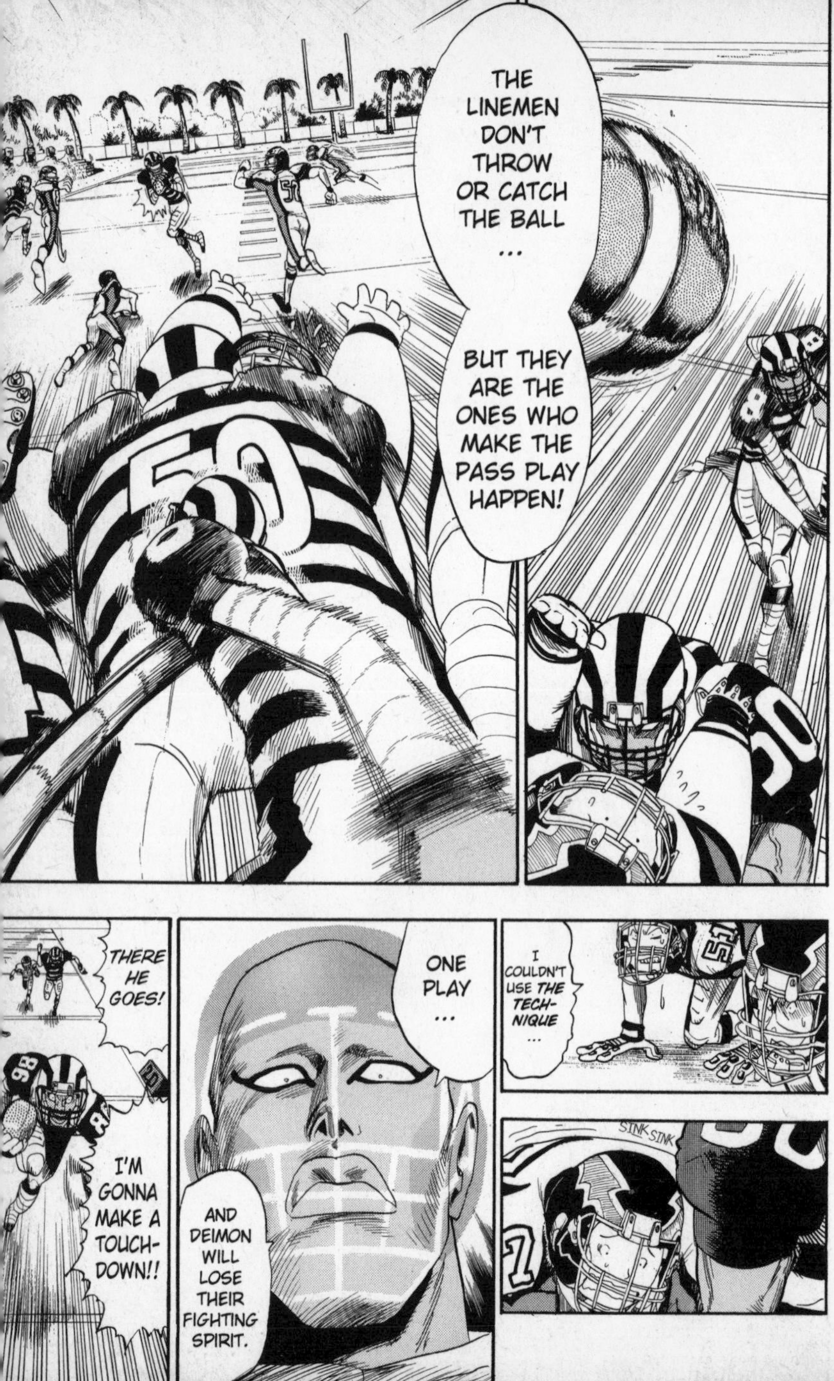
THE LINEMEN DON'T THROW OR CATCH THE BALL...
BUT THEY ARE THE ONES WHO MAKE THE PASS PLAY HAPPEN!
I COULDN'T USE THE TECHNIQUE...
SINK SINK
ONE PLAY...
AND DEIMON WILL LOSE THEIR FIGHTING SPIRIT.
THERE HE GOES!
I'M GONNA MAKE A TOUCHDOWN!!

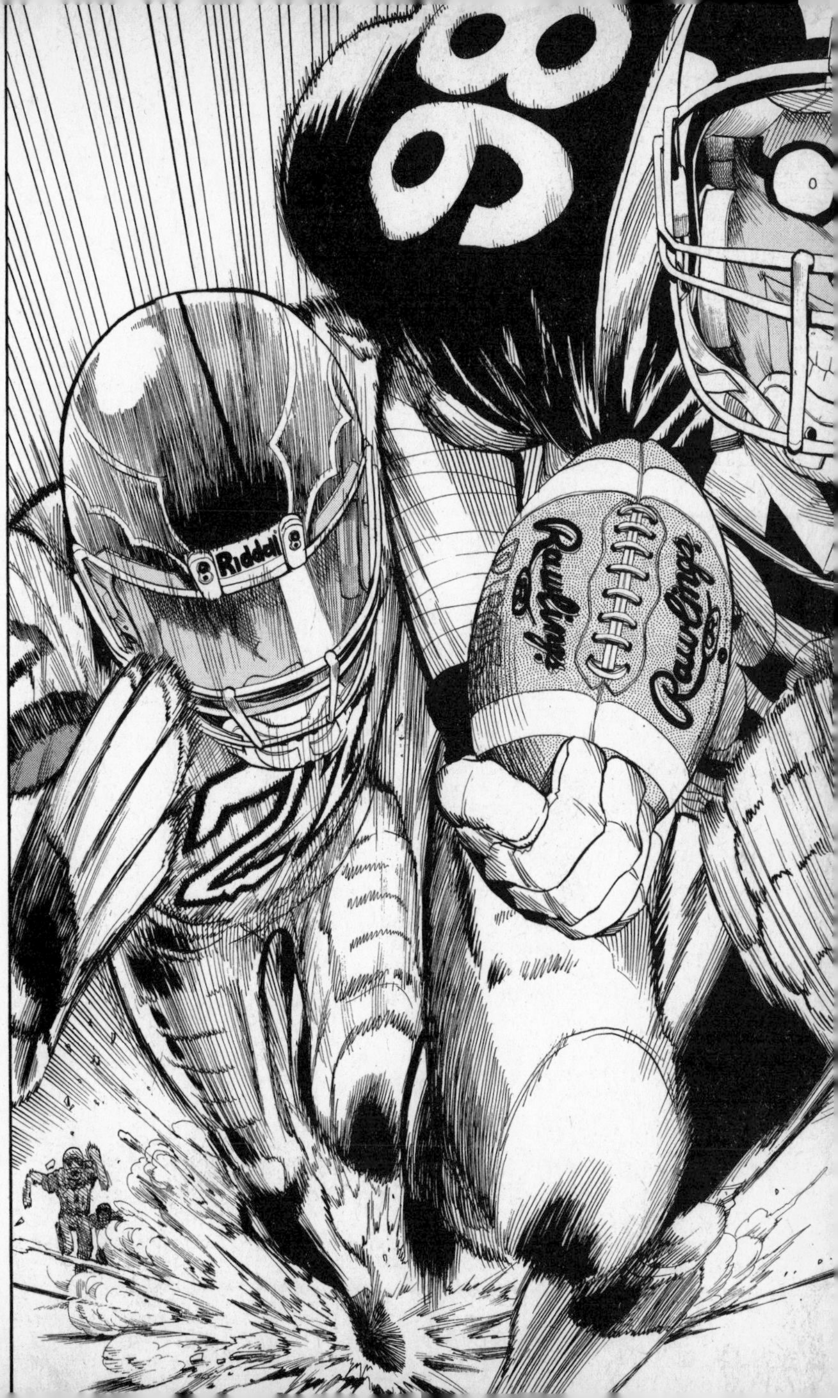
Riddell
Rawlings
Rawlings

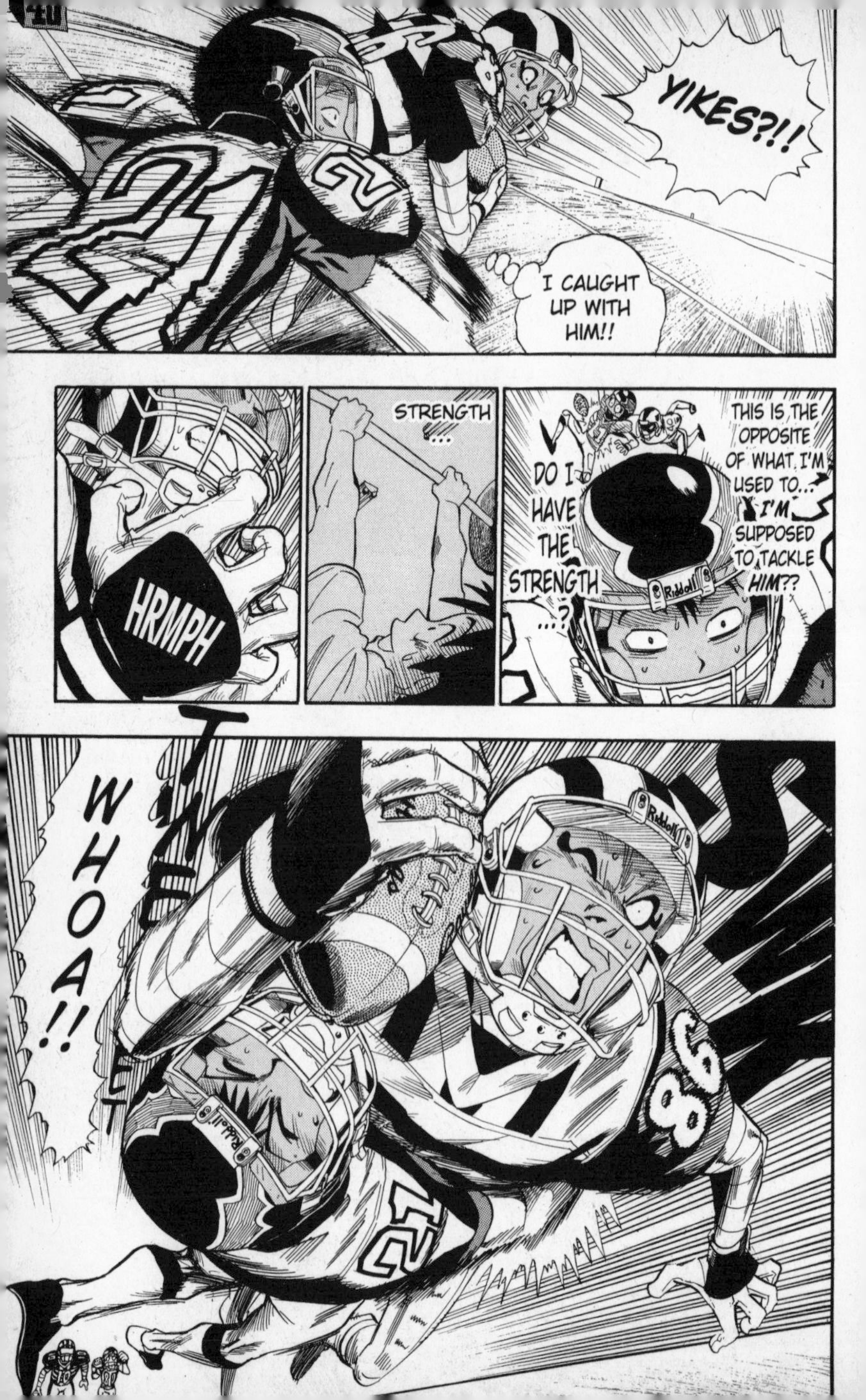
YIKES?!!
I CAUGHT UP WITH HIM!!
THIS IS THE OPPOSITE OF WHAT I'M USED TO... I'M SUPPOSED TO TACKLE HIM??
DO I HAVE THE STRENGTH ...?
STRENGTH ...
HRMPH
WHOA!!

DEIMON HIGH SCHOOL

SURPRISE SCHOOL BAG INSPECTION

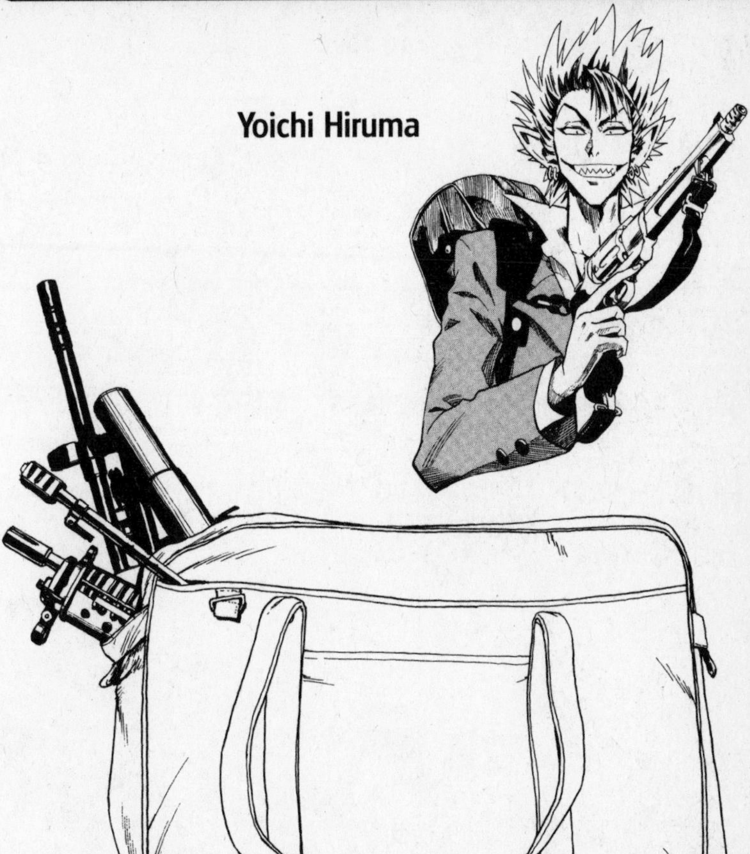
Yoichi Hiruma

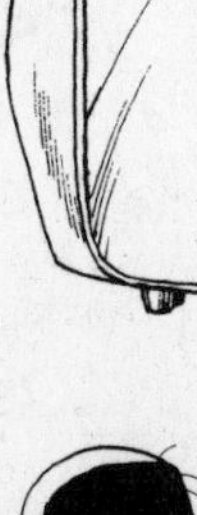
UH...YOU'RE FINE.
GO ON, NOW...

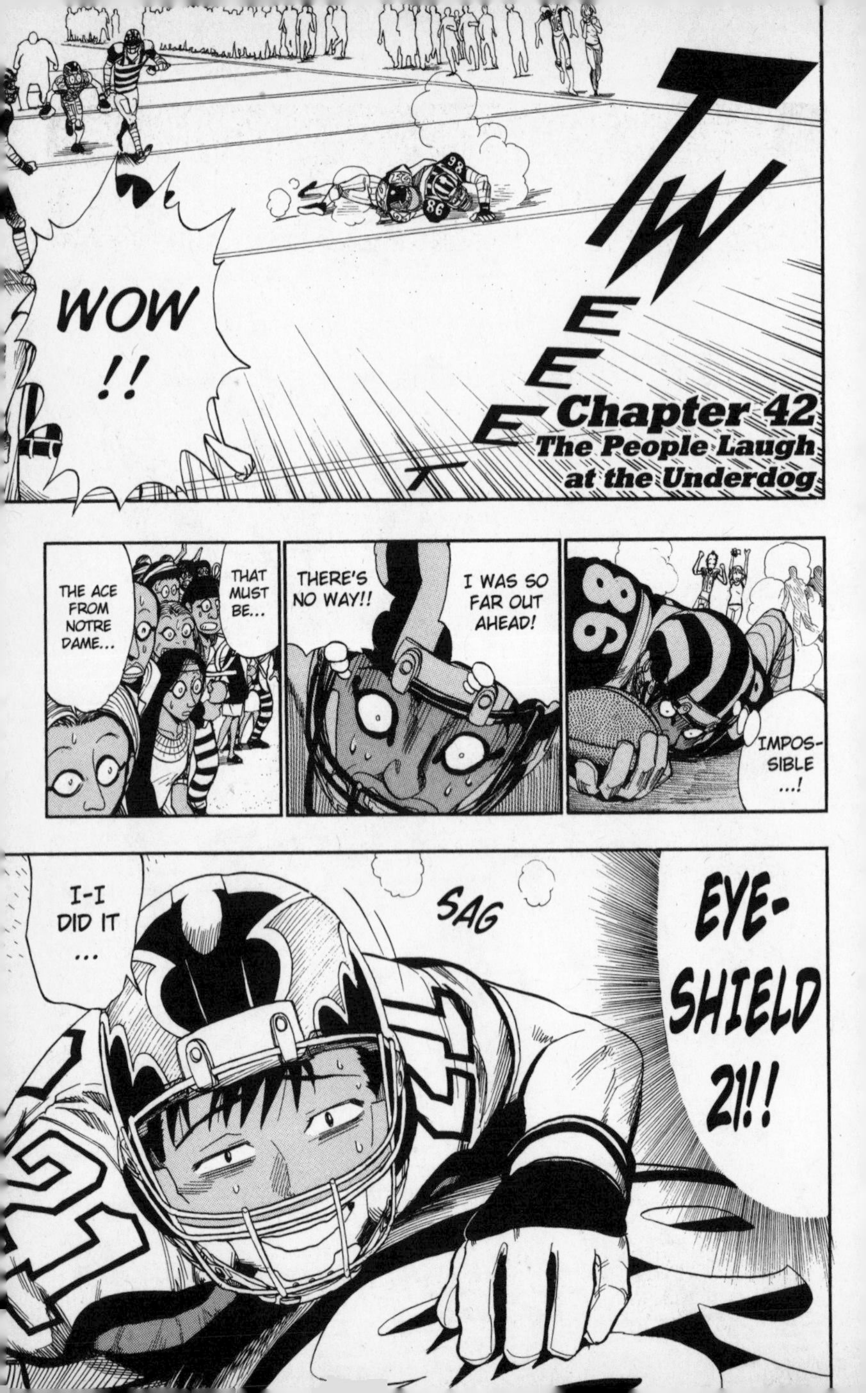
TWEEEEET
Chapter 42
The People Laugh at the Underdog
WOW !!
IMPOS-SIBLE ...!
I WAS SO FAR OUT AHEAD!
THERE'S NO WAY!!
THAT MUST BE...
THE ACE FROM NOTRE DAME...
EYE-SHIELD 21!!
SAG
I-I DID IT ...

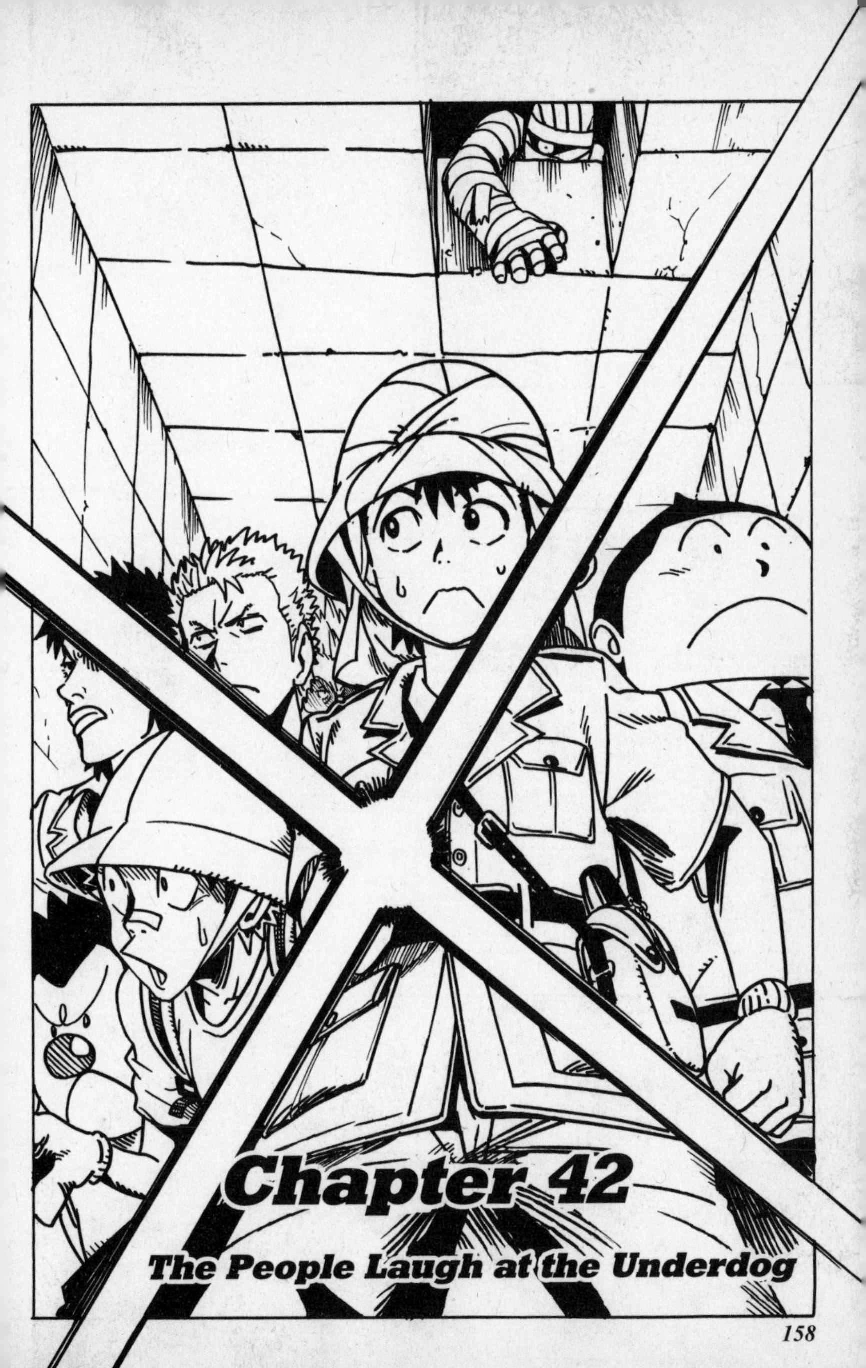

Chapter 42

The People Laugh at the Underdog

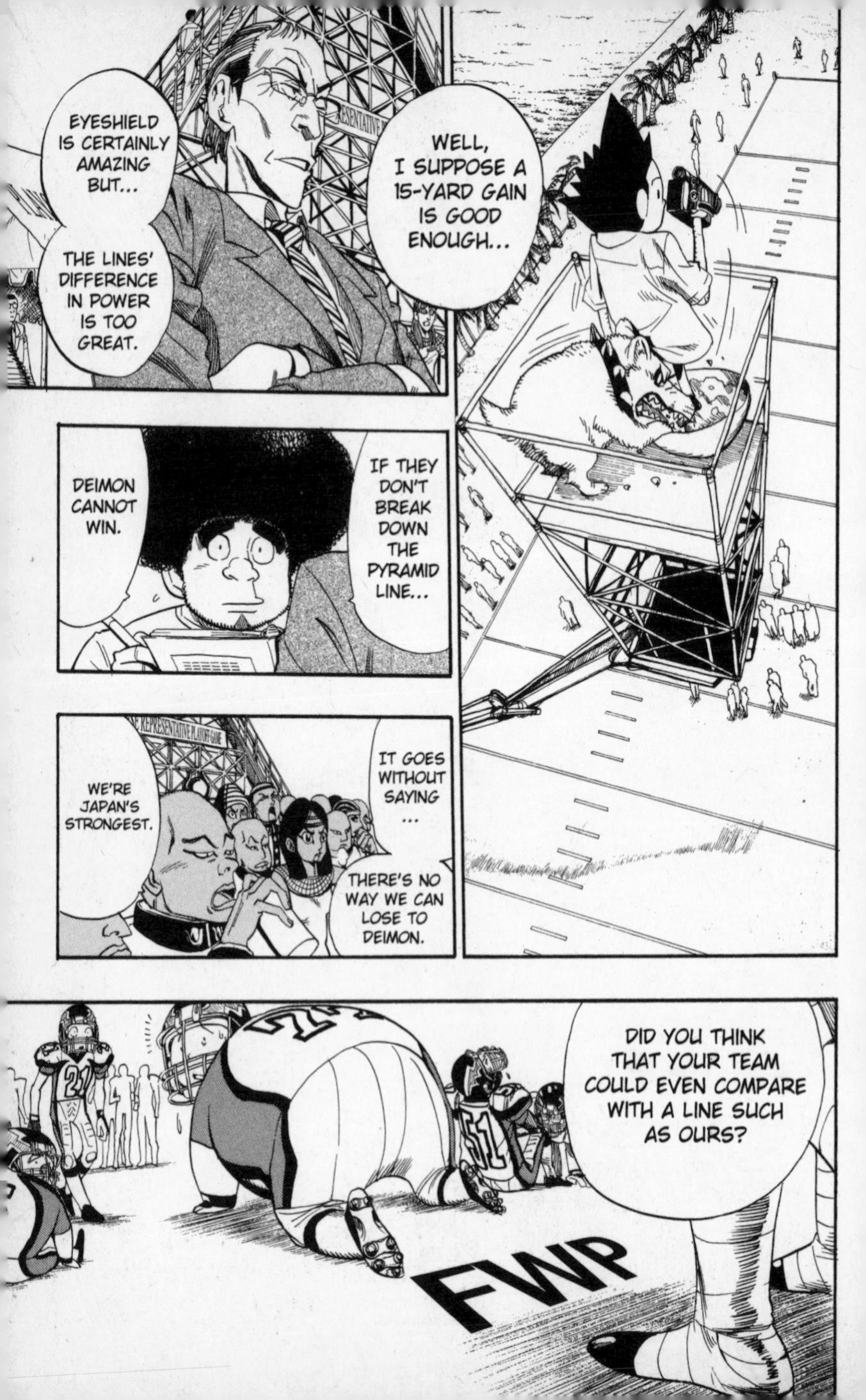
WELL, I SUPPOSE A 15-YARD GAIN IS GOOD ENOUGH...
EYESHIELD IS CERTAINLY AMAZING BUT...
THE LINES' DIFFERENCE IN POWER IS TOO GREAT.
IF THEY DON'T BREAK DOWN THE PYRAMID LINE...
DEIMON CANNOT WIN.
IT GOES WITHOUT SAYING ...
WE'RE JAPAN'S STRONGEST.
THERE'S NO WAY WE CAN LOSE TO DEIMON.
DID YOU THINK THAT YOUR TEAM COULD EVEN COMPARE WITH A LINE SUCH AS OURS?
FWP

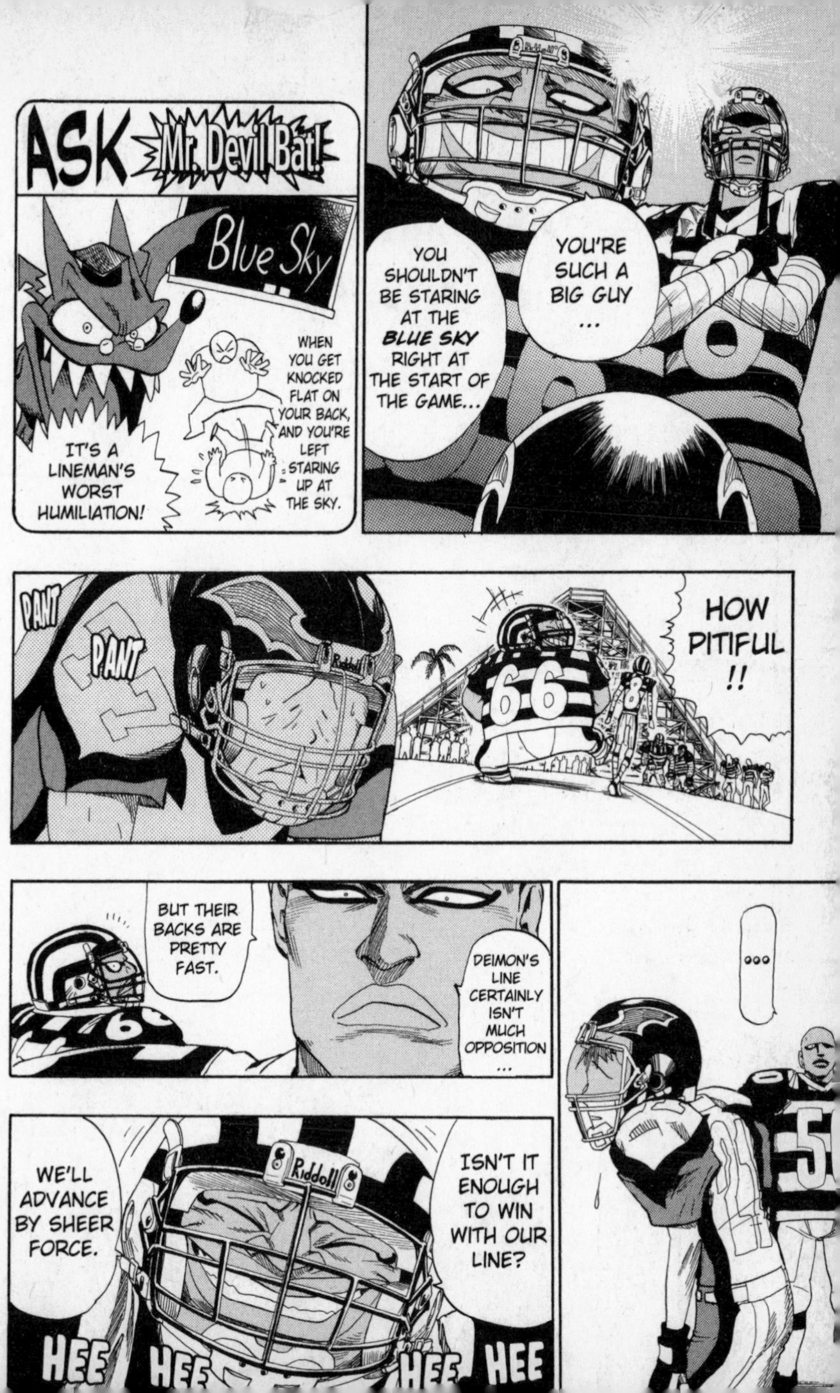
YOU'RE SUCH A BIG GUY ...
YOU SHOULDN'T BE STARING AT THE BLUE SKY RIGHT AT THE START OF THE GAME...
ASK Mr. Devil Bat!
Blue Sky
WHEN YOU GET KNOCKED FLAT ON YOUR BACK, AND YOU'RE LEFT STARING UP AT THE SKY.
IT'S A LINEMAN'S WORST HUMILIATION!
HOW PITIFUL !!
PANT
PANT
...
DEIMON'S LINE CERTAINLY ISN'T MUCH OPPOSITION ...
BUT THEIR BACKS ARE PRETTY FAST.
ISN'T IT ENOUGH TO WIN WITH OUR LINE?
WE'LL ADVANCE BY SHEER FORCE.
HEE HEE HEE HEE

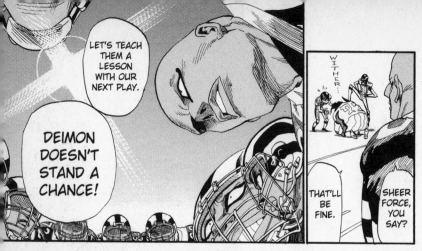

WITHER...
SHEER FORCE, YOU SAY?
THAT'LL BE FINE.
LET'S TEACH THEM A LESSON WITH OUR NEXT PLAY.
DEIMON DOESN'T STAND A CHANCE!
SET!
RAH
RAH
Taiyo Sphinx
56 yards to goal line
THAT DAMN FATTY!
HE'S COMPLETELY LOST HIS NERVE!
HUT!

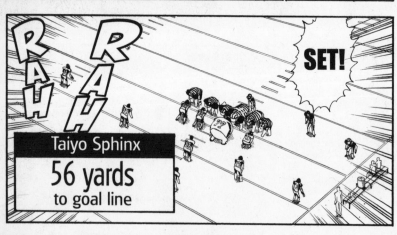

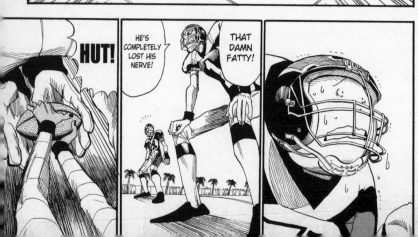

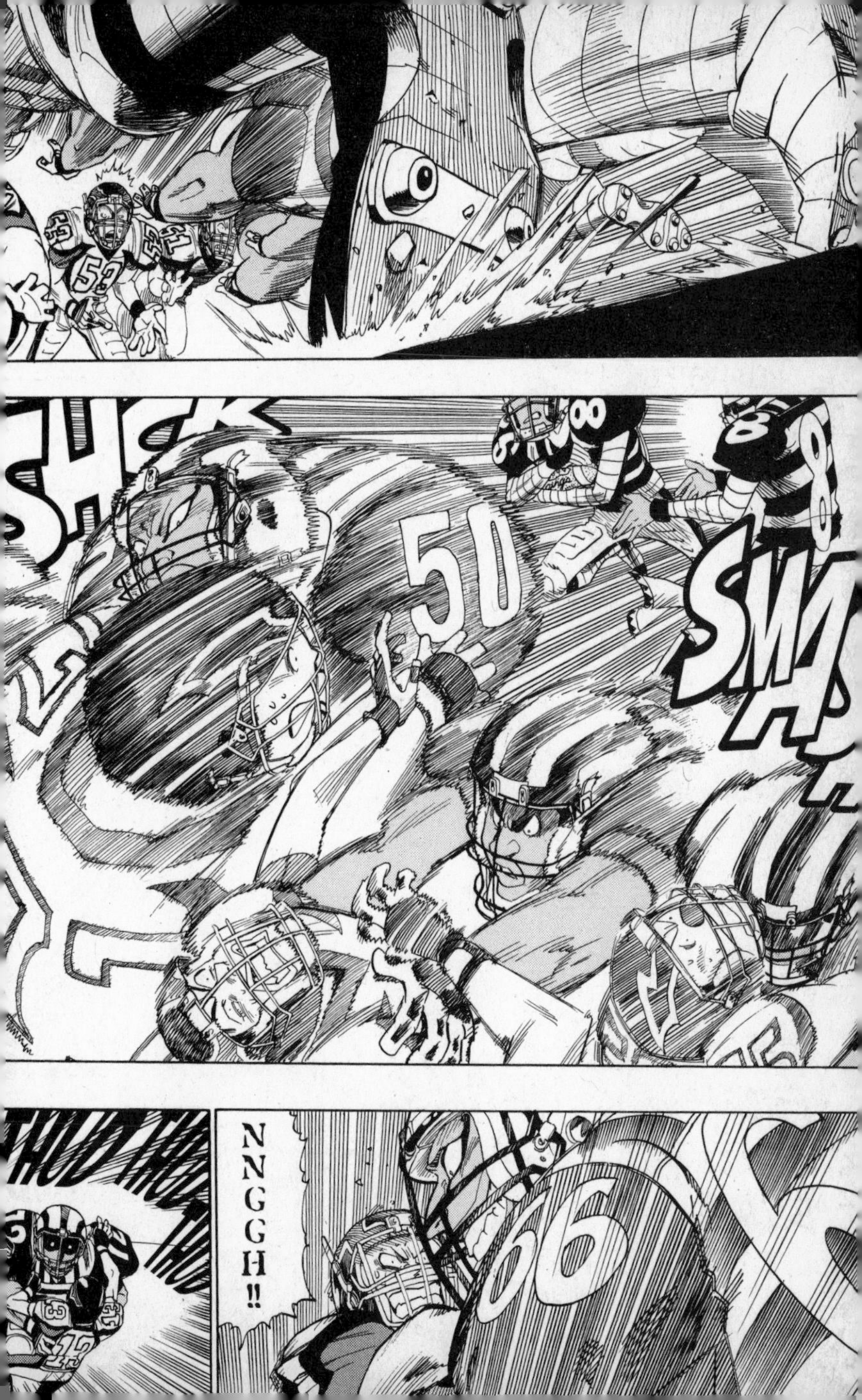
NNGGH!!
THUD THUD THUD

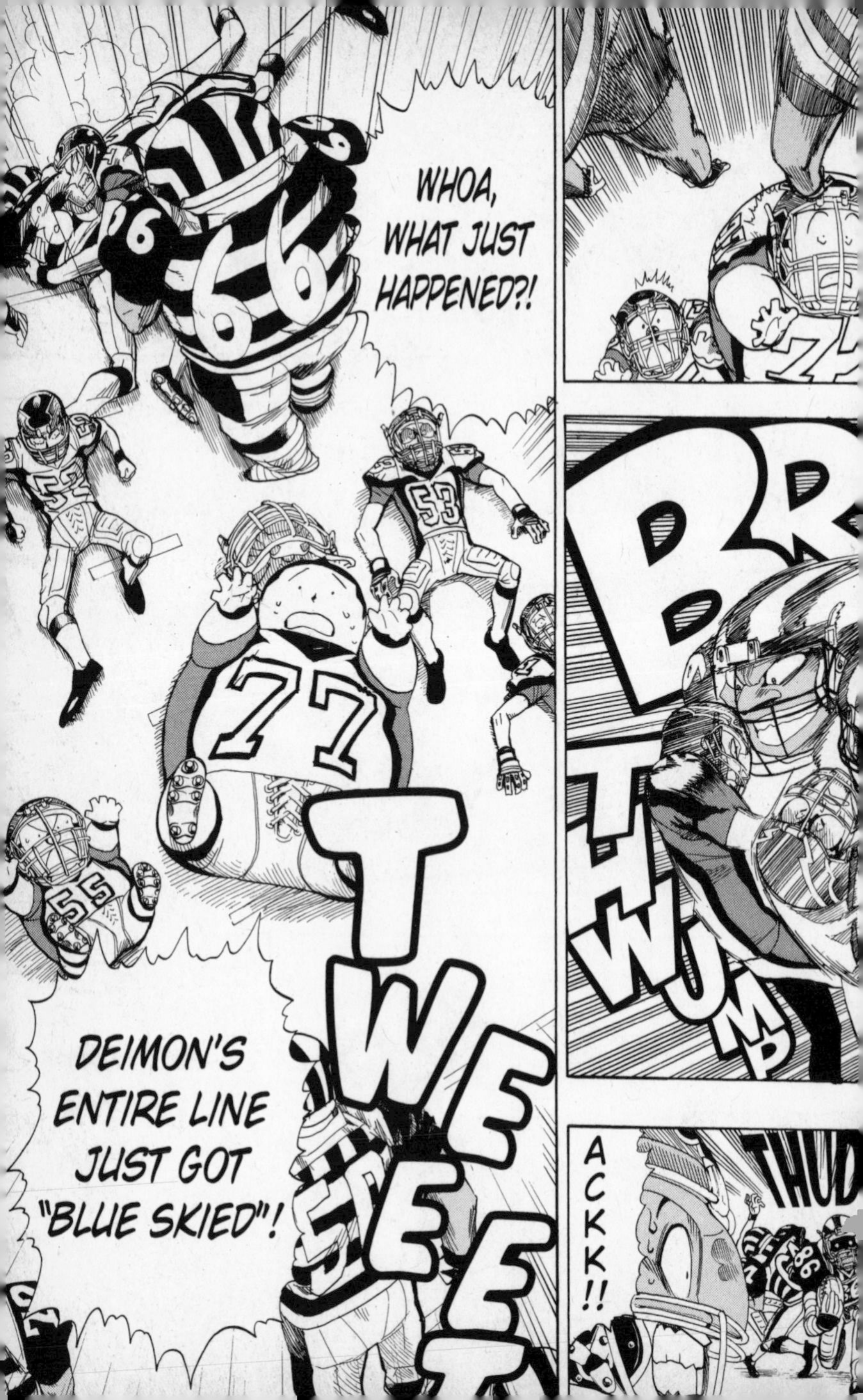
BR
THWUMP
ACKK!!
THUD
WHOA, WHAT JUST HAPPENED?!
DEIMON'S ENTIRE LINE JUST GOT "BLUE SKIED"!
TWEEE

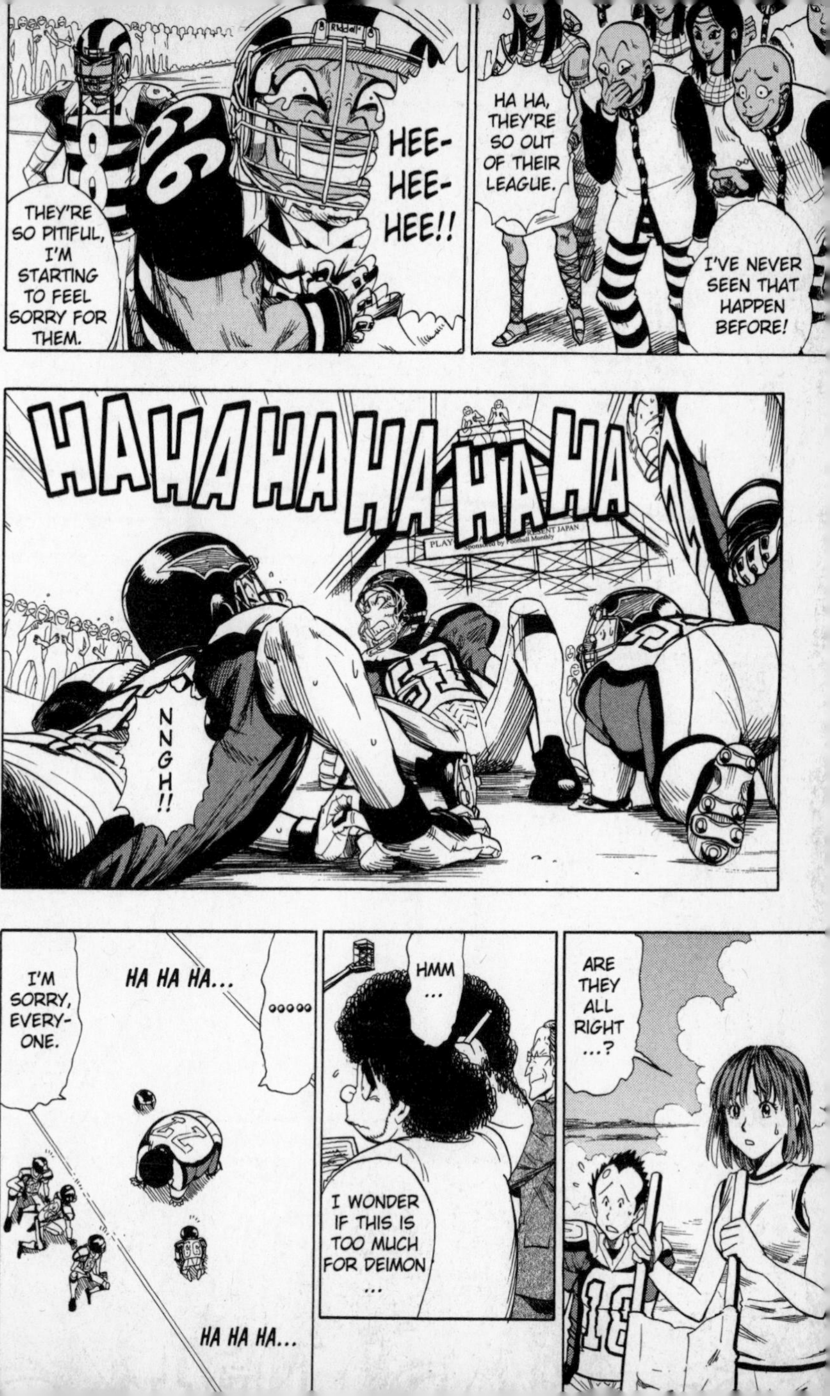
HA HA, THEY'RE SO OUT OF THEIR LEAGUE.
I'VE NEVER SEEN THAT HAPPEN BEFORE!
HEE-HEE-HEE!!
THEY'RE SO PITIFUL, I'M STARTING TO FEEL SORRY FOR THEM.
HAHAHAHAHAHAHA
NNGH!!
ARE THEY ALL RIGHT...?
HMM...
I WONDER IF THIS IS TOO MUCH FOR DEIMON...
.....
HA HA HA...
I'M SORRY, EVERY-ONE.
HA HA HA...

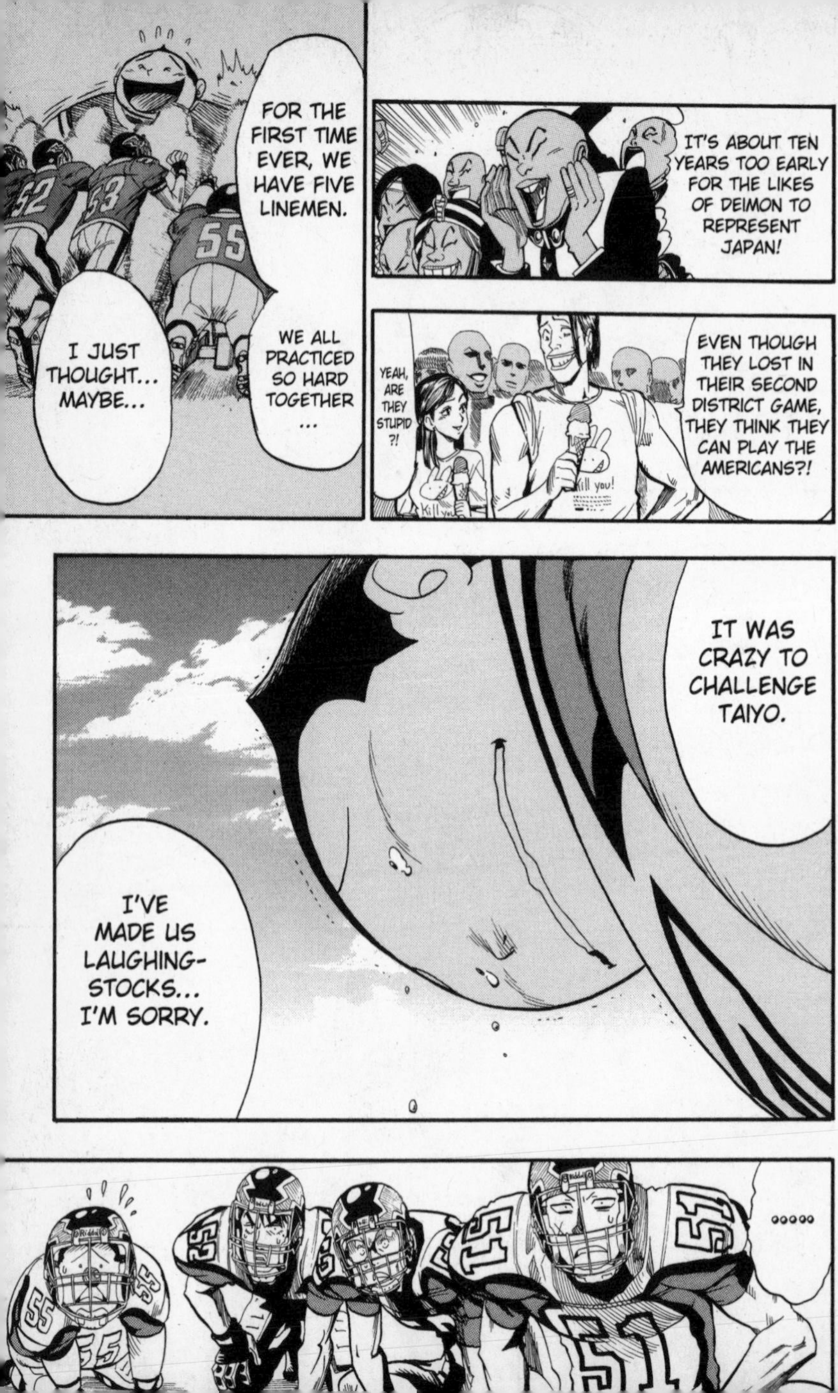
IT'S ABOUT TEN YEARS TOO EARLY FOR THE LIKES OF DEIMON TO REPRESENT JAPAN!
EVEN THOUGH THEY LOST IN THEIR SECOND DISTRICT GAME, THEY THINK THEY CAN PLAY THE AMERICANS?!
YEAH, ARE THEY STUPID ?!
Kill you!
FOR THE FIRST TIME EVER, WE HAVE FIVE LINEMEN.
WE ALL PRACTICED SO HARD TOGETHER ...
I JUST THOUGHT... MAYBE...
IT WAS CRAZY TO CHALLENGE TAIYO.
I'VE MADE US LAUGHING-STOCKS... I'M SORRY.
.....

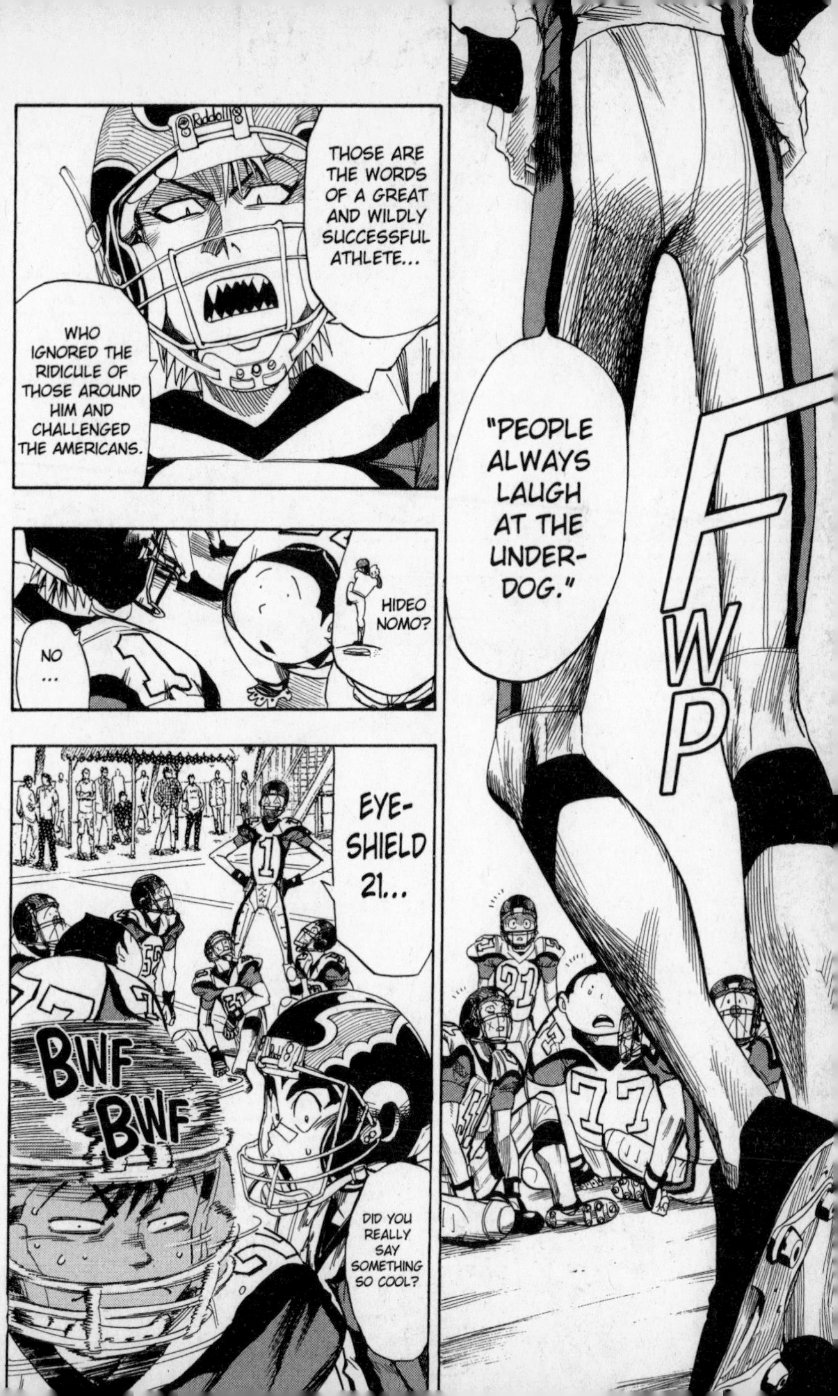
"PEOPLE ALWAYS LAUGH AT THE UNDER-DOG."
FWP
THOSE ARE THE WORDS OF A GREAT AND WILDLY SUCCESSFUL ATHLETE...
WHO IGNORED THE RIDICULE OF THOSE AROUND HIM AND CHALLENGED THE AMERICANS.
HIDEO NOMO?
NO ...
EYE-SHIELD 21...
BWF
BWF
DID YOU REALLY SAY SOMETHING SO COOL?

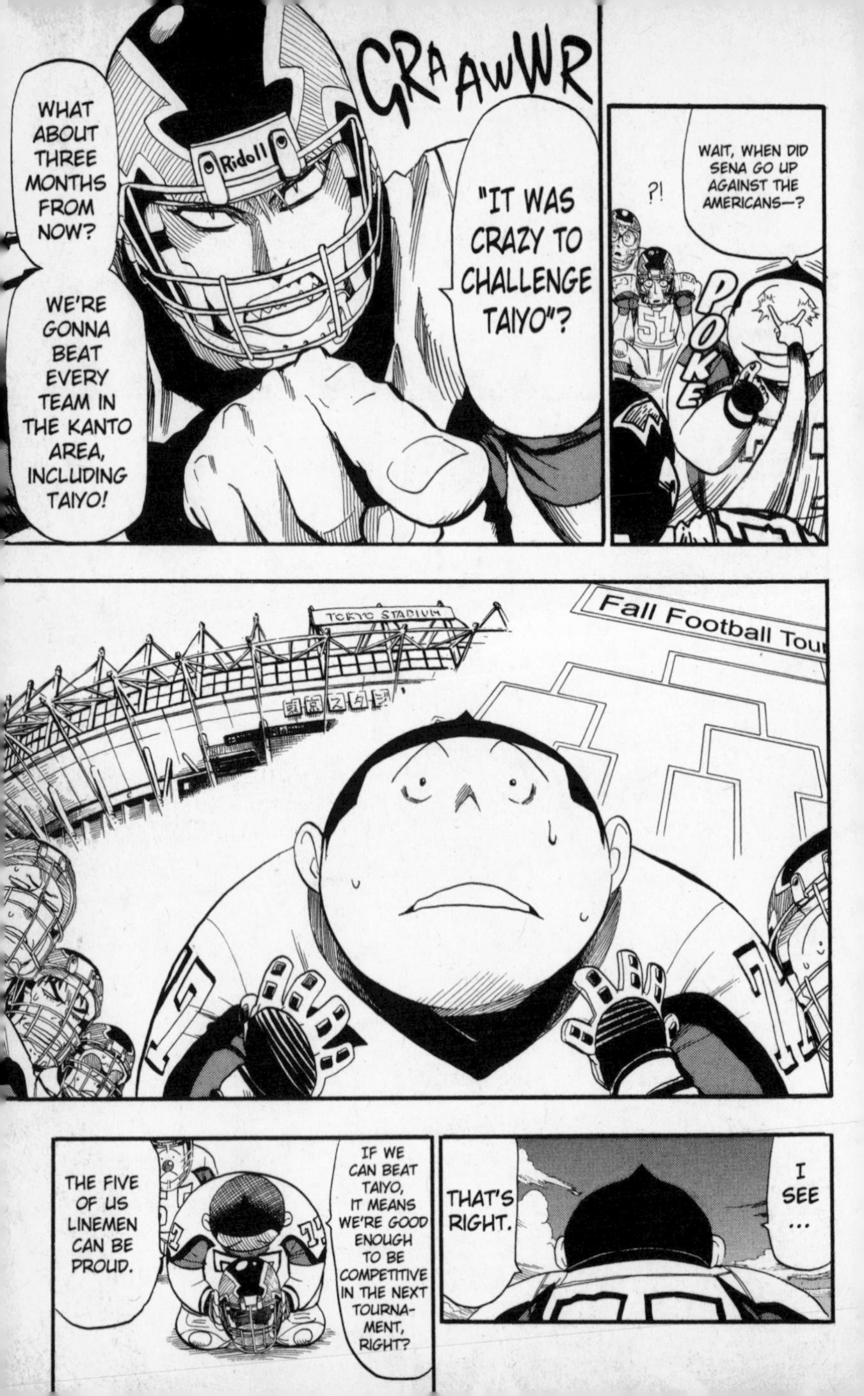
?!
WAIT, WHEN DID SENA GO UP AGAINST THE AMERICANS—?
POKE
GRAAWWR
"IT WAS CRAZY TO CHALLENGE TAIYO"?
WHAT ABOUT THREE MONTHS FROM NOW?
WE'RE GONNA BEAT EVERY TEAM IN THE KANTO AREA, INCLUDING TAIYO!
Fall Football Tou
TOKYO STADIUM
I SEE...
THAT'S RIGHT.
IF WE CAN BEAT TAIYO, IT MEANS WE'RE GOOD ENOUGH TO BE COMPETITIVE IN THE NEXT TOURNAMENT, RIGHT?
THE FIVE OF US LINEMEN CAN BE PROUD.

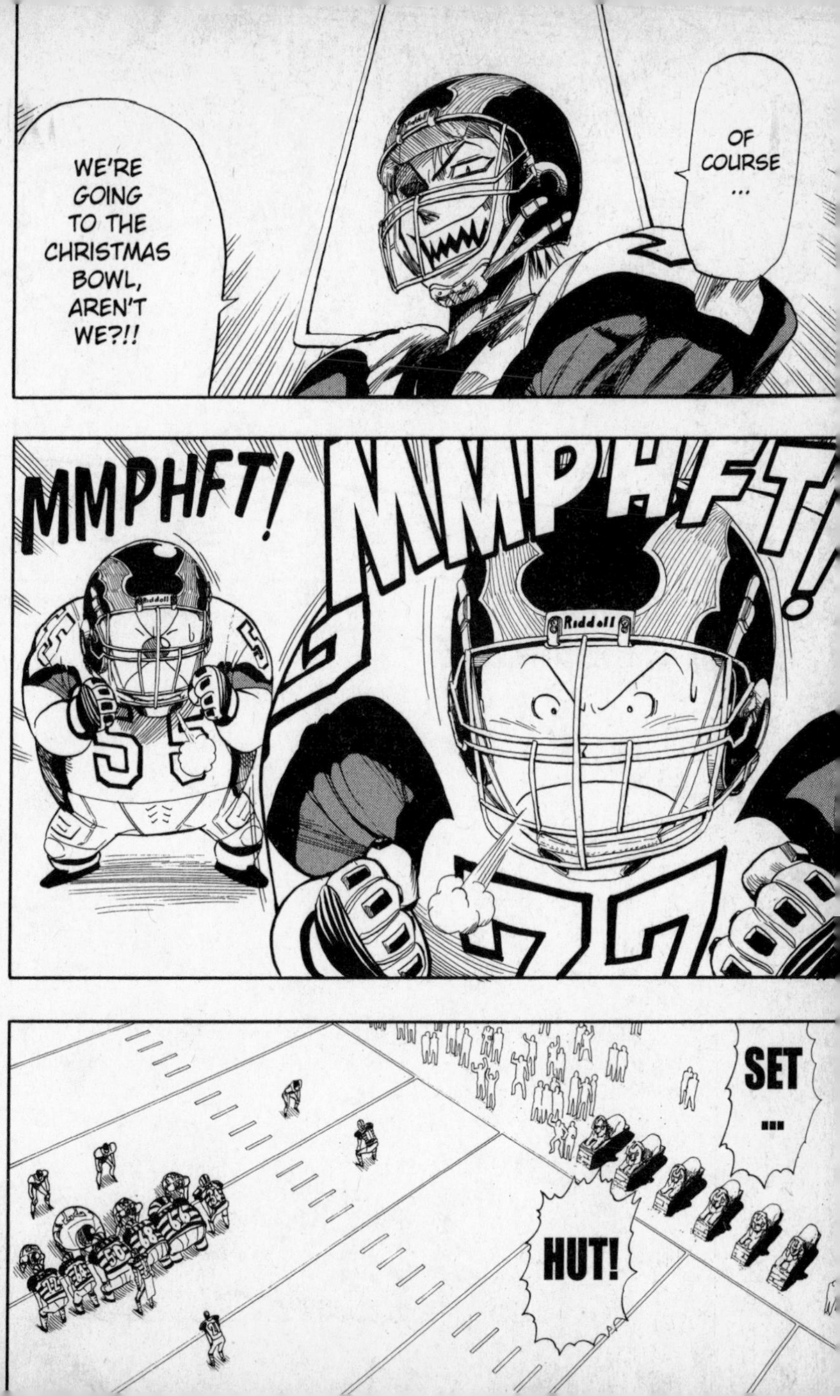
OF COURSE ...
WE'RE GOING TO THE CHRISTMAS BOWL, AREN'T WE?!!
MMPHFT!
MMPHFT!
SET ...
HUT!

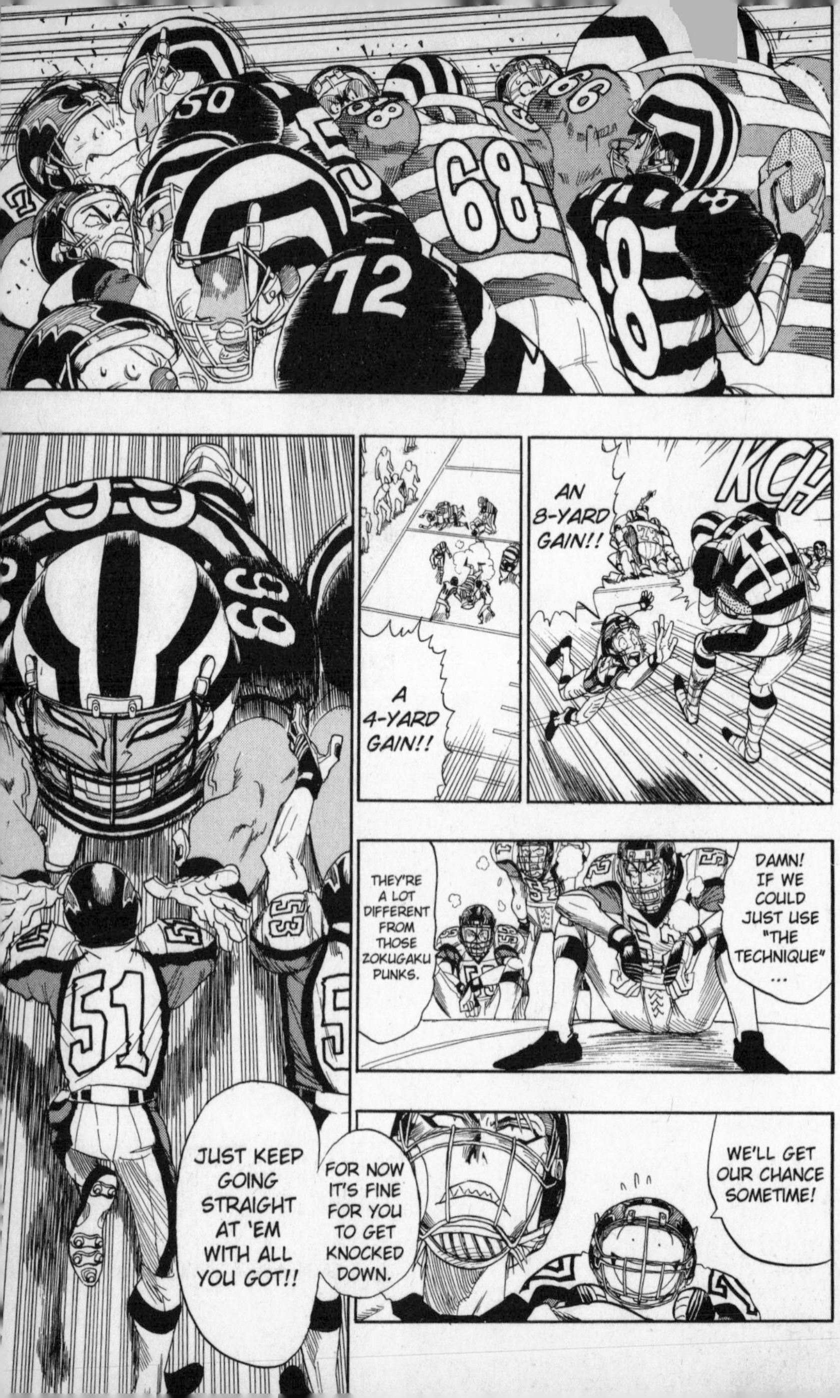
KCH
AN 8-YARD GAIN!!
A 4-YARD GAIN!!
DAMN! IF WE COULD JUST USE "THE TECHNIQUE" ...
THEY'RE A LOT DIFFERENT FROM THOSE ZOKUGAKU PUNKS.
WE'LL GET OUR CHANCE SOMETIME!
FOR NOW IT'S FINE FOR YOU TO GET KNOCKED DOWN.
JUST KEEP GOING STRAIGHT AT 'EM WITH ALL YOU GOT!!

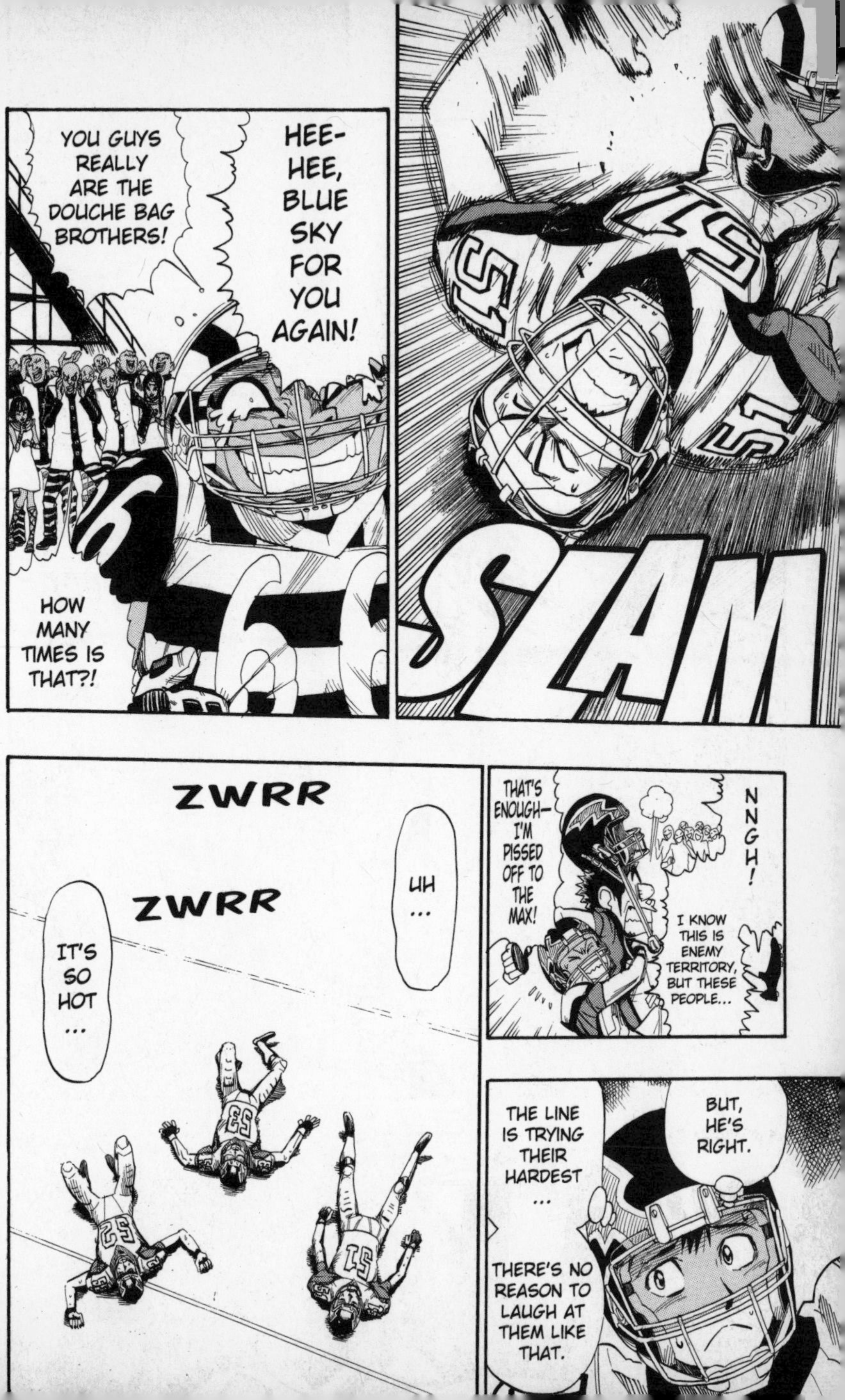
SLAM
HEE-HEE, BLUE SKY FOR YOU AGAIN!
YOU GUYS REALLY ARE THE DOUCHE BAG BROTHERS!
HOW MANY TIMES IS THAT?!
NNGH!
THAT'S ENOUGH— I'M PISSED OFF TO THE MAX!
I KNOW THIS IS ENEMY TERRITORY, BUT THESE PEOPLE...
BUT, HE'S RIGHT.
THE LINE IS TRYING THEIR HARDEST...
THERE'S NO REASON TO LAUGH AT THEM LIKE THAT.
ZWRR
UH...
ZWRR
IT'S SO HOT...

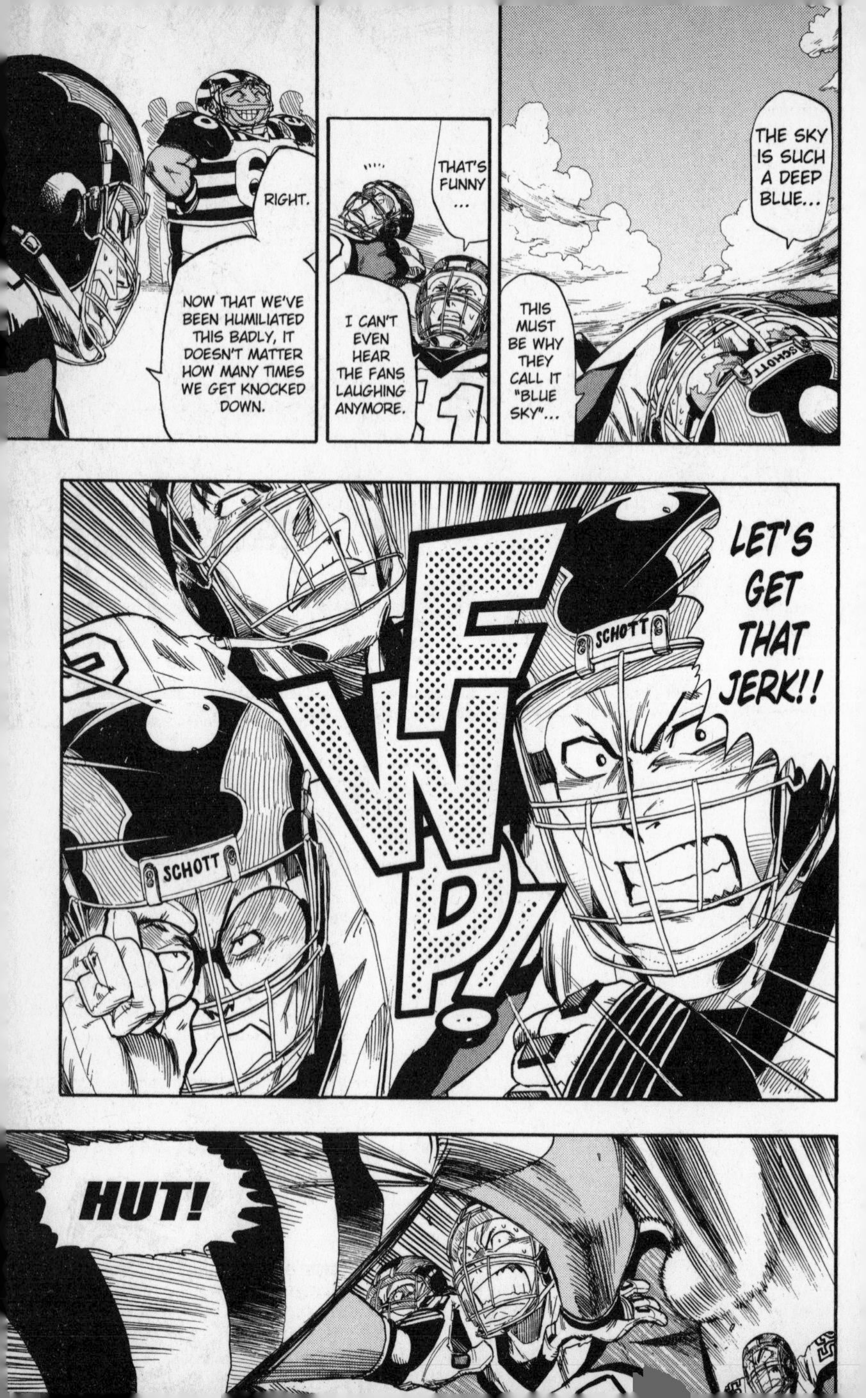
THE SKY IS SUCH A DEEP BLUE...
THIS MUST BE WHY THEY CALL IT "BLUE SKY"...
THAT'S FUNNY...
I CAN'T EVEN HEAR THE FANS LAUGHING ANYMORE.
RIGHT.
NOW THAT WE'VE BEEN HUMILIATED THIS BADLY, IT DOESN'T MATTER HOW MANY TIMES WE GET KNOCKED DOWN.
LET'S GET THAT JERK!!
FWP!
HUT!

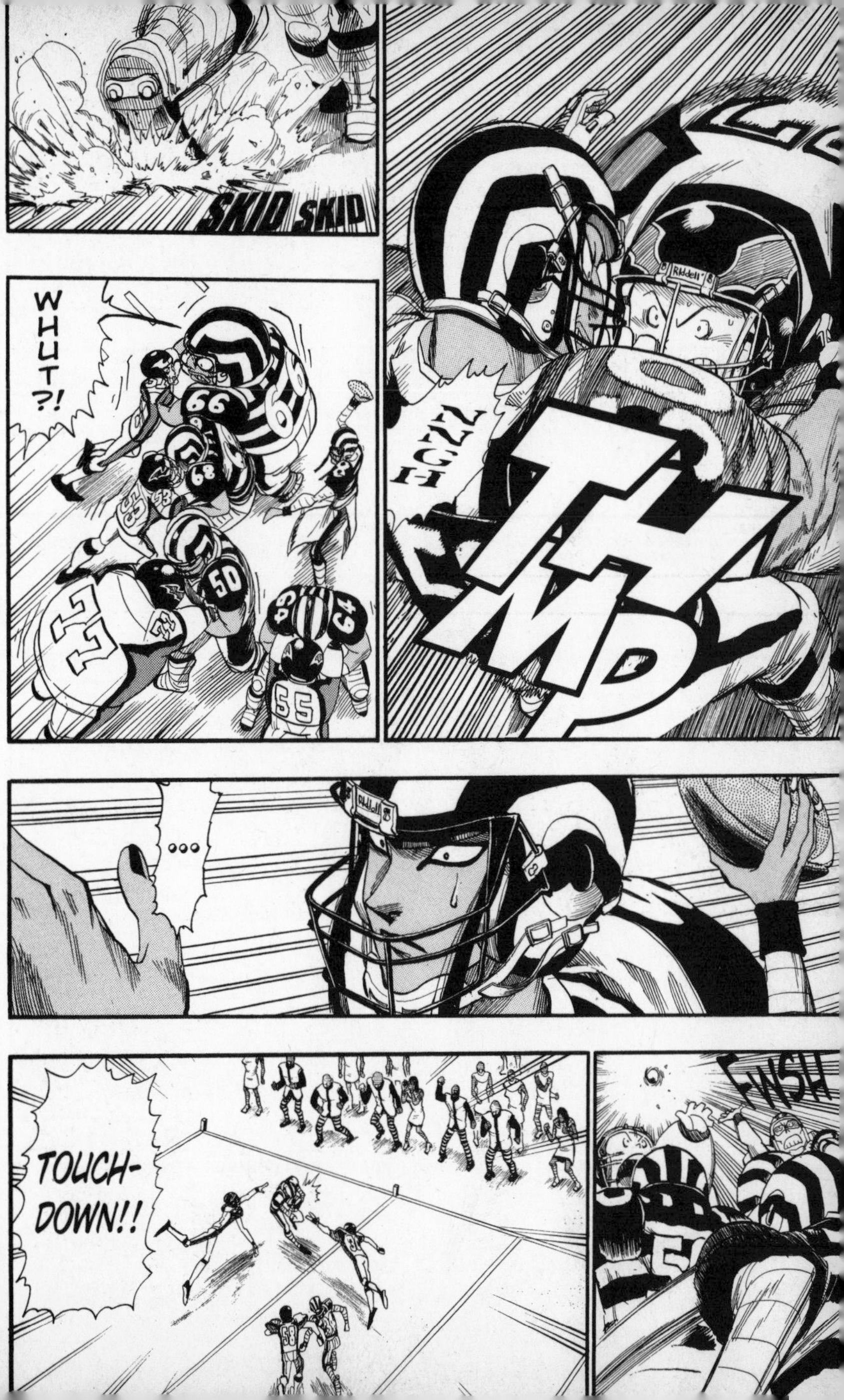
NNGH
THMP
SKID SKIP
WHUT?!
...
FWSH
TOUCH-DOWN!!

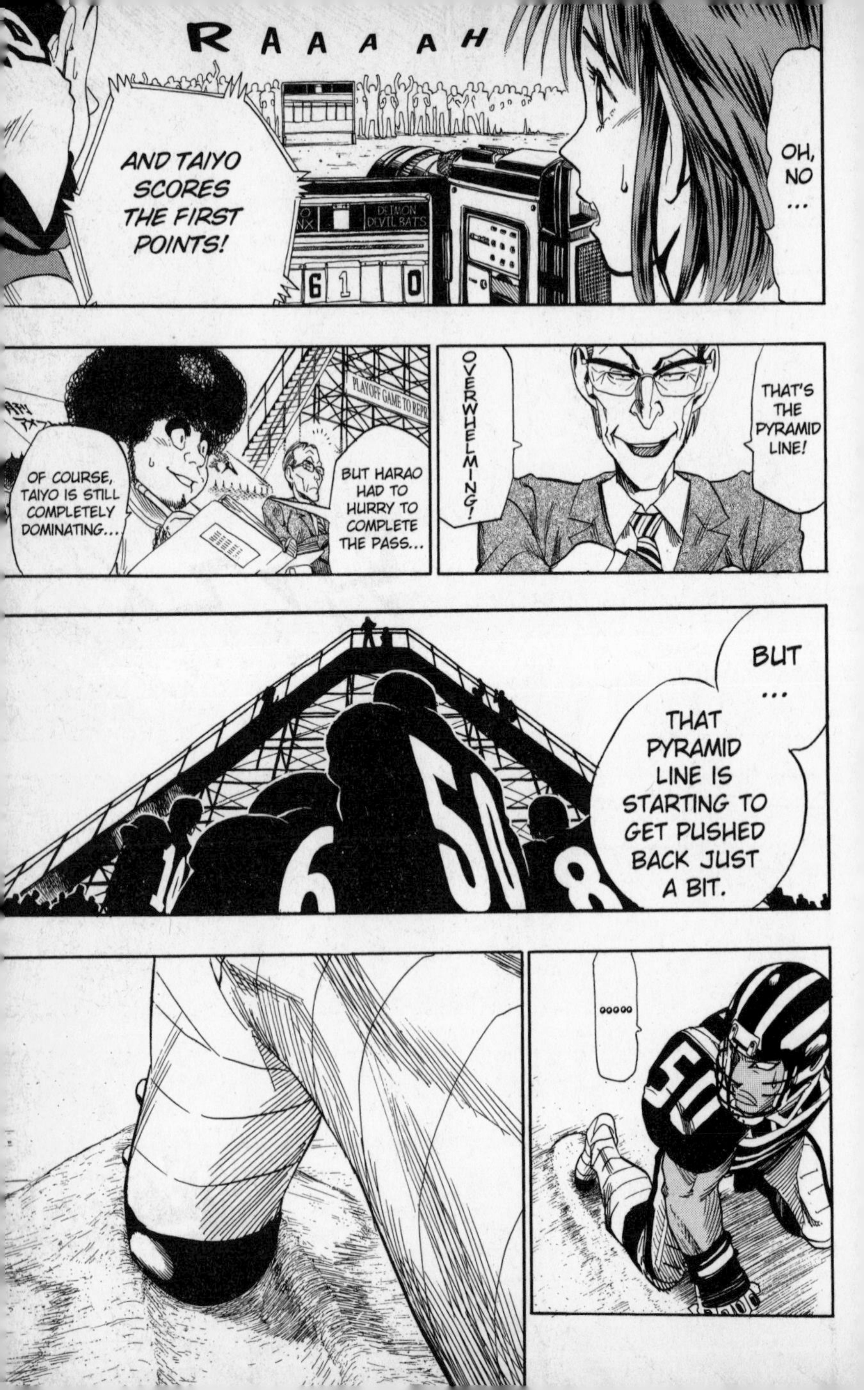
RAAAAH
OH, NO ...
AND TAIYO SCORES THE FIRST POINTS!
DEIMON DEVIL BATS
THAT'S THE PYRAMID LINE!
OVERWHELMING!
BUT HARAO HAD TO HURRY TO COMPLETE THE PASS...
OF COURSE, TAIYO IS STILL COMPLETELY DOMINATING...
BUT ...
THAT PYRAMID LINE IS STARTING TO GET PUSHED BACK JUST A BIT.
.....

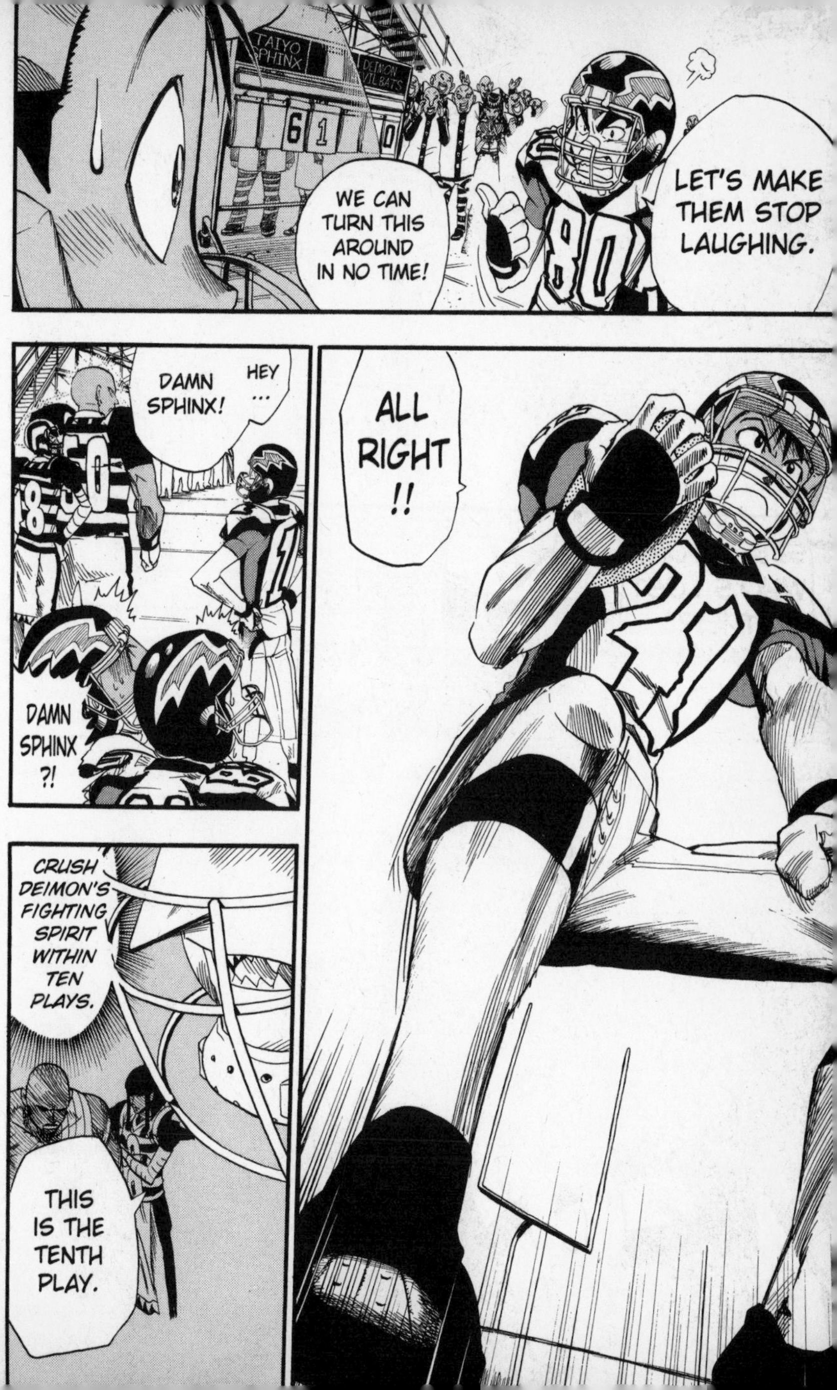
TAIYO SPHINX
LET'S MAKE THEM STOP LAUGHING.
WE CAN TURN THIS AROUND IN NO TIME!
ALL RIGHT!!
HEY...
DAMN SPHINX!
DAMN SPHINX?!
CRUSH DEIMON'S FIGHTING SPIRIT WITHIN TEN PLAYS.
THIS IS THE TENTH PLAY.

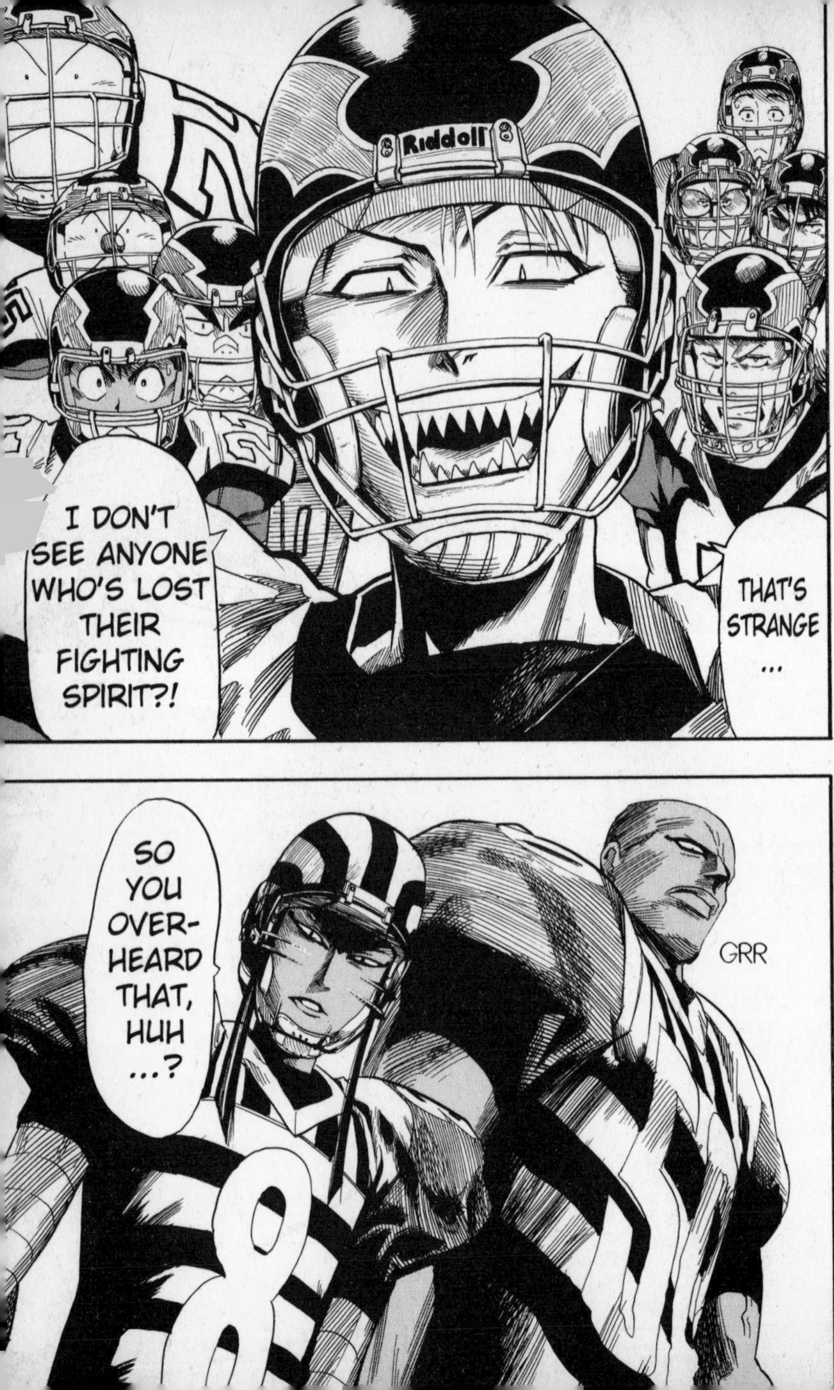
THAT'S STRANGE ...
I DON'T SEE ANYONE WHO'S LOST THEIR FIGHTING SPIRIT?!
GRR
SO YOU OVER-HEARD THAT, HUH ...?

DEIMON HIGH SCHOOL
SURPRISE SCHOOL BAG INSPECTION

Daikichi Komusubi

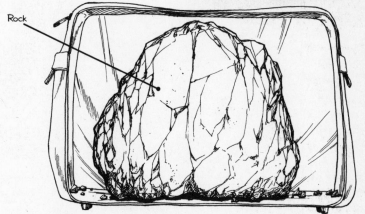

Rock

TR-TRAINING!!

...I SEE...

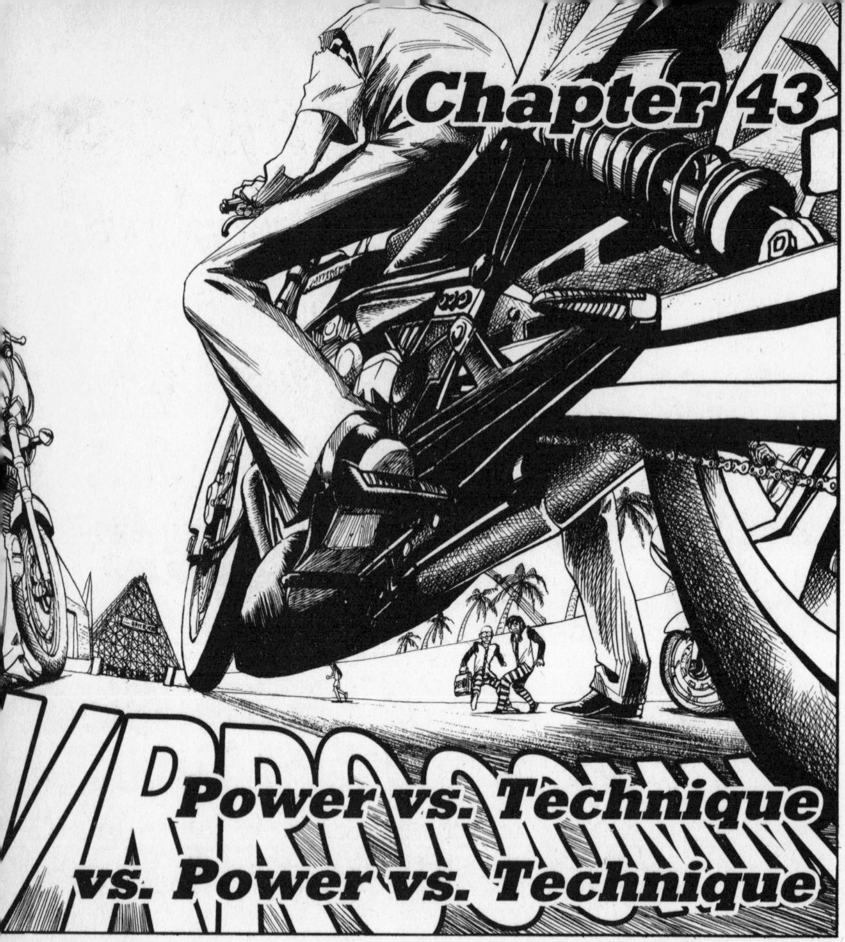
Chapter 43
Power vs. Technique vs. Power vs. Technique

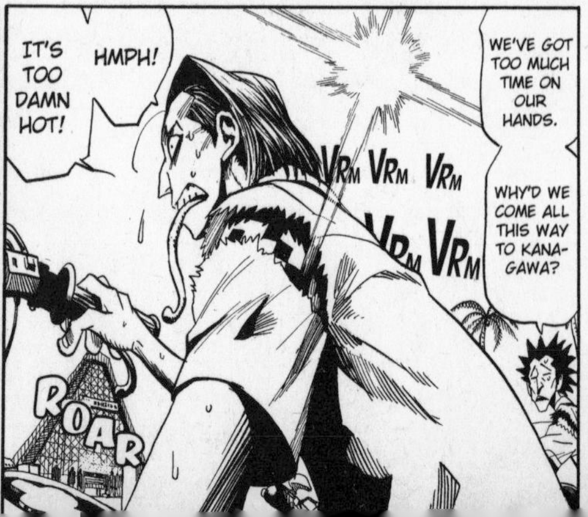
WE'VE GOT TOO MUCH TIME ON OUR HANDS.
WHY'D WE COME ALL THIS WAY TO KANAGAWA?
HMPH!
IT'S TOO DAMN HOT!
VRM VRM VRM
VRM VRM
ROAR

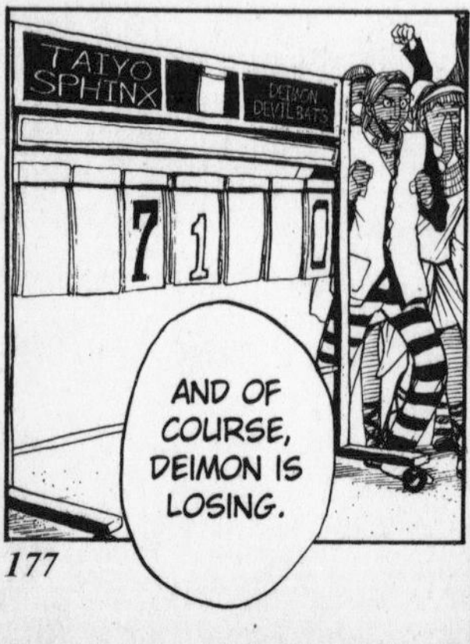
TAIYO SPHINX
DEIMON DEVILBATS
7 1 0
AND OF COURSE, DEIMON IS LOSING.

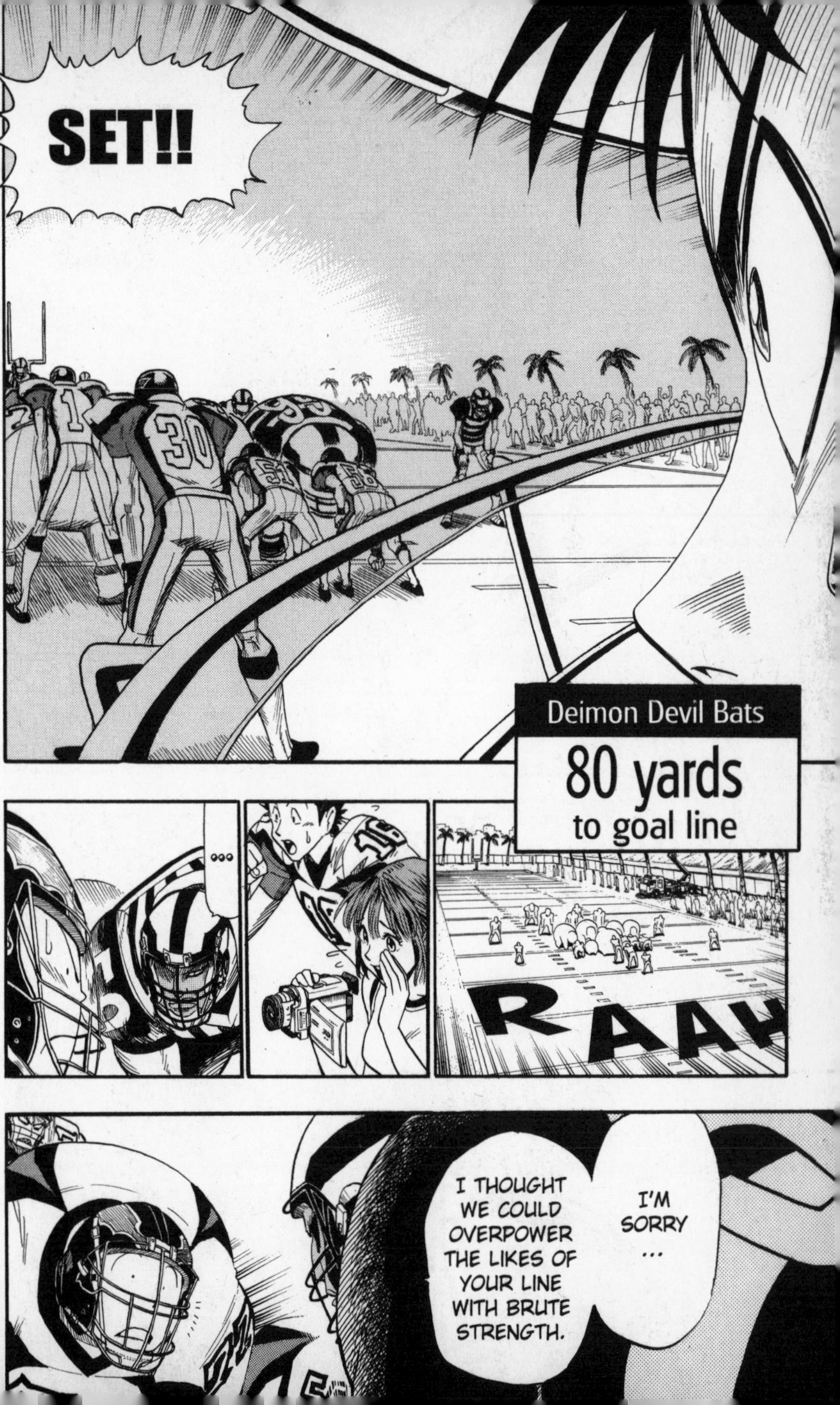
SET!!
Deimon Devil Bats
80 yards
to goal line
RAAH
...
I'M SORRY ...
I THOUGHT WE COULD OVERPOWER THE LIKES OF YOUR LINE WITH BRUTE STRENGTH.

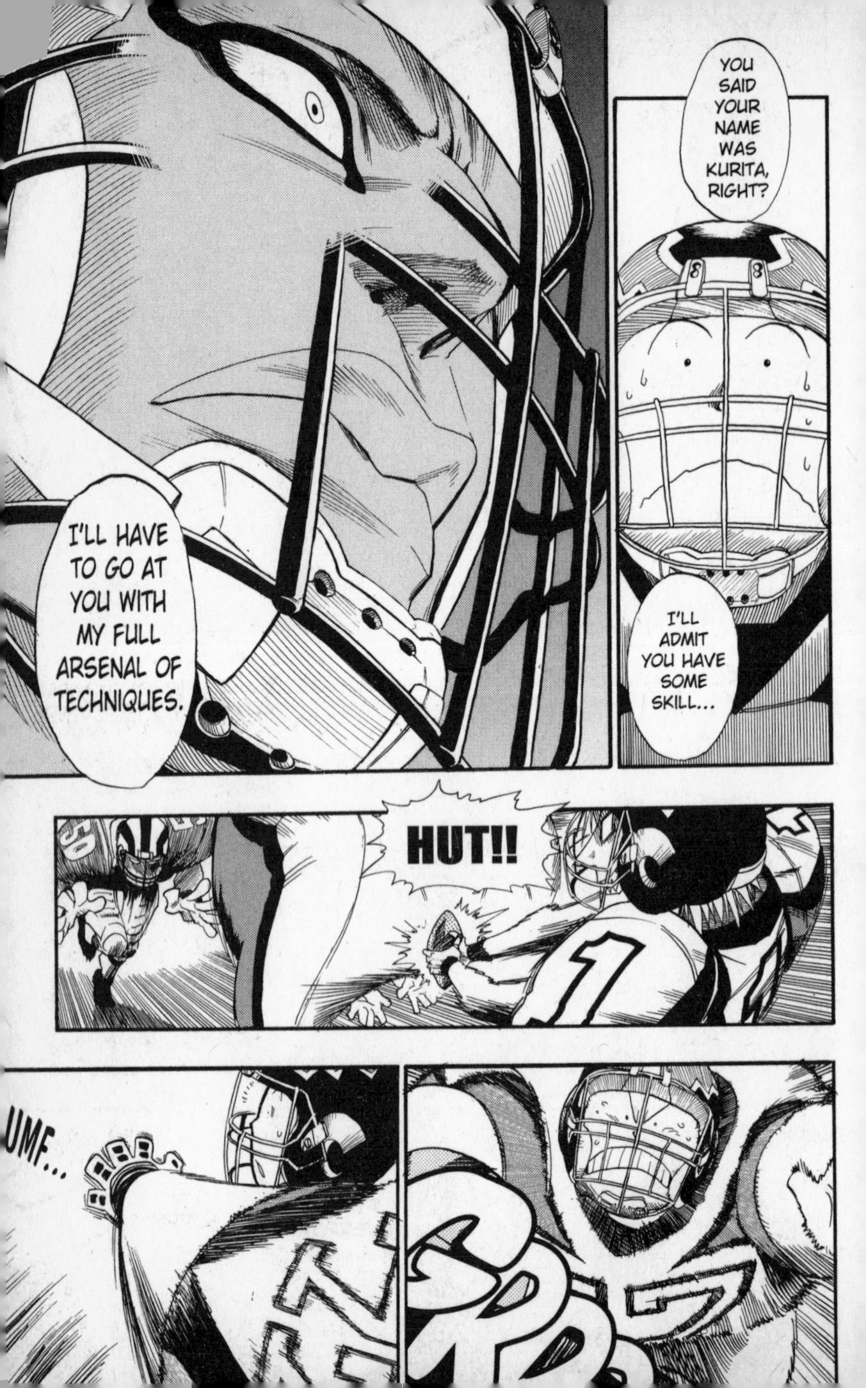
YOU SAID YOUR NAME WAS KURITA, RIGHT?
I'LL ADMIT YOU HAVE SOME SKILL...
I'LL HAVE TO GO AT YOU WITH MY FULL ARSENAL OF TECHNIQUES.
HUT!!
UMF...

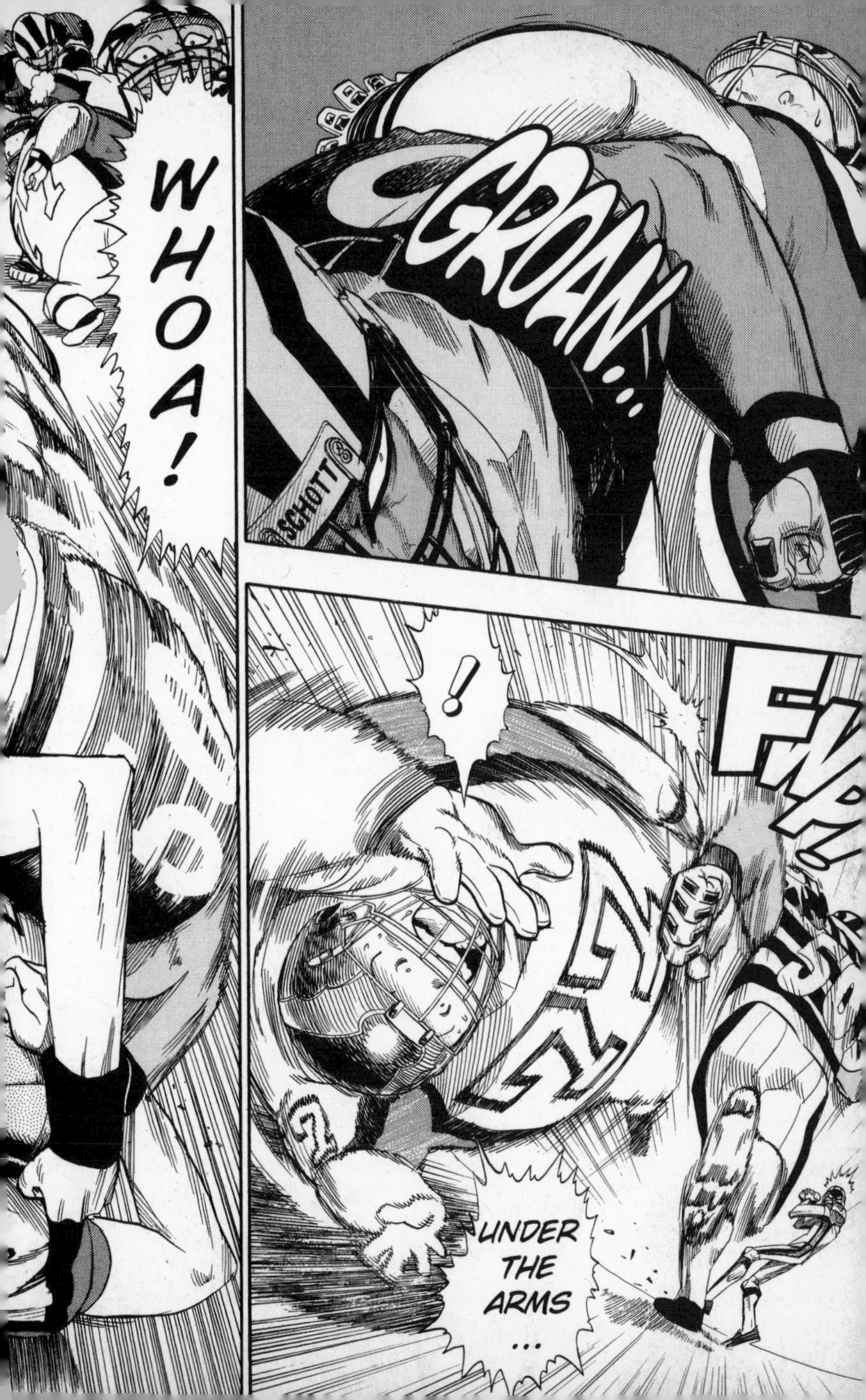
GROAN...
!
FWP!
UNDER THE ARMS ...
SCHOTT
WHOA!

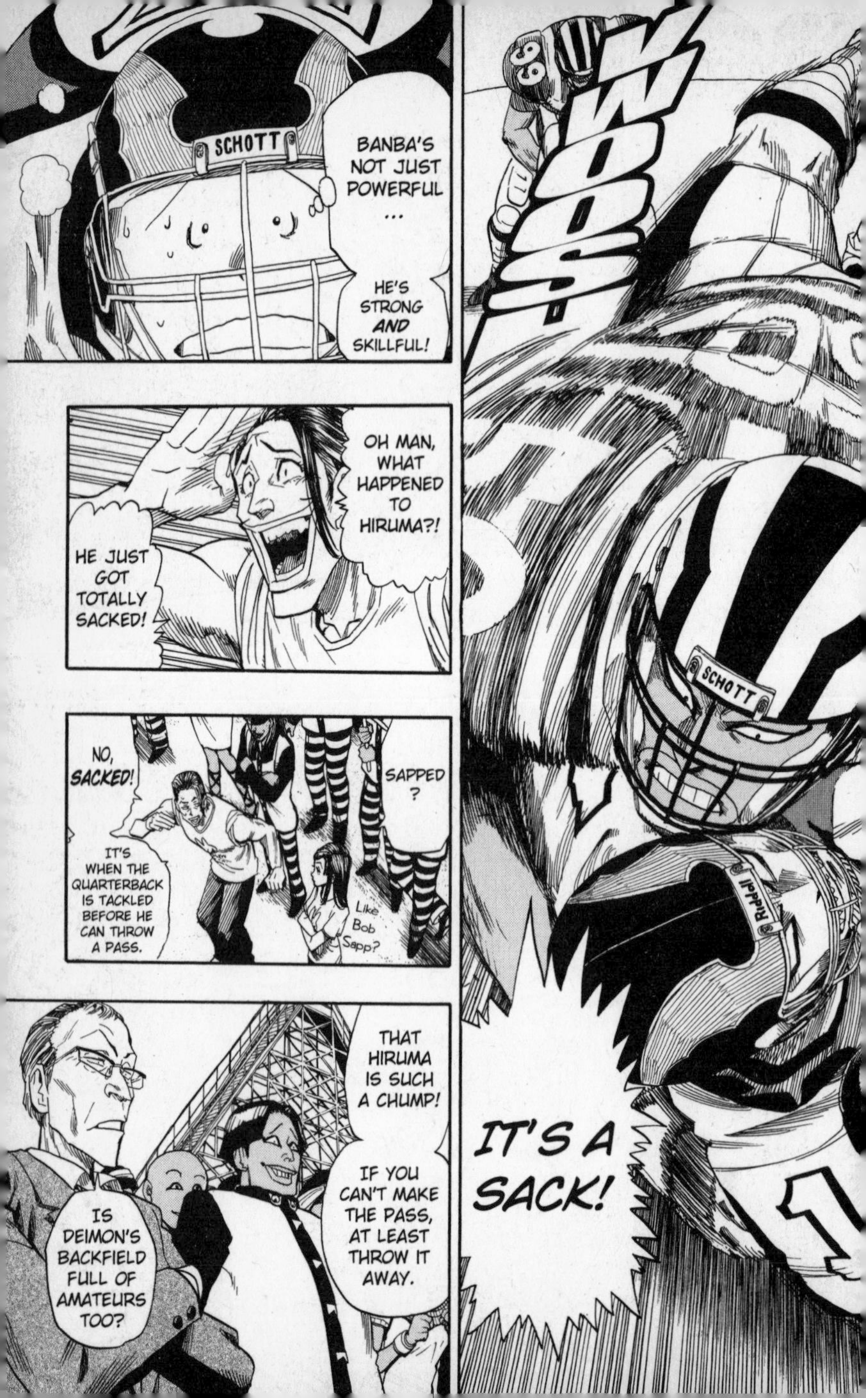
IT'S A SACK!
BANBA'S NOT JUST POWERFUL ...
HE'S STRONG AND SKILLFUL!
OH MAN, WHAT HAPPENED TO HIRUMA?!
HE JUST GOT TOTALLY SACKED!
SAPPED?
NO, SACKED!
IT'S WHEN THE QUARTERBACK IS TACKLED BEFORE HE CAN THROW A PASS.
Like Bob Sapp?
THAT HIRUMA IS SUCH A CHUMP!
IF YOU CAN'T MAKE THE PASS, AT LEAST THROW IT AWAY.
IS DEIMON'S BACKFIELD FULL OF AMATEURS TOO?

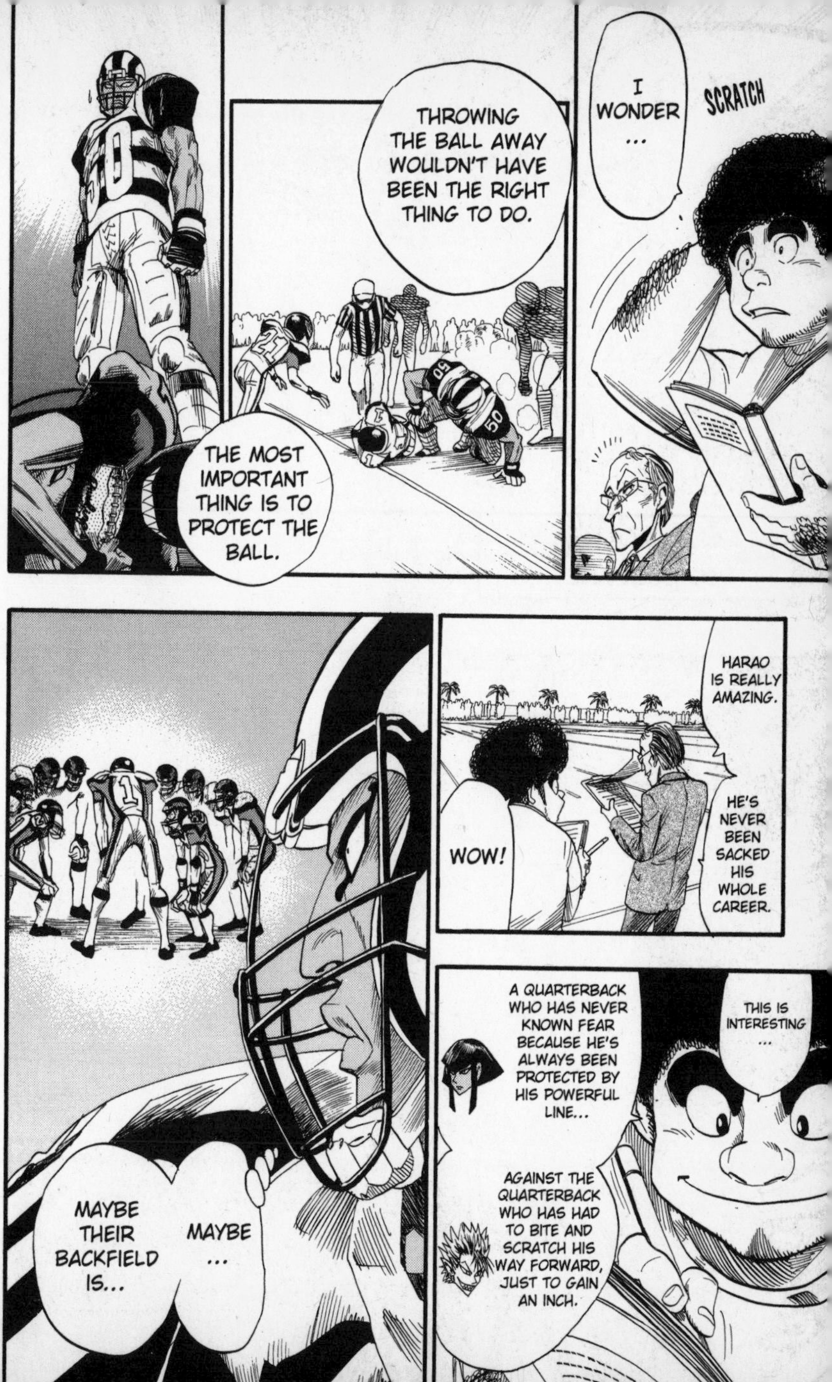
I WONDER ...
SCRATCH
THROWING THE BALL AWAY WOULDN'T HAVE BEEN THE RIGHT THING TO DO.
THE MOST IMPORTANT THING IS TO PROTECT THE BALL.
HARAO IS REALLY AMAZING.
HE'S NEVER BEEN SACKED HIS WHOLE CAREER.
WOW!
THIS IS INTERESTING ...
A QUARTERBACK WHO HAS NEVER KNOWN FEAR BECAUSE HE'S ALWAYS BEEN PROTECTED BY HIS POWERFUL LINE...
AGAINST THE QUARTERBACK WHO HAS HAD TO BITE AND SCRATCH HIS WAY FORWARD, JUST TO GAIN AN INCH.
MAYBE ...
MAYBE THEIR BACKFIELD IS...

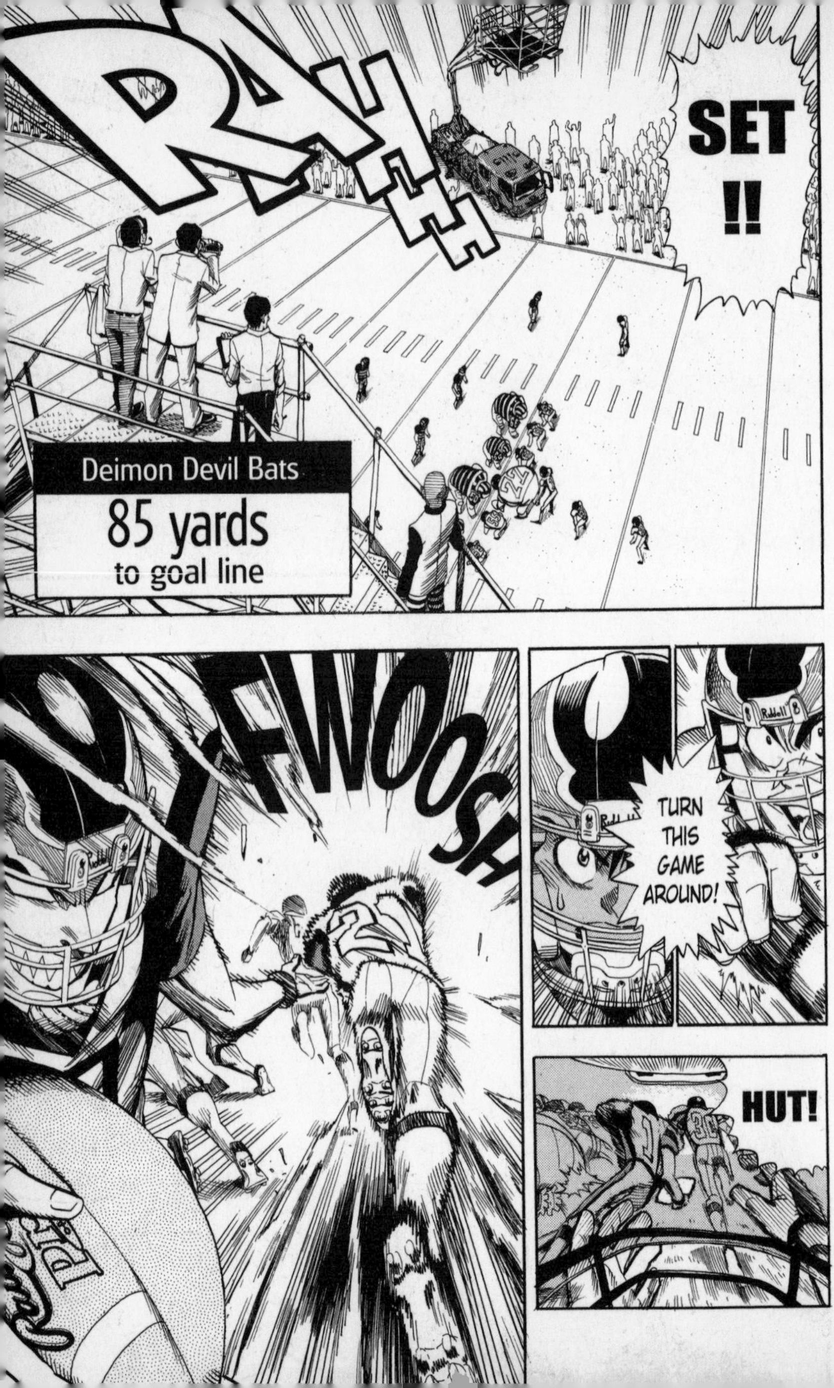
SET!!
RAHHH
Deimon Devil Bats
85 yards to goal line
TURN THIS GAME AROUND!
HUT!
FWOOSH

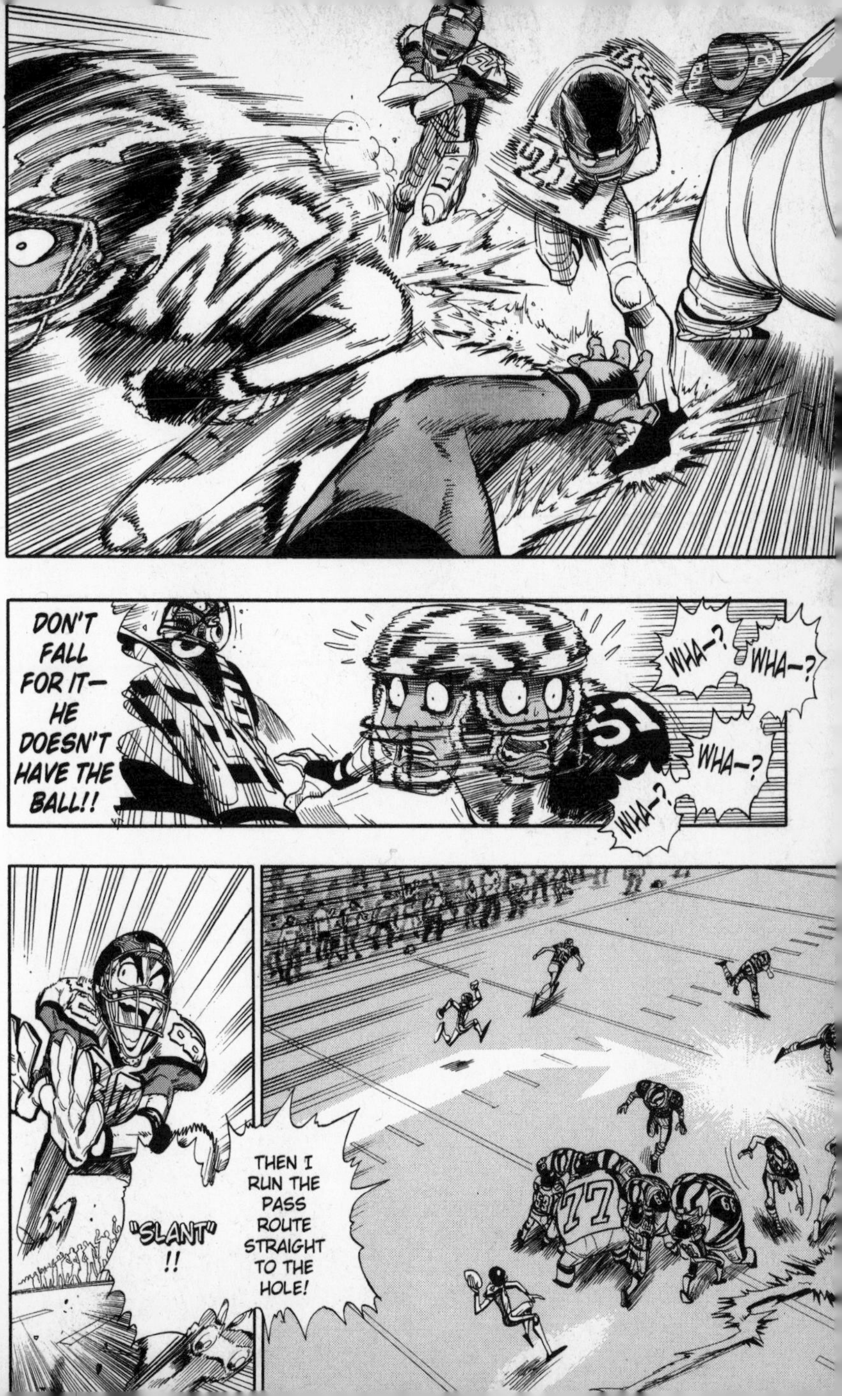
WHA-?
WHA-?
WHA-?
WHA-?
DON'T FALL FOR IT— HE DOESN'T HAVE THE BALL!!
THEN I RUN THE PASS ROUTE STRAIGHT TO THE HOLE!
"SLANT" !!

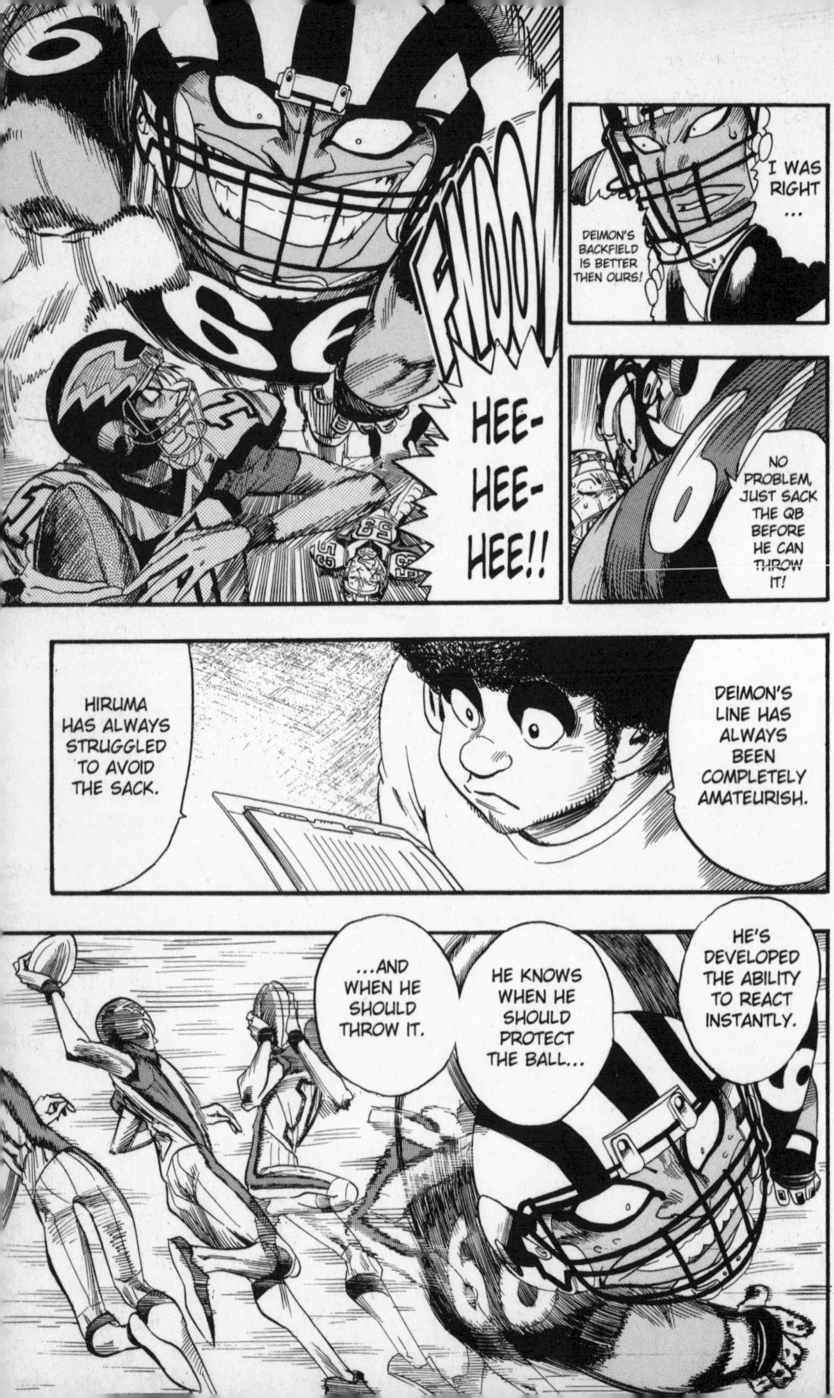
I WAS RIGHT ...
DEIMON'S BACKFIELD IS BETTER THEN OURS!
NO PROBLEM, JUST SACK THE QB BEFORE HE CAN THROW IT!
HEE-HEE-HEE!!
DEIMON'S LINE HAS ALWAYS BEEN COMPLETELY AMATEURISH.
HIRUMA HAS ALWAYS STRUGGLED TO AVOID THE SACK.
HE'S DEVELOPED THE ABILITY TO REACT INSTANTLY.
HE KNOWS WHEN HE SHOULD PROTECT THE BALL...
...AND WHEN HE SHOULD THROW IT.

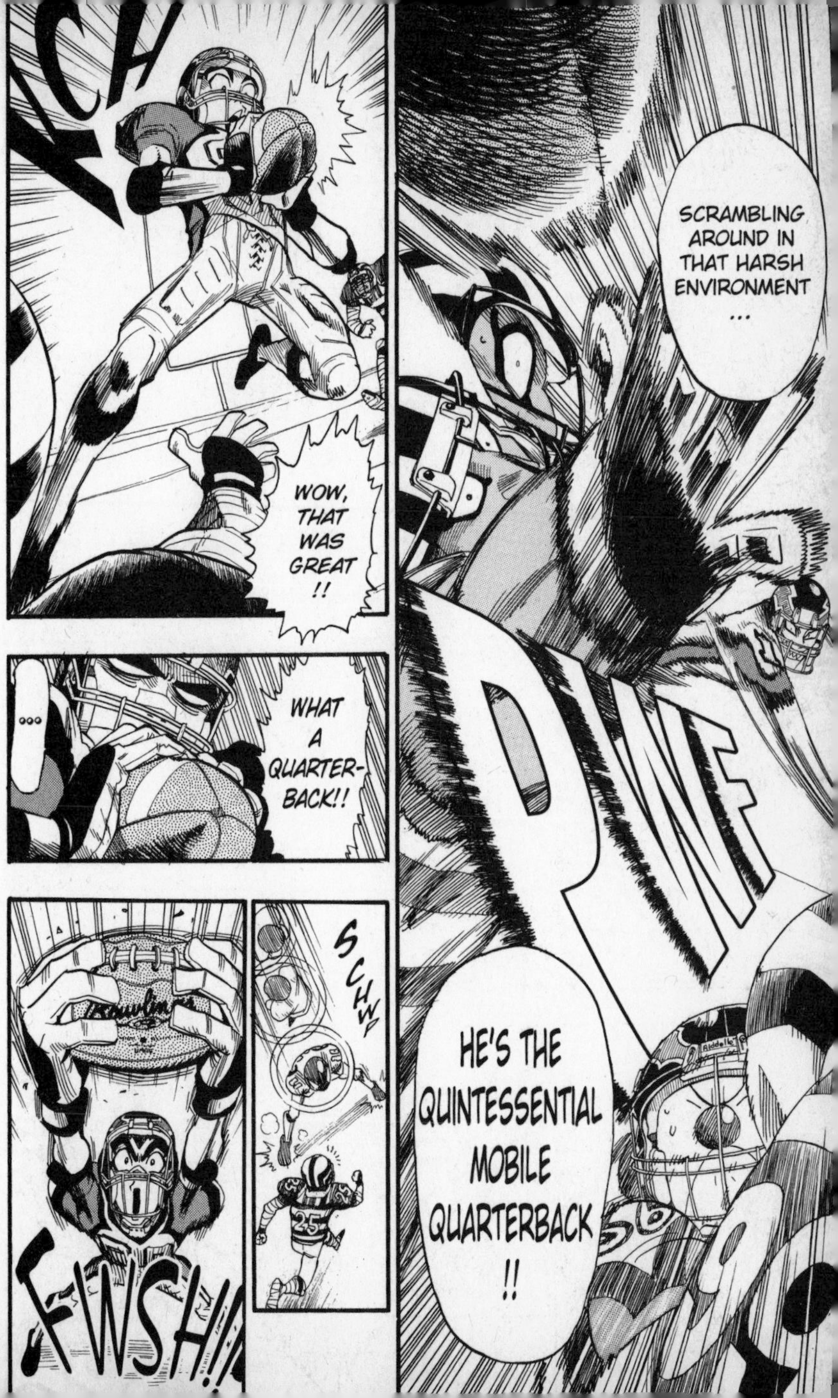
SCRAMBLING AROUND IN THAT HARSH ENVIRONMENT ...
HE'S THE QUINTESSENTIAL MOBILE QUARTERBACK !!
WOW, THAT WAS GREAT !!
...
WHAT A QUARTER-BACK!!
FWSH!!

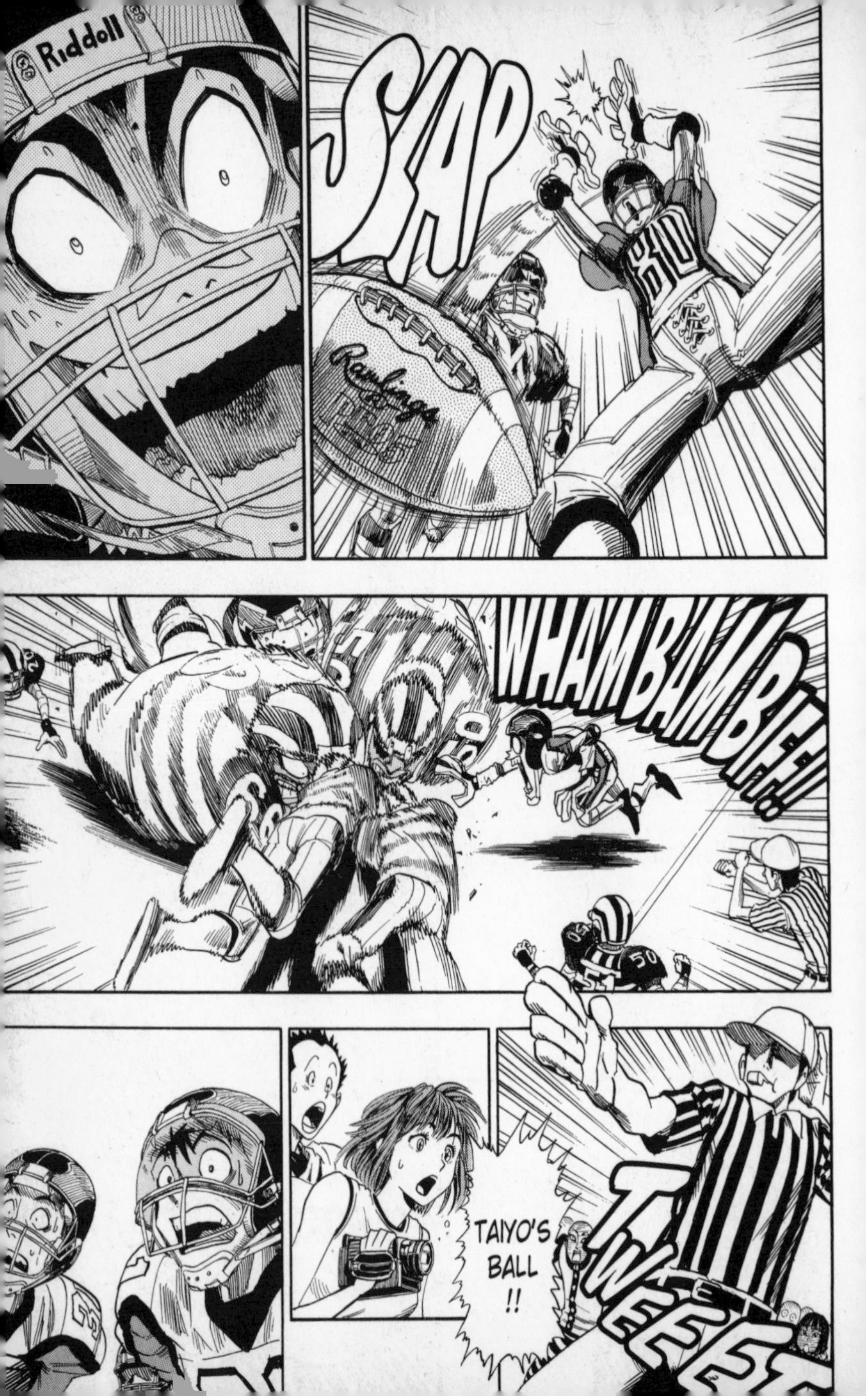
SAP
Riddoll
WHAM BAM BAM!!
TWEEET
TAIYO'S BALL !!

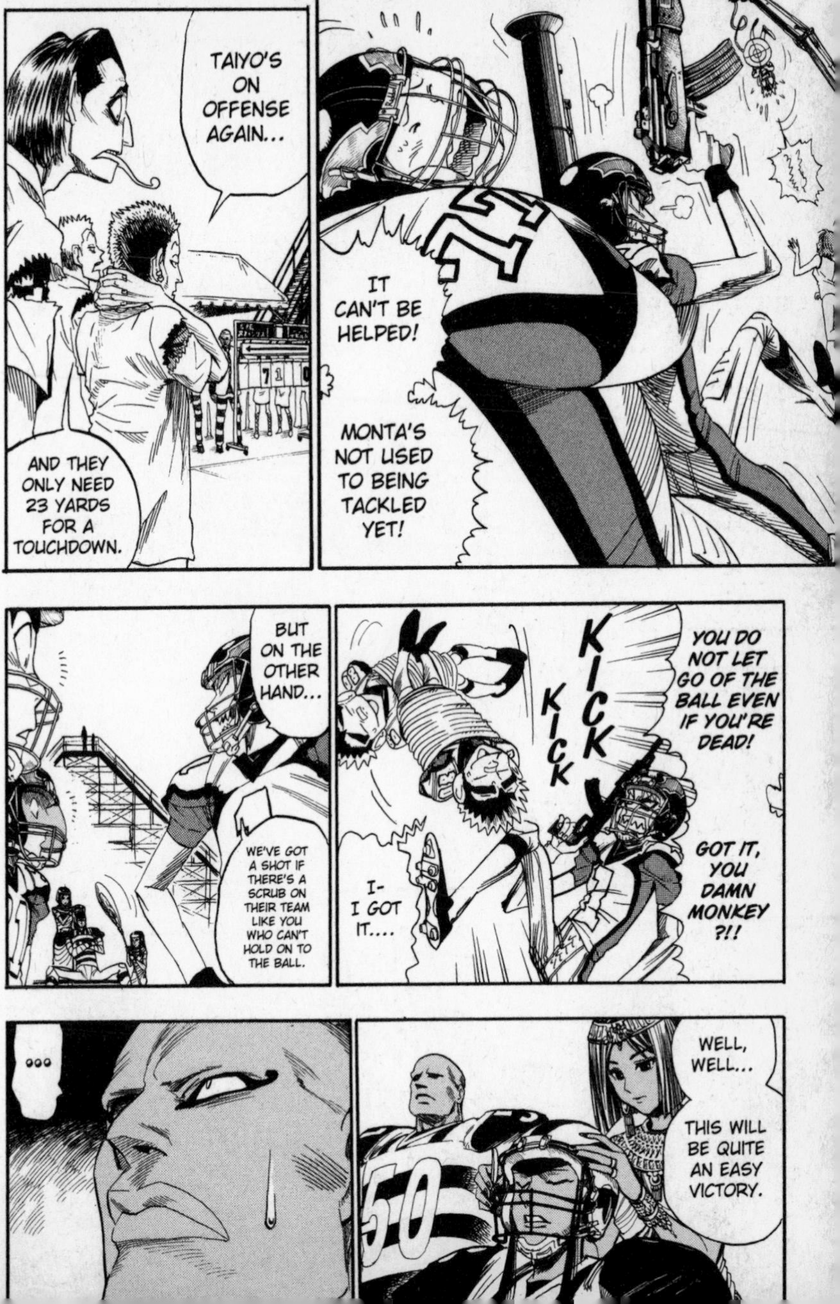
IT CAN'T BE HELPED!
MONTA'S NOT USED TO BEING TACKLED YET!
TAIYO'S ON OFFENSE AGAIN...
AND THEY ONLY NEED 23 YARDS FOR A TOUCHDOWN.
YOU DO NOT LET GO OF THE BALL EVEN IF YOU'RE DEAD!
KICK
KICK
GOT IT, YOU DAMN MONKEY ?!!
I- I GOT IT....
BUT ON THE OTHER HAND...
WE'VE GOT A SHOT IF THERE'S A SCRUB ON THEIR TEAM LIKE YOU WHO CAN'T HOLD ON TO THE BALL.
WELL, WELL...
THIS WILL BE QUITE AN EASY VICTORY.

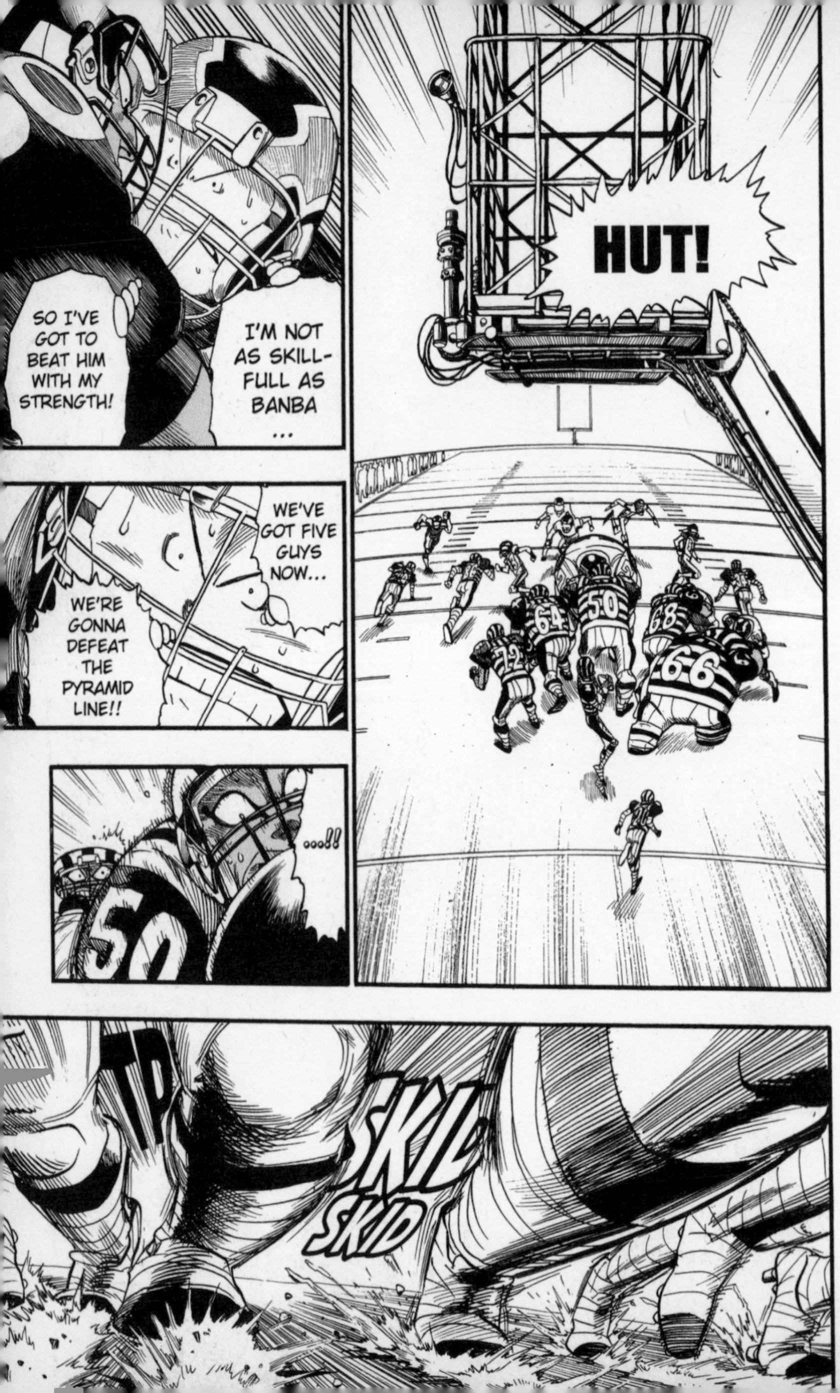
HUT!
I'M NOT AS SKILL-FULL AS BANBA ...
SO I'VE GOT TO BEAT HIM WITH MY STRENGTH!
WE'VE GOT FIVE GUYS NOW...
WE'RE GONNA DEFEAT THE PYRAMID LINE!!
...!!
SKID
SKID

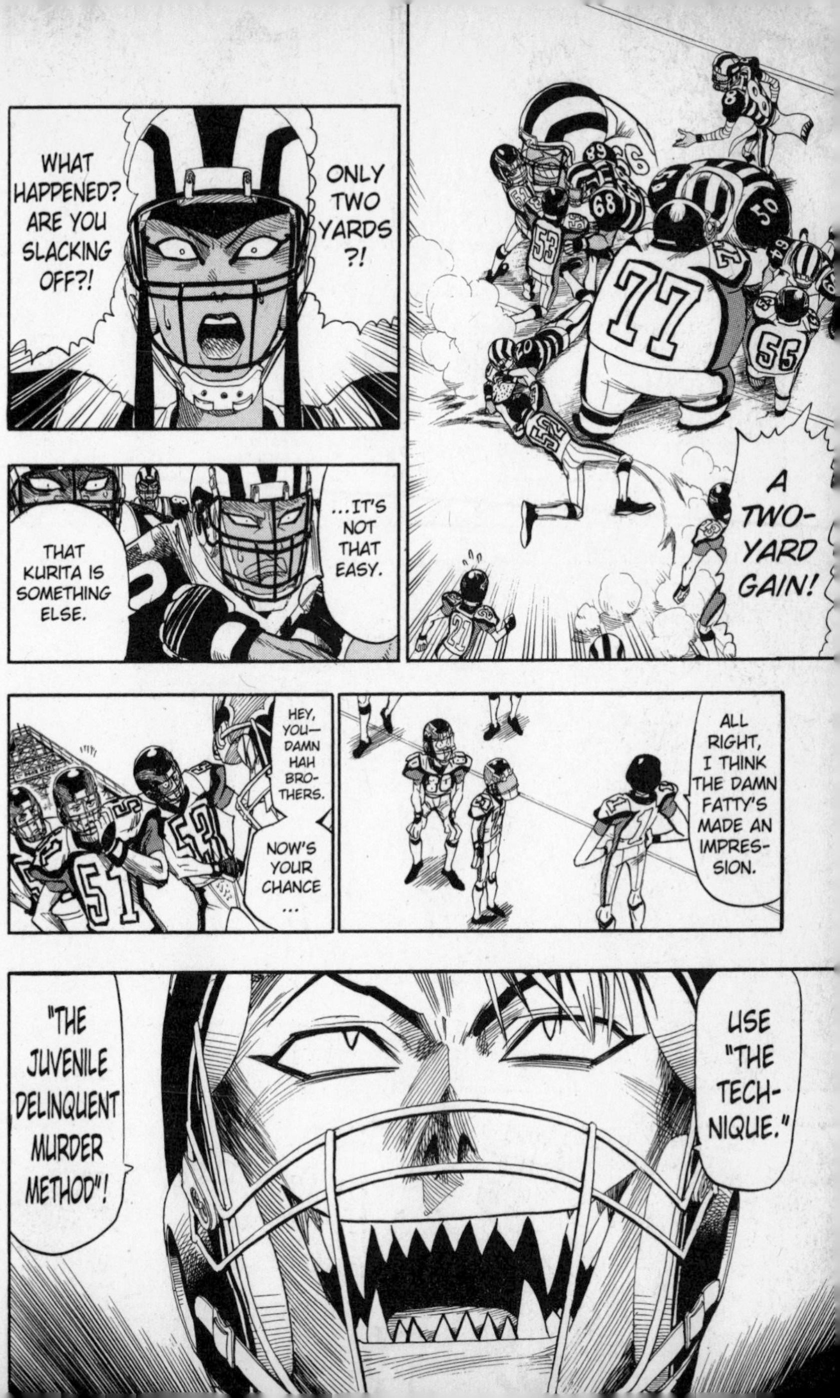
A TWO-YARD GAIN!
ONLY TWO YARDS?!
WHAT HAPPENED? ARE YOU SLACKING OFF?!
...IT'S NOT THAT EASY.
THAT KURITA IS SOMETHING ELSE.
ALL RIGHT, I THINK THE DAMN FATTY'S MADE AN IMPRESSION.
HEY, YOU—DAMN HAH BROTHERS.
NOW'S YOUR CHANCE...
USE "THE TECHNIQUE."
"THE JUVENILE DELINQUENT MURDER METHOD"!

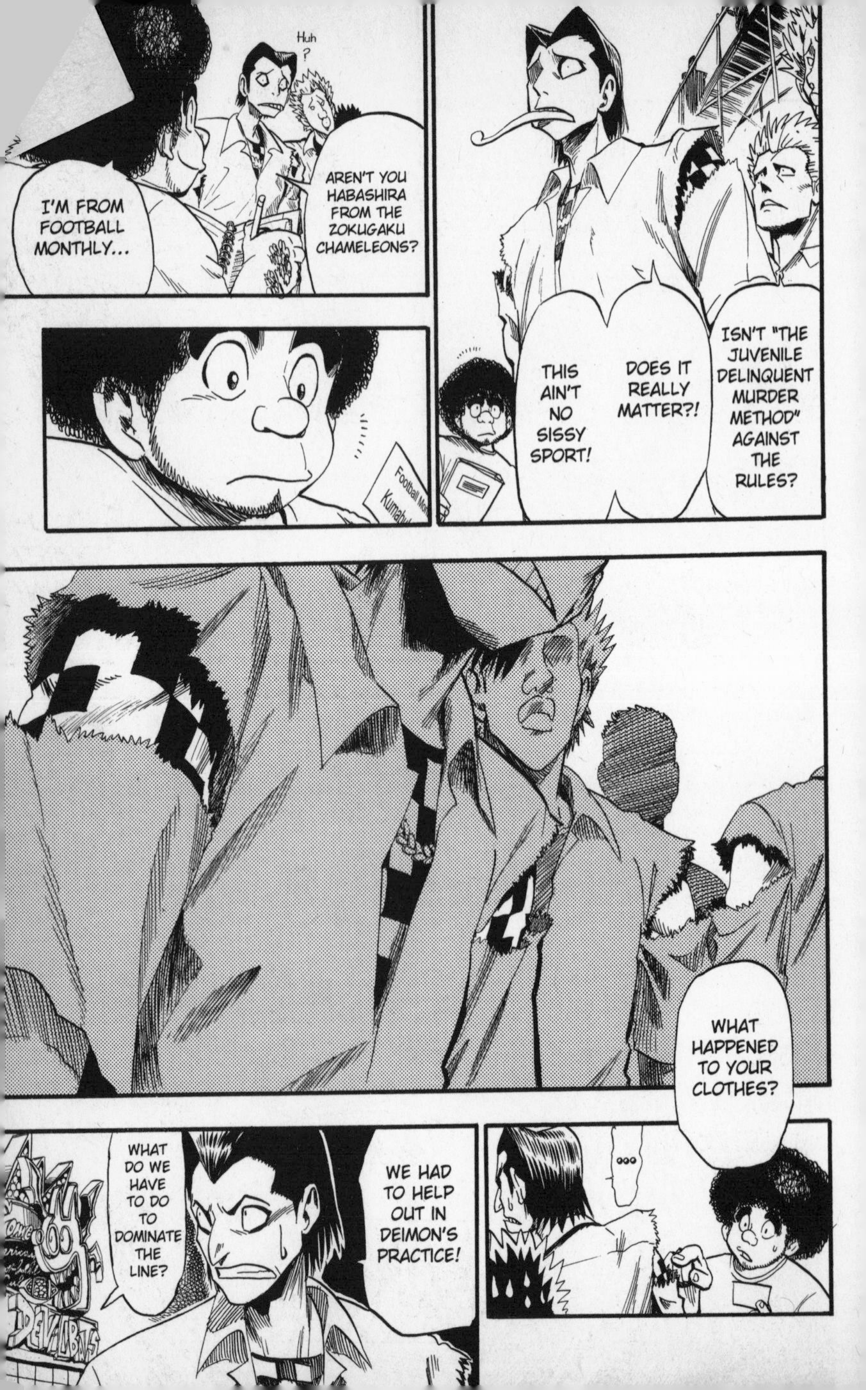
ISN'T "THE JUVENILE DELINQUENT MURDER METHOD" AGAINST THE RULES?
DOES IT REALLY MATTER?!
THIS AIN'T NO SISSY SPORT!
Huh ?
AREN'T YOU HABASHIRA FROM THE ZOKUGAKU CHAMELEONS?
I'M FROM FOOTBALL MONTHLY...
WHAT HAPPENED TO YOUR CLOTHES?
...
WE HAD TO HELP OUT IN DEIMON'S PRACTICE!
WHAT DO WE HAVE TO DO TO DOMINATE THE LINE?
DEVILBATS

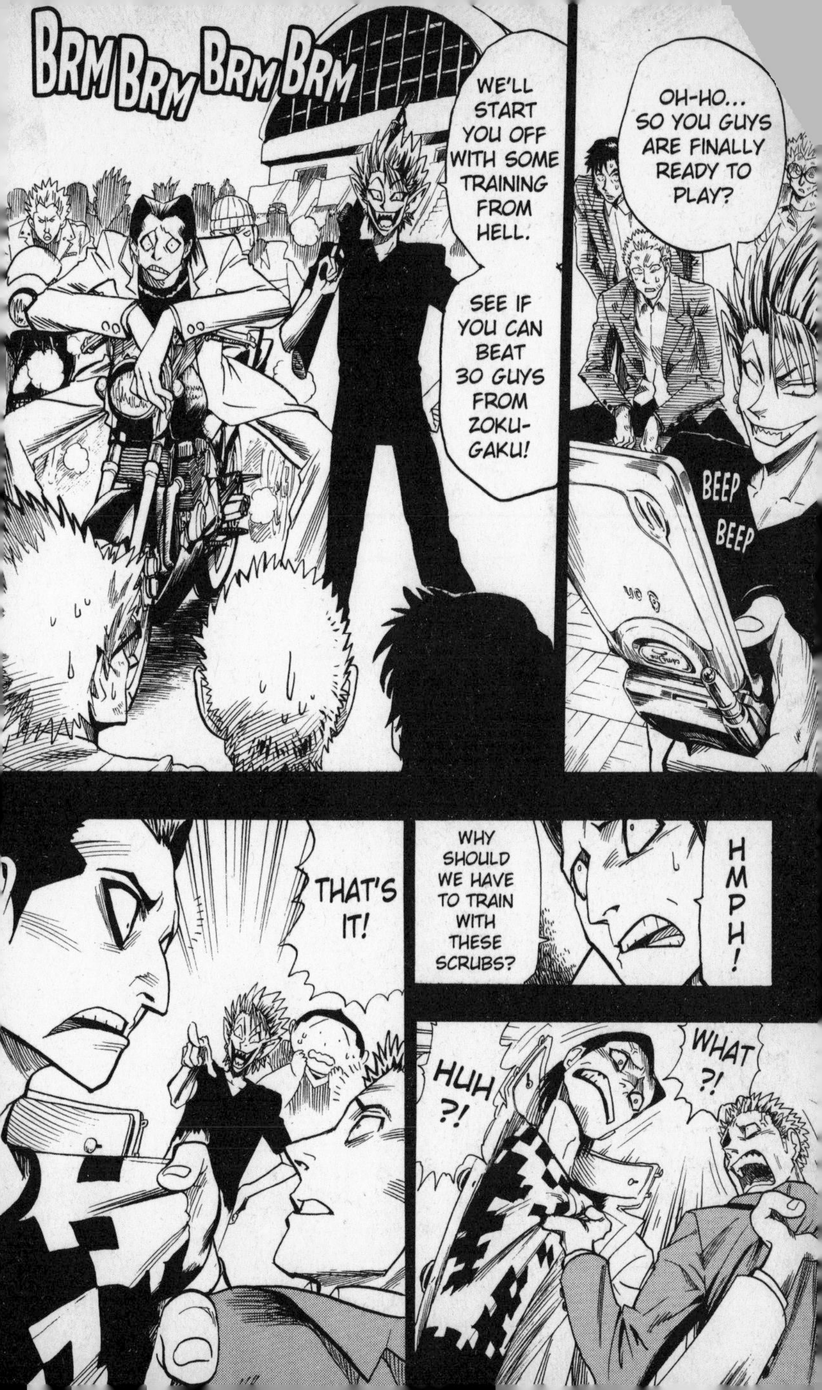
OH-HO... SO YOU GUYS ARE FINALLY READY TO PLAY?
BEEP BEEP
BRM BRM BRM BRM
WE'LL START YOU OFF WITH SOME TRAINING FROM HELL.
SEE IF YOU CAN BEAT 30 GUYS FROM ZOKU-GAKU!
HMPH!
WHY SHOULD WE HAVE TO TRAIN WITH THESE SCRUBS?
WHAT?!
HUH?!
THAT'S IT!

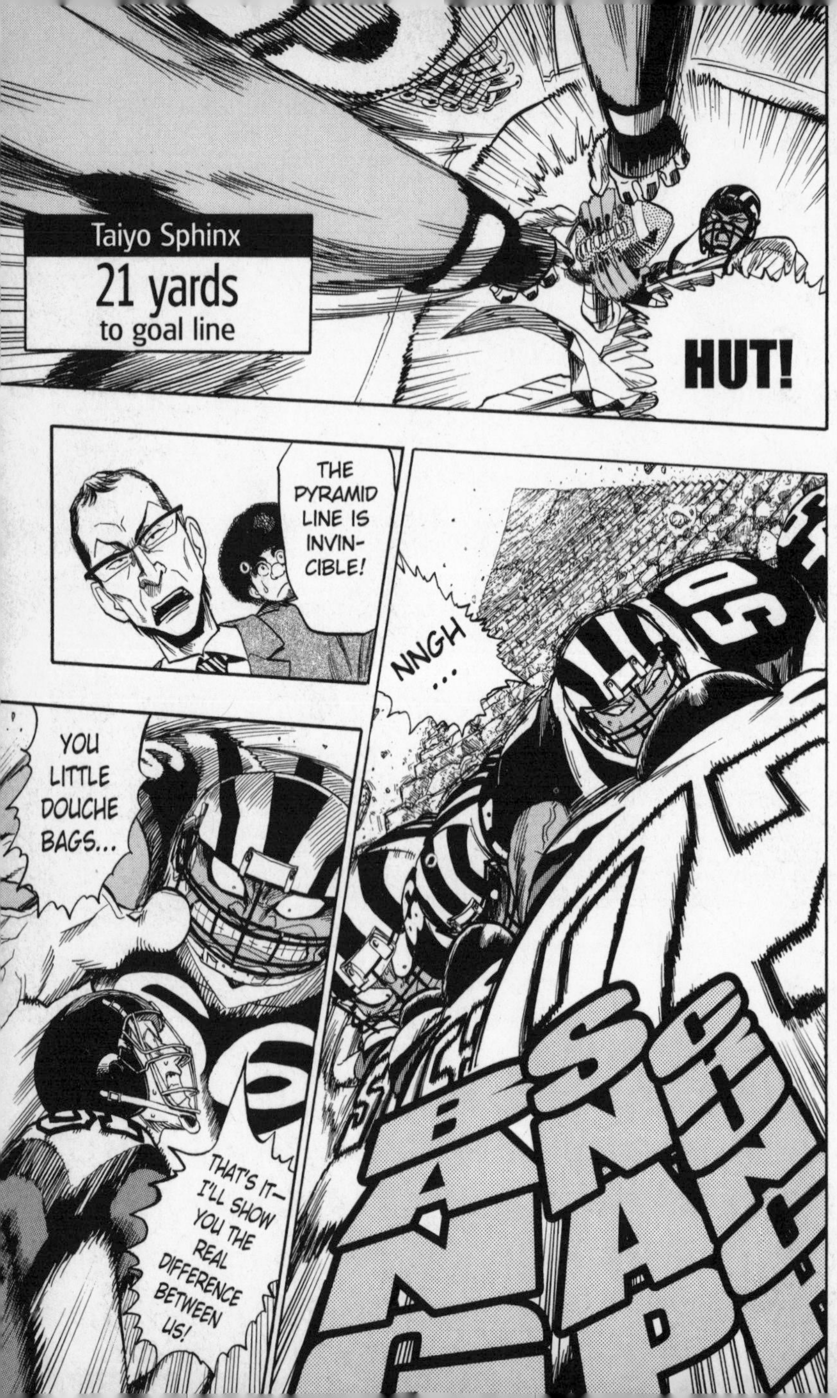
Taiyo Sphinx
21 yards
to goal line
HUT!
NNGH...
THE PYRAMID LINE IS INVINCIBLE!
YOU LITTLE DOUCHE BAGS...
THAT'S IT— I'LL SHOW YOU THE REAL DIFFERENCE BETWEEN US!

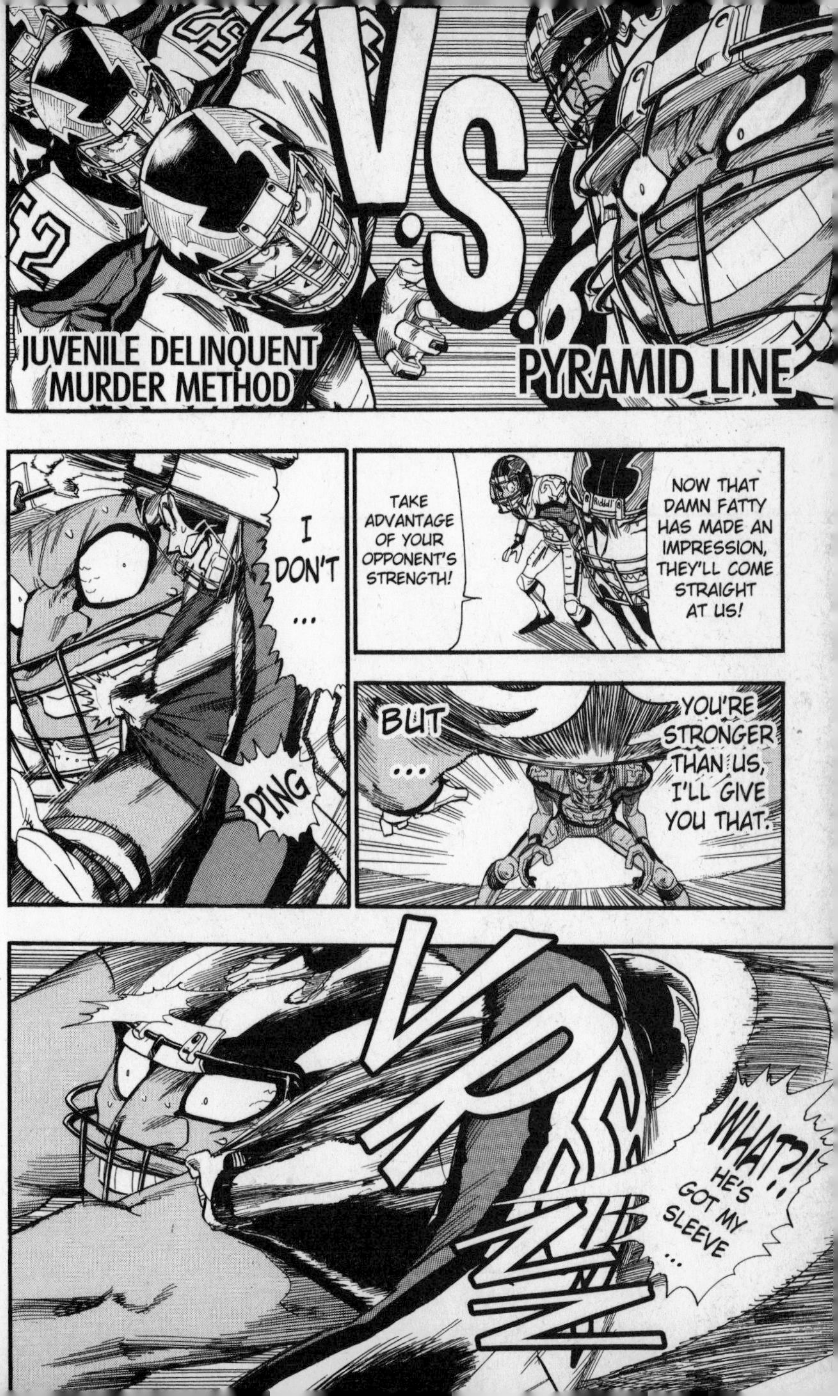
PYRAMID LINE
V.S.
JUVENILE DELINQUENT MURDER METHOD
NOW THAT DAMN FATTY HAS MADE AN IMPRESSION, THEY'LL COME STRAIGHT AT US!
TAKE ADVANTAGE OF YOUR OPPONENT'S STRENGTH!
YOU'RE STRONGER THAN US, I'LL GIVE YOU THAT.
BUT ...
I DON'T ...
PING
WHAT?!
HE'S GOT MY SLEEVE ...

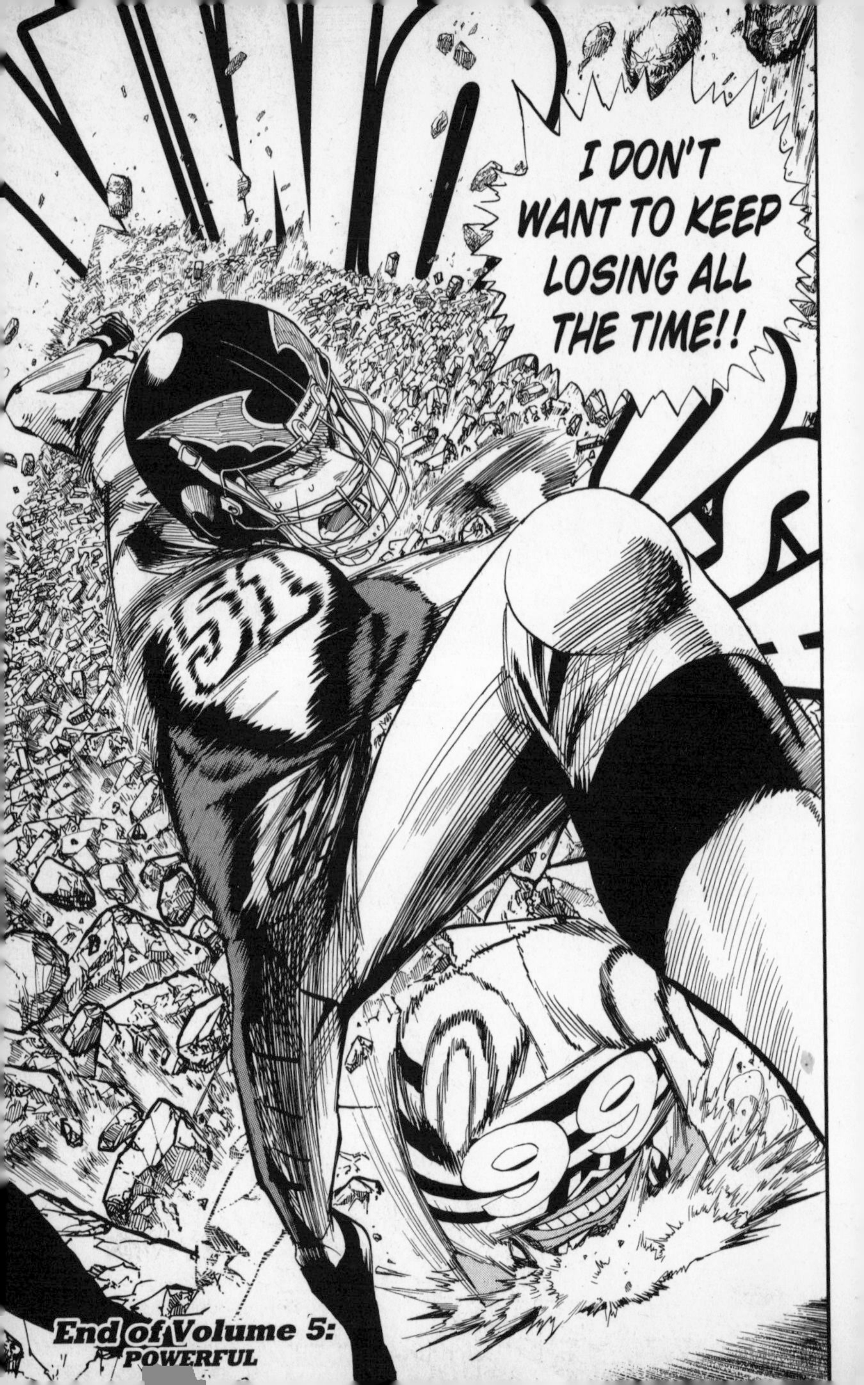
I DON'T WANT TO KEEP LOSING ALL THE TIME!!
End of Volume 5:
POWERFUL

A THANKLESS TASK

Deluxe Biographies of the Supporting Cast

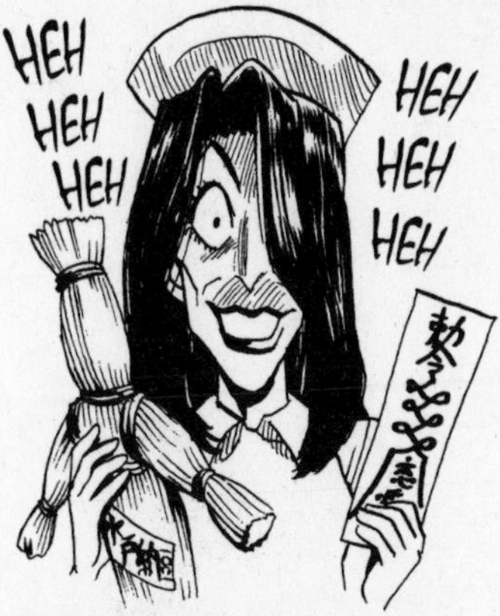
HEH HEH HEH
HEH HEH HEH

Head Nurse Oka

She is known for making mysterious remarks like recommending surgery via straw dolls or rearranging the location of beds according to what her "powers" are telling her.

But the bigger mystery—how did someone like her get to be head nurse?

Taiyo Prefectural High School

Principal Yoshiji Sakumura, who is an expert in archaeology, wanted to encourage his students' interest in archaeology too, but he got carried away with the design.
Now it's more like a theme park than an archaeological monument.

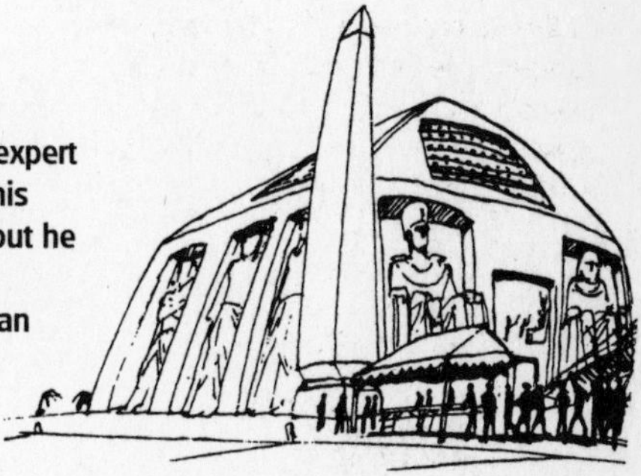

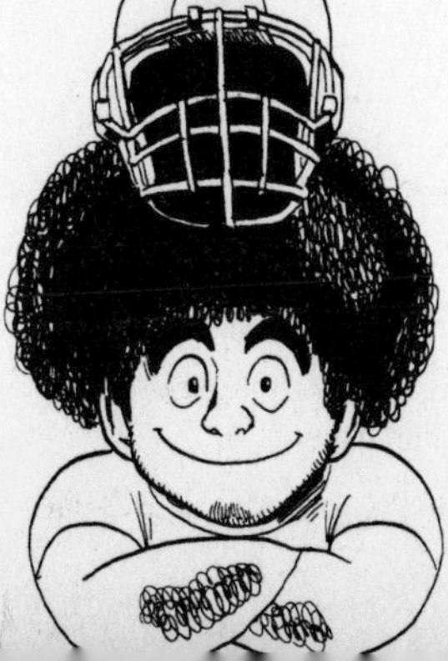

Kumabukuro the Journalist

He played football when he was in high school.
He used to hate the way that his helmet always flattened down his hair. Now his hairstyle seems to overcompensate for that.

The Wild Gunmen Cheerleaders

The Seibu High School cheerleading team was more of a typical athletic squad when it was formed, but they got caught up in the coach's enthusiasm for the Wild West. Before they knew it, this is what they were wearing.

Maybe enthusiasm makes for a happier life…

The Computer Room Operator

At the office, he's a shy guy who never expresses himself at all, but on the internet he transforms into a long winded chatterbox!! His online name is "Black Squall"… It's kind of pitiful…

The Guy in the Ladder Truck

Hiruma found out there was gambling going on in the firehouse, and made the ladder truck guy his pawn by threatening to tell the press about it.

But Hiruma put slot machines in the football clubhouse…

It just goes to show that knowledge is power.

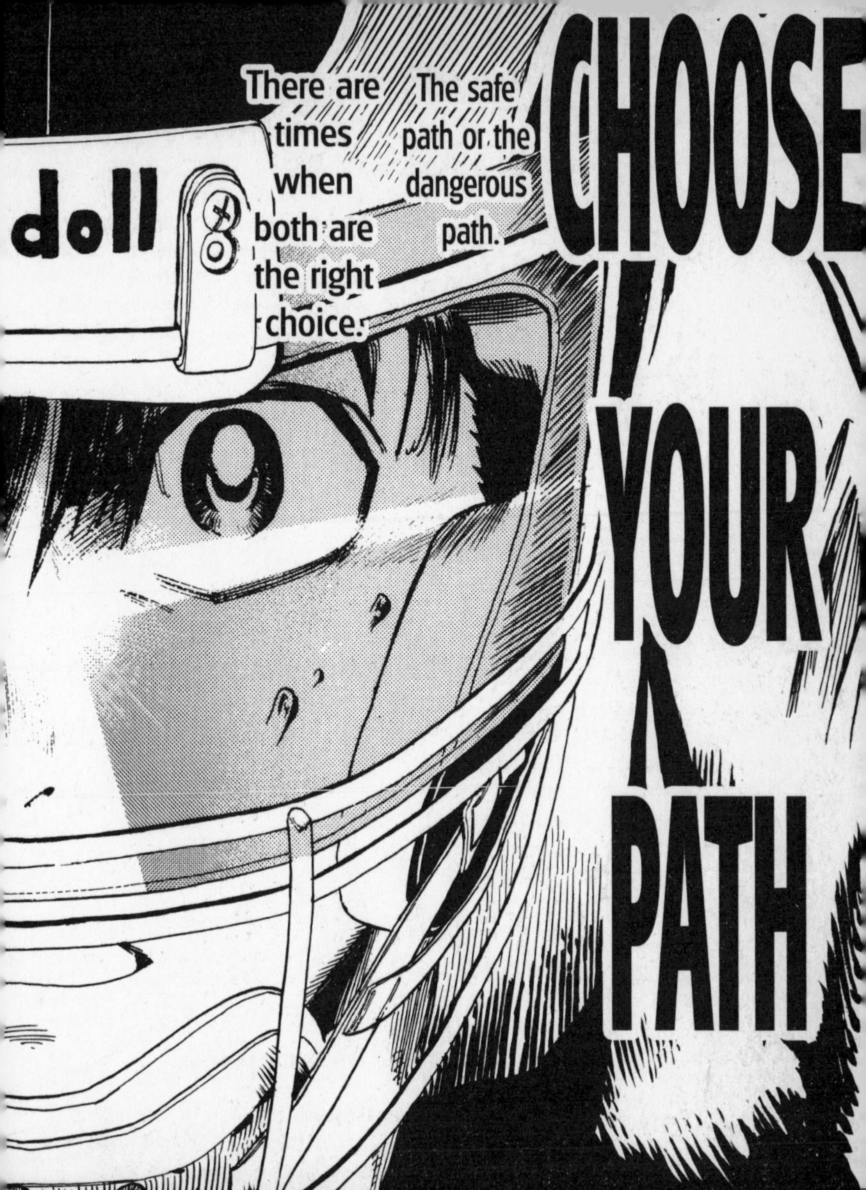
CHOOSE YOUR PATH
The safe path or the dangerous path.
There are times when both are the right choice.
doll

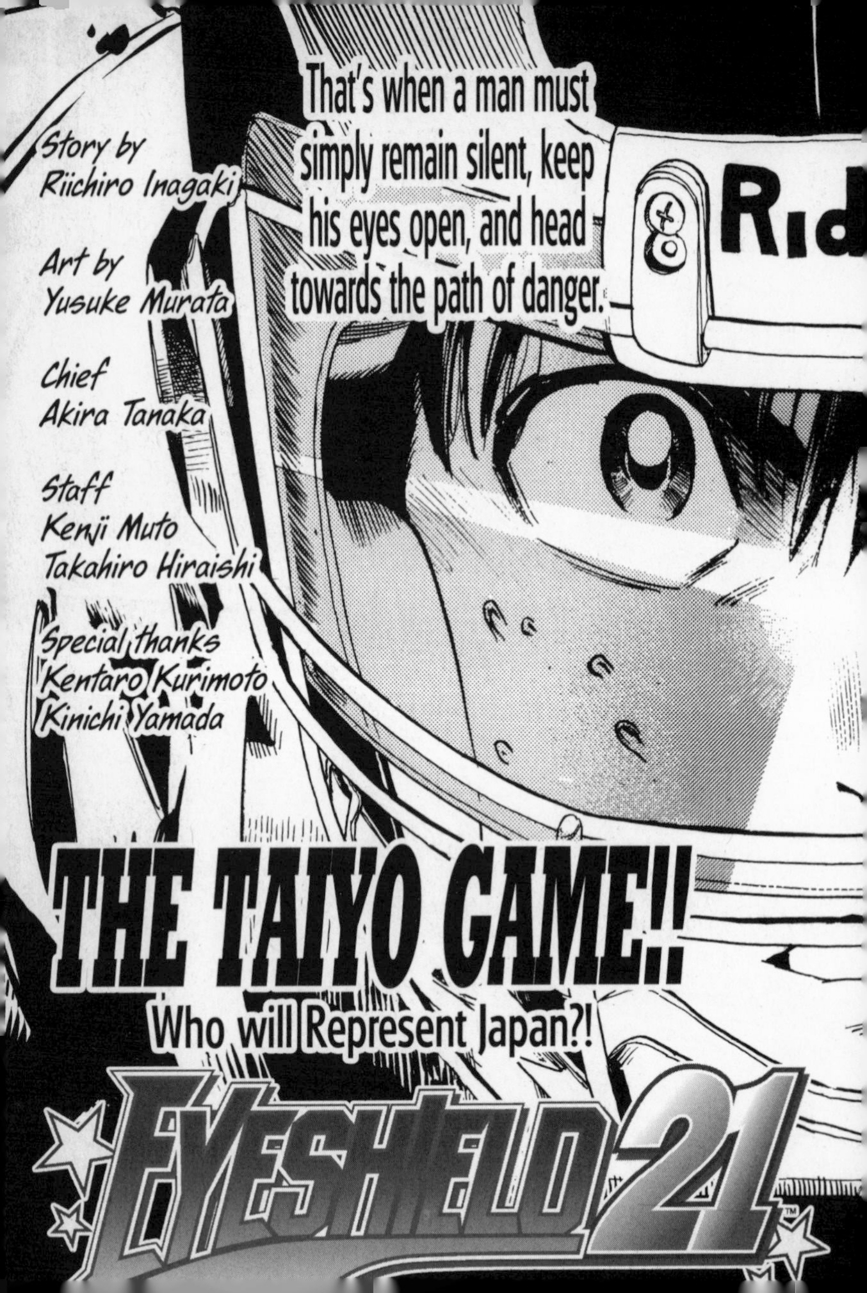
That's when a man must simply remain silent, keep his eyes open, and head towards the path of danger.
Story by Riichiro Inagaki
Art by Yusuke Murata
Chief Akira Tanaka
Staff Kenji Muto Takahiro Hiraishi
Special thanks Kentaro Kurimoto Kinichi Yamada
THE TAIYO GAME!!
Who will Represent Japan?!
EYESHIELD 21™

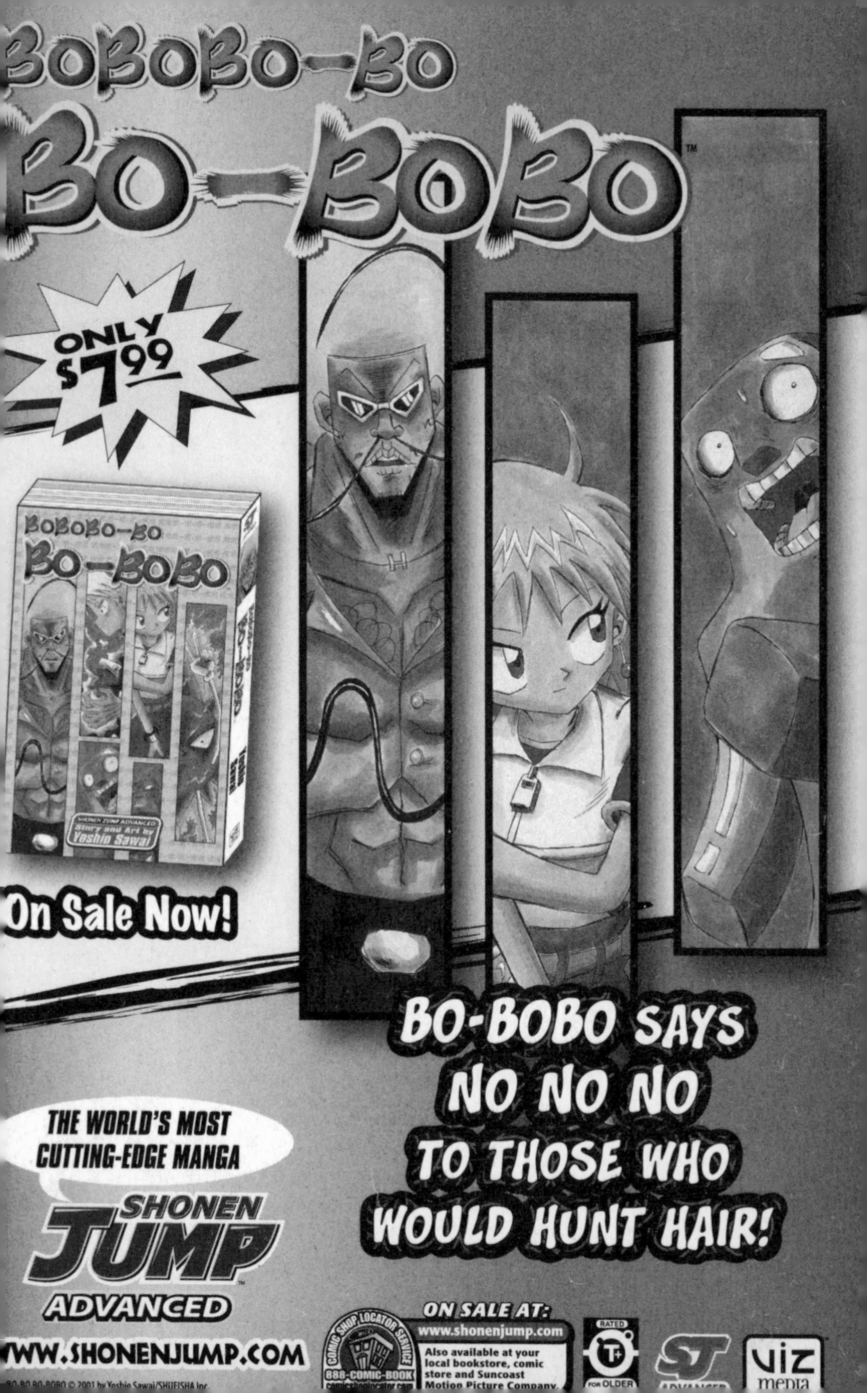
BOBOBO-BO
BO-BOBO™
ONLY $7.99
BOBOBO-BO BO-BOBO
SHONEN JUMP ADVANCED
Story and Art by Yoshio Sawai
On Sale Now!
BO-BOBO SAYS NO NO NO TO THOSE WHO WOULD HUNT HAIR!
THE WORLD'S MOST CUTTING-EDGE MANGA
SHONEN JUMP™ ADVANCED
WWW.SHONENJUMP.COM
ON SALE AT:
www.shonenjump.com
Also available at your local bookstore, comic store and Suncoast Motion Picture Company.
COMIC SHOP LOCATOR SERVICE
888-COMIC-BOOK
RATED T+ FOR OLDER
viz media
BO-BO BO-BOBO © 2001 by Yoshio Sawai/SHUEISHA Inc.

FREE PREVIEW ISSUE! of SHONEN JUMP Magazine!

THE REAL ACTION STARTS IN... SHONEN JUMP

THE WORLD'S MOST POPULAR MANGA

www.shonenjump.com

SHONEN JUMP Magazine: Contains Yu-Gi-Oh!, One Piece, Naruto, Shaman King, YuYu Hakusho and other HOT manga - STORIES NEVER SEEN IN THE CARTOONS!
Plus, get the latest on what's happening in trading cards, video games, toys and more!

Check out this ultra cool magazine for FREE! Then when you decide you must have SHONEN JUMP every month we will send you 11 more issues (12 in all) for only $29.95. A Price so low it's like getting 6 issues FREE!

But that's not all: You'll also become a member of the *SJ* Sub Club with your paid subscription!

Check us out on the web!

www.shonenjump.com